CANADA
AND UN PEACEKEEPING

Cold War by Other Means, 1945-1970

CANADA
AND UN PEACEKEEPING

Cold War by Other Means, 1945-1970

SEAN M. MALONEY

Foreword by LtGen (Ret'd) Romeo A. Dallaire, CMM, MSC, CD

Vanwell Publishing Limited
St. Catharines, Ontario

Vanwell Publishing acknowledges the financial support of the Government of Canada through the Book Publishing Industry Development Program for our publishing activities.
Cover Design by Renée Giguère

Vanwell Publishing Limited
1 Northrup Crescent
P.O. Box 2131
St. Catharines, Ontario L2R 7S2
sales@vanwell.com
tel: 905-937-3100
fax: 905-937-1760
Printed in Canada

National Library of Canada Cataloguing in Publication
Maloney, Sean M. (Sean Michael), 1967-

    Canada and UN peacekeeping : Cold War by other means,
1945-1970 / Sean M. Maloney.

Includes bibliographical references and index.

ISBN 1-55125-088-8
    1. Peacekeeping forces--Canada--History--20th century.
2. United Nations--Peacekeeping forces--History--20th century.
I. Title.

JZ6377.C3M34 2002   327.1'72   C2002-901196-5

TABLE OF CONTENTS

CHAPTER 8

CHAPTER 9

CHAPTER 10

CHAPTER 11

CONCLUSION

BIBLIOGRAPHY

INDEX

ABOUT THE AUTHOR

LIST OF MAPS

This book is dedicated
to my uncle,
WO Michael J. Maloney, CD
UNEF
UNEFII

Although my neighbours are all barbarians,
And you, you are a thousand miles away,
There are always two cups on my table.

- *Tang Dynasty poem*

1950s or 1990s?

I have referred to the dangerously false thinking now in the ascendant at UN meetings...the type of thinking which confuses a mere declaration of aspirations with a real improvement in human rights, which would substitute an empty resolution to outlaw war for the slow, heart-breaking work of trying to remove the causes of war....In short, I mean the whole mechanistic, declaratory approach which constantly evades or overlooks the fundamental point that resolutions and declarations of this nature are merely a cruel deception.

(H.H. Carter, 1951)

Because of our own internal stresses, the habit of compromise and the doctrine of the 'middle way' have become so ingrained in us that we find it hard to make up our minds. On the other hand our growing strength and our activist foreign policy are pushing us out into a world where we may-horrible viau-be forced to do so. If we fail to make up our minds there will be discernible within the husk of our voting record (a brilliant phrase) no grain of principle but merely the dead air created when opposing forces are reduced to zero; in itself a form, though a lowly one, of expediency...Can we do this so long as we are a member of NATO? Can we have our cake and eat it?

(External Affairs memorandum, 1956)

In 1954 and 1955 nobody blessed the United Nations Truce Supervision Organization in Palestine as a peacemaker, possibly because it was not peacemaking but at best a peace-keeping organization. Sometimes its members were referred to as international policemen, but they were policemen without truncheons. They were actually more like watchmen, watching on behalf of the Security Council of the United Nations for breaches of the General Armistice Agreements of the Council's cease-fire order.

(General E.L.M. Burns, 1957)

I have reluctantly come to the conclusion that, so long as the present management is in charge on the 38th floor, we may have eloquent expressions of philosophy and an admirable tone of high aspiration, but I would have hesitations about entrusting to them any substantial operational responsibility involving Canadian personnel.

(George Ignatieff, 1967)

The civil war has been fought in a primitive and brutal fashion, in jungle terrain with which Canadian troops are not familiar. It might be disastrous to commit Canadians to an unfamiliar environment where the political situation is tense and the necessary guarantee that they will not have to defend themselves against unruly tribesmen is, at best, uncertain.

(Cabinet discussion over Biafra, 1968)

FOREWORD

It is a pleasure to contribute the foreword to Sean Maloney's *Canada and UN Peacekeeping: Cold War by Other Means, 1945-1970*. His energy, thorough research and fair approach to Canadian military history, traits for which he already has a formidable reputation, are well applied to this subject. And what of that subject? Clearly, for those of us who practice peacekeeping there is a dearth of scholarship, specifically with regard to its history, origins and early development. Is it not strange that Canada, the prime practitioner and arguably the inventor of UN peacekeeping, has until now, not produced a history detailing her involvement in this critical role? Think of the lessons we might have learned and applied!

I, for one, am extremely proud of our hard-won reputation and I want Canadians to display similar pride. This work will help us understand how it was done in the early days and explain in detail the difficult journey Canadian policymakers undertook in search for security in the nuclear age. It was not always heroic: it could be tedious, frustrating, and dangerous. Canadian politicians, soldiers and diplomats sometimes had to adopt questionable methods to get the job done during the dark days of the Cold War: the author does not shirk his duty in his examination of them. Yet UN peacekeeping was one means by which we protected ourselves, our allies, and even our enemies from annihilation. There should be no apologies for what we did or how we did it. Canadians made the world a better place.

We were and remain important players on the stage of global conflict. The threat in the 1950s and 1960s was perhaps different from that of the 1990s. Yet we can no longer uncritically fall back on our reputation. We did that in the 1990s and had problems adapting to the new strategic environment. This was a new era, one which demanded that we jettison old methodologies in policy formulation, leadership, doctrine, training, officer development and civil-military relations. It was a period of trial and error, just as our predecessors in the 1950s and 1960s conceived and developed UN peacekeeping by trial and error. They had the formidable task of using peacekeeping to freeze brushfire conflicts before they could expand into nuclear war. We now have the task of making peacekeeping evolve to a higher state of conflict resolution, and stabilizing the world from anarchy, warlordism, and ethnic violence. In the past, peacekeeping was an adjunct to our containment efforts. Peacekeeping now must become part of a multi-disciplinary approach: diplomatic, humanitarian, and stabilization fields must work in harmony as they never have before. To do this, we must understand the 1950s and 1960s before we can understand the 1990s, and then we can move forward to this new state we seek. Sean Maloney's book is the first step.

Lt Gen (Ret'd) Romeo A. Dallaire, CMM, MSC, CD

ACKNOWLEDGEMENTS

I would like to thank several colleagues who read and provided critiques on the draft manuscripts. Such a service, though time consuming, is invaluable in ensuring that the proper forest-to-trees perspective is maintained. Therefore my hat goes off to Dr. Michael A. Hennessy, Dr. Scot Robertson, Major John Grodzinski, and Major Gord Ohlke who ploughed through the draft with fervor, Major Brent Beardsley, and to my students from War Studies 512 and 514 at RMC as well as Major David Last and his peacekeeping course, who all served as "crash test dummies" for the ideas contained herein. It would not do to ignore the vital administrative support provided by the Royal Military College War Studies Program and the History Department. I would especially like to thank Dr. Brian McKercher and Dr. Ronald Haycock for their support and encouragement. Serge Campion at the Fort Frontenac library also provided a variety of services without which this project would have been less successful.

Archival research is impossible without accessing vital teams of specialists. I would especially like to thank the staff of the National Archives of Canada, particularly Tim Dubé, Dan German, George Lafleur (who was seconded to the PCO), Paul Marsden, and all the Access to Information personnel who suffered through my endless requests. I would also like to thank Joan Champ at the Diefenbaker Centre, David Haight and all the staff at the Dwight D. Eisenhower Library, and Regina Greenwell at the Lyndon B. Johnson Library.

This project also had the critical assistance of Dr. Marilla B. Guptil, Chief, Archives Unit, at the United Nations in New York. This invaluable and underused resource proved critical time and again.

At the Directorate of History and Heritage I would especially like to single out Isabelle Campbell, Donna Porter, and Andrea Schlecht for their attention to detail and ceaseless pursuit of obscure material on my behalf; I would also like to thank Dr. Serge Bernier, Jean Morin, and especially Michael Whitby.

I undertook field research in the Middle East in preparation of this and other works on Canadian UN peace-keeping. Assistance for these endeavors was provided by the Canadian Forces and the United Nations and I am most grateful to both organizations. I would like to particularly single out the redoubtable Lieutenant Colonel J. Michael Snell, military advisor to Canada's mission to the UN in New York. Without his encouragement and assistance, I would not have been able to travel to visit UNFICYP, UNDOF, and UNTSO, and thus put faces, events, and locations to these sometimes obscure UN acronyms. Though a detailed order of battle is impossible here, the personnel conducting these missions took a significant amount of time out of their normal duties to assist me and I hold them in particularly high esteem:

UNFICYP: Colonel C.M.B. Coats (UK Army), Captain and Mrs. Rob Cooper and family (Cdn Army), Captain Vicki Walker (UK Army), RSM L. McGrath (Irish Army), BSM Miller (UK Army), Sgt Paul Hodgins (Cdn Army) and all the members of 42 Battery, Welsh Gunners and their neighbours, the marines from the Argentinean Contingent, who all rolled out the red carpet on the so-called "island of love."

UNDOF: MGen H.C. Ross (Cdn Army), Colonel Michael Jordan (Cdn Army), Captain Bernard Hudson (Cdn Army), Capt Barb Krasij (Cdn Air Force) and the men and women of LOGBATT, particularly all the members of the WO and Sgt's Mess who, after their interrogation to ensure I was not in from Ottawa to spy on them, really know how to show first time visitors to the Golan a good time.

UNTSO: Major Charles Brunet (Cdn air force).

It is absolutely critical that I not neglect Colonel Gary Furrie, the Canadian military attaché at the Canadian embassy in Tel Aviv and his assistant Sgt Joellen McNeil (thanks for the loan and advice, Jo!). My travels in the region would have been impossible without their hospitality, assistance and understanding. Finally, I want to thank Gayle Fraser at the Canadian Institute for International Affairs for supplying me with photographs and for allwing me access to John Holmes papers.

This project was financially supported by the Social Sciences and Humanities Research Council of Canada and I would once again like to thank the individuals of that institution for demonstrating the foresight to back my work in this field.

INTRODUCTION

I believe in peacekeeping, not policing. I am Joe and I am Canadian.
- Molson beer advertisement, circa 2000

Canadians have participated in the creation of a national peacekeeping myth. Canadian policymakers, consequently, have an exaggerated impression of the importance and role of UN peacekeeping in Canadian national security policy. This impression is an outgrowth of a lack of historical understanding as to why Canada involved herself with UN peacekeeping during the onset of the Cold War.

This myth sometimes drove Canada to commit to dubious peacekeeping operations throughout the 1990s: the highly damaging operation in Somalia (1993) for which no detailed official explanation is given of Canada's involvement; the murderous debacle in Rwanda (1994); and the embarrassing Operation ASSURANCE in Zaire (1996). The myth has reached the point where it may constrain Canada from acting unilaterally. It also constrains us from acting in coalitions which enhance Canadian prestige and provide economic benefits. The minimalist participation in the Persian Gulf War of 1990-91 is one example of senior Canadian policymakers and the loyal opposition's concern that involvement in the land campaign would damage Canada's peacekeeping image.[1] In another case, the mistaken belief that Canada had participated in every UN peacekeeping operation was a factor in high-level discussions over Canadian participation in the United Nations Observer Mission in Liberia in 1993.[2]

The myth has the potential to damage the structure of the armed forces by limiting their ability to operate across the spectrum of military operations commensurate with Canadian interests. On one occasion, Canadian forces operating with the UN in the former Yugoslavia were prohibited (unlike the Danish contingent) from having Leopard main battle tanks, from using TOW Under Armour vehicles or self-propelled mortars for anything other than observation and illumination.[3] The inability of the Canadian contingent to defend itself in turn restrained its use of airpower to support Canadian maritime forces conducting an embargo of the Serbian coast. These factors ultimately hampered Canada's diplomatic role during efforts to resolve a very dangerous conflict.[4]

Undoubtedly, the myth will continue to drive us into operations that have no bearing on defined Canadian interests. Yet the origins of Canadian peacekeeping are firmly rooted in Canada's attempt to exert international influence during the Cold War.

It is tempting to view our UN and NATO commitments as separate and even contradictory expressions of Canadian national security policy. Peacekeeping implies impartiality, and since many of the crises involving Canadian peacekeeping occurred during the Cold War, it is equally tempting to view Canada as quasi-neutral in this long twilight struggle. Similarly, the proliferation of Canadian peacekeeping deployments have by their sheer number overshadowed the larger and more important Cold War Canadian NATO deployments. Those policymakers in the 1970s seeking to present the Third World with a non-colonial, non-imperialistic all-Canadian image generally considered Canada's NATO commitments, encumbered with all those nasty nuclear and conventional weapons, as the mad sibling locked in the basement whenever polite company came over for dinner.

The infatuation in Canadian policy circles with the "new" peacekeeping, human security and "soft power" in the post-Cold War 1990s reinforced these notions and obscured the true political origins and diplomatic purposes underlying Canadian participation in UN peacekeeping operations. In the 1950s and 1960s, however, Canadian peacekeeping operations were generally conceived as complementary to Canada's NATO policy. Further examination of the decision-making processes for many Canadian UN peacekeeping operations reveals that co-ordination for some of these operations was conducted in NATO circles first and UN circles later. There were even discussions as early as 1956 for the creation of a NATO peacekeeping force separate from the UN forces, a debate which continued into the 1960s.

Placed in the context of today's situation in the former Yugoslavia in which a UN peacekeeping force became a NATO peacekeeping force, this project will provide a new look at a significant Canadian contribution to world peace, security, and the protection of Canadian interests. In essence, this book will argue that Canadian peacekeeping operations were a means to project Canadian power for national security interests, interests which included economic, military and diplomatic components, and that this power projection was in most cases directly related to, and even subordinated to, Canada's NATO policy.

The bulk of the literature dealing with Cold War foreign policy tends to ignore non-American and non-British aspects of the Cold War. The body of work examining NATO usually focuses on the various internal NATO crises and most particularly on NATO nuclear strategy and issues related to the defence of NATO's Central Region. As for the vast literature on the United Nations, most of it is too laudatory and the rest hypercritical of this attempt of a functional world government to provide Canadians with an adequate context. Works dealing with specific UN peacekeeping missions are so focused on their subjects that the overall picture eludes us. Consequently, the role of United Nations peacekeeping operations during the Cold War is misunderstood.

The best lens from which to view this is through Canada's participation in UN peace-keeping. Canada, whose Department of Foreign Affairs and International Trade (DFAIT) continuously boasts that it is the world's foremost peacekeeper, is also a charter NATO member. During the Cold War, the United States, the United Kingdom, and France, all permanent members of the Security Council, remained aloof in several difficult circumstances as a sort of plausible deniability. Canada was the West's champion in the Cold War UN arena.

To do this effectively, however, the Government of Canada had to conceal the realities as much as possible, even from its own electorate. This produced a situation whereby Canadian cultural imperatives seized on UN peacekeeping as a prime component of a fragile but burgeoning Canadian identity, particularly in the 1960s and 1970s. UN peacekeeping became part of an ideology of Canadian Exceptionalism. Eventually the original subordination of UN peacekeeping operations to NATO strategic primacy was lost, and Canada's NATO and UN policies were viewed (and continue to be viewed by some) as contradictory.

Since Canada was a prime practitioner of UN peacekeeping as NATO strategy by other means, analysis of the strategy has remained buried and the reality of the issue has been denied to policymakers in Canada and elsewhere. References in American and British literature to Canada and UN peacekeeping are diffuse and sporadic, which in turn has contributed to a loss of understanding of the role that UN peacekeeping played in support of NATO's Cold War objectives. It is only when these pieces are brought together and placed within the proper conceptual framework that the reality of the strategy finally emerges.

The stakes were high. The Cold War outside of the NATO area is best characterized as a chess game, of which bloc controlled what area and which ideology influenced the inhabitants of the contentious regions in the Third World. This affected the day-to-day ideological and economic conflict which also affected the deterrence of nuclear war in two ways. First, there were international crises in these areas which had the potential to escalate into superpower confrontation which might have included nuclear weapons use, with the obvious global consequences. Second, many of these areas had to be secured as bases from which NATO military forces (conventional in some cases, nuclear in others) could operate in wartime. The demonstrated ability to operate such forces effectively in peacetime contributed to the overall deterrent in any event. In every large UN peacekeeping operation during this period, either one factor or both were in play and Canada was involved as a NATO representative supporting alliance needs.

This book is organized chronologically. The first chapter examines the Canadian peace-keeping myth in an effort to explain why and how our collective view on it has become distorted. In particular it will highlight the problems of peacekeeping terminology and how this has blurred the debate. The following chapters look at how each government from Louis St Laurent to Pierre Trudeau viewed peacekeeping within the larger context of Canadian national security policy. Interspersed with these discussions are closer examinations of specific Canadian peacekeeping operations conducted during those administrations and why and how Canada chose to get involved with them.

This is not meant to be an operational history of Canadian peacekeeping, and the missions themselves will not received detailed examination. That is the subject of a future companion work. The focus here is on UN peacekeeping. Canada's involvement in Vietnam is a separate, greatly debated subject which has in fact received more historical examination than Canada and UN peacekeeping.[5] Canada's involvement with the ICCS and ICSC will only be touched on as it relates to the issues of peacekeeping as policy by other means.

It should be noted here that there is little Canadian peacekeeping historical literature per se.[6] For a country which prides itself on the belief that it created interpositionary peacekeeping, this major omission is utterly remarkable—and the deficiency must be rectified.

1. Access to Information, DND (25 Feb 91), memorandum to DGMPO, "Kuwait-Peacekeeping," (10 May 91) Briefing Note to MND, "Canadian Participation in UNIKOM."

2. Saner heads prevailed and noted that "our record is probably unsustainable (and largely unimportant) in any event." See ATI DND (25 Aug 93), memo DG Pol Ops to Assoc ADM (Pol and Comm) "United Nations Observer Mission in Liberia (UNOMIL)."

3. Sean M. Maloney, *War Without Battles: Canada's NATO Brigade in Germany, 1951-1993* (Toronto: McGraw-Hill Ryerson, 1997), Ch. 7.

4. Sean M. Maloney, "The Hindrance of Military Operations Ashore: Canadian Participation in Operation SHARP GUARD, 1991-1993," *Canadian Military History.*

5. There are no less than five: Douglas Ross, *In The Interests of Peace: Canada and Vietnam, 1954-73* (Toronto: University of Toronto Press, 1984); Victor Levant, *Quiet Complicity: Canadian Involvement in the Vietnam War* (Toronto: Between the Lines Press, 1986); James Eayrs, *Indochina: Roots of Complicity* (Toronto: University of Toronto Press, 1983); Charles Taylor, *Snow Job: Canada. The United States, and Vietnam* (Toronto: Anansi, 1973); Ramesh Thakur, *Peacekeeping in Vietnam: Canada, India, Poland, and the International Commission* (Edmonton: University of Alberta Press, 1983).

6. For example, the only overview is Fred Gaffen's, dated (1989) *In the Eye of the Storm* (Ottawa: Deneau, 1989). It is anecdotal and operational in orientation. There are three or four picture books but nothing which explains why Canada is engaged in peacekeeping.

CHAPTER 1

CANADIAN EXCEPTIONALISM AND UN PEACEKEEPING: MYTHS AND ANTECEDENTS

*Without a doubt the greatest injury of all was done by basing morals on myth.
For, sooner or later, myth is recognized for what it is and disappears.
Then morality loses the foundation on which it has been built.*

- Herbert Louis.

The lap dog disguised himself as a lamb, but tried to hunt with the wolves.

- Dag Hammarskjöld, *Markings*

Of the twelve peacekeeping operations Canada was involved in from 1945 to 1970, only two included Canadian combat troops. Five missions had signals and/or service support troops as the primary Canadian force committed. Six were unarmed observer missions. (CF Photo)

WHAT IS THE GREAT CANADIAN PEACEKEEPING MYTH?

We tend to confuse ideals with historical reality. We prefer not to examine the motives behind political decision-making: we prefer to deal with the results of actions based on those motives, particularly if they fit into a positive framework.

The myth of Canadian peacekeeping is directly related to the concept of Canadian Exceptionalism, which suggests that our identity is based on Canada being demonstrably different from and morally superior to the United States. There are several tenets to the ideology of Canadian Exceptionalism, an ideology which has been carefully maintained by successive governments, nationalist commentators, and particularly Canadian popular culture over the past thirty years. They are, as they relate to national security policy:

1) Canada is an unmilitary nation and by inference made up of non-violent people who eschew the use of military force except as a last resort.[1]

2) Canada was a neutral or quasi-neutral during the long Cold War. Canada's role was to function as a reluctant American instrument or to restrain the Superpowers to prevent nuclear war.[2]

3) Canada has no territorial ambitions and by inference no serious economic ambitions outside North America.

4) Canada is not a colonial power and never has behaved abhorrently, like the European colonial powers.[3]

5) Canadians are a nice, inoffensive, altruistic people who are welcome anywhere around the world in part because they do not behave like Americans.[4]

6) Canadians are morally superior to others, particularly Americans since they are not racist or xenophobic.[5]

From these larger tenets, there are a number of implications that relate to national security policy during the Cold War and are promulgated by cultural means:

1) Canada's primary military activities have, since 1945, been peacekeeping and humanitarian aid operations.

2) Canadian participation in NATO is, at best, a necessary evil.

3) The UN is a purely idealistic entity which should replace, supersede, and be free from superpower influence. Canadian military activity should always be conducted within this framework.

4) Canada is and always has been a proponent of disarmament, be it nuclear, biological, chemical, or conventional weapons. The Canadian disarmament effort is the centre-piece of Canadian foreign policy.

A prime component of Canadian Exceptionalism ideology in examining UN peacekeeping is that Canada does not normally project power for national purposes, and does so reluctantly in exceptional circumstances such as the First and Second World Wars. Canada does, in fact, have a rich history of power projection: a 100-year strategic tradition called Forward Security. Forward Security is designed to prevent overseas conflicts from affecting Canadian interests and to use those conflicts to further Canadian objectives in other areas of coalition and alliance relations. These interests include the physical protection of Canadians and the preservation and maintenance of their economic prosperity.[6]

In addition to the Red River Expedition (1870) and the Northwest Rebellion (1885), the Canadian government formed and deployed the Yukon Field Force (1898-1900) to Yukon Territory to exert a presence, support the North West Mounted Police, and maintain order on the American-Canadian border. This 200-man formation, which was as large as or larger than most Canadian UN peacekeeping contingents, conducted what can be called a strategic deployment from Upper Canada to the Canadian northwest, a distance of over 6000 kilometres (or the same distance Canada's First and Second World War forces traveled from North America to Europe).[7]

Canada's participation in The South African War (1899-1902) could be considered in light of the Canadian Exceptionalism mold. On the surface, the strategic deployment of 7384 troops to the Dark Continent appears to have been undertaken reluctantly by the Canadian government, an Imperial exercise in which significant pressure was exerted by London. In fact, the government was split on the matter whereas a majority of Canadians supported the war. It was, for them, an expression of national power and more than symbolic of Canada's place in Empire (with its attendant economic benefits), something which was celebrated, not deplored by most of the Canadian people.[8]

Yet another example of power projection occurred in the wake of the destructive First World War. The Russian Revolution generated a chaotic situation with disparate factions working at cross purposes to Allied objectives which were, in the main, to keep Russians fighting Germans so that the latter would not fight Canadian, British, French and American forces on the Western Front. The Western allies intervened in several locations on the Russian periphery, with Canadian forces operating in Siberia and out of Archangel. Canadian motives for projecting power in this case were an amalgam of Imperial obligations, security needs related to the war directly, the prevention of a 'radical engine' in central Europe,[9] and, as C.P. Stacey remarked, "Extraordinary as it now appears, an element in the decision to send Canadian troops to Siberia was calculations...of postwar economic advantage in that region."[10]

Other examples of unilateral power projection are found in the Caribbean and Latin America. On twelve occasions between 1915 and 1993 Canadian naval forces were used for "Gunboat Diplomacy" in the region, to "exert a delicate and discrete threat [short of declared war] to secure national objectives." Notable operations included Mexico (1915), Costa Rica (1921), El Salvador (1932), St. Lucia (1958), and Haiti on multiple occasions since 1963.[11]

These examples demonstrate that power projection in the form of Forward Security is not foreign to national policymakers and that Canada has a significant heritage in such operations.

Another source of the Canadian peacekeeping myth is a series of three trends in the international affairs analysis community that acted as a framework for burgeoning interest in peacekeeping. These trends were manifested through an increase in popular and specialist writings on the UN and peacekeeping, coupled with public pronouncements on the increased requirement for international community—usually UN—intervention.

Efforts undertaken during and immediately after the Second World War promoted a popular interest in international organizations like the Organization of American States, the European Coal and Steel Community, the Western Union Defence Organization, the Rio Pact, and even NATO. There was an excited surge in popular interest in the League of Nations' successor, the United Nations. Even popular culture in the form of espionage and science fiction movies depict the UN as a de facto functional world government that aliens and madmen trying to take over the world must deal with. The UN brought with it new possibilities, a fresh approach that was on the surface democratic, egalitarian, anti-colonial, and anti-fascist, the very things Canada fought for during the Second World War. This belief in the efficacy of the UN waned in the late 1940s, during the Arab Israeli War of 1948-49 and the Korean War, though the legitimacy provided by the organization did not.[12]

The second trend occurred between 1957 and 1967. It was driven by the impressive personality of UN Secretary General Dag Hammarskjöld, the deployment of the United Nations Emergency Force in 1956, the bestowal of a Nobel Peace Prize on Lester Pearson, and the proliferation of UN peacekeeping operations between 1958 and 1964. This trend waned during the withdrawal of UN forces from the Congo and the demand by Colonel Gamel Nasser for UNEF to leave the Sinai in 1967 prior to the start of the Six Day War.[13]

The third resurgence of interest in UN peacekeeping activities occurred after the Cold War ended in 1990-91, when some analysts and diplomats believed the UN would be unfettered by Superpower confrontation and could take its rightful place as world mediator. There was an explosion of literature within the international relations community, and more significantly the popular press, about peacekeeping operations. This coincided with the proliferation of UN peace operations between 1990 and 1996. However, once UN operations went drastically wrong (particularly in Rwanda and Somalia, and in some respects, the UNPROFOR operation in the former Yugoslavia), faith in the UN's ability to intervene waned again as NATO took up the peacekeeping torch in Bosnia and then in Kosovo.[14]

Ignorance of the UN's role in peacekeeping and the motives for Canadian involvement during the Cold War led to confusion in the early 1990s: was the use of a light armour battlegroup to deliver humanitarian aid in the Bosnian civil war "peacekeeping"?

(Author's Collection)

In Canadian popular culture, the second and third peacekeeping trends produced two widely read memoirs which brought home for Canadians what their peacekeepers were doing. The first was Lieutenant General E.L.M. Burns's 1966 book, *Between Arab and Israeli*, followed by the 1993 bestseller, *Peacekeeper: The Road to Sarajevo* by Brigadier General Lewis Mackenzie.

The fact that General Burns moved from commanding UNEF to taking a seat at the table of the non-UN but UN-affiliated nuclear disarmament talks in Geneva possibly contributed to a sense in the popular mind that peacekeeping and disarmament activities were interchangeable. Burns, for example, favoured the use of UN forces to observe military reductions between NATO and the Warsaw Pact in Europe.[15] Burns' books critiquing nuclear weapons, most notably *Megamurder* (1966); his other work on disarmament, *A Seat at the Table*; and *Between Arab and Israeli*, might also have contributed to this perception.

In the Canadian academic world, there has been resounding silence on the topic of peacekeeping history. As far as can be determined, there are only three books devoted to the history of Canadian peacekeeping, two of which are popular works.[16] Peacekeeping has, from time to time, popped up in professional writings prior to the 1990s, but it was the 1990s resurgence in interest that in part prompted the creation of the Pearson Peacekeeping Centre and its literary output. Peacekeeping, apparently, is just something Canada is involved with naturally, without discussion. The UN asks and Canada does, or so the Department of Foreign Affairs and International Trade would have us believe.

Many professional analysts, particularly those with access to the mass media, are generally anti-NATO, if not anti-military, as much as they are pro-UN. The primary representations of this view are the images by Gwynne Dyer in the *War* documentary series which postulated that NATO military operations in the Central Region were futile. The series served to bolster the arguments of those who wanted to keep Canada's NATO commitments at arms length and ridiculed those who believed otherwise.[17]

Gwynne Dyer also narrated the National Film Board series *Protection Force*, on Canadian peacekeeping in the former Yugoslavia, which praised the Canadian contribution to peacekeeping outside its Cold War context. The production and widespread distribution of Lewis Mackenzie's superb documentary *A Soldier's Peace* further cemented the notion of Canada as peacekeeper in the popular culture at home and abroad.[18]

Indeed, anyone reading Mackenzie's best-selling autobiography *Peacekeeper: The Road to Sarajevo* would come away with the perception that NATO had little impact on Mackenzie's career or experiences since it was, in his words, "boring."[19] There are no NFB or CBC productions examining Canada's long-standing contributions to NATO or NORAD as positive aspects of Canada's heritage. Similarly, the Heritage Minute pieces seen in theatres and on television do mention the Avro Arrow interceptor aircraft, but say nothing about NORAD or NATO. There is a piece, however, on UNFICYP in Cyprus.

In general, the apparent hostility directed against Canada's NATO experience by many in the academic and media communities is more intense than criticisms of Canada's role in the UN. These perceptions also serve to overshadow NATO's role in Canadian national security policy and enhance the UN peacekeeping image. In essence, Canada's role in NATO is tinged with guilt by association with the so-called military industrial complex since there is a predominant view that NATO is merely an extension of American national security policy.[20] The UN on the other hand is seen to be an egalitarian expression of worldly brotherhood, not dominated by superpower intrigue, a forum in which Canada can create counterweights to balance American dominance and push for the peaceful resolution of disputes.

NATO was a hybrid conventional-nuclear deterrent and warfighting force, aggressive and active. UN peacekeeping is a passive, conciliatory activity in which nuclear weapons are not involved (apparently). This view appeals to Canadians with an idealistic, altruistic view of man and his affairs, with a false moral superiority over those who must be prepared to deter and fight on behalf of Canada's interests in the real world.

The Canadian government has seen fit to erect a monument to peacekeeping which appears on currency, postcards, and medals. The Canadian ten-dollar bill has been modified to include a female soldier wearing a Blue Beret. No such monument or commemoration is planned for Canada's Cold War NATO or NORAD contribution, which were arguably more important mechanisms for keeping the peace during the Cold War. It is as if these commitments never existed. There can be no greater message sent to the Canadian public.

THE TRANSFORMATION OF UN PEACEKEEPING

One very important aspect of the myth is the misunderstanding or misuse of terminology. It is quite common for the popular press to describe any UN activity as 'peacekeeping.' Such a perception is quite understandable, since the images transmitted back to domestic audiences consist of large groups of people from a variety of countries wearing blue berets and shoulder armbands bearing the UN symbol. The confusion is also understandable from a historical perspective since in the early days, there was sometimes little or no distinction made by the practitioners between types of operations.[21]

The Canadian Army, for example, did not formally differentiate between peace mission types until 1996, when it produced its first doctrinal pamphlet, *Peacekeeping Operations*, which established four types of peace operations:

PEACE ENFORCEMENT: Conventional military operations to establish a deterrent to aggression against a target country and to fight if necessary to prevent conflict escalation.

PEACEKEEPING: Multinational military formations interposed between parties in a conflict to permit political negotiations to take place.

PEACE OBSERVATION: The deployment of military observers to a region to monitor compliance of parties with a truce, accord, or other international agreement.

HUMANITARIAN ASSISTANCE: The use of military forces under UN auspices to provide humanitarian and disaster relief. [22]

Cultural overemphasis on Canadian UN peacekeeping has obscured the fundamental pillar of Canadian national security during the Cold War: the "hard" power of the North Atlantic Treaty Organization and the salient Canadian contribution to it. Without her willingness to confront totalitarianism through NATO, Canada would have had no political or operational credibility in UN operations.

(CF Photo)

Note that these are not the only mission types Canadian military forces are involved in. Between 1948 and 1964, Canadian military personnel were involved in all four of these mission types, yet the popular press and even the professional analytical community generally referred to all of them as "peace-keeping" operations. This was despite the fact that such operations required different mixes of personnel, different levels of risk, and different international and national objectives.

UN peacekeeping was not a static activity in the 1950s and 1960s. The first UN missions were what we would call peace observation missions (UNTSO and UNMOGIIP). The deployment of UNEF during the Suez Crisis in 1956 fits into the peacekeeping category, but UNOGIL in Lebanon in 1958 was peace observation. The next big UN mission, ONUC in the Congo from 1960 to 1964, was similar to NATO missions in Bosnia in the 1990s: it was much closer to counterinsurgency or peace enforcement than UNEF-like interpositionary peacekeeping. UNTEA in West New Guinea, UNIPOM in India-Pakistan, and UNYOM in The Yemen during the early 1960s were peace observation missions. UNFICYP in Cyprus was a hybrid: it started off as a stabilization mission in 1964, nearly became a counterinsurgency or peace enforcement mission that year, and then evolved into an interpositionary peacekeeping mission by 1974. In other words, there was no clear evolution of peacekeeping operation types, despite some analysts' attempts to impose such a framework during the 1990s to explain the activities of that decade.

UN peacekeeping operations which emerged in the 1950s and 1960s had specific historical contexts which broadly fit into two superimposed categories. First, and most important, was the Cold War (east-west) competition between what amounted to an American-led empire and a Soviet-led empire. Both empires had the ability to cause mass devastation through nuclear weapons use, which essentially froze the conflict in place and discouraged traditional warfighting methods to resolve disputes in critical areas.[24]

The second category was decolonization (north-south). The re-ordering of the world after the Second World War produced areas where Western colonial control was loosened (Soviet control over its colonial areas in central Asia was not in doubt until the war in Afghanistan in the 1980s). Many of these areas contained valuable resources by dint of their geography, demography, or geology. Soviet-supported challenges in these areas aggravated problems which existed under colonialism but were now in play. Consequently, the link between the Cold War and decolonization turned these areas in Africa, the Middle East, and Asia into battlegrounds for the two empires.[25]

UN peacekeeping in its broadest sense was a mechanism to ensure that situations in these areas did not escalate into empire confrontation which would involve nuclear weapons use. It also served to provide an alternative to an attractive but violent and repressive Communist ideology and thus fill power vacuums as they emerged. This view of UN peacekeeping only appeared in 1947, after Canadian policymakers considered the 1945 UN experiment as a failure in collective global security since it could not contain aggressive Soviet activity. This failure was the foundation for the creation of NATO. Similarly, the use of UN peacekeeping as a surrogate force in the 1950s and 1960s was considered to have run its course by 1967, particularly after the Congo affair and the forced withdrawal of UNEF. The expansion of the UN General Assembly during the decolonization period completely altered the complexion of UN deliberations and the organization shifted from one dominated by the West to one dominated by post-colonial nations subject to Soviet manipulations. By the mid-1970s, the Western powers were on the ropes in the Cold War and the UN was part of the problem, not the solution.

Unfortunately, the Canadian exceptionalist ideologists and particularly those championing Canada's involvement in UN peacekeeping in the 1990s had no clear understanding of these matters. In effect, the foreign policy elite and the academic constituency that pursued the human security and soft power agendas in the 1990s was trapped in an ossified vision of UN peacekeeping that ignored the complex relationship between each separate 1950s and 1960s UN mission and the Cold War. They focused on a single event and held it up as the standard:interpositionary peacekeeping of the UNEF model, mostly because a Canadian received the Nobel Peace Prize for his ostensible creation of it. This distortion contributes to the myth that policymakers must deal with today, for peacekeeping as we knew it no longer exists. Military forces in the NATO-led IFOR, SFOR, and KFOR missions in the Balkans and the UN-led missions in Sierra Leone, Liberia, and Somalia operate more like counterinsurgency forces than peacekeeping forces like UNEF or UNIFYCP in its post-1974 incarnation.[26]

Interpositionary peacekeeping in the 1990s was a rare event. Of the thirty or so UN missions from 1990 to 2000 that Canada was involved in, only UNFICYP in Cyprus; UNMEE in Ethiopia and Eritrea; and UNPROFOR I in Croatia had, as part of their primary mission, Canadian combat troops interposed between belligerent forces.[27]

THE REALITIES OF CANADIAN COLD WAR PEACEKEEPING

There is nothing inherently wrong with or dishonourable about Canadian participation in UN peacekeeping, or the use of peacekeeping operations to project power for Forward Security. Peace support operations were and remain critical components of Canadian national security policy. It is vital, however, that the distorted view which has been generated by the myth receive attention. It must be placed in the proper historical context. UN peacekeeping was not the primary expression of Canadian national security policy during the Cold War: NATO and NORAD were the fundamental building blocks on which Canadian UN peacekeeping was constructed.

The Canadian Army from 1945 to 1950 consisted of a single brigade group (about 5000 men) dedicated to the defence of Canada against small-scale ground incursions. The ability to rapidly expand the Army was suspect, and demonstrably so when an entire brigade group had to be raised from the street to combat Communism in Korea from 1950 to 1955. It was only with the four-fold expansion of the Army to handle NATO commitments in Europe during 1951 that enough trained and experienced manpower and suitable equipment and transport became available for global operations later in the 1950s and 1960s. If Canada's NATO commitments had not existed, there would not have been a force structure capable of conducting UN peace-keeping operations, nor would there have been any strategic lift to transport them. Canada's military credibility was continuously demonstrated during NATO warfighting and deterrent exercises in Europe, and through its combat role in Korea. Without that level of credibility, Canadian forces employed on UN peacekeeping missions would not have been as respected or as effective in their dealings with belligerent forces. The fact that Canada's armed forces were nuclear-capable in the 1960s gave added weight to this credibility, not by posing any direct or indirect threat of their use, but by enhancing prestige and demonstrating that powerful allies trusted Canada to possess such a capability.

Let us examine the UN versus NATO or NORAD in terms of public visibility. To an untrained observer, the sheer number of Canadian UN peacekeeping operations alone (practically all of them) would be remarkable. The exotic locales for such operations also stimulate the imagination, with Canadian soldiers wearing the Blue Beret from West New Guinea, to Cambodia, to Afghanistan, Iraq, the Golan Heights, Cyprus, the Sahara and Honduras. Canada's NATO forces were clustered in northern Europe or at sea, while the NORAD commitments were generally in isolated portions of northern Canada and the Arctic. Secrecy surrounded their work, particularly since Canada's NATO and NORAD forces were equipped with nuclear weapons and were part of highly classified war planning involving the United States.

The numbers of Canadians involved in UN peacekeeping seem impressive, but appearances can be deceiving. The bulk of UN peacekeeping commitments for the period covered by this book (1945-1970) were short-term operations with small numbers of Canadian participants. Some of these missions only had one Canadian officer involved (for example, the Dominican Republic observation mission in 1965). If we break down Canadian UN missions by mission type, we find that only two are actual peacekeeping operations in that they involve Canadian combat troops in formed units (UNEF and UNFICYP) separating belligerent forces. The bulk of the missions are peace observation or peacekeeping support commitments (missions involving Canadian support or service units but without combat troops). (see Chart 1) It is an inescapable conclusion that from 1945 to 1970, Canada supported UN peacekeeping rather than kept the peace using Canadian forces.[28]

Chart 1: Canadian Peacekeeping Operations by Type, 1945-1970

MISSION	PEACE OBSERVATION (Military Observers)	INTERPOSITIONARY (Combat Troops)	PEACEKEEPING SUPPORT (Service Support Troops)
UNCURK	X		
UNMOGIIP	X		
UNTSO	X		
ICSC	X		
UNEF		X	X
UNOGIL	X		
ONUC			X
UNTEA			X
DOMREP	X		
UNYOM			X
UNFICYP		X	
UNIPOM			X

The vast majority of Canadian forces were committed to Europe, the Atlantic, or the continental defence of North America. On any given year throughout the 1950s and 1960s, of the 100,000 to 120,000 personnel in the armed forces, there were approximately 12,000 Canadian soldiers and airmen stationed in Europe as part of NATO. The rest were either at sea or stationed in Canada defending North America or preparing to rotate with the Europe-based NATO forces. The peak UN peacekeeping deployment year for Canada was 3399 personnel in 1964 and that lasted for only one year: 1200 of those were stationed on one ship that spent a limited period on one operation. From 1948 to 1955, the total number of Canadians committed to UN peacekeeping never exceeded twenty. If we accept that an average of 2000 Canadian troops were deployed overseas annually on UN duties in the 1960s, it is still a fraction of those deterring Soviet forces in central Europe and in North America.[29]

Similarly, the amount of money and industrial effort (and thus job production for Canada) expended on NATO and NORAD commitments greatly exceeds that spent on UN peacekeeping. UN peacekeeping has no direct industrial benefit to Canadians in the way NORAD and NATO commitments did, particularly in the critical aerospace and shipbuilding industries which employed thousands of Canadian voters building fighter aircraft and anti-submarine destroyers.

Where, exactly, did NATO primacy in Canadian national security policy come from and why was UN peacekeeping subordinated to it? The origins lie in the failure of the UN as an institution, a failure identified as early as 1947 by Canadian policymakers led by Lester Pearson and General Charles Foulkes.

Notes for Chapter 1

1. George Stanley, *Canada's Soldiers: The Military History of an Unmilitary People*, revised ed. (Toronto: Macmillan and Co., 1960), 1.

2. Gwynne Dyer and Tina Viljoen, *The Defence of Canada: In the Arms of the Empire 1790-1939* (Toronto: Macmillan, 1990); Blair Fraser, *The Search for Identity: Canada Postwar to Present 1945-1967* (Toronto: Doubleday, 1967); Phillip Resnick, "Canadian Defence Policy and the American Empire," in *Close the 49th Parallel etc: The Americanization of Canada* (Toronto: University of Toronto Press, 1970), 94-115.

3. Pierre Berton, *Why We Act Like Canadians: A Personal Exploration of our National Character* (Toronto: Penguin Books, 1982), 34-52; Charles Hanly, "The Ethics of Independence," in *An Independent Foreign Policy for Canada?* Stephen Clarkson, ed. (Toronto: McClelland & Stewart, 1968), 17-28.

4. Douglas LePan, "In Frock Coat and Moccasins,"*Canada: A Guide to the Peaceable Kingdom*, William Kilbourn, ed. (Toronto: Macmillan, 1970), 3-7; Gerald L. Caplan and James Laxer, "Perspectives on un-American Traditions in Canada," in *Close the 49th Parallel etc: The Americanization of Canada* (Toronto: University of Toronto Press, 1970), 305-320.

5. Hugh Hood, "Moral Imagination: Canadian Thing," *Canada: A Guide to the Peaceable Kingdom*, William Kilbourn, ed. (Toronto: Macmillan, 1970), 29-35.

6. See Sean M. Maloney, "Helpful Fixer or Hired Gun: Why Canada Goes Overseas"; IRPP conference, "Challenges to Governance: Military Interventions Abroad and Consensus at Home," Montreal, November 2000.

7. Brereton Greenhous and Bill McAndrew, "The Canadian Military Marches North: The Yukon Field Force 1998-1900," *Canadian Defence Quarterly* Vol 10 No. 4 (Spring 1981), 30-41; Brereton Greenhous (ed) *Guarding the Goldfields: The Story of the Yukon Field Force* (Toronto: Dundurn Press, 1987).

8. Carmen Miller, *Painting the Map Red: Canada and the South African War, 1899-1902* (Kingston: McGill-Queen's University Press, 1993), Ch 1 & 2.

9. Lloyd Ambrosious, *Wilsonian Statecraft: theory and Practice of Liberal Internationalism during World War I* (Wilmington: Scholarly Resources Inc, 1991), Ch. 4; Stanley, *Canada's Soldiers*, 332-336; Levin, Woodrow Wilson and World Politics, Ch 3.

10. C.P. Stacey, *Canada and the Age of Conflict Volume 1: 1867-1921* (Toronto: University of Toronto Press, 1984) p. 277.

11. The fact that some of the missions had the appearance of comic opera, particularly San Salvador in 1932, should not detract from the fact that the forces were expressly used to project Canadian pressure. See Richard A. Preston, "The RCN and Gun-Boat Diplomacy in the Caribbean," *Military Affairs*, Vol 36, No. 2 (April 1972), 41-44; Sean M. Maloney, "Maple Leaf Over the Caribbean: Gunboat Diplomacy, Canadian-Style?" conference paper presented at the Halifax Naval Conference on the Diplomatic Uses of Canadian Naval Forces, June 1998.

12. H. Nicholas, *The United Nations as a Political Institution* (London: Oxford University Press, 1967), Ch. 4; Stanley Meisner, *United Nations: The First Fifty Years* (New York: Atlantic Monthly Press, 1995), Ch 1 & 2; Lester B. Pearson, *Mike: The Memoirs of the Rt. Hon. Lester B. Pearson volume 2 1948-1957* (Toronto: University of Toronto Press, 1973), 32, 35, 37.

13. H.G. Nicholas, "The United Nations in Crisis," *Survival*, vol 7 (1965), 257-262; Philippe Ben, "The Limits of the UN," *Survival*, Vol 8, No. 4 (1966), 130-133; Alfred O. Hero Jr., "The American Public and the UN, 1954-1966," *Conflict Resolution* Vol 10, No. 4, 436-475.

14. For example, there were at least ten separate works on UN peacekeeping operations published between 1993 and 1996, in addition to the establishment of the academic journal *International Peacekeeping*.

15. Albert Legault and Michel Fortmann, *A Diplomacy of Hope: Canada and Disarmament 1945-1968* (Kingston: McGill-Queens University Press, 1992), Ch 3, 4 & 5.

16. These are: J.L. Granatstein and David Bercuson, *War and Peacekeeping: From South Africa to the Gulf-Canada's Limited Wars* (Toronto: Key Porter Books, 1991); Fred Gaffen, *In the Eye of the Storm: A History of Canadian Peacekeeping* (Ottawa: Deneau and Wayne, 1989); Alastair Taylor, ed. *Peacekeeping: International Challenge and Canadian Response* (Toronto: University of Toronto Press, 1968). There are numerous political science works on peacekeeping, but these usually do not use rigorous historical methodology or documentation.

17. Gwynne Dyer, *War* (Toronto: Stoddart, 1985), Ch 8 & 9.

18. *Protection Force* Volumes I-III, National Film Board of Canada, 1996; *A Soldier's Peace* Canadian Broadcasting Corporation, 1995.

19. Lewis Mackenzie, *Peacekeeper: The Road to Sarajevo* (Toronto: Douglas and McIntyre, 1993).

20. See for example Howard Peter Langille, *Changing the Guard: Canada's Defence in a World of Transition* (Toronto: University of Toronto Press, 1990); and Dan Smith, *Pressure: How The US Runs NATO* (London: Bloomsbury, 1989).

21. There were attempts in the literature to differentiate, but these were informal in nature and not universally accepted. See Inis L. Claude Jr, "United Nations Use of Military Force," *Conflict Resolution* Vol 7, No. 2, 117-129.

22. As quoted in Sean M. Maloney, "Insights into Canadian Peacekeeping Doctrine," *Military Review*, (March-April 1996), 12-23. To further confuse the issue, Canadian Army doctrine in the 1960s viewed peacekeeping as another form of counterinsurgency operations.

23. Even David Wainhouse's early but comprehensive work *International Peace Observation* (Baltimore: John Hopkins University Press, 1966) groups peacekeeping and peace observation together.

24. See John Lewis Gaddis, *We Now Know: Rethinking Cold War History* (Oxford: Clarendon Press, 1977), Ch. 2.

25. See D.A. Low, *Eclipse of Empire* (Cambridge: Cambridge University Press, 1991); and John Keay, *Last Post: The End of Empire in the Far East* (London: John Murray, 1997).

26. The author's experiences in the Balkans and the Middle East confirm this view. See also Robert Young Pelton, The Hunter, *The Hammer, and Heaven: Journeys to Three Worlds Gone Mad* (Guilford: The Lyons Press, 2002) particularly the first section on Sierra Leone; and Martin Stanton, *Somalia on $5.00 a Day: A Soldier's Story* (Novato: Presidio Press, 2001).

27. See Sean M. Maloney, "Directorate of Peacekeeping Policy Study 00/01:Canada and UN Commanded Operations, 1948-2000," 20 October 2000.

28. Ibid.

29. Ibid.

CHAPTER 2

OUT OF ISOLATIONISM: CANADIAN NATIONAL SECURITY POLICY AND PEACE OPERATIONS TO 1951

Armed might alone will not stop the spread of Communism. In a sense, our volunteer firemen are now lined up to beat out the flames at any point where they might begin to spread. We have failed to realize, however, that we are fighting a fire that can suddenly climb over the heads of the helpless firemen and race vast distances through the treetops. What about the condition of the forests on the other side of the line? Are we sufficiently aware that tremendous expanses of the areas we have a duty to protect are tinder dry and can kindle with a single spark?

- Trygve Lie, UN Secretary General, 1945-52.

General Andrew McNaughton (left), Ambassador Charles Ritchie (second from left) and John Holmes (right), worked together on numerous occasions to protect Canadian interests, in this case in the 1948 Kashmir crisis. Holmes, the eventual head of External Affairs' UN Division, was particularly wary when it came to excessive reliance on the UN as a security instrument.

(CIIA Photo)

Canadian national security policymakers in the 1990s would recognize the problems faced by their predecessors in the mid-1940s. The Second World War and its aftermath generated a new world order which had blurred shape and dimensions, where the implications for world peace were at best uncertain and perhaps not achievable. There was pressure from the Canadian public for a "peace dividend." Threats to security existed and the policymaking community was divided on how to interpret—let alone deal with—these threats. There was proliferation of weapons of mass destruction, particularly to a despotic unstable world leader. The lessening of the old order's grip on the developing nations promoted ethnicity-based warfare. When open warfare prompted the UN to attempt peace initiatives, as in the 1990s, between the new political/ethnic entities, it underestimated the depth of long-standing ethnic animosities by assuming a state-to-state model of conciliation. This short term mediation was mistaken for a long term solution.

Unlike the 1990s, Canada achieved a new prominence on the world stage: her soldiers fought gallantly throughout the European theatre, her sailors kept the sea lanes in the Atlantic open, and her airmen helped to pulverize and burn the heart out of the Nazi war machine. The road to a lasting peace was not clear: it was littered with the debris of the old order and, if the Canadian Government wanted to get what Canadians wanted, the leaders would have to stickhandle through the mess. Proselytizers exhorted the public with "never agains" and "no mores": More practical—perhaps even cynical—men knew better, particularly after the full extent of the damage wrought by the Hiroshima and Nagasaki bombs was revealed.

What of the inevitable regional conflicts in the new world order? How were the great nations to handle them? The Second World War had released new energies like democracy, self determination and freedom. What would happen to the colonial world? How could great powers make room at the table for the new? There were no easy answers. What role could or should Canada play in the series of international dramas which would unfold? Canadian policymakers had first to determine what Canada wanted.

The relative disinterest in world affairs exhibited by Prime Minister Mackenzie King's government did not impress General Charles Foulkes, whose staff developed a UN peacekeeping force concept as early as 1947. Even Defence Minister Brooke Claxton was cautious about Canadian global involvement.

(CF photo)

CANADA AND THE NEW WORLD ORDER, CIRCA 1945

The men who would define Canada's global interests in the mid-1940s generally had the Second World War as a common experience. The elected officials included the Prime Minister, William Lyon Mackenzie King; Louis St Laurent, his Quebec-born foreign minister (who would replace King as Prime Minister in 1948); and Brooke Claxton, the "lion tamer" in the newly formed Department of National Defence. These men were hand-picked by King to implement the new order: they were quite distinct from those who fought alongside King in his wartime Cabinet.

Then there were the unelected officials, such as the members of the Department of External Affairs who were on the whole brought into the system by O.D. Skelton. Skelton was an influential figure in the creation of Canadian bureaucracy, particularly in those entities engaged in national security policy formulation. He enjoyed a long standing relationship with the equally long standing Prime Minister Mackenzie King prior to Skelton's death in 1941. The so-called "Ottawa Men" included Bob Bryce, economic genius and doyen of the Privy Council Office; Lester B. "Mike" Pearson, former ambassador to the United States during the war; John Holmes, ambassador to the United Nations; Norman Robertson, Pearson protégé and eventual Undersecretary of State for External Affairs; Hume Wrong; Escott Reid; and others. These men saw what Canada was capable of achieving and decided that the time was ripe to capitalize on her new global influence.[1]

Serving military men were also part of this group of policymakers. The Second World War ushered in an era where there was increased responsibility for those who "took the King's shilling." The term "civil-military relations" was relatively new in 1945, but the incredible cooperative effort necessary to fight the war left its indelible mark. The situation was so different and the unknowns too great to keep the military on a short leash in the dog house until the politicians/diplomats declared war. The most politically and strategically astute individual was Chief of the General Staff, Lieutenant General Charles Foulkes, the man who had beat out the over-rated Guy Granville Simonds for the job. Unlike his counterparts, who were focused on trying to limit the damage caused by the inevitable slash of Claxton's budget axe, Foulkes strove to understand the intricate workings of the system in Ottawa and had enough curiosity to monitor international trends and retain situational awareness, whatever might come.[2]

General A.G.L. McNaughton, formerly the Chief of the General Staff in the 1930s and later head of the Canadian Army overseas and ultimately Minister of National Defence, was installed by Mackenzie King as Canada's representative at the United Nations in January 1948.[3]

It was fairly clear to Canadians that the King government was planning to make good on its wartime claims that it would establish a functioning welfare state. Economic gains during the war allowed for this and the government was generally focused on meeting its obligations. Fortunately, on the international front, King had no intention of retreating into total isolationism. Post-war prosperity and international engagement were not seen as incompatible. It was a question of the degree of the engagement.

During the war, Canadian policymakers projected that the Soviet Union would replace Nazi Germany as a global threat. There were too many instances of Soviet-supported subversion and espionage directed against Canada and her allies to ignore this, particularly after the Gouzenko Affair exposed an extremely damaging Soviet spy ring operating in Canada. What really gave the diplomats pause was the Gouzenko Affair, as well as the Soviet occupation of Eastern Europe and the complete lack of significant Red Army demobilization. Then the Greek Civil War shifted into high gear with covert Soviet backing for the Communist guerrillas, followed by bellicose Soviet threats directed at Turkey, and unacceptable Soviet military interference in Iran. When Stalin announced in February 1946 that the Communist bloc and the "capitalist" bloc were incompatible and that conflict was inevitable, the Cold War was effectively declared.[4]

Had not Canada just fought a war to ensure freedom? Lester Pearson put it best:

The main and very real threat during the first years of the Cold War was the armed might, the aggressive ideology, and the totalitarian despotism of the communist empire of the USSR and its satellite states under the iron hand of one of the most ruthless tyrants of all time. To ignore this danger, or to refuse to accept any commitments for collective action to meet it, while playing our part in positive action in the United Nations or elsewhere to bring about a better state of affairs, would have been demonstrably wrong and perilously short-sighted.[5]

Though these words are drawn from Pearson's 1972 memoirs, they accurately reflect the mind-set in Canadian national security policy formulation bodies of the day. In light of the situation, Louis St Laurent provided a firm policy framework at a 1947 lecture. The principles of Canada's international engagement during the Cold War were: national unity; political liberty; the rule of law in international affairs; the values of Christian civilization; and Canada's responsibility to play her part.[6] The Prime Minister had to be won over because he was concerned with the political problems of deploying military forces overseas. Before too long, however, St Laurent was Prime Minister and Pearson was running External Affairs.

Peace, freedom, and prosperity for Canadians. These were legitimate objectives of Canadian national security policy. How best to secure them? Canada had four primary venues in which to do so, three of which were outgrowths of the war.

The first was the British Commonwealth, of which Canada was a charter member. Originally conceived as a means of retaining British influence in the increasingly independent-minded former colonies, and using that influence to compete with the USSR, the United States, or the French Empire, the Commonwealth was in the process of overhaul in the wake of the war. In general terms, the Commonwealth members shared a common system of government and ideals, and could coordinate their economic, military, and diplomatic movements if they felt it was in their best interests. It was a loose organization with a declining imperial defence aspect after 1945, and one which would not have a formalized structure until the 1960s.[7]

The primary Canadian objective within the Commonwealth was to influence the British by mobilizing collective opinion from like-minded states. In addition, Canada attempted to straddle the world economic order split between the sterling bloc (British) and the gold bloc (American). In a wider sense, the Commonwealth could also act as a counterweight to American influence if necessary.[8]

The second venue was the wartime Canada-US Permanent Joint Board on Defence (PJBD) and its Cold War secret sub-component, the Military Co-operation Committee (MCC). These organizations provided Canada with a special relationship to the United States which even exceeded that of the much-trumpeted British-American special relationship. The Joint Board allowed constant co-operation in matters related to continental defence to be handled discretely at the diplomat-foreign service level, while the MCC was a formal link between the US Joint Chiefs of Staff and the Canadian Chiefs of Staff Committee and their respective Joint Planning Staffs. Though the aim was not to generate wide influence with the Americans, the Joint Board allowed friendships to develop which had economic and political benefits for both countries.[9]

Canada's participation in the PJBD was a yearly summit event, while the work of the MCC was a very low key day-to-day affair handled by the Joint Staff in Ottawa. The larger purpose of the exercise was to retain influence over continental defence matters which could have an impact on Canadian sovereignty.[10]

The third venue was related to the first and second: the American-British-Canadian or ABC relationship. ABC was a loose series of arrangements between those three English-speaking powers. The first level was a series of standardization committees relating to items from screw threads to radio frequencies to rifle calibres. Another level was the ABC intelligence sharing relationship where the information collected as well as the intelligence derived from it were traded. There was also significant ABC cooperation related to nuclear energy and nuclear weapons developments. For the purpose of this study, however, the most important aspect of the ABC relationship was the coordination of global war planning. Prior to the establishment of NATO in 1949, the ABC members' joint planning staffs co-ordinated their planned moves in the event of war with the Soviet Union at an unprecedented level.[11]

As with the PJBD and MCC, Canadian participation in the ABC relationship allowed access to technological and intelligence benefits from the larger allies. It also afforded Canada the opportunity to peer into the black chamber of American defence planning. It was a low-key affair, not unlike the MCC, but with even less formality.[12]

The final venue was the United Nations. It is worth noting here that the Second World War anti-fascist alliance commonly known as "The Allies" was technically called the "United Nations." President Roosevelt suggested this name for the post-war world-wide organization which would be led by the Big Four powers: Britain, the United States, the Soviet Union, and China. As originally conceived, the UN was to be the guarantor of the peace. It later took on humanitarian functions (like the UN Relief and Rehabilitation Agency) but the primary function was to act as a diplomatic intermediary and intervene if international disputes escalated to the point of open conflict. Initial talks included the concept of an international UN army to carry out the UN's purpose in such interventions. This concept may have been raised by Norman Robertson as early as 1945, who favoured establishing something similar to a UN French Foreign Legion to be placed at the disposal of the planned Security Council.[13]

As part of the victorious alliance, Canada was invited to become a founding member of the UN, a significant event in Canada's journey from colony to nation. The diplomats were split, however, on what Canada's larger aims should be. Some favoured a limited approach which viewed the UN as a larger and more effective League of Nations. Others had a more utopian view in which the UN was a functioning (not virtual) world government to ensure control over nuclear weapons, disarm the world and make it safe. Pearson took a middle of the road approach. Terms like "functionalism" were thrown about in External Affairs, but what it all boiled down to was that the UN forum could be used, not unlike the Commonwealth, as a means for the smaller powers to exert pressure on the larger powers. In theory, this applied to all the larger powers, but in practice Canadian diplomats saw the Soviet Union as the main target for diplomatic pressure. Canada, in one view, would function as a "middle power" between the two groups. The reasons or purposes of that middle power were, however, left ill-defined by the Canadian policymakers.[14]

Note that Canadian participation in these forums in the 1940s was mutually supporting. The policies pursued in one venue did not generally contradict the policies pursued in the others. This was the result of having a coherent, coordinated policymaking apparatus in Ottawa. The system was not perfect, but it allowed for a certain flexibility. Prior to 1948, the preference was to have some form of "UN primacy" because of the publicity benefits to be reaped from the perceived global legitimacy created by the signing of the UN Charter in 1945, but this was not formalized by the government in Ottawa at the time. With the Commonwealth and the ABC relationship, Canada retained strong connections with the British. The ABC and PJBD/MCC relationships gave Canada access to the Americans. The United Nations put Canada on the international world stage and provided another outlet which could be used if and when it was necessary.

In Cold War terms, the PJBD and MCC defended Canada from direct physical attack from the Soviet Union, while the ABC relationship allowed Canada to go on the offensive alongside its allies if it became necessary to do so. The Commonwealth could be used to back up its weaker members (particularly in the economic and diplomatic arenas) to make them more resistant to Soviet-inspired Communist encroachment, while the UN was a forum which had enough legitimacy to apply direct (and public) international diplomatic pressure on the Soviet Union. In the future, it was assumed by many, a UN Army would police the world. Consequently, any action taken by Canada in the peacekeeping realm was only one part of a multi-faceted Canadian policy gestalt.

UN ARMY CONCEPTS, COLLECTIVE SECURITY, AND PEACE OPERATIONS

The primary means by which some Canadian diplomats believed world peace could be generated was through the UN's Military Staff Committee and a UN Army. Canadian perspectives on these bodies in the mid-1940s bear some examination since the inability of the UN to implement them had a direct bearing on the creation of NATO and on the early development of UN peace operation forces.

The legal UN basis for military forces is buried in several sections of the UN Charter. Chapter VI, Article 43 permits the Security Council to investigate and make recommendations on a response to aggression. Chapter VII, Article 39 places the Security Council in charge of UN military reactions to acts of aggression. Article 42 permits military action by forces placed at the disposal of the Security Council, while Article 51 ensures that the right of self defence is not impaired by UN inactivity. Finally, Article 47 establishes a Military Staff Committee drawn from members of the permanent members of the Security Council which in turn is responsible to the Security Council.[15]

The first time the UN tried to deal with blatant aggression was in 1946 when the Greeks asked for assistance against Communist guerrillas operating across the Bulgarian border during the Greek Civil War. The Soviet member of the Security Council vetoed any action proposed by the other members because the Soviets themselves had inspired and were supporting the operation.[16] As for an international UN force, the Americans and the Soviets could not agree on its composition or how it would be funded. The Americans wanted an integrated, international, multi-division amphibious force with lots of air support, while the Soviets favoured a small force composed of national elements which, incidentally, were too small to threaten Soviet interests in Asia or Eastern Europe. UN Military Staff Committee meetings became, according to analyst Anthony Verrier, "one of those pantomime acts which the UN can well do without."[17]

What of the Canadian view? The Chiefs of Staff Committee Joint Planning Committee thought that the UN should forgo the creation of a large standing army in favour of:

> A more moderate requirement to make available to the United Nations a small force to deal with a series of disputes of a minor nature which have arisen since the war of 1939-45: Indonesia, Palestine, and Kashmir. In each of the above cases all of the elements which might lead to a general conflict exist *and the presence of a small accredited United Nations Force in these theatres would, by the moral force of its presence, exert an effect out of all proportion to actual members.* [author's emphasis][18]

This 1948 report was generated by the joint planners in response to communication from the Undersecretary of State for External Affairs, Lester Pearson, who forwarded the report of the Military Staff Committee to the Canadian Chiefs of Staff Committee for comment on Canadian implications.[19]

It is unfortunate that the names of the planners who wrote the JPC report have been lost to history since the report appears to be the first formal Canadian expression of UN peacekeeping's purpose and general structure. The study was sent to the Cabinet secretariat in the East Block where it undoubtedly was read by Pearson.[20]

The failure of the UN's Military Staff Committee notwithstanding, Secretary General Trygve Lie continued his efforts to establish a UN military force. Generally, these efforts flowed from problems encountered by the UN in the frustration of the Military Staff Committee deadlock and notably from the situation in Palestine (the subject of the next section). In any event, Lie announced at a Harvard University speech in June 1948 that a small UN Guard Force was to be established under the Security Council. This Guard Force was to provide traffic control for the UN's Palestine operations, but Lie also thought it could be used to guard polling stations during plebiscites or guard small UN trust territories.[21]

Various numbers and structures were discussed inside the Secretary General's office. The idea stabilized at 600 to 1000 men, which would be recruited internationally. The United Nations Guard would be mounted in jeeps and would be equipped with small arms. Lie saw the creation of this force as a "foot in the door" with the Military Staff Committee and the Security Council to force their hand on the issue of a UN Army.[22]

Pearson was kept informed of these developments by Canadian diplomats at the UN. He concluded, however, that professional military advice was required before Canada could formulate a policy on the matter. Escott Reid, General Foulkes and the Chiefs of Staff Committee were asked to examine the matter and concluded that it was "desirable" as an interim measure. Such a force should consist of a brigade group with appropriate air support and sea lift. Foulkes was unenthusiastic since the Canadian Army was not large enough to participate due to massive cutbacks in 1946. He expressed concern about External Affairs committing the army to UN missions which it could not fulfill. If Canada was to participate, the government needed to expand the armed forces.[23]

The UN Guard Force idea gained support in External Affairs. Norman Robertson thought that such an organization could be based on the Second World War Canada–US Special Service Force (The Devil's Brigade) or the French Foreign Legion. It would provide an outlet "for the restless and adventurous young men in small countries who otherwise stay at home and 'make revolut' [sic] like Joao Alberto."[24] Similarly, the Joint Planning Committee did a detailed study on structure and training using a Canadian Provost Corps (Military Police) company as a model, but equipping it with scout cars, jeeps, and trucks.[25]

Over time the concept was watered down to a field service of technical staff and security guards. It was unclear whether the force would be under the Charter, and whether it contravened national sovereignty. Escott Reid, for one, was concerned about Communist infiltration. The Chiefs of Staff Committee were concerned about whether or not the force would be equipped with nuclear weapons. The question of who was going to pay for the force drove the final nail into the coffin, though a 49-man multinational technical and security team was eventually formed and sent to Jerusalem.[26]

THE MIDDLE EAST, 1948: CANADA AND THE FIRST UN PEACE OPERATION

Between 1945 and 1948 the UN was peripherally involved in several disputes which affected the superpowers: Iran, the Greek Civil War, the Anglo-Albanian Corfu Channel case, and the problems between the Dutch and their Indonesian subjects. In one of these cases, the UN created the UN Special Committee on the Balkans (UNSCOB), a select group of civilian observers, to examine the political situation and report back to the UN Secretary General. It was during these initial steps that the UN organization began deploying people to trouble spots to provide information so that the UN members could use diplomacy to resolve the disputes before they could escalate into war.[27] The fine line between peace mediation and peace operations involving military personnel was finally crossed by the UN in 1948 when it sent military observers to Palestine.

The origins of the volatile situation in the Middle East are the subject of great debate which has in time determined a plethora of causes and could easily be taken back to Biblical times, when Joshua and the Israelites reconnoitered and defeated the inhabitants of the region after leaving Egypt, or to the "ethnic cleansing" of the Israelites by the Romans. Others blame the spread of Islam and its wars with the Crusaders in the 1000s or the conquering of Islam by the Ottoman Empire. Perhaps the rise of Zionist ideology in the 1870s was to blame, or the British defeat of the Ottoman Empire which provided for a Jewish homeland but did not establish its location or extent. One could easily suggest the violently anti-semitic Arab revolt of 1936-39 and the subsequent retaliatory Jewish terrorist campaign of the 1940s as more proximate causes. The after effects of the Holocaust only aggravated an already untenable situation in the region.[28]

For their part, the British were worn out after the Second World War and were tired of terrorist operations conducted against British forces in Palestine. They did not relish the prospect of Sir Winston S. Churchill in Opposition criticizing the government in Parliament and the media then comparing Great Britain to Nazi Germany. The problem was that the Attlee Government wanted to back the Arab nations, particularly those in the oil-rich Persian Gulf, while their closest ally and competitor, the United States led by Harry Truman, was under extreme public pressure in an election year to back the creation of Israel. Several Anglo-American meetings took place. Both countries recognized that the Soviet Union would capitalize on the situation if it became public. This might lead to the introduction of unwanted Soviet presence into the Arab world which would "bring about chaos from Casablanca to Pakistan" (specific Anglo-American strategic concerns will become apparent later). The best method to handle the situation was to stop arms shipments to all sides and institute a peace plan through UN mediation.[29]

The UN's first Secretary General was former Norwegian foreign minister, Trygve Lie. Lie was a compromise candidate for the position since Paul Henri Spaak of Belgium was considered too "pro West" by the Soviets, who in turn thought they could gain influence with potentially semi-neutral but geographically important Norway. Operating from the temporary UN headquarters located in a former Sperry electronic plant at Lake Success, Long Island, New York, Lie and the fledgling UN staff were soon embroiled in the Palestine situation which had almost literally been dumped at their doorstep by the British in March 1947. The complex matter was passed by Lie to Ralph Bunche, his modest and hardworking special assistant. Bunche was an extremely able African American with a PhD in Political Science and wartime OSS experience, a man deeply concerned about the process and subsequent effects of decolonization.[30]

The UN followed its existing pattern of sending a civilian commission to the region and sent the UN Special Commission on Palestine (UNSCOP) to investigate and make recommendations in 1947. Lester Pearson was supposed to be the Canadian representative, but his candidacy was vetoed by the Prime Minister.[31] The UNSCOP members were decidedly mediocre. Canada's contribution to peace mediation featured Justice Ivan Rand, who, according to Bunche, was "grumbling, neurotic, eccentric and garrulous....A one man sabotage team. He relates everything to Canada and talks incessantly,"[32] though Pearson found him respectable.[33]

The UNSCOP plan recommended that two partitioned enclaves be formed, one Jewish, one Arab, and that they be unified economically. Jerusalem would be an open city under UN control. UNSCOP did not, however, establish exactly what the partition borders would be. In any event, the Arab and Jewish communities were intermixed.[34]

Then violence in the region accelerated into open warfare. The massacre at Deir Yassin, conducted by a Jewish irregular force, touched off a wave of what would later be called "ethnic cleansing": 720,000 Palestinian refugees left Israeli-controlled territory. The war prompted the UN to establish a Truce Commission in Jerusalem of local diplomats. They were to be available if a ceasefire were generated. Full-scale war was on the horizon as both sides fought to expand their control over land before a peace settlement could be made.[35]

Count Folke Bernadotte of Sweden, an old friend of Secretary General Trygve Lie, was appointed by him to act as mediator. The two men had attempted to negotiate with Nazi Germany in 1945 to allow neutral humanitarian aid into the concentration camps. Ralph Bunche became Lie's special representative in Palestine. In a white DC-3 bearing the UN symbol and the Red Cross, Bernadotte and Bunch conducted shuttle diplomacy between the belligerents to secure a truce.[36]

It took time. The first truce established in late June-early July 1948 prompted some movement on a UN observation force. Of the 300 men requested, 68 Belgian, French, and American officers arrived over a three-week period. By July their numbers were fewer than 105. Then the truce was broken and not re-established till the fall. By this point the concept had evolved into a regional observation force and a UN protection force for a (planned) demilitarized Jerusalem. The force was also supposed to be capable of monitoring arms imports and patrolling the ceasefire lines on all fronts.[37]

Bernadotte wanted US Marines to form the Jerusalem protection force. He went so far as to meet with Admiral Forrest Sherman, commander of the US Sixth Fleet, and almost got 125 Marines to act as military observers. The reaction from the State Department was that the introduction of American troops into the Middle East might prompt the Soviets to deploy forces unilaterally to interfere and dilute the functions of the UN force, though the Central Intelligence Agency (CIA) favoured a strong UN operation. The United States and France also supplied four destroyers for UN coastal patrol operations, while the US Air Force (USAF) gave the UN three C-47 transports. These commitments formed the basis of the United Nations Truce Supervisory Organization (UNTSO).[38]

St. Laurent and Pearson were exceptionally concerned. There would be "bloodshed and chaos" in the Middle East if some means to reduce the tension was not found quickly. The partition plan was the only politically viable solution since the British, Americans, and Soviets were deadlocked in the UN. If there were no solution, "it would have placed even greater strain on Anglo-American relations and an increased danger of exploitation of the situation by the USSR."[39] It is important to note that Israel was not necessarily viewed as a pro-Western state at this time since it consisted mostly of people of Eastern European origin, Czechoslovakia had a substantial arms deal with Israel, and there was potential for the new nation to shift into or be influenced by the Soviet camp.[40]

Mackenzie King, on the other hand, was still not enthusiastic about any Canadian involvement in Palestine, no matter what the larger benefits. It was, in his view, a British problem. As he saw it, introducing a UN army into the region was the only real solution. If Canada backed anything remotely resembling such action, it would be called to send troops. He was unwilling to even entertain such suggestions which would lead to damaged relations with Britain.[41] This clash of views prevented Canada from participating in the mounting of the first real UN peace operation.

The Zionist "Stern Gang" eventually assassinated Count Bernadotte in an effort to prevent the UN from accepting his partition plan. By 1949 the shaky truce was superseded by formal armistice agreements and several Mixed Armistice Commissions (MACs) were created by the UN as confidence-building machinery. UNTSO supported the MACs which acted as forums for the belligerents to resolve local disputes. Partition was now a reality as Arabs were driven from and/or voluntarily left Israeli-occupied areas during the military operations that followed. The armistice was not a peace, however, and the conflict would smoulder until the next outbreak in 1956.[42]

Though Canada would play a significant role in UNTSO during the 1950s, it is clear that Canada's first involvement with peace operations was an inauspicious debut. On the plus side, the UN was successfully used as a vehicle to ensure that an Anglo-American dispute could be resolved discretely while at the same time preventing the Soviets from using the situation to further their aims. If Canada's objective was to assist her two closest allies in heading off a situation which could affect the conduct of the Cold War, that objective was achieved.

THE KASHMIR, 1948-49: UNCIP AND UNMOGIIP

UN involvement in Kashmir, like Palestine, was directly related to British decolonization operations conducted in the context of the Cold War. Like Palestine, India was a multi-ethnic state and, similar to Palestine, British colonial control of India was in part facilitated by playing off ethnic factions against each other. The Muslims were in the minority to the Hindus, and there were other ethnic groups including the Sikhs. As Churchill once put it, the "Hindu-Muslim feud [was] the bulwark of British rule in India."[43]

It became apparent in London during the war that Britain would have to give India its independence. Again as in Palestine, freedom and self-determination projects had to be carried out if Britain and the West were to retain the moral high ground during the Cold War. The Muslims were, quite naturally, concerned that the Hindu majority would be in a position of control after independence. Hindu leaders like Pandit Nehru were quite open about this. The level of intercommunal violence skyrocketed throughout 1946-47: even the

Royal Indian Navy mutinied, an event which may have been stimulated by Communist agents. The British wanted a "self supporting nation which would play a key role in...future plans for security in Asia." British Foreign Minister Ernest Bevin was candid: the Soviets would probably intervene if Britain abandoned India without warning.[44]

Lord Louis Mountbatten was brought in to take charge of the decolonization process. A hastily conceived partition plan was implemented whereby there would be a Muslim-dominated country called Pakistan, and a Hindu-dominated nation called India. Unfortunately, the plan did not take into account certain complications in multi-ethnic areas like the Princely States which had a unique relationship to the British Crown. Mountbatten cajoled, flattered, threatened and manipulated most of their leaders into signing on with the new program. The exception was Kashmir, which had a Muslim majority ruled by a Hindu leader. Mountbatten thought Kashmir should be part of Pakistan, or failing that, the province should be partitioned first and the parts incorporated into each country later. The problem was that Nehru was from Kashmir and was emotionally connected to the region.[45]

The issue of Kashmir remained unresolved. Ethnic clashes escalated after independence in 1947: 5.5 million Hindus and Sikhs went from Pakistan to India, while 5.8 Muslims left India for Pakistan, all amidst waves of bloodshed. Muslim irregulars flooded into Kashmir, which prompted the Indian Army to move in, and the fighting began.[46]

The situation did not bode well for Western trade and security concerns in Asia. The Dutch were engaged in a military campaign to retain the region eventually called Indonesia. The French were fighting the Communist Viet Minh in Indochina. The British were taking on a Communist Chinese-backed guerrilla movement in Malaya. The Chinese Civil War was ongoing (and the Communist Chinese led by Mao were winning), and, to the west, Iran was smouldering. The European nations, economically devastated by the Second World War, needed to reap what benefits they could from their overseas holdings in order to prevent a depression, which could provide a breeding ground for further Communist agitation and revolution in the home countries.[47]

External Affairs developed increased interest in Communist activities in Asia throughout 1948. The Soviets were organizing and infiltrating Australian, Siamese, Indian and Malaysian youth groups using Yugoslav proxies led by Vladimir Dedier (Ambassador Robert Ford referred to Dedier as "courageous, intelligent, and completely unscrupulous").[48] China and Tibet received more attention because of their proximity to the Kashmir crisis. There was recognition in Ottawa that the Communists would win the Chinese Civil War which in turn could threaten India.[49]

The UN's handling of the Kashmir dispute followed the pattern established for Palestine. The United Nations Committee on India and Pakistan (UNCIP) was formed in July 1948. UNCIP had Argentinean, Belgian, Columbian, Czech, and American membership. They recommended ceasefire and truce agreements, followed by demilitarization and a plebiscite, all handled under UN auspices.[50] The problem was that neither side wanted to demilitarize the Kashmir, which was a precondition to carrying out a plebiscite since the presence of troops would influence the vote in each occupied region. Behind the scenes, the British,

American, and Canadian governments "called for a single negotiator to be granted broad authority by the Security Council to mediate between India and Pakistan," and Canadian representative General Andy McNaughton was nominated.[51]

The British government felt this behind the scenes maneuvering was necessary since its direct involvement would be perceived as biased by the belligerents. The Attlee government, therefore, wanted "to avoid assuming the overt leadership in any progress adopted by the [UN] Security Council."[52] American and British views were "very similar" on Kashmir, with the Americans advocating Canadian involvement to forestall Soviet criticism which might be directed at the effort.[53]

The Department of External Affairs initially did not want to get involved, in part since "it was feared that the Indian Government might regard such a move as an indication of 'ganging up'." This view changed over time as Escott Reid pointed out to Pearson that the Commonwealth as an institution was at risk if the Kashmir crisis degenerated into a "chronic conflict on the Indian sub-continent: the dispute could well spread alarmingly were India and Pakistan to go to war. Pakistan has already uttered vague threats that in the event of war help would be sought 'elsewhere'," presumably from the USSR.[54]

McNaughton was able to bring the belligerents together at Lake Success. He convinced the two representatives that Kashmir needed policing during demilitarization, and until the plebiscite was held. The Pakistani representative, Sir Mohammed Zafrullah Khan, suggested that a Commonwealth international force handle this operation, in essence "sub-contracted" to the UN. By August 1948 both sides had accepted the UNCIP plan, but the Kashmir situation bogged down again. McNaughton was then able to get the belligerents to accept a military observer force to monitor the existing balance of military power on both sides of the line and report to negotiating sessions if the situation deteriorated. This was also accepted and the military observer force, later called United Nations Military Observer Group in India Pakistan (UNMOGIIP), was formed.[55]

Putting together the UNMOGIIP observer force took some time. The nations eligible to contribute had to be those with no Asian possessions. Argentina, Brazil, Belgium, Canada, and the United States were courted by Secretary General Lie. UNMOGIIP's leader, Belgian General Maurice Delvoie, was aging and UNCIP wanted a younger man as his deputy. The British were for some reason eager to have Canadian Army General Dan Spry, the Deputy Chief of the General Staff, fulfill this role. The Americans also pushed to have McNaughton take over as the plebiscite administrator, but Pearson was not enthusiastic since he wanted to send "someone with the stature of [Count] Bernadotte" and for whatever reason McNaughton didn't appeal to him. Cabinet concurred. American Admiral Chester Nimitz was nominated instead.[56]

Pearson and Defence Minister Brooke Claxton nominated Lieutenant Colonel H.H. Angle, a Militia officer from Kelowna, BC with wartime experience, as Delvoie's deputy. Seven other Canadian officers made up the first Canadian UNMOGIIP contingent. However, UNCIP neglected to establish the cease fire line, which prompted the belligerents to shuffle their forces around to gain local tactical advantages. When General Delvoie arrived in January 1949, the situation was starting to deteriorate again. The 42 UNMOGIIP members, 15 Americans, 8 Belgians, 6 Mexicans, 5 Norwegians and the Canadian contingent had tremendous difficulty trying to monitor a fluid line in a mountainous region about half the size of New Brunswick.[57]

Pearson does not appear to have been overly impressed with the Kashmir crisis. His apparent motives for deploying Canadian observers were at first glance to "comply with the Secretary General's request, since Canada is still represented on the Security Council."[58] It is curious that Kashmir, UNCIP, and UNIIMOG hardly feature in Pearson's autobiography. Louis St. Laurent's biographer as well scarcely mentions these operations: there is a short explanation that Canada became involved because St. Laurent thought a strong India would be an example to other Asian nations that democracy could work.[59] Pearson's biographer, John English, hardly discusses what is essentially Canada's first peace operation. Even US Secretary of State Dean Acheson is silent on the subject in Present at the Creation. McNaughton's biographer does make some mention, but deals curtly with the decision by the Canadian Government not to employ him in the region in a prominent post. The Annual Report of External Affairs for 1949 is similarly sketchy. Why the silence?

Canada's actual role in UNMOGIIP, had it been revealed at the time, would have proved extremely embarrassing to the Canadian government and its successors. The Kashmir and Palestine disputes continue today: when most of these biographies and autobiographies were written, the crises were still flashpoints.

The Canadian UNMOGIIP contingent included intelligence personnel, one of whom reported to the Directorate of Military Intelligence in Ottawa. There were also two Royal Canadian Air Force (RCAF) intelligence officers. Arrangements were made with External Affairs (which caused some discomfort for the members of the High Commission in New Delhi!) whereby information acquired by the field personnel was sent via diplomatic bag back to Canada. In other cases oral reports were given to embassy personnel by Brigadier Angle and these were forwarded through the External Affairs cipher and communications system. The information appears to have covered a variety of political and military topics, the value of which was disputed by External Affairs personnel in India. The ultimate destination and use of the information remains obscure.[60]

On 17 July 1950, Brigadier H.H. Angle and members of his staff were aboard an Indian National Airways aircraft when it crashed. He was the first Canadian to die (in the service of peace). Rumours immediately started that the plane had been sabotaged and Angle assassinated. Instead of conducting his own investigation, the acting High Commissioner for Canada almost one year later merely asked the Civil Air Advisor of the British High Commissioner what happened and was told that the automatic pilot was engaged during a severe storm which resulted in a loss of control.[61] There is no mention of the loss or even the name of the first Canadian to die on UN operations in any memoir or biography produced by the Ottawa Men. No larger Canadian investigation appears to have been conducted and the affair was quietly forgotten, probably since the Korean War had only just started.

The question remains: why were Canadian UNMOGIIP officers gathering intelligence?

What no one could explain publicly in any detail at the time was the relationship between the Kashmir crisis, the partition of Palestine, and ABC global war planning. Between 1947 and the creation of NATO in 1949, the American, British, and Canadian Chiefs of Staff created a series of plans to fight a war against the Soviet Union if its forces invaded Western Europe. The first of these was called Plan BROILER (British title: DOUBLEQUICK), approved in 1948 for use in the 1948-49 time frame. This plan later evolved in 1949 into Plans DOUBLESTAR (US), SPEEDWAY (British), and BULLMOOSE (Canadian version). The basis for these plans was that part of Western Europe would be lost to the Soviet advance. The enemy would also make serious efforts to invade Iran and cut off Persian Gulf oil. Since the West did not have enough forces to hold at the Iron Curtain, a withdrawal would take place. Four large base areas would be secured and developed on the Soviet periphery. America's small nuclear force would deploy to these four areas and commence the atomic bombing of the USSR, while conventional forces were to build up in these base areas and prepare to return to the continent to drive the Soviets out.[62]

These four base areas were: Great Britain, French North Africa, the Middle East (Egypt-Palestine) and Karachi, which was now part of Pakistan (see Figures 1 and 2). In some versions of the plans the Karachi base area is omitted, while in others Palestine is omitted, depending on the year, yet the broad outline of the plan's execution is clear. It is important to recall that the USAF Strategic Air Command was not yet capable of global thermonuclear war on short

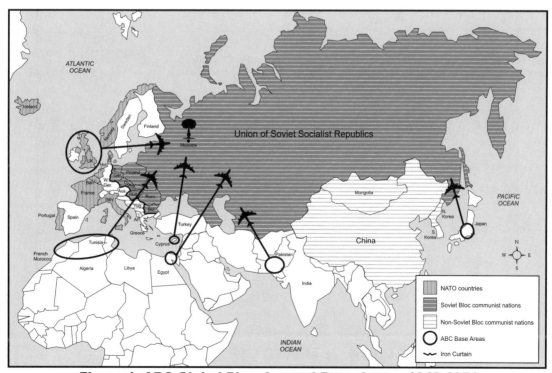

Figure 1: ABC Global Planning and Base Areas, 1948-1951

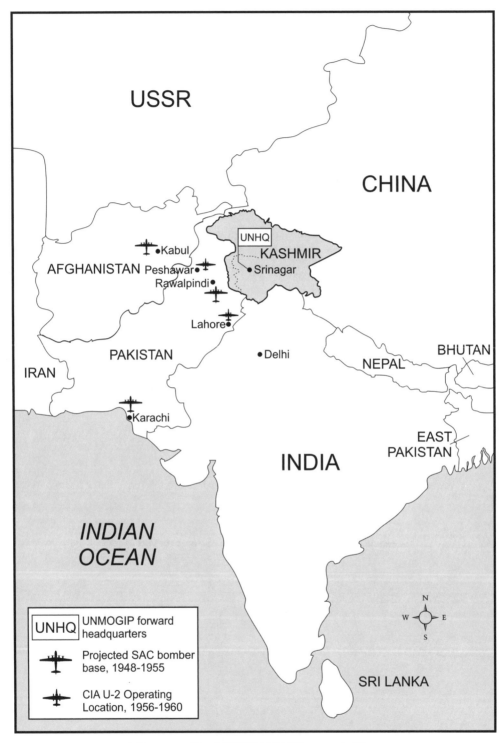

**Figure 2: UNMOGIP and the
Kashmir Dispute, 1948 to present**

notice. SACs bombers were not jet powered, could not refuel in the air, the nuclear weapons they carried were few and relatively limited in yield. Air bases in Karachi and the Middle East were critical for the success of any strategic bombing campaign directed at the USSR at this time. There was even an unmanned recovery base for USAF bombers in Afghanistan.[63]

Some might question Canada's role in strategic planning. How much did the people in External Affairs know, and more importantly did it affect decisions related to Canadian policy in Palestine and Kashmir? The ABC planning arrangements were extremely sensitive and were not widely distributed. What is clear is that Canadian military planners were part of the planning process: this is evident from an analysis of the plans themselves, particularly the sections dealing with North American defence and the naval campaign for the Atlantic sea lanes.[64] External Affairs retained a highly classified file dealing with Plan BULLMOOSE, yet it remains unavailable to the public at this time. This is somewhat surprising since the American and British versions of the same plan were declassified in the 1980s.

The benefits gained in securing the Middle East and Karachi base areas are obvious. It is equally clear that political instability in the planned base areas would prevent their use, both from a political and a practical operational view. Allowing the USSR or their surrogates to deploy peace observation forces alongside Western forces would undermine the security of the regions. The UN was therefore used as a forum in an attempt to establish stability in both regions on Western terms. The military and political motives for doing so were intertwined: denying the areas to Soviet political influence in peacetime was as important as being able to operate atomic bombers from these sites in wartime.

This in turn was linked to the Commonwealth agenda. There was serious concern that if the India-Pakistan dispute was not resolved or ameliorated, the Commonwealth itself would break up and the nations be subjected to Soviet pressure and influence, which would deny Canada the ability to influence the British and prevent the British from using the Commonwealth as a counterweight to American influence. In the case of Palestine, ongoing instability in the region could have a damaging effect on Anglo-Egyptian relations, which would affect not only the ability of SAC to operate there in war but also affect the vital Suez Canal, a critical economic and military feature both in terms of fighting the Cold War in Asia and in a global war against the USSR.

An astute realist such as Lester Pearson would not have flagrantly disregarded such a calculus. Why would Canada get involved in peace operations in Palestine and Kashmir but stay out of the Netherlands-Indonesia conflict? Or why was there so much Canadian reluctance to become involved with Korea in the critical early days that conflict? Indonesia and Korea were not as critical to Canadian interests prior to 1950 since they lay outside the Commonwealth and ABC spheres.

AT THE CREATION: CANADA AND NATO, 1948-49

Canadian skepticism about the utility of the UN was called into question more and more throughout the late 1940s. Pearson thought:

The UN, through the Security Council, could not guarantee the peace....Collective security could not, in fact, be organized on a basis of world-wide agreement. We knew that this hard fact must lead to changes in our policies.. While we actively supported the UN, we had no illusions about its weaknesses, especially about the growing tendency to substitute propaganda for constructive debate and action.[65]

Most observers were reluctant to publicly label Secretary General Trygve Lie as a weak leader.[66] The Soviets frequently abused their veto power in the Security Council to frustrate the other members, particularly in matters like the development (or lack thereof) of the UN's Military Staff Committee, supposedly the venue for collective security. Disarmament initiatives were also adversely affected.[67] Similarly, as early UN Secretariat member Brian Urquart noted, "The statesmanlike attitudes of the early meetings soon gave way to competitive point-scoring, and on many critical issues, the level of the debate sank to name calling, polemics, and abuse, rendering a positive outcome precarious, if not impossible."[68]

There were other, larger problems. The UN was unable to prevent or influence Soviet behaviour which produced the Czechoslovakian coup in 1948. Canadian diplomat George Ignatieff, representing Canada in the UN, recalled:

> I sat in the UN General Assembly listening to the Ukrainian representative denouncing Canada for supposedly giving sanctuary to fascist and nazi war criminals when suddenly I heard a soft but distinct voice behind me say: "Canada is as fascist as Czechoslovakia is communist." I turned around and saw that I was sitting in front of Jan Masaryk, Czechoslovakia's universally beloved and respected foreign minister, whose so-called suicide following the communist putsch shocked the civilized world. Those were the last words I ever heard him say.[69]

Unlike the faceless thousands who died in such events, Jan Masaryk was one of the diplomats' own circle. The circumstances surrounding his death could not fail to have a profound personal effect on Canadian diplomats.

The Czech Crisis was immediately followed by the Berlin Blockade which in turn produced the very real possibility that the Soviets would invade Western Europe. The Joint Intelligence Committee in the UK was convinced that the communist movement in France "could seize power in 48 hours."[70] Reports of Soviet machinations in Italy also abounded, as did concerns that Norway would "go neutral" like Finland. Canadian Charge D'Affairs in Moscow, John Holmes, sent back chilling dispatches regarding the character and nature of Soviet totalitarianism.[71]

Pearson discussed these matters with his subordinates. Should some form of regional European security pact replace or supplement the UN? The Brussels Pact was in the works, as was the Western European Defence Organization. These were concrete examples of the recognition that the UN had failed.[72]

The product of all this angst was the North Atlantic Treaty and the North Atlantic Treaty Organization (NATO). The UN, Pearson reasoned, was still useful as a means of putting diplomatic pressure on the Soviets, but useless as a means to secure Canadian objectives in

Europe. The primary objective was to collectively deter war against Canada's closest economic and cultural allies, and then collectively defend the North Atlantic Area if war broke out. There was also the counterweight role in which NATO membership permitted Canada to balance out American and British global influence by building diplomatic allies within the Organization and applying pressure when necessary.[73] These ideas were not unique. All NATO members had ulterior motives in signing the treaty relating to the need to protect their interests outside of what would become the defined NATO Area.[74]

After the North Atlantic Treaty was signed by Canada in 1949, General Charles Foulkes set out to influence the form of NATO's military structure, something which would have long term implications for Canadian national security policy when NATO debated how the Middle East would fit into the NATO Area. Foulkes' view was:

> The natural development of NATO, particularly from the political aspect, is a gradual growth of an organization comprising of all those countries which wish to defend themselves from the infiltration of the Russian form of communism. Following from the political desire of these nations to be associated in such a pact would naturally stem the defensive aspect of a purely military point of view.[75]

Most intelligence analysis concurred in 1949 that the period of maximum danger would come around 1954 or 1955, once the Soviets had built up an atomic bomb stockpile and developed the means to deliver it. NATO had to have the military forces to deter all other avenues of attack, including defence against massive conventional attack.

Others naively thought that the mere existence of a defensive alliance might be enough to deter Soviet aggression in its many guises. These men were about to learn in the cauldron of the Korean War that words had to be backed up with credible military force.

KOREA, CANADA AND THE UN

Canada's initial involvement in Korea during 1947 was a case study in isolationism under Mackenzie King. The peninsula was artificially divided at the end of the Second World War between the USSR and the United States, since both nations were responsible for disarming and repatriating Japanese forces stationed there. In effect, American forces left the south while the Soviets used the time to install communist cadres throughout the north. The idea of a UN trusteeship was then proposed to re-unifythe two parts. Since Korea had been an occupied nation under the Japanese for decades and had no functional higher government, the communists in 1946 played on Korean suspicion of the Japanese to block the trusteeship concept and demand a vote. In September 1947, the Americans turned the whole issue over to the UN.[76]

The "UN commission pattern" was put in play once again and, once again, Canada was asked by Trygve Lie in December 1947 to send a commissioner. Mackenzie King was away at a conference in Britain, so St. Laurent and Pearson selected Dr. G.S. Patterson as Canada's United Nations Temporary Commission on Korea (UNTCOK). UNTCOK's mandate was to supervise free elections and then observe the withdrawal of the USSR and US armed forces of occupation.[77] On his return, Mackenzie King stormed that Canada had no interests in

Korea, that the UN was a communist propaganda forum, and that Pearson was an American tool. The counter argument was that Canada was a member of the Security Council and as such had an obligation to provide firm participation and leadership. What was wrong with supporting the idea of free elections for all? The debate over UNTCOK produced a serious Cabinet split which in turn drew in bitter Liberal party politics as Mackenzie King and St. Laurent threatened each other with resignations. In the end, Patterson became the Canadian UNTCOK representative and by the end of the year Mackenzie King had stepped down.[78]

UNTCOK rapidly discovered that the Korean situation was hopelessly deadlocked. The Soviet— and now Chinese — backed communist north would never allow free elections. They also discovered that American support for the south had hardened to the point where the occupation forces collaborated with the South Koreans to manipulate UNTCOK and influence its final report. The matter went to the UN and free elections were held in the South, while the North created a "People's Democratic Republic". UNTCOK admitted that it had failed on the first aspect of its mandate. As for occupation forces withdrawal, UNTCOK was a perceived success, though the USSR announced their withdrawal first by January 1949 thereby gaining obvious propaganda value in forcing the Americans to appear obstinate by leaving last.[79]

A protracted low-intensity border campaign began after the Soviet withdrawal in 1949. This campaign was characterized by small raids, incursions, and blatant intelligence gathering. A United Nations Commission on Korea (UNCOK) was then formed to investigate guerrilla operations. UNCOK was a military observer force much like UNTSO and UNMOGIIP and, once again, Canadian military participation was requested by the Secretary General in April-May 1950. As with UNMOGIIP, Canada planned to send intelligence officers embedded in the Canadian contingent on the recommendation of the Joint Intelligence Committee. However, UNCOK was scuttled by the communist invasion of the Republic of South Korea in June 1950.[80]

The Soviet-supported invasion of South Korea, it should be kept in mind, came on the heels of the Berlin Blockade, the loss of China, and the detonation of the first Soviet atomic bomb in late 1949. The Korean War and the UN response to it prompted a serious re-appraisal of Canada's national security policy which had long term ramifications. Prior to Korea, there was a belief in Ottawa that Soviet-inspired communism could be handled through diplomatic and economic means and that the military means needed to be kept in the background. Now the military aspects of deterrence and defence moved forward to take an equal footing in Canadian national security policy.

That said, External Affairs was not happy with the way the United Nations got involved in military operations in Korea. Many participants in the process, including Pearson, made great public play of how Canada was almost shamed (or dragooned) into participating in the Korean ground war by her allies. The initial Canadian response before the pressure for ground troops really began was to send three destroyers (called "the three tokens" by American diplomats), a risk-adverse minimalist enterprise which Canada would repeat in the 1990-91 Gulf War. By not participating in Korea, the St. Laurent government had the potential to slide back into

Mackenzie King's isolationism. There was much more at play, however, all of which had a direct impact on Canada's later peace operations and their link to national security policy.

Initial estimates conducted by the Joint Intelligence Committee and circulated to External Affairs, the Chiefs of Staff Committee, and later Cabinet, concluded that the Korean War did not entail a larger war with the Soviet Union. This changed when Korea's importance received more scrutiny. The Chiefs of Staff Committee, for example, realized that:

> South Korea is important politically because it is a United Nations creation. Its unchallenged demise would be a serious blow to the United Nations as an effective world organization.
>
> It is additionally important in the eyes of Southeast Asia and Europe as a proving ground for the promises of the United States and the democracies to give aid as assistance to the newly-formed states against communist expansion.[81]

An External Affairs analysis provided to UNCOK observers suggested that "this unfortunate country and its unhappy occupants may well be likened to Poland and its people in their struggle for independence,"[82] perhaps indicative of an External Affairs mindset which saw Korea as a trigger for larger conflict. The Chiefs of Staff Committee and External Affairs also collaborated in the production of a series of estimates throughout 1950 which culminated in a unified approach to Cabinet in December 1950 while it was deliberating the deployment of Canadian ground troops.

The debate centred around whether or not the Soviets were orchestrating the Korean War through a North Korean or Chinese proxy. There was no substantive conclusion on this in Canadian circles. All agreed, however, that whatever the stimulus, in the future "the Soviet Union can be expected to exploit and probably to intensify the exploitation of local wars with the object of expanding Soviet control while dissipating Western resources." This would occur "in those areas where there is little likelihood of United Nations action being taken; eg., Colonial Areas ie: Malaya and Indochina [and] Internal Dissension Areas, ie., Greece, Iran."[83]

Once the Chinese entered the war later in 1950, more attention was paid to the implications of the Korean War on NATO. There was a strong possibility that the drain on American and British military resources in defence of Korea would reduce the West's ability to protect Western Europe under Article 5 of the North Atlantic Treaty ("an attack against one is an attack against all"). This vulnerability could prompt the Soviets to attack, there and in the Middle East. There was a possibility that the mere possession of the atomic bomb in limited numbers would not be enough to deter such action. The original period of maximum danger, set for 1954-55, was now changed to 1952 or earlier.[84]

Brooke Claxton and Lester Pearson presented their case to Cabinet. Fighting in Korea was one key aspect of the larger Cold War in 1950. If aggression was allowed to continue, there was a strong possibility that parts of Asia and Europe would fall to "the forces of Soviet imperialism" and that "the position of North America will eventually become serious...worse than in 1940." The area that was most at risk was Western Europe, though the defeat of the UN forces in Korea would probably encourage open warfare in Indochina with spill-over effects on British Malaya and Indonesia and thus Australia. India and Pakistan's position "would be most precarious." China might attack Formosa.[85]

The immediate Canadian military reactions to the 1950 crisis which flowed from this series of Cabinet discussions, the deployment of 25 Canadian Infantry Brigade to Korea and 27 Canadian Infantry Brigade to Europe, are covered in other works.[86] Korea and the 1950 crisis demonstrated to Canadian national security policymakers that the UN had totally failed to prevent war, perhaps even assisted in exacerbating the situation, and that NATO was rapidly becoming the stronger pillar of Canadian national security policy. Therefore Canadian peace operations in the 1950s and 1960s should be examined from this perspective, not one which suggests that the UN was the cornerstone of Canada's national security policy. Canada's UN operations were subordinated to Canada's interests as defined through the North Atlantic prism. How this view solidified in the policymaking establishment is the subject of Chapter 3.

Notes to Chapter 2

1. See J.L. Granatstein, *The Ottawa Men* (Toronto: University of Toronto Press, 1982).

2. James Eayrs, *In Defence of Canada: Peacemaking and Deterrence* (Toronto: University of Toronto Press, 1972) 1-75.

3. See John Swettenham, *McNaughton: Volume 3 1944-1966* (Toronto: Ryerson Press, 1969).

4. John Lewis Gaddis, *The United States and the Origins of the Cold War 1941-1947* (New York: Columbia, University Press, 1972) 299; see particularly Bruce R. Kuniholm, *The Origins of the Cold War in the Near East: Great Power Conflict and Diplomacy in Iran, Turkey, and Greece* (Princeton: Princeton University Press, 1980) and Denis Smith, *Diplomacy of Fear: Canada and the Cold War 1941-1948* (Toronto: University of Toronto Press, 1988).

5. Pearson Memoirs, Vol II, p. 25.

6. Ibid., p. 26.

7. David Adamson, *The Last Empire: Britain and the Commonwealth* (London: I.B. Taurus and Co. Ltd., 1989) 6-7; Andrew Walker, *The Commonwealth: A New Look* (Toronto: Pergamon Press, 1978) Ch 1; Alastair Buchan, "Commonwealth Military Relations," in W.B. Hamilton et al. *A Decade of the Commonwealth 1955-1964* (Durham: Duke University Press, 1966) 194-207.

8. John Holmes, *The Shaping of Peace: Canada and the Search for World Order Vol. I 1943-1957* (Toronto: University of Toronto Press, 1979) Ch. 5; Eayrs, *In Defence of Canada: Peacemaking and Deterrence*, Ch. 4.

9. C.P. Stacey, *Canada and the Age of Conflict Vol. II 1921-1948* (Toronto: University of Toronto Press, 1981) Ch. 10.

10. Ibid.

11. Sean M. Maloney, *Securing Command of the Sea: NATO Naval Planning 1948-1954* (Annapolis: Naval Institute Press, 1995) Ch. 2.

12. Sean M. Maloney, *"Learning to Love The Bomb: Canada's Cold War Strategy and Nuclear Weapons, 1951-1968"* (forthcoming) Ch. 1.

13. Stanley Meisner, *United Nations: The First Fifty Years* (New York: The Atlantic Monthly Press, 1995) Ch. 1; Holmes, *The Shaping of Peace Vol. I,* 233.

14. Ibid., Ch. 8; Eayrs, *In Defence of Canada: Peacemaking and Deterrence* Ch. 2; Stacey, *Canada and the Age of Conflict Vol. II* 378-386; Pearson Memoirs, Vol II, p. 132.

15. Leland M. Goodrich, *The United Nations* (New York: Thomas Y. Crowell, 1959) 159-163, and Appendix B, "Charter of the United Nations".

16. Ibid., p. 164.

17. Anthony Verrier, *International Peacekeeping: UN Forces in a Troubled World* (London: Penguin Books, 1981) xx.

18. DHH, file 193.009 (D 53) (2 Sep 48) JPC, "United Nations Military Staff Committee."

19. DHH, file 193.009 (D 53) (18 Aug 48) memo Under-secretary of State for External Affairs to Secretary, Chiefs of Staff Committee, "United Nations Military Staff Committee."

20. DHH, file 193.009 (D 53) (2 Sep 48) memo COSC to DL, "United Nations Military Staff Committee."

21. NAC RG 25 vol. 6214 file 5475-DK-40 pt. 1.1, (Jul 48) Minute on Despatch No. 68 of June 21.

22. NAC RG 25 vol. 6214 file 5475-DK-40 pt. 1.1, (21 Jun 48) memo CANDELUN to Secretary of State for External Affairs.

23. DHH, 193.009 (D 53) (27 Aug 48) letter Pearson to Foulkes; (9 Sep 48) COSC, 430th Meeting. Note that the Canadian Army was down to one brigade group from a two-corps army, with minimal mobilization stocks. See Sean M. Maloney, "The Mobile Striking Force and Continental Defence," *Canadian Military History Vol. 2* No. 2 (Autumn 1993), 75-88.

24. NAC RG 25 vol. 6214 file 5475-DK-40 pt. 1.1, (n/d) "Observations by Mr. Robertson."

25. NAC RG 25 vol. 6214 file 5475-DK-40 pt. 1.1, (15 Sep 48) COSC JPC, "Observations on the Establishment of a United Nations Guard Force."

26. NAC RG 25 vol. 6214 file 5475-DK-40 pt. 1.1, (11 Aug 48) memo to UN Division from Reid, "United Nations Guard Force"; (30 Oct 48) memo COSC to UN Division, External Affairs; (21 Jun 48) message CANDELUN to Secretary of State for External Affairs."

27. Richard Hiscocks, *The Security Council: A Study in Adolescence* (New York: The Free Press, 1973) 116-133.

28. For two exceptional overviews of the situation see Charles D. Smith, *Palestine and the Arab-Israeli Conflict, 3rd ed.* (New York: St. Martin's Press, 1996) and also Ian J. Bickerton and Carla L. Klausner, *A Concise History of the Arab-Israeli Conflict, 2nd ed.* (New York: Prentice Hall, 1995).

29. Amitzur Ilan, *Bernadotte in Palestine, 1948: A Study in Contemporary Knight-Errantry* (New York: St. Martin's 1989) 70-71; Avi Beker, *The United States and Israel: From Recognition to Reprehension* (Toronto: Lexington Books, 1988) 31-36.

30. Trygve Lie, *In the Cause of Peace: Seven Years with the United Nations* (Toronto: Macmillan Co., 1954) Ch. 1.

31. Dale C. Thompson, *Louis St Laurent: Canadian* (Toronto: Macmillan of Canada, 1967) 221.

32. Brian Urquart, *Ralph Bunche: An American Life* (New York: W.W. Norton, 1993) 142.

33. Pearson Memoirs, Vol II, 213.

34. Urquart, *Ralph Bunche: An American Life,* 149-150.

35. See Bickerton and Klausner, *A Concise History of the Arab-Israeli Conflict 2nd ed.*

36. Urquart, *Ralph Bunche: An American Life*, 159-161.

37. Ibid., 169-171.

38. Ilan, *Bernadotte in Palestine, 1948,* 150-156.

39. Ibid., 214.

40. David Schoenbaum, *The United States and Israel* (New York: Oxford University Press, 1993) 54-55.

41. Thompson, *Louis St Laurent: Canadian*, 221; Pearson Memoirs, Vol II, 215.

42. E.L.M. Burns, *Between Arab and Israeli* (Toronto: Clark Irwin and Co., 1962) 22.

43. Lawrence James, *Raj: The Making and the Unmaking of British India* (London: Little Brown and Co., 1997), 540.

44. Ibid., 590, 594, 599, 606.

45. Philip Ziegler, *Mountbatten* (London: Harper and Row, 1985) 405-414.

46. James, *Raj,* 635-637.

47. Andrew Rotter examines this in his analysis of Anglo-American Asian trade policy arrangements but the argument applies equally to the other cases. See *The Path to Vietnam: Origins of the American Commitment to Southeast Asia* (Ithaca: Cornell University Press, 1987) particularly Ch. 3.

48. NAC RG 25 vol 4767 file 50072-40 Pt. 1, (27 Apr 48) letter Robertson to Pearson.

49. NAC RG 25 vol 4767 file 50072-40 Pt. 1, (16 Aug 48) letter Davis to Pearson, "Communist Activities in South East Asia."

50. Josef Korbel, "The Kashmir Dispute and the United Nations," *International Organization Vol. II* (1949), 278-287.

51. Robert J. McMahon, *The Cold War on the Periphery: The United States, India, and Pakistan* (New York: Columbia University Press, 1994) 59-60.

52. U.S. State Department, *FRUS 1948 Vol. V: The Near East South Asia, and Africa Part 1* (Washington D.C.: US GPO, 1975) 272, (6 Jan 48) message to State Department.

53. Ibid., 276 (10 Jan 48) memcon with Lord Ismay; 281-283, (14 Jan 48) message US representative UN to Secretary of State.

54. DFAIT, *Documents on Canadian External Relations Vol. 15 1949* (Ottawa: Supply and Services, 1995) (13 Sep 49) memo A.D.P. Heeney to Pearson, "Recent Developments in the Kashmir Dispute," (20 Oct 49) memo Escott Reid to Pearson, "The Kashmir Question."

55. Swettenham, *McNaughton Vol. 3*, 132-137, 154-160.

56. NAC RG 25 vol. 6214 file 5475-CX-2-40 Pt. 1.1, (11 Dec 48) memo for Acting Secretary of State for External Affairs, "Military Advison United Nations Commission for Kashmir."

57. Sylvain Lourie, "The United Nations Military Observer Group in India and Pakistan," *International Organization Vol. IX* (1955), 19-31.

58. NAC RG 25 vol. 6214 file 5475-CX-2-40 Pt. 1.1, (18 Jan 49) memo Pearson to Claxton.

59. Thompson, *Louis St Laurent: Canadian*, 279.

60. NAC RG 25 vol. 6292 file 11380-40 pt. 1, (14 Jul 49) memo Crean to Brindle; (1 Oct 49) letter Brindle to George; (9 Jun 50) letter Brindle to Mackay.

61. NAC RG 25 (no volume number) 5475-CX-2-40 vol. 3, (3 May 51) message for Pearson, "Crash of Indian National Airways plane on July 17, 1950."

62. Maloney, *Securing Command of the Sea*, Ch. 2.

63. Ibid; Henry S. Bradsher, *Afghanistan and the Soviet Union* (Durham: Duke Press Policy Studies, 1983) 30.

64. Sean M. Maloney, "Learning to Love The Bomb" Ch. 1.

65. Pearson Memoirs, Vol II, 30, 133.

66. Holmes, *The Shaping of Peace Vol. II* 301.

67. Escott Reid, *Time of Fear and Hope: The Making of the North Atlantic Treaty 1947-1949* (Toronto: McClelland and Stewart, 1977) 185.

68. Brian Urquart, *A Life in Peace and War* (New York: W.W. Norton, 1987) 109.

69. George Ignatieff, *The Making of a Peacemonger: The Memoirs of George Ignatieff* (Toronto: University of Toronto Press, 1985) 98-99.

70. DHH, file 193.009 (D53) (21 Apr 48) memo to COSC, "Partisan Movements in Europe."

71. Reid, *Time of Fear and Hope* 17-21.

72. Pearson Memoirs, Vol II, 31; Reid, *Time of Fear and Hope* 32-33.

73. John English, *The Worldly Years: The Life of Lester B. Pearson 1949-1972* (Toronto: Vintage Books, 1992) Ch. 1; Pearson Memoirs, Vol II, Ch. 3.

74. The best work examining these aspects of NATO is Winfried Heinemann's *Vom Zusammenwaschen des Bundnisses: Die Funktionsweise der NATO in ausgewahlten Krisenfallen 1951-1956* (Munchen: Oldenbourg, 1998). It is to the detriment of NATO historiography that this work has not yet been translated into English.

75. DHH, The Raymont Collection, file 3170, (17 Jul 51) memo Raymont to Mackay.

76. Herbert Fairlie Wood, *Strange Battleground: The Official History of the Canadian Army in Korea* (Ottawa: Queen's Printer, 1966) 4-7.

77. NAC RG 25 vol. 5475-CX-3-40 vol. 1, (1 Oct 53) Far Eastern Division, "UNTCOK 1948-Efforts Toward Unification of Korea."

78. Thompson, *Louis St Laurent: Canadian*, 218-227; English, *The Shadow of Heaven: The Life of Lester Pearson Volume 1 1897-1948* (Montreal: Vintage UK, 1989) 326-328.

79. NAC RG 25 vol. 5475-CX-3-40 vol. 1, (1 Oct 53) Far Eastern Division, "UNTCOK 1948-Efforts Toward Unification of Korea."

80. NAC RG 25, vol. 5475-CX-3-40 vol. 1, (23 May 50) memo for Defence Liaison Division; (12 May 50) memo for Menzies from Cleveland; (15 May 50) memo for Pearson.

81. DHH, file 193.009 (D53) (12 Jul 50) Chiefs of Staff Comittee Papers No. 19(50), "The Strategic Importance of South Korea."

82. NAC RG 25, vol. 5475-CX-3-40 vol. 1, (5 Jul 50) memo and brief historical annex on Korea for the Use of Military observers Nominated by Canada for service with UNCOK."

83. NAC RG 25 vol. 7928 file 50028-AK-40 pt. 1, (2 Aug 50) "Appreciation of the Imminence of War."

84. NAC RG 25 vol. 7928 file 50028-AK-40 pt. 1, (24 Oct 50) "Imminence of War," (28 Dec 50) memo to Cabinet, "The International Situation."

85. NAC RG 25 vol. 7928 file 50028-AK-40 pt. 1, (28 Dec 50) memo to Cabinet, "The International Situation."

86. Wood, *Strange Battleground*; Maloney, *War Without Battles*.

CHAPTER 3

EAST OF SUEZ:
CANADIAN PEACE OPERATIONS POLICY,
1951-1955

Ship me somewheres east of Suez, where the best is like the worst,
Where there aren't no Ten Commandments an' a man can raise a thirst.

- Rudyard Kipling, *Mandalay*

The UN has been effective in a measure. If it can't bite at least it can snap.
If it can't bait the bear, it can scare hell out of some of the rats.
The UN will have to work up to bears, have to grow and develop.

- Spivey Pierce, Canadian diplomat

Led by General E.L.M. Burns, Canadian observers had joined the United Nations Truce Supervision
Organization (UNTSO) in the Middle East by 1954. The St. Laurent government was keen on moving
Canada forward into global engagement rather than plodding along the isolationist path.

(UNTSO Photo)

The security environment generated by the ongoing Korean War was quite different from the environment that existed in 1946. The first multi-megaton-yield hydrogen device (not a deliverable bomb) was tested by the United States in 1952, closely followed by the Soviet test of their first boosted bomb in 1953 (300-500 kilotons) and a full-scale thermonuclear test in November 1955. Both American and Soviet worldwide delivery capabilities continued to expand as intercontinental bombers of increasing range were introduced: the prospect of a nuclear holocaust was no longer a science fiction fantasy. The stalemate continued in Europe as NATO expanded its small deterrent forces and equipped them with tactical nuclear weapons to offset crushing Soviet numerical superiority. The national security focus for NATO was fine-tuned to the defence of North America, the Atlantic sea lines of communication, and Western Europe.

However, the unwillingness of the Americans to use atomic weapons in the Korean War demonstrated to all that conflicts of a lower intensity could be fought under the nuclear umbrella, though it was equally clear that such conflicts could escalate into global war involving the use of nuclear weapons. If the Soviet Union or China chose to support these new conflicts, the world would become a more dangerous place.

The opportunities for interference were almost unlimited. Decolonization efforts by European nations produced scores of friction points, many in critical geographic areas. The British were preoccupied with the Malayan Emergency throughout the 1950s, and the Mau Mau insurgency that gripped Kenya from 1952 to 1956. Agitation for *enosis*, or reunification, with Greece drove the creation of the EOKA in Cyprus: this "dirty little war" started in 1952 and would last until 1959.

The French, embattled in Indochina since 1945, would admit defeat fighting the communist Viet Minh at Dienbienphu in 1954. The loss of Vietnam precipitated problems in the new nations of Laos and Cambodia. The FLN in Algeria initiated a campaign that would transform the Casbah into a vicious, squalid battlefield from 1954 well into the 1960s. Even Portugal was at odds with India over Goa in 1954. The American sphere of influence was not untouched. The Philippine government was fighting communist Hukbalahap rebels, while closer to home it appeared as though Guatemala would shift into the communist orbit. A confrontation with communist China over the defeated nationalist Chinese occupation of Formosa's offshore islands in 1954 had nuclear overtones. The only positive event for the West between 1951-55 was that the Germans in the communist-occupied zone revolted in 1953, prompting a violent confrontation with the USSR: Iran was also secured from communist control in 1954.

Not all of these little wars were fought by communist elements and that was the problem for Western nations. Were they nationalist insurgencies? Were they communist insurgencies supported from Peking and/or Moscow? Were they communist insurgencies pretending to be nationalist? Were they nationalist insurgencies pretending to be communist? It was difficult for Western policymakers to make such determinations and it was better to be safe than sorry. Any incident at any friction point could be used: by the UN, for example, to gather support from newly-created nations, to convince nations to form alliances or accept bases or foreign aid. This was the nature of the Cold War in the mid-1950s and Canada had to adapt to it. UN policy could not be divorced from other foreign policies which were increasingly driven by the need to solidify NATO in the face of a multi-faceted threat.

CANADA, THE UN AND NATO DURING THE KOREAN WAR

In May 1950, H.H. Carter, a Canadian diplomat at the UN, sent a rather eloquent but scathing memo to John Holmes which, along with the Korean War, initiated a re-examination of Canada's UN policy. Carter's frustration with the UN machinery was evident since, on his part there was "a greater realization of how comparatively few are our allies in the cause of common sense." Carter was an idealist who had run into the cold, hard wall of political reality:

> I have referred to the dangerously false thinking now in the ascendant at UN
> meetings... the type of thinking which confuses a mere declaration of aspirations with
> a real improvement in human rights, which would substitute an empty resolution to
> outlaw war for the slow, heart-breaking work of trying to remove the causes of war...
> In short, I mean the whole mechanistic, declaratory approach which constantly evades
> or overlooks the fundamental point that resolutions and declarations of this nature are
> merely a cruel deception... Our own country's history-with its background of pragmatic
> and workable, but superficially illogical political arrangements-clearly refutes the
> validity of this doctrinaire approach.[1]

He lamented "the substitute of rhetoric for action" and was concerned that the Canadian public would find out that the system was flawed, with subsequent loss of credibility for the Canadian government. Carter "didn't think this would have been the case if the public had been told from the beginning that the world organization had only a circumscribed jurisdiction and that its effectiveness depended entirely on the willingness of the states to use the machinery it provided." In words which would have far ranging echoes in the 1990s, Carter noted that "Continuing illusions on this basic point may lead to a soporific attitude with dangerous consequences."[2]

Holmes passed the memo along with his own views to A.D.P. Heeney. One of his recommendations was that "we use our influence to restrain United Nations bodies from drafting declarations and conventions which are merely declarations of Utopian intention."[3] During the Korea War, Holmes conferred with Escott Reid. Holmes was frustrated by his failed attempts to get the Americans to stop or delay military operations in Korea (after the Inchon landings) so that diplomatic pressure could be brought to bear on North Korea.[4] This drove him to suggest to John Ford of the United Nations Division at External Affairs that a far reaching examination of Canada's UN policy be conducted.[5]

Ford had a realistic view, that is, "it is impossible to admit that we are prepared to apply collective security to one area and not another but if a show down came it would have to be done." Furthermore, "I fail to see...how the United Nations could avoid at least trying to apply collective security , even if the North Atlantic Treaty Organization countries had decided that certain areas were indefensible." Therefore, Ford argued, the UN could be used by the West in areas that other collective security organizations couldn't protect, such as nations outside the defined NATO Area. The specific areas Ford referred to included Finland, Yugoslavia, Greece, Turkey (not yet a member of NATO), Iran, Pakistan, India, and Indochina ("This is more complex and the situation is so confused, it might be possible to avoid applying collective security"). If nothing practical could be done in these situations or in Korea, Ford noted, "the United Nations should make the gesture of applying collective security, knowing that whatever it did would be far too late. This may be cynical..."[6]

Escott Reid then asked Holmes to undertake the study. The importance of this UN policy study is not the ultimate fate of the various drafts but the discussion it generated and what that discussion tells us Pearson and his External Affairs men were thinking in the early 1950s.

Holmes tipped his hat to the "successes" of Kashmir and Palestine since UN machinery was used to contain the fighting which "could have set off a world war." That said, those in the know had to admit that UN interventions "were on the periphery of the main conflict between the Soviet world and the democratic world." The same methods would not work in that forum. This, however, could not be publicly acknowledged since it would "shake confidence not only in the expanded pretensions of the [UN], but also in its previous limited mandates...it is less likely now that the [UN] could exert pressure on Arabs or Jews or Pakistanis, when it has not been able to exert pressure on Russians or Chinese." In the future "all conflicts now will probably be direct products of the main conflict."[7]

Canada's view should be a realistic one since:

It is conceivable that the United Nations could exert its force in areas where trouble had been provoked by Soviet agents but by such remote control from Moscow that these agents could, if necessary, retire without too much loss of face from the Kremlin....The question arises as to the extent to which those countries which must take a lead in defending democracy can follow a policy of using the UN as an instrument for creating an anti-cominform coalition.[8]

Holmes was equally blunt about American policy, which was to do exactly that. The Americans would decide:

which countries can be defended and which must be abandoned. The rest of us may continue to exert some influence, but this influence will be exerted directly in Washington, rather than through the UN, although we may find the meeting place of the UN useful channels to rally support....for our resistance.[9]

This paper was distributed to senior Canadian diplomats for comment. Their responses are revealing. For example, members of the Canadian Permanent Delegation in Geneva agreed with Holmes and even amplified what he said:

Before our eyes are dilated by the heat of another crisis we should attempt with our [NATO] partners to prepare a plan for global strategy and decide which areas we must and can defend by force, and which we can only try to hold with words, or bluff if you

will: that is, which areas are essential in terms of our resources and which are not...
it does mean serious work by us and our friends behind closed doors...This cannot be
our idea of how the [UN] *should* operate, but it would be unrealistic to hide our head
in the sand...someday we must make the [UN] or something like it work effectively or
accept the probable alternative of being blown to atomic bits.[10]

Basil Robinson, head of the United Nations Division, agreed that a more realistic approach
was necessary. In his view, "in seeking to inform the public we should pin our hopes for effective
measures of defence on NATO rather than upon the United Nations [while] at the same time
attempting to stress the fact that NATO's purposes are essentially UN purposes." Canada had to
"adjust ourselves to more subtle and honest propaganda" when it came to the UN. Negotiation
functions should be emphasized "for public consumption."[11] These views were echoed by
Canada's man in Washington, Hume Wrong: "[NATO] and not the United Nations is the major
international instrument that has been forged for the application of collective security."[12] Saul Rae
from the Office of the High Commissioner for Canada in London said it best:

In the period in which we now find ourselves, when the threat of aggression is great and
our resources limited, the steps which we take to meet specific acts of aggression what
appear to be a "local" scale must be based not upon irresponsible Assembly majorities,
but on secret and precise military planning in light of longer term strategic considerations
as to where the main threat lies and how it can be met. We are reaching the point
where (barring one or two marginal cases) further acts of aggression will be Soviet-
inspired and where as a consequence the collective security machinery of the United
Nations will in fact operate as an anti-Communist coalition.[13]

Where should such planning take place? As we saw in the previous chapter, Canada was
a member of an American-British-Canadian global planning arrangement. The ultimate
Canadian expression of this planning resided in the 1948 BULLMOOSE plan. Once NATO
was formed in 1949, however, the emphasis shifted away from Canadian participation in
ABC planning. Pearson was concerned that ABC would be viewed with envy by other NATO
members, so the relationship was toned down temporarily. NATO planning was the focus, in
the treaty-defined NATO Area. The original NATO planning structure, which was created by
General Charles Foulkes and accepted by NATO's Military Committee and Standing Group in
early 1950, broke the NATO Area down into several Regional Planning Groups: Canada-US,
North Atlantic Ocean, Northern Europe (Norway, Denmark), Western Europe (UK, France,
Belgium, Netherlands, Luxembourg), and Southern Europe (the Western Mediterranean,
including French Algeria).[14]

The planning groups consisted of military representatives of the nations choosing to
commit forces to each region: Canada initially committed to the Canada-US and the North
Atlantic Group, and then later to the Western European Regional Planning Group. Under the
pressures of the Korean War, however, NATO decided that formal military headquarters and
commands had to be established, and military forces formally assigned and deployed in
"peacetime" to deter Soviet activity. The result was the creation of Supreme Allied

Commander Europe (SACEUR) in 1951 and Supreme Allied Commander Atlantic (SACLANT) in 1952. The regional planning groups disappeared except for the Canada-US region, which effectively was the Military Cooperation Committee wearing a NATO "hat".[15]

NATO strategy in 1950 was formalized in a rather vague document called MC 14.[16] The global context of MC 14 envisioned a war in which the Soviets would attack Western Europe, the North Atlantic Sea Lanes, North America, and the Middle East. Prior to such a war, however, MC 14 confirmed that the NATO nations would "oppose, by all measures short of war, any peacetime attempts by the USSR or her satellites to increase their threat against the Treaty nations, meanwhile initiating measures exploiting Soviet weakness."[17] Though MC 14 took into account regional planning, it did not take into account NATO enlargement which in turn was related to the problems of making NATO planning work in a global context. The ambiguous relationship between NATO planning and global war planning by the ABC powers remained ambiguous with MC 14.

NATO strategy then changed again. Greece and Turkey joined NATO in 1951, which enlarged the NATO Area into the eastern Mediterranean and the Middle East. Lester Pearson opposed this move, though his memoirs do not explain the full extent and reasons for his opposition.[18] The broader unstated issue was that enlargement would dilute the North Atlantic character of the NATO and "force" the Alliance to deal with thorny matters such as how the Middle East related to NATO. This was a moot point since NATO planning evolved again to incorporate Greece and Turkey. Turkey's strategic importance was obvious: it controlled the Bosporus Straits which blocked Soviet naval forces in the Black Sea from sorties into the Mediterranean in wartime, and was directly adjacent to Soviet territory which would facilitate the conduct of the nuclear air campaign if deterrence failed.[19]

Essentially, NATO's new strategic concept, MC 14/1, was the European portion of the existing ABC DOUBLESTAR-SPEEDWAY-BULLMOOSE plan. MC 14/1's initial concept of operations was to counter any enemy offensive action directed against NATO nations, then "Ensure Allied ability to carry out strategic air attacks promptly," and "Secure, maintain, and defend...main support areas...essential to these undertakings." Mobilization would flow into the main support areas and the ground war would be fought.[20]

The primary holding actions were to be in Scandinavia, Western Europe and Turkey. Turkey was now critical to NATO strategy since enemy advances "would give access to the Mediterranean and greater freedom of operation against the Middle East. In particular it would threaten important Allied oil producing areas." The main support areas for NATO offensive action included North America and the British Isles. NATO member territories in the Mediterranean basin were also key: "[the] defence of bases in Gibraltar, Malta, Cyprus, Northwest Africa, Libya, and Egypt supporting the strategic air offensive or serving vital allied lines of communication." French Algeria was singled out for special mention because it was "a base area for the Allied strategic air offensive."[21]

It is important to note that NATO strategic concepts were not imposed on Canada. Canada wielded its influence in the NATO forums which generated the concepts and took an active part in fine tuning them as its representatives saw fit. Consequently MC 14/1's precepts were known to the highest levels of the External Affairs community as well as the Chiefs of Staff Committee, a body which had an External Affairs representative present for important meetings.[22] Canadian comments on MC 14/1, both External and the Chiefs of Staff, were limited to concern that "the paper did not appear to take sufficient account of the effect of atomic weapons and other weapons of mass destruction"[23] since this directly affected North America: Canadian concerns were addressed in MC 14/1's replacement strategic concept. Other than that, both External Affairs and National Defence accepted and agreed that MC 14/1 constituted NATO, and thus Canadian, strategy.[24]

The nagging part of NATO strategy development was how NATO, and thus Canada, interacted with areas that lay outside the defined NATO Area. Canada had almost committed two divisions to defend the Middle East during ABC global strategy discussions at the height of the Korean crisis when Brooke Claxton stopped any progress in this area (Canada hardly had enough troops for NATO and Korea at the time). Once MC 14/1 was accepted as a strategic concept, Dana Wilgress (the Under Secretary) fell under some pressure by Pearson to determine where Canada stood on the question of the Suez Canal and the use of the area as a Main Support Area in NATO strategy.[25]

The Joint Planning Committee duly examined the strategic aspects of the Suez area for External Affairs. Simply put, the JPC concluded:

> In the event that Europe is completely overrun and the UK neutralized, a large operational base in the Middle East would be of immense value to NATO for counter offensive operations against the Soviet Union and also for the defence of Africa which would be invaluable during the build up for an offensive to liberate Europe.[26]

Most importantly, "Should a base in the Middle East be given up it might prove impossible to prevent Soviet conquest of the area with...grave consequences" which included the disruption of the oil supply, allowing Soviet naval forces into the Mediterranean, the blockage of communications with the Far East, and the fact that the other main support area, French North Africa, would

The United Nations and other diplomatic forums were themselves battlegrounds as the Soviet Union and allies attempted to manipulate that new weapon, world opinion, for their purposes. Effective participation in NATO and UN peacekeeping afforded Canada the ability to influence events in these theatres of the Cold War.

(CIIA Photo)

be exposed.[27] It is very clear that External Affairs knew why the Suez Canal area was important to NATO, and thus Canadian, interests.

General Foulkes, in setting up the original NATO organizational structure, attempted to include global planning but was unable to do so since "it was realized that to attempt to formalize any such regional arrangements would endanger the United Nations Organization." The fallback plan was to have the United States involved in a series of regional arrangements which "could be welded together into an effective organization in the event of an outbreak of war and/or a breakup of the [UN]."[28]

In 1951 and 1952, however, the possibility that the Korean conflict would trigger a global war coupled with the projected development of thermonuclear weapons forced several concurrent re-examinations of western global planning. The British produced an influential study called the Global Strategy Paper (GSP) in mid-1952, which was distributed to Canada and the United States for comment. This document formed the basis of British strategy and was the launching pad for a new NATO strategy in 1954-55.

In essence, the GSP argued that the main effort was in the NATO Area. The best way to deter the Soviets there was to produce a mixed conventional-nuclear force structure and plan for nuclear war.[29]

The problem, the British planners noted, was that:

Outside the NATO area there exists no effective organization for co-ordinating the efforts of the free nations. Proposals for a Middle East Defence Organization are under examination but have been delayed by events in Egypt. Resistance to Communist threats and aggression in the Far East is disjointed.[30]

The Middle East was absolutely critical to western military planning during Cold War positioning. It was the link between Europe, the oil-rich Persian Gulf and the resource-rich Far East, and it was the only way by which enemy forces could get at nuclear bomber bases in French North Africa. Most importantly, since Turkey was now a NATO member, "it is of great importance to retain the Moslem world—from Pakistan to Morocco—in the Western orbit...the Middle East and its bomber bases are essential to the Allied Strategic Air Offensive." In the Far East, British planners believed, the spread of communism threatened the right flank of the Middle East, although they "do not regard China as a Soviet satellite; indeed she is a menace on her own account."[31]

Canadian views on the British study are revealing. The matter was brought to the Cabinet which agreed that it did not "affect present Canadian defence planning."[32] This appraisal was based on Brooke Claxton's summation of the Global Strategy Paper. The problem was that Claxton did not explain to Cabinet the global implications, only those that dealt immediately with the NATO Area.[33] The External Affairs views on the GSP were still in process, however.

The British were proposing that greater ABC co-operation on global planning be conducted. The Americans were suspicious, particularly General Omar Bradley who thought that "the paper was dictated by the UK slim pocket book than real strategical considerations."[34] A.D.P. Heeney, Canada's representative to NATO, was involved in detailed discussions going on in the back rooms of Paris. Heeney worked through the options. There could be a formal command established to link NATO and similar planned regional organizations in the Middle and Far East. This was not feasible "because it would involve [nations] in areas where they have no direct strategic interests." Should NATO formally evolve into this global planning agency? If not, could NATO handle this job tacitly? The situation was serious, since "it is now clear that the Soviet threat is not limited to the Atlantic area and indeed that the threat to NATO countries might well develop in other areas."[35]

Foulkes' solution to this issue harked back the creation of a NATO entity which evolved into the Standing Group. The Standing Group consisted of the British, American, and French members of the NATO Military Committee: in fact, the Military Committee had to have its planning confirmed and endorsed by the Standing Group before it was approved by the political level, the North Atlantic Council. In this way, NATO planning could be co-ordinated with the "Big Three" in global deterrence and war planning. Pearson did not like the idea of the Standing Group, since it formalized the notion that some NATO members were more important than others. Canada was invited to join the Standing Group, but Pearson declined. If Canada was part of it, Canada could not create "counterweights" to American and British influence with the other NATO members since Canada would be overly-identified with the "Big Three."

Foulkes and Heeney conferred frequently on the matter and Dana Wilgress and Lester Pearson were kept informed of developments. Foulkes had extensive conversations with his American counterpart, General Bradley, who agreed but needed the assent of the National Security Council. In effect, global strategy outside the NATO Area was co-ordinated from within NATO through the Standing Group. In the Canadian view this was acceptable, but the planners were not to make any requests for concrete Canadian military commitments.[37]

During this time Pearson was exploring (in response to questioning in the House of Commons by Howard Green, later to become Secretary of State for External Affairs under Diefenbaker) how a relationship could be forged between NATO and the newly-formed Australia-New Zealand-United States (ANZUS) defence pact, a NATO-like structure in the Pacific.[38] How did NATO relate to regional defence in the Pacific? Foulkes' views were solicited. Foulkes believed Pearson had to decide what his aim should be. Was his aim to have representatives in these organizations who could observe and report back to Ottawa, or should Canada actually participate in them? There were dangers to both and no middle ground was possible. Either Canada was involved, or was not. Canada did not have the forces to participate, and should not get locked into one regional organization outside of NATO. It should, Foulkes thought, be in a position to back up any regional organization wherever communist aggression occurred, as in Korea: "militarily we have no more interest in South East Asia than we would have in an outbreak of communist aggression in Iran or Pakistan." Ad hoc and informal relationships seemed the best policy in these areas.[39]

ECONOMY OF FORCE: CANADIAN PEACE OPERATIONS IN ASIA

It would be too easy to divorce Canadian peace operations in Asia and treat them as events unconnected to the main thrust of Canadian national security policy in NATO. Yet new Canadian involvement in Indochina and increased Canadian commitments to the Kashmir were indicative of the new policy of "economy of effort" in the wake of the acceptance of MC 14/1. Economic support to new Commonwealth members in Asia, designed to speed development of those nations, flowed as a result of the Canada-backed Columbo Plan and, like the Marshall Plan's relationship to NATO, Canada and Great Britain could not allow their monetary investment to be threatened by Communist insurgency[40] (See Figure 3).

The Joint Intelligence Committee's appreciation of the situation in Asia in the early 1950s suggested that Indochina was an increasingly important Communist target. If the French lost in Indochina, the resulting strain on their economy could affect their ability to participate in the NATO defence of Europe. If the French armed forces in Indochina succeeded or if there was a non-military solution to the conflict, then they could be repatriated. However, "the possession of Indo-China by the Communists would greatly facilitate campaigns against Thailand and Burma...[this] would seriously endanger the British position in Malaya and directly threaten India and Pakistan."[41] If the British lost Malaya their economy would suffer, threatening economic support to the Commonwealth and affecting the utility of that body as an anti-communist entity.[42]

Between 1951 and 1953, while the West was at war in Korea and building up in Europe, the French forces in Indochina were slowly succumbing to the Chinese and Soviet-backed Viet Minh. More and more American military aid was required. The French pressured the Americans, arguing that if support did not continue, France could not support the European Defence Community initiative, which was critical to normalizing West Germany in the NATO system and bolstering the NATO deterrent forces in Europe.[43] The climactic battle at Dienbienphu in 1954 had serious implications. The Americans had successfully used nuclear threats to bring about an armistice in Korea, which may have prompted the Eisenhower administration to consider using two or three kiloton-yield nuclear weapons to break the Viet Minh siege: plans were made with the French to do so. Conventional operations to assist the beleaguered garrison were also explored.[44]

Canadian analysis of the situation expressed serious concern that American intervention, in whatever form, would trigger Chinese intervention in Indochina and result in the mass use of nuclear weapons in that theatre. Pearson's view was that the UN should be involved but such a move was inextricably linked to the thorny issue of whether the People's Republic of China should be recognized by the UN as a legitimate government (no small feat in the year following the Korean armistice).[45]

In the end the Eisenhower administration was unable to gain enough support from its allies for a combined Australian, New Zealand, British and Canadian expedition to Indochina (the "United Action" concept). The nuclear option disappeared into the murky shadows and the Americans supported the French in their efforts to withdraw as gracefully as possible.

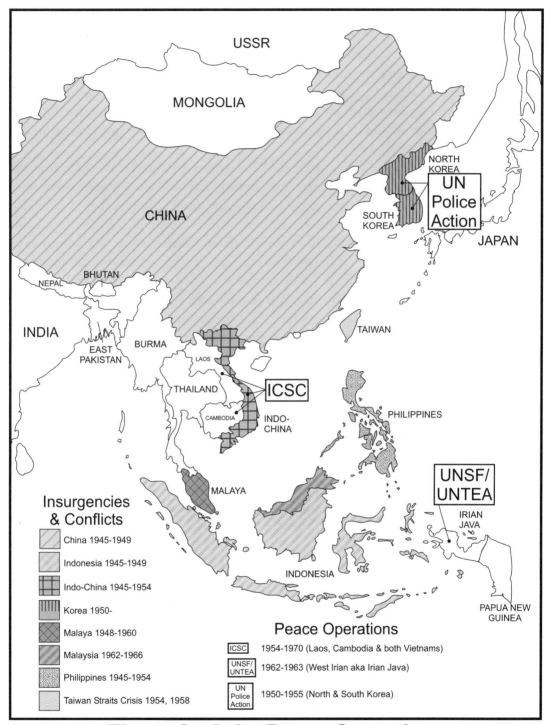

**Figure 3: Asia, Peace Operations
and the Cold War, 1950-1962**

However, Canada did become involved in the May-July 1954 Geneva talks which confirmed French defeat and divided Vietnam, Korea-like, into a Communist north and a Western-backed south.[46] Canada was part of another diplomatic meeting in Geneva dealing with Korea. The Canadian delegation consisted of Pearson, Holmes, and Charles Ronning. These talks included China, the Soviets, the North Koreans, France, Britain, the United States, as well as some of the other powers committed to Korea (keep in mind that although there was an armistice in Korea, there was no formal peace). Canada participated in the "Indochina phase" of the talks.

The Indians, through the Chinese, invited Canada to join what became known as the International Commission for Supervision and Control (ICSC), the peace observation force designed to monitor the Geneva Agreement in Indochina (now split into Laos, Cambodia, and North and South Vietnam). India was instrumental in swaying the Chinese to support Canadian participation: the Americans wanted Belgium. Canada was the compromise candidate.[47] The ICSC consisted of Indian, Canadian, and Polish delegations and monitors. The organization was not intended to be an impartial UN-style peace observation mission. It was abundantly clear from the start that Poland represented the communist world, India the "non-aligned" world, and Canada was the West's champion.[48]

Canada's ICSC contingent arrived in the region aboard RCAF North Star transports in the fall of 1954. Overall, Canada contributed 150 military personnel for monitoring duties, although there were an additional 50 civilians, some drawn from External Affairs, providing support and diplomatic capabilities. The ICSC, divided into fixed and mobile teams, had several tasks. The priority was to monitor the withdrawal of the French Army from the region and the repatriation of prisoners of war. Once this was accomplished, the ICSC was to monitor the region to report on arms shipments to the four new political entities. The main problem was who the ICSC reported *to*, since there was no UN "analogy." In theory the ICSC reported to the Joint Commission, but the Joint Commission was not a diplomatic forum like the UN or Commonwealth. There was, therefore, ample room to maneuver for those interested in ensuring that the ICSCs effectiveness was reduced.[49] In the meantime, however, relative peace was brought to the region.

While Canadian ICSC monitors went about their work in the jungles, changes were occurring at the UN. The embattled Trygve Lie had resigned in November 1952 in part because of his ostracisizm by the UN's Communist-bloc representatives over his handling of Korea. Lie's ability to place a firm grip on the bloated UN bureaucracy was also suspect. Cold War machinations by the Soviets ensured that Lester Pearson, supported by the French, British and Danes, was out of the running to replace Lie. By spring 1953, the redoubtable Swedish Foreign Minister, Dag Hammarskjöld had assumed the mantle of Secretary General.

The son of a diplomat, Hammarskjöld earned a PhD in economics and by the age of thirty had become under secretary of state for finance. He was a highly ethical civil servant, a man steeped in the art of impartiality, a trait which would serve him well in his seven years as UN Secretary General. He already knew that the UN was a flawed organization requiring special handling in a very dangerous world and he was able to bring his personal qualities of asceticism, dedication to duty, and self-sacrifice to bear in tight situations.[50]

A confidential assessment of Hammarskjöld provided to Pearson indicated that the Secretary General had a "cultivated impartiality in his references to men and affairs, but it was a constructive and positive impartiality rather than static or negative...This kind of 'neutrality' can be very creative." The man could "mix discretion and frankness behind a blandly animated exterior with a sure instinct for the limits beyond which he should not go."[51]

Hammarskjöld's objectives were difficult to gauge in the early years of his tenure. He was kept busy moving from crisis to crisis, such as preventing the shooting down of an American B-29 near Korea from fanning the flames in the region. Handling the diplomatic aftermath of the American covert intervention in Guatemala competed with Hammarskjöld's time spent on UN deliberations over whether to recognise the Chinese, the offshore island dispute, the American Seventh Fleet, and the possible use of nuclear weapons against the Chinese forces threatening Taiwan. Everything in the region was connected.[52]

Discussions between Hammarskjöld and Pearson during 1954 revealed the Secretary General's intense interest in resolving the Korean situation, and the possible spillover effects in Asia if this was not done soon. Middle East conflicts troubled him greatly: he felt that the UN's "prestige...in the Middle East was extremely low and unfortunately, the influence of the three countries with long standing interests there [US, UK, France] was even less." The UN was the only body that could "coordinate those forces which might work towards the establishment of conditions under which peace was possible." Technical assistance to the developing world was absolutely critical but this was also linked to internal UN reorganization.[53]

And what of NATO-UN relations? Hammarskjöld did not want to see NATO become "a kind of Atlantic UN" (as implied in the Canadian-championed NATO Article 2), but he felt:

> There might be areas where NATO could encourage a degree of co-operation for which the UN under the present Charter was not too well equipped. [Hammarskjöld was]sympathetic to more elaborate techniques within NATO for the pacific settlement of disputes.[54]

On the whole, Canada's relationship with Hammarskjöld developed into a fairly close one, with Pearson rated as a significant political confidant.[55]

Canada's UN policy was also evolving at this time, though not dramatically. External Affairs analysts correctly noted in 1955 that the UN was more and more likely to become involved as a prime player in decolonization efforts. As the Western nations relinquished more and more control over their colonial possessions and new states emerged, these regions would likely become Cold War battlegrounds. Similarly, the West would come under increased attack by the Soviet bloc and a formal UN anti-colonial policy might emerge which would threaten Western interests. How should Canada respond? How should Canada facilitate the transition to peace in the UN forum? One issue related to this was the actual legal wording of the UN Charter. Could it be applied broadly and still be advantageous to Western interests?[56]

The areas under discussion were the French colonies of Tunisia, Morocco, Algeria, the Dutch colony of West Irian, and the British colony of Cyprus. With the exception of West Irian, all of these areas corresponded to critical areas in NATO military planning for global war. The French and British were fighting counterinsurgency campaigns in Algeria and Cyprus respectively. External Affairs' UN Division argued that it would damage Canadian interests to have a "rigid and legalistic policy" since it "would relegate to second place or even rule out altogether the equally vital political considerations."[57] The area that particularly concerned External Affairs was Algeria, since it was technically part of Metropolitan France and was recognized as such under the North Atlantic Treaty. It would prove highly embarrassing to have a blanket policy, so the recommendation was to have a policy which would be based "on our usual devious and liberal interpretation" of the UN Charter.[58]

Internal External Affairs memoranda sum up the dilemma:

> Because of our own internal stresses, the habit of compromise and the doctrine of the 'middle way' have become so ingrained in us that we find it hard to make up our minds. On the other hand our growing strength and our activist foreign policy are pushing us out into a world where we may—*horrible viau*—be forced to do so. If we fail to make up our minds there will be discernible within the husk of our voting record (a brilliant phrase) no grain of principle but merely the dead air created when opposing forces are reduced to zero; in itself a form, though a lowly one, of expediency...Can we do this so long as we are a member of NATO? Can we have our cake (NATO) and eat it (ECOSOC, Columbo Plan, SUNFED)? We probably can so long as our national interest isn't directly touched.[59]

Robert Ford was even more blunt: Cyprus and Algeria "go to the heart of the conflict between political necessity and domestic jurisdiction; they also cut across our general acknowledgment of the principle of self-determination...and our growing realization of the strategic political requirements of the Western powers."[60] Marcel Cadieux, in a note to John Holmes on a talk being prepared for NATO journalists, was even more frank: Canadian policy on colonialism should be "slanted in such a way that while a member of NATO, our 'colonial' policy in the UN is based upon the assumption that we take the organization seriously."[61] Pearson in the end acknowledged that Canadian policy should remain ambiguous in his instructions to the Canadian UN delegation in 1955.[62]

This policy was reflected on the Kashmir front, where there had been little movement. The 1951 plebiscite never came off: neither the Pakistani nor Indian governments nor the political entities in the region had the will to conduct it despite UN backing. Over time, "the long continued delays over this question has of course hardened public opinion on both sides; so that neither Government feels able to make any further concessions to the other without loss of face."[63] Nehru was intransigent and there had been no real demilitarization of the Kashmir: paramilitary police forces deployed by both sides were as well armed as military forces.[64]

Despite the deadlock, Canada's reasons for being involved remained the same. Canada maintained between seven and nine military observers with UNMOGIP in the Kashmir (the second "I" had been dropped by this point). External Affairs' confidential briefing notes sum up that organization's attitude towards UNMOGIP:

> UNMOGIP is considered to work most effectively without public attention and the United Nations wishes as little publicity as possible to be given to the operation. Because of this, and because the Kashmir issue is a delicate and embarrassing question in terms of Commonwealth relations, it has been our practice not to mention UNMOGIP except when necessary.[65]

Though the possibility of Soviet or Chinese intervention in the India-Pakistan dispute receded somewhat, there were still serious concerns expressed by Canadian military observers and diplomats that if UNMOGIP's presence were withdrawn or reduced, a larger conflict in the region would be precipitated between the two Commonwealth countries with dire effects elsewhere.[66]

UNMOGIP and ICSC were Canada's "economy of force" peacekeeping operations "east of Suez". Like these other operations, UNTSO in the Middle East smouldered away throughout the early 1950s but received far more Canadian scrutiny in the wake of the adoption of a Canadian strategic concept in 1954.

CANADA, NATO'S NEW LOOK, AND THE MIDDLE EAST

The nuclear backdrop to Canadian peace operations during this phase of the Cold War is extremely important. The Soviet nuclear threat to North America was growing alarmingly and the Warsaw Pact conventional threat to Europe remained massive in its dimensions. Canada's national security strategy prior to 1957 was, in the main, directed towards deterrence and then warfighting if deterrence failed. Conflict prevention at the regional level was in its infancy, though its formal connection to national strategy was getting stronger. The link had not yet been made between crisis diplomacy and strategic concepts emphasizing deterrence.

The British Global Strategy Paper influenced NATO strategy development from 1952 to 1954. At the same time, the Americans were conducting analyses which would become known as "The New Look" by October 1953. In NATO, the Supreme Headquarters Allied Powers Europe (SHAPE) created the New Approach Group in 1954. All of these initiatives were examining how the hydrogen bomb and nuclear deterrence affected all aspects of Western national security policy and strategy. These efforts would coalesce into a defined NATO strategy by November 1954. Canada's involvement in these processes eventually had an impact on the role of peace operations in Canadian national security policy.[67]

One recurring theme was the relationship between the NATO Area and the non-NATO areas. The cultural gap between the diplomats and soldiers was apparent in their approach to global planning and strategy. External Affairs chose to define global strategy as an "assessment of the military threat in all areas in relation to 'holding the ring'" while global planning was "the more detailed problem of distributing the forces to be contributed in any area."[68]

The Chiefs of Staff Committee, on the other hand, did not make such a distinction. This difference reflected the concerns about the peacetime process of committing Canadian military forces to fight outside of the NATO Area in wartime.

External Affairs personnel thought that "NATO should be involved in global strategy but not global military planning since we have a clear and direct interest in ensuring that NATO (and Canada) are informed."[69] What happened, however, if there was a threat from outside the NATO Area? The view in NATO circles was that a regional non-NATO organization should handle such a threat. Such organizations could include the Middle East Defence Organization/Baghdad Pact/CENTO, ANZUS, or South East Asia Treaty Organization (SEATO). If they failed and NATO had to be brought in, "Canada would likely then extend her [NATO] commitments beyond the NATO area."[70] To Canada's ambassador to NATO A.D.P. Heeney, this was only a worst case scenario, however. Heeney noted there was a belief that the larger powers (Britain, France, and the United States) "would take on the responsibility." Heeney and General Foulkes, however, had some problems with this since it might "weaken" the UN and smack of colonialism.[71]

Further attempts to create formal global planning and strategy organizations within NATO were subject to a variety of problems that militated against any larger formal concept of NATO involvement outside of the NATO Area. The French pushed for a political version of the Standing Group that would coordinate all global planning and strategy within NATO. Others wanted a formal ANZUS and NATO link. The problem was further aggravated by the inability within NATO to define whether such a group should confine itself to Cold War activities or hot war activities. Using the status quo NATO organization "might be at best a cause for acute embarrassment to the United Kingdom and the Americans," particularly since the two nations were re-examining their roles in the Middle East.[72]

Several factors were in play. Arab nationalism had grown exponentially since 1945, particularly after the defeat of Arab forces during the first Arab-Israeli war. Colonel Gamel Abdul Nasser's 1952 coup in Egypt added fuel to the fiery anger directed at the West and its support for the Arabs' primary antagonist, Israel. Syria and Iraq were unstable, while Iran teetered on the brink of accepting a pro-Soviet government. The only pillars of strength were NATO-member Turkey, British-supported Trucial States, British-backed Jordan, American-backed Saudi Arabia, and French-backed Lebanon. NATO-style solutions like CENTO were unworkable in such an environment, although attempts to create them proceeded, as did attempts to link Middle East command organizations with NATO ones.[73]

These matters appear to have been completely secondary to the realization in the United States that North America could be directly attacked with thermonuclear weapons. The American policy emphasis was to shift to North American air and naval defence efforts, as well as strengthening the nuclear deterrent in Europe. The Middle East, however, retained its importance since the USAF Strategic Air Command still needed forward bases to operate effectively against the USSR if deterrence failed.[74]

The details of how NATO developed its 1954 strategic concept and the adoption of MC 48 as Canada's Cold War strategic policy are dealt with in another work.[75] In effect, the document known as MC 48 or "The Most Effective Pattern of NATO Military Strength for the Next Few Years" (which had extensive Canadian contributions) became the basis for NATO strategy well into the 1960s. MC 48 was based on the principle that nuclear weapons would be used immediately upon the outbreak of a war with the Warsaw Pact if deterrence failed. Such a war would have two phases: in Phase I, nuclear weapons would be used until one side ran out of them. In Phase II, the war would be concluded on conventional terms after a "broken backed" period of reorganization and repair. Initially it was thought Phase I would last up to thirty days, while Phase II could have no fixed duration. MC 48 did not explain what would happen to trigger such a war, a point we will come back to later.[76]

The primary Soviet threat in MC 48's conceptualization, was that of "intensive atomic strategic air attacks against the vital centres and atomic bases of NATO" followed by "widespread attacks by the Soviet army and tactical air forces against NATO countries in Europe" as well as an intense naval campaign directed at NATO sea lines of communications. NATO's primary aim, as MC 48 reiterated time and again was:

> Now more than ever before, to prevent war. This aim can only be achieved if the Allied nations are so powerful in the vital elements of modern warfare that the enemy will conclude that he has little hope of winning a war involving NATO. This means that NATO must be able to withstand the initial Soviet onslaught, to deliver decisive atomic counter-attacks against the war-making capacity of the enemy, and to prevent the rapid overrunning of Europe.[77]

NATO's first line of defence, therefore, was the strategic deterrent and all that entailed. SAC's B-47 bombers and KC-97 aerial tankers, and later Royal Air Force Bomber Command's V-Force Victor, Vulcan, and Valiant nuclear bomber squadrons, had to be ready at a moment's notice to strike their targets inside the Soviet Union. It was critical that the bases from which these aircraft were to operate were secure to permit maximum flexibility, unpredictability and surprise, the essence of the deterrence strategy. A similar situation held true for American and British aircraft carrier task forces equipped with nuclear-capable aircraft. These forces had to have secure facilities so that they would be ready for H-Hour. Many of these bases were in the Mediterranean, the Middle East, and the Far East, volatile areas during the Cold War, areas vulnerable to Soviet proxy or nationalist activity.

Pearson, who along with Foulkes was integral to the process by which MC 48 was accepted by NATO, requested an extensive analysis of MC 48 in the spring of 1955.[78] The first thing the study noted was that the explicit threat to use nuclear weapons to respond to Communist aggression carried an increased "risk of turning local hostilities into general war" no matter where those hostilities took place. The Americans wanted some form of overall deterrence, but External Affairs thought that the West had to "be in a position to distinguish between aggressions of less directness and magnitude from all-out threats and they must also be in a position to control the putting into action of NATO plans." This essentially was a recognition that some form of crisis could occur which could trigger nuclear war and that crisis management needed to be an element in the deterrent strategy[79] Given that that was the case:

If in any given case the risks of all out or nuclear war are not justified, and yet important interests of the free world are involved, it is essential that the Western Powers should be prepared to deal with limited wars with limited means and within limited objectives. Canada itself would not participate in such limited or local wars unless by a decision of the United Nations which it had accepted.[80]

Similarly,

The Communist threat and methods vary from area to area according to available resources and the weaknesses and contradictions which they can exploit; allied strategy must therefore combine political and economic rather than military measures to deter the indirect threats which may be posed by the Communists in an effort to outflank the nuclear deterrent.[81]

Did this bring Canada full circle to the pre-1950 concepts embodied in NATO's Article 2 and initiatives like the Columbo Plan? Not necessarily:

Canada's own security interests lie primarily in North America and the North Atlantic Treaty Area....Canada's interests would not be involved directly in the holding of any particular areas around the Soviet periphery in the Far-East or Middle East...even though Canada may not be directly involved in such peripheral and local wars, she cannot escape certain consequences if the United States were involved especially because of the interdependence of the two countries in air defence; such local and limited wars are therefore of concern to Canada.[82]

In effect, the fact that both sides had nuclear deterrence would stabilize the main confrontation area, Europe. The Cold War of position and influence would shift to areas peripheral to the NATO Area, where the Soviets would attempt to disrupt and outflank NATO with the overall objective of developing a better posture in the event of all-out war, generated by accident or design, and denying NATO geographical advantage if that war occurred. The methods used would vary, but they had to be opposed through a combination of American, British and French military force, Commonwealth economic aid, and the use of the United Nations in crises resolution when it could be used.

External Affairs MC 48 analysis suggested that in ideal circumstances steps should be taken to bolster regional organizations outside the NATO Area. The problem was that "the recognition of mutual security interests" and "determination to join together" were factors that were "lacking, for a variety of reasons, in the areas of South East Asia and the Middle East" though an Iraqi-Turkish arrangement with American and British participation was imminent. Canada could play a role in "increased diplomatic representation in threatened areas, increased contributions to United Nations activities in the non-military sphere."[83]

Not surprisingly then, the area that received the largest increase in Canadian activity from 1954 to 1963 was the Middle East. Even though the bulk of this activity occurred after the introduction of United Nations Emergency Force I during the Suez Crisis of 1956, the roots were laid much earlier. The Mackenzie King Government was unwilling to get involved with the creation and initial deployment of UNTSO. St. Laurent was preoccupied with Asian and NATO matters. UNTSO, with its staff reduced and total international military observer strength hovering around forty to fifty officers, fit neatly into the economy of force category of UNMOGIP and ICSC.

An External Affairs analysis conducted for Pearson in early 1957 would have been equally applicable two years earlier, despite its proximity to the Suez Crisis. Simply put, Canada had "limited prospects for trade," because of high shipping costs. Canada did not need any raw materials from the region, though oil was imported from the Gulf to make up shortfalls in Canadian production. The Middle East was not "an important reservoir of population for immigration," the exception being Lebanon since there was a sizable Lebanese community in Canada.[84]

But Canadian security interests were at issue. The primary Canadian diplomatic representatives in the region were located in Beirut. Their analysis was that "as the defence of the Western world becomes more and more interlocked, the importance of protecting the vital interests of our friends, notably with regard to their oil supply, becomes more of a matter of concern to us." Most importantly,

> The preservation of peace in the area is of highest importance to Canada. Apart from the danger that a Middle East conflict might degenerate into a world conflict, our attitude must be influenced by the need to preserve the prestige of the United Nations and the rule of law…[there is also] the task of combating the spread of Communism and Soviet influence in the area…[Canada] has a useful potential role to play in showing peoples of the area that the West is not made up exclusively of powers dominated by "imperial interests."[85]

Dag Hammarskjöld conducted a Middle East tour in 1953 and concluded that UNTSO should be expanded because tensions between Egypt and Israel had increased dramatically. After conversations with Lester Pearson and Brooke Claxton, Hammarskjöld was informed in June 1954 that Canada could contribute five observers and, most importantly, Hammarskjöld's request that a Canadian general assume the position of Chief of Staff was granted. Unlike traditional military hierarchies, the Chief of Staff UNTSO is the highest military position in that organization. These Canadian commitments were not discussed in Cabinet, for reasons which remain obscure.[86] Canadian interest in the region stemmed, in part, from Pearson's belief that "the lack of direct representation in the area has been a handicap to us in many respects" in the United Nations since "it has been particularly difficult for Canada to take part in the many discussions of Middle Eastern questions."[87] Thus, having a Canadian lead UNTSO was vital.

UN peace operations in the Middle East were extremely difficult since ethnic animosity was so virulent in the wake of Israel's successful War of Independence. The man selected by Canada to lead UNTSO was the dour Lieutenant-General E.L.M. "Tommy" Burns. A Royal Military College graduate and signals officer during the First World War and a Corps commander in the Second World War, Tommy Burns had also been Deputy Minister for

Veterans' Affairs. He eventually became a part of the Canadian delegation to the UN in 1949. How and why exactly Burns was selected by the Canadian Government to command UNTSO remains unclear: Pearson's memoirs merely state that it was done and Burns provides no clues in his own UNTSO and UNEF memoir, *Between Arab and Israeli*.

Upon taking command of UNTSO in 1954, Burns noted:

> In 1954 and 1955 nobody blessed the United Nations Truce Supervision Organization in Palestine as a peacemaker, possibly because it was not peacemaking but at best a peace-keeping organization. Sometimes its members were referred to as international policemen, but they were policemen without truncheons. They were actually more like watchmen, watching on behalf of the Security Council of the United Nations for breaches of the General Armistice Agreements of the Council's cease-fire order.[88]

UNTSO had been deployed into the region to supervise a truce, which then became an armistice (established by Ralph Bunche, for which he received the Nobel Peace Prize), but there was no formal peace treaty between Israel on one side and Jordan, Syria, Lebanon, and Egypt on the other. UNTSO's initial objectives were to facilitate communication between the military forces of the belligerents in contact with each other, and report local incidents to Mixed Armistice Commissions with the hope of avoiding larger reactions.

In theory, UNTSO would have withdrawn, but that was conditional on an actual peace treaty being signed by the belligerents. UNTSO was now caught in a quagmire of no war, no peace. There were innumerable breaches of the cease fire, breaches which included raids of increasing size and sophistication across the Armistice Demarcation Lines, ambushes, random shootings, mortar attacks, and interference with the civil populations in all areas. UNTSO investigations became commonplace as all sides denied the cross-border activity and interfered with UNTSO's ability to mediate. And, like Canadian European Community and United Nations military observers in Bosnia forty years later, UN military observers were routinely shot at, detained and taken hostage.[89]

Operating from UNTSO HQ located in the former UK Government House on the so-called "Hill of Evil Council" in Jerusalem overlooking the Temple Mount, Burns was dismayed at UNTSO's limitations and requested more military observers. Jerusalem was divided and there were not enough mobile patrols to police the line, nor were there enough to escort convoys to the isolated but strategically important Israeli enclave of Mount Scopus deep in the Jordanian zone. Five more Canadian UNMOs were sent (for a total of ten) out of the 300 or so UNTSO UNMOs.[90] More unarmed observers were not the answer, however, since the Israelis "had gotten accustomed to pushing UN Military Observers around."[91]

Belligerent military activity became so intense in the Middle East throughout October 1955 that Burns was contacted while on leave in Ottawa by Secretary General Hammarskjöld's assistant, Andrew Cordier. The Israelis raided a police fort at El Kuntilla, in retaliation for an Egyptian raid which was in turn retaliation for an Israeli raid in the Gaza Strip. In a London meeting on 4 November, Burns had talks with British Minister for Foreign Affairs Anthony Nutting, who was more and more concerned with the security of the Suez

Canal zone, since the Nasser regime was developing closer relations to the Soviets, including an arms agreement. Burns and Hammarskjöld hoped to get British diplomatic assistance in the Security Council to persuade the Americans to put pressure on Israel to back off, something the Eisenhower administration was not interested in doing. As Burns noted,

> We discussed the possibility of introducing United Nations troops between the armed forces of the parties. I said I thought that it would take extraordinary pressure to get the Israelis out of the El Auja [demilitarized] zone, and that I did not think it would be possible to get UN troops in without a prior military intervention by the Great Powers.... The conclusion was that nothing more than the proposals of the Secretary General could be advanced at that time.[92]

The situation in the Middle East was about to come to a head the following year, in 1956. What, then, was the state of Canadian peace operations and their role in Canadian national security policy on the eve of the Suez Crisis?

Peace operations involving UN military forces were conceptualized by the Canadian Chiefs of Staff Committee's Joint Planning Committee in 1948. This conceptualization was read by Lester Pearson in his capacity as Undersecretary of State for External Affairs in the government of Mackenzie King. King's government was extremely reluctant to get involved in UN peace operations, to the extent that the Americans organized the first mission, UNTSO, in 1948. Canada did not participate in that mission prior to 1954. Despite a change of government from King to St. Laurent, actual Canadian participation in peace operations was relatively small in numbers: 5 to 10 for UNTSO, 4 to 9 for UNMOGIP, and 150 for ICSC, though Canadian generals commanded two of the three operations.

Despite the small numbers, all three missions functioned as vital "economy of force" missions under Canadian national security policy. Canada and the West could not militarily defend against communism everywhere at once, but nuclear war could be averted through the careful use of peace operations. All the while, however, Canadian peace operations were subordinated to Canada's main national security policy effort, NATO. Finally, the concept of interpositionary UN peace operations in the Middle East using military forces were suggested by Canadian General E.L.M. Burns in 1955 as a solution to the troubles in that region.

Notes to Chapter 3

1. NAC RG 25 vol. 6460 file 5475-FA-40 Pt. 1, (18 May 50) memo Carter to Holmes.

2. Ibid.

3. NAC RG 25 vol. 6460 file 5475-FA-40 Pt. 1, (25 May 50) memo Holmes to Heeney.

4. Clearly, Holmes did not understand that the momentum behind a military operation cannot be just 'turned off' like a light switch. NAC RG 25 vol. 6460 file 5475-FA-40 Pt. 1, (29 Dec 50) memo Holmes to Reid.

5. NAC RG 25 vol. 6460 file 5475-FA-40 Pt. 1, (29 Dec 50) memo Ford to distribution list, "The Role of the United Nations in Maintaining Collective Security."

6. Ibid.

7. NAC RG 25 vol. 6460 file 5475-FA-40 Pt. 1.2, (29 Dec 50) "A Re-examination of the United Nations in the light of the reverse in Korea."

8. Ibid.

9. Ibid.

10. NAC RG 25 vol. 6460 file 5475-FA-40 Pt. 1.2, (18 Jan 51) message CANDEL Geneva to UnderSecretary of State for External Affairs, "A Re-examination of the United Nations in the light of the reverse in Korea."

11. NAC RG 25 vol. 6460 file 5475-FA-40 Pt. 1.2, (12 Jan 51) memo Robinson to Holmes.

12. NAC RG 25 vol. 6460 file 5475-FA-40 Pt. 2.2, (20 Jun 51) message Wrong to Undersecretary of State for External Affairs.

13. NAC RG 25 vol. 6460 file 5475-FA-40 Pt. 3 (5 Sep 51) message Rae to Undersecretary of State for External Affairs, "Role of United Nations in maintaining collective security."

14. Maloney, *Securing Command of the Sea* (Annapolis: Naval Institute Press, 1995) Ch. 2.

15. Ibid.

16. The details about the creation of MC 14 can be found in Maloney, *Securing Command of the Sea*, Ch. 2; and Maloney, *Learning to Love The Bomb*, Ch. 2.

17. North Atlantic Military Committee, (28 Mar 5) "MC 14: Strategic Guidance for North Atlantic Regional Planning."

18. Pearson Memoirs, Volume II, p. 85.

19. George McGhee, *The US-Turkish-NATO Middle East Connection: How the Truman Doctrine and Turkey's NATO Entry Contained the Soviets* (London: Macmillan, 1990), Ch. 6.

20. North Atlantic Military Committee, (9 Dec 52) "MC 14/1: Strategic Guidance."

21. Ibid.

22. See Maloney, *Learning to Love The Bomb*, Ch. 2.

23. NAC RG 25 vol. 4495 file 50030-E-1-40 pt. 1, (1 Dec 52) memo for Defence Liaison 1, "NATO December Military Meeting."

24. NAC RG 25 vol. 4495 file 50030-E-1-40 pt. 1, (19 Nov 52) "Brief for the 7th Meeting Military Committee December 1952."

25. PRO, DEFE 6/11 (14 Oct 49) British Joint Planning Staff "ABC Meeting"; DHH, file 193.009 (D 53) (29 Sep 53) Extract from Minutes of 544th Meeting of the Chiefs of Staff Committee Meeting."

26. DHH, file 193.009 (D 53) (11 Sep 53) JPC Report, "Suez Canal Base."

27. Ibid.

28. DHH, Raymont Collection, file 434, (9 Feb 53) letter Foulkes to Wilgress.

29. Alan Macmillan and John Baylis *Nuclear History Program, Occasional Paper 8: A Reassessment of the British Global Strategy Paper of 1952* (Center for International and Security Studies at Maryland School of Public Affairs, University of the Maryland, 1994).

30. Ibid.

31 . Ibid.

32. NAC RG2 Cabinet Conclusions, 15 October 1952.

33. MAC RG 24 vol. 20710 csc 232, (7 Oct 52) memo to the Cabinet Defence Committee, "Canadian Comments on UK Views on Global Strategy and Defence Policy."

34. National Security Archive, (15 Sep 52) memo from Foulkes to Claxton, "Notes on Discussion with General Bradley held in Washington on 10 September 1952."

35. DHH, Raymont Collection, file 434, (13 Jan 53) message Heeney to Pearson, "NATO and Global Planning."

36. Maloney, *Learning to Love The Bomb*, Ch. 1 and 2.

37. DHH, Raymont Collection, file 434, (9 Feb 53) letter Foulkes to Wilgress; (24 Feb 53) message Wilgress to CANDEL NATO, "NATO and Global Defence Problems"; NAC RG 25 vol. 4903 file 50115-P-40 pt. 2, (28 Feb 53) memo "Global Strategy and Organization of Security in the Pacific Ocean Area."

38. DHH, Raymont Collection, file 434, (3 Mar 53) letter Wilgress to Foulkes, "Global Strategy and Organization of Security in the Pacific Ocean Area."

39. DHH, Raymont Collection, file 434, (10 Mar 53) letter Foulkes to Wilgress.

40. See Holmes, *The Shaping of Peace*, vol. 2 and Pearson memoirs vol. 2 for discussions on the origins and purpose of the Columbo Plan. See also NAC RG 25 vol. 4767 file 50072-40 pt. 1 (30 Dec 49) Cruickshank study to Pearson, "Outline of Communist Strategy in South East Asia."

41. DHH, file 193.009 (D 53) (21 Dec 50) JIC "Intelligence Appreciation-Indo-China."

42. These conclusions were reached by some analysts as early as 1949 during the Bukit Serene Conference of the Colonial Governors, data which was forwarded to Ottawa which formed part of the analysis. NAC RG 25 vol. 4767 file 50072-40 pt. 1 (21 Nov 49) memo Shannon to ADP Heeney, "Bukit Serene Conference." See also Victor Levant's *Quiet Complicity: Canadian Involvement in the Vietnam War* (Toronto: Between the Lines Press, 1986), Ch. 2 and 3 for his take on Western economic interests as a factor in Canadian decision making.

43. George McT. Kahin, *Intervention: How America Became Involved in Vietnam* (Garden City: Anchor Books, 1987) Ch. 2.

44. Richard Immerman, "Between the Unattainable and the Unacceptable: Eisenhower and Dienbienphu," in Melanson and Mayers, eds, *Reevaluating Eisenhower: American Foreign Policy in the Fifties* (Chicago: University of Illinois Press, 1989), 120-154; for American nuclear involvement in Korea, see Rosemary Foot, *The Wrong War: American Policy and the Dimensions of the Korean Conflict, 1950-1953* (Ithaca: Cornell University Press, 1985), Ch. 6.

45. Douglas Ross, *In the Interests of Peace: Canada and Vietnam 1954-73* (Toronto: University of Toronto Press, 1984), 60-64.

46. I am referring to Victor Levant's *Quiet Complicity*, James Eayrs, *Indochina: Roots of Complicity* and Douglas Ross, *In the Interests of Peace*. Even George McT. Kahin's *Intervention* is somewhat sketchy on the origins of the Geneva conference and how it evolved.

47. English, *The Worldly Years, 93-96*; Ross, *In the Interests of Peace*, Ch. 3; Eayrs, *Indochina: The Roots of Complicity*, 49.

48. DHH, Raymont Collection file 3351, (2 Jun 69) "Report of the Viet Nam Working Group."

49. John E.G. de Domenico, *Land of a Million Elephants: Memoirs of a Canadian Peacekeeper* (Burnstown: General Store Publishing house, n/d) see Appendix "A"; DHH, Raymont Collection file 3351, (2 Jun 69) "Report of the Viet Nam Working Group"; Fred Gaffen, *In the Eye of a Storm: A History of Canadian Peacekeeping* (Ottawa: Deneau and Wayne, 1987) Ch. 11.

50. Brian Urquart, *Hammarskjöld* (New York: W.W. Norton, 1994), 23-29.

51. NAC RG 25 vol. 6394 file 5475-6-40 pt. 3, (19 Jul 56) letter Max Cohen to Pearson.

52. Urquart, *Hammarskjöld*, Ch. 5.

53. NAC RG 25 vol. 6394 file 5475-6-40 pt. 2.2, (22 Mar 54) memo Pearson to distribution list, "Visit to Canada of UN Secretary-General."

54. NAC RG 25 vol. 6394 file 5475-6-40 pt. 3, (19 Jul 56) letter Max Cohen to Pearson.

55. Urquart, *Hammarskjöld*, 36.

56. The background to this debate is contained in NAC RG 25 vol. 6460, file 5475FA-40 pt. 4, (n/d) "Charter Review Studies: Article 2(7) of the United Nations Charter."

57. NAC RG 25 vol. 6460, file 5475FA-40 pt. 4, (9 Sep 55) Cadieux to Holmes, "Canadian Policy on the Competence of the General Assembly to discuss colonial items and matters of domestic jurisdiction."

58. NAC RG 25 vol. 6460, file 5475FA-40 pt. 4, (n/d) "Canadian Policy with Reference to Article 2(7)."

59. NAC RG 25 vol. 6460, file 5475FA-40 pt. 4, (10 Sep 56) memo Commonwealth and Middle East Division to European Division, "Canadian Policy on Colonial Issues in the United Nations."

60. NAC RG 25 vol. 6460, file 5475FA-40 pt. 4, (29 Aug 56) memo European Division to United Nations Division, "Canadian Policy Concerning Colonial Issues in the United Nations."

61. NAC RG 25 vol. 6460, file 5475FA-40 pt. 4, (29 Aug 56) memo Cadiex to Holmes, "Talk on the UN to visiting NATO Journalists."

62. NAC RG 25 vol. 6460, file 5475FA-40 pt. 4, (21 Sep 55) message to the Chairman, Canadian Delegation to the Tenth Session of the General Assembly from Undersecretary of State for External Affairs, "Article 2(70) of the Charter."

63. NAC RG 25 file 5475-CX-40 pt. 3.2, (31 Jul 52) message Reid to Wilgress, "Canadian Military Observers in Karachi."

64. Escott Reid, *Envoy to Nehru* (Toronto: Oxford University Press, 1981), Ch. 8 and 9; NAC RG 25 vol. 6848 file 5475-CX-2-40 pt. 6, (31 Aug 56) memo Commonwealth and Middle East Division, "Return to Canada of UN Observers from Kashmir."

65. NAC RG 25 vol. 5137 file 5475-CX-2-40 pt. 8, (28 Apr 61) House of Commons Committee on External Affairs, "United Nations Military Observer Group in India and Pakistan (Kashmir)."

66. NAC RG 25 file 5475-CZ-2-40 vol. 5, (17 May 55) memo to file, "Interview with Major Maclelland-UNMOGIP Observer from Kashmir."

67. Maloney, *Learning to Love The Bomb*, Ch. 2.

68. NAC RG 25 vol. 4903 file 50115-P-40 pt. 2, "Political Implications of New Proposals on Defence Planning and Global Strategy."

69. Ibid.

70. Ibid.

71. NAC RG 25 vol. 4903 file 50115-P-40 pt. 2, (24 Feb 53) message Heeney to Under Secretary of State, "NATO and Global Defence Problems," (10 Mar 53) message Heeney to Under Secretary of State, "NATO and Global Defence Problems."

72. NAC RG 25 vol. 4903 file 50115-P-40 pt. 2, (4 Jun 53) letter Foulkes to Wilgress, "Global Planning."

73. Michael A. Palmer, *Guardians of the Gulf: A History of America's Expanding Role in the Persian Gulf, 1833-1992* (New York: The Free Press, 1992), 52-59; Maloney, *Securing Command of the Sea,* Ch. 5.

74. NAC RG 25 vol. 4903 file 50115-P-40 pt. 2, (9 Feb 54) Joint Planning Committee, "A Study of Recent Changes and Trends in United States Defence Policy and the Implications it Might Have on Canadian Defence Policy," (25 Feb 54) message CANDEL NATO to Under Secretary of State, "Implications of US Strategy."

75. See Maloney, *Learning to Love The Bomb.*

76. North Atlantic Military Committee, (22 Nov 54) "Decision on MC 48: The Most Effective Pattern of NATO Military Strength for the Next Few Years."

77. Ibid.

78. DHH, Raymont Papers (uncatalogued), (22 Dec 54) Foulkes note to file "Note on Negotiations for Approval of MC 48."

79. NAC RG 25 vol. 4495 file 50030-E-1-40 pt. 1, (26 Mar 55) "The Strategic Concept of the Nuclear Deterrent."

80. Ibid.

81. Ibid.

82. Ibid.

83. Ibid.

84. NAC RG 25 file 12554-40 pt. 1.1, (30 Apr 57) message Canadian Delegation, Beirut to Secretary of State for External Affairs, "Canadian Interests in the Middle East."

85. Ibid.

86. Urquart, *Hammarskjöld*, 133-136; Pearson Vol. II, 217; NAC RG 25 vol. 6948 file 5475-CX-2-40 pt. 6, (2 May 56) memo for Acting Minister, "Request for Five Additional Canadian Military Observers with the United Nations Truce Supervision Organization in Palestine."

87. NAC RG 25 vol. 6293 file 11852-40 pt. 1.1, (13 Oct 53) message Pearson to Canadian High Commissioner, London, "Canadian Representation in the Middle East."

88. E.L.M. Burns, Between Arab and Israeli (Toronto: Clarke, Irwin and Co., 1962), 22.

89. Ibid., pp. 23-32; Kennet Love, "Burns—the Man in the MIddle," *Globe and Mail* (18 November 1955); "General Burns is Always on the Spot, " *Weekend Magazine* (10 December 1955); see also E.H. Hutchison, *Violent Truce: A Military Observer Looks at the Middle East Conflict, 1951-1955* (New York: Devin Adair Co., 1956).

90. NAC RG 25 vol. 6948 file 5475-CX-2-40 pt. 6, (2 May 56) memo for Acting Minister, "Request for Five Additional Canadian Military Observers with the United Nations Truce Supervision Organization in Palestine."

91. Burns, *Between Arab and Israeli*, 273.

92. Ibid., 98.

CHAPTER 4

SUEZ: THE RETREAT TO PEACE, 1956-1957

Said England unto Pharaoh, "I must make a man of you,
that will stand upon his feet and play the game;
That will Maxim his oppressor as a Christian ought to do,"
And she sent old Pharaoh Sergeant Whatsisname.
It was not a Duke nor Earl, nor yet a Viscount-
It was not a big brass General that came;
But a man in Khaki kit who could handle men a bit
With his bedding labeled Sergeant Whatsisname.

- Rudyard Kipling, *Pharaoh and the Sergeant*

Though credited with inventing UN peacekeeping, Secretary of State for External Affairs Lester B. Pearson had built on existing concepts and proposals in consultation with others who were equally concerned about preventing Soviet expansion into the Third World. Pearson confers with John Holmes and others during the UN General Assembly Emergency Meeting of 5 November 1956 at the height of the Suez Crisis.

(CIIA Photo)

In the Middle East and in Europe, 1956 was a year of extreme tension. The cancellation of American support for the Aswan Dam project, Nasser's nationalization of the Suez Canal, renewed violence on the Armistice Demarcation Lines and the International Frontier, and Anglo-French contingency planning, all informed the UN Security Council debate throughout October 1956. Even though the Security Council was prepared to assist in the mediation of the Suez Canal dispute, the Soviet Union vetoed any such diplomatic action that might have provided machinery to forestall Anglo-French military action.

Both the United States and Canada had maintained uncoordinated diplomatic pressure on their allies in the North Atlantic Council to work through the UN to resolve the issues at hand, but this means was now blocked. Despite dire warnings that the use of force by the United Kingdom and France against Egypt would cause serious rifts in NATO and in the Commonwealth,[1] the British and the French developed a secret agreement with Israel. By going to war with Egypt, Israel would create a "threat" to the Canal, prompting the intervention of an Anglo-French peacekeeping force to "protect" the Canal and separate the "belligerent" forces. Israel would thus acquire a buffer zone in Sinai, while the British and the French prevented Egyptian interference with vital European oil shipping traffic through the Canal.[2] On 29 October, Israel invaded Egypt; which was immediately followed by an Anglo-French "ultimatum" to the belligerents. At the same time the UN Security Council called on the British and French to refrain from the use of force. The Anglo-French air campaign against Egypt commenced nonetheless on 31 October.[3]

Early on 1 November, Canadian Prime Minister Louis St. Laurent sent a message to Anthony Eden, the British Prime Minister. St Laurent emphasized that the Anglo-French action was not justified and that there was the strongest possibility of war, regional or worldwide, if the action continued. This action, St. Laurent noted, would split the Commonwealth and—more importantly—NATO. The Soviets would also exploit this and destroy everything the West had accomplished since 1948. St. Laurent urged Eden to find some way of stopping the operation. There was no reply to his communication. St. Laurent then conferred with Canadian Secretary of State for External Affairs, Lester Pearson. Pearson suggested that some form of legitimate international force could be used to replace the Anglo-French force waiting offshore, thus allowing the British and the French to withdraw from their publicly stated position that they were a "peace force." This was urgent, Pearson emphasized. The West could not afford wholesale condemnation of the UK and France by the UN General Assembly. This would also be exploited by the Soviets for the purposes of propping up their prestige and influence in the Third World.[4]

The Americans were, at the same time, trying to find ways to keep the conflict from spreading. However, the State Department had been warned that "any purely United States attempt to force [the UK and France] to break off hostilities...would be useless and would merely widen dangerous fissures in [NATO]."[5] President Eisenhower then met with Secretary of State John Foster Dulles and instructed him to use all means to prevent "harshly worded" condemnations of the Anglo-French action within the UN forum, and to "develop a final resolution that would represent the considered judgment of the United Nations" to prevent Anglo-French humiliation.[6]

The problem once again was with the Soviet Union. Any action taken in the UN would come under Soviet scrutiny and be subject to their intervention. Belgian foreign minister (later NATO Secretary General) Paul Henri Spaak flew to Moscow to see if he could break the Soviet deadlock. This mission failed: the Soviets wanted maximum humiliation and disruption in the NATO camp.[7] On the positive side, the Yugoslav delegation to the UN was successfully able to move the debate from the Security Council to the General Assembly (so that the French, British, or Soviets could not veto UN actions).

On 2 November, the General Assembly issued a resolution urging a ceasefire and withdrawal of Israeli forces. Before this meeting, Pearson approached UN Secretary General Dag Hammarskjöld with the suggestion of replacing the Anglo-French intervention force with an international one. Hammarskjöld did not think it was practical,[8] though he understood that the West was in trouble. The Soviets had taken the opportunity to crack down on dissent in Hungary and he was "determined to do everything he could to re-knit the essential web of western solidarity, so badly torn by this ill-judged, ill-fated action" in Egypt. He was privately concerned that the Israelis might massacre Palestinians in the now-occupied Gaza Strip and was prepared to ask the United States to intervene with its Sixth Fleet.[9]

At this point the Canadians and Americans started to coordinate their efforts more closely. Canadian Ambassador to the United States, A.D.P. Heeney, conveyed Canadian thinking to Dulles. Pearson's objective, Heeney said, was to help get the British and French "off the hook".[10] Before suggesting a solution in the UN, Canada wanted US and British input. Pearson wanted to create a temporary force made up of Canadian and American troops, with a token number of French and British troops, to stabilize the situation. This force would be followed by a more diverse international force, which would be part of a larger settlement of the dispute.

The primary objective was "to restore as quickly as possible the United States-United Kingdom alignment," albeit in an undefined way.[11] Could the Americans back off until Pearson could get British approval? Dulles agreed, but was unsure exactly how a police force would be formulated; he was concerned about the appearance of collusion, an appearance which would be punctuated by the introduction of an Anglo-French-Canadian-American intervention force onto Egyptian territory. Heeney thought that UNTSO should be expanded in some way, with Burns in charge, and Dulles concurred. Later that day during a meeting of the UN General Assembly Dulles formally asked the Canadian representative to formulate and introduce a concrete proposal for an international intervention force. There were two problems, the Suez invasion and the ongoing Arab-Israeli dispute. Perhaps Burns and UNTSO could form the basis of a solution to both.[12] The Canadians contacted Selwyn Lloyd to see if the British were amenable to the idea.[13]

While the Americans and Canadians worked into the night, Anthony Eden publicly announced that the Anglo-French forces would stop military action if the following conditions were met: 1) Egypt and Israel would accept a UN force to keep the peace; 2) the UN would put such a force together for the duration of the two disputes (the Canal and Arab-Israeli border problems); and 3) that such a UN force would have a French and British component.[14] The situation was now even more complicated. There was a danger that the Canadian proposal would have the appearance of collusion to get the French and British "off the hook"—keeping in mind that there really was the intent to do so, evidenced by Pearson's motives and by contact with the British beforehand. The modified American view was that the proposed Anglo-French components of such a force would have to be eliminated to maintain appearances.[15]

The Canadian and American delegations to the UN met once again to formulate a joint approach to the problem. The Eden statement could not be supported, yet long term negotiations would not work. Short term action was required.[16] The US Joint Chiefs of Staff had concluded that there were definite Soviet interests and objectives in the crisis which included disrupting NATO and the tottering Baghdad Pact; prolonging and expanding the Middle East conflict; and disrupting the oil flow to the West. Unless something was done and done quickly, the West's position in the Cold War could be irretrievably damaged.[17]

To get around the problems posed by Eden's statement and Soviet intransigence, the Canadians proposed to the American delegation that a five-nation UN advisory committee[18] examine the creation and implementation of a UN police force and advise the Secretary General within forty-eight hours.[19] This would ensure that there was some form of multi-national consultation, rather than imposition of an idea by the great powers or the West in general. Both delegations agreed that a division-sized force equipped with an airborne element and air support was needed, though the delegates wisely understood that the details of such a force structure should be left up to military professionals. To be credible, the force needed freedom of movement and it had to be able to act without the consent of the belligerents, (an item vetoed by Hammarskjöld later on, that caused no end of problems throughout UNEF's deployment). Notably, the delegates concurred that "for greater efficiency this force must be drawn from a few countries with the most up-to-date forces rather than from many countries with less advanced armies"[20] and that forces could not be drawn from Britain, France, the US or USSR, or countries

The architects of peace in the Middle East, General E.L.M. Burns and UN Secretary General Dag Hammarskjöld, meet at last at UNEF HQ the Sinai. Burns' contention, long before the 1956 Suez crisis, that combat forces should be used to maintain peace in the region were finally accepted by Hammarskjöld when the world tottered on the edge of the nuclear abyss.

(CF photo)

retaining colonies. Both delegations agreed that Canada should ideally sponsor the proposal in the General Assembly, but there was residual concern that the Afro-Asian bloc would perceive the whole effort as a face saving exercise and block it.[21]

The advisory committee proposal evolved over the next twenty-four hours. In conversations with Hammarskjöld, Pearson learned that the Secretary General was also concerned about Afro-Asian impressions, but agreed that the emergency force had to be drawn from Scandinavia, Latin America, North America, and Asia. In Hammarskjöld's view, the force should be inserted into separate Egyptian and Israeli forces and should police an Israeli withdrawal from Egypt (Operation MUSKETEER, the Anglo-French parachute and amphibious landings, had not yet occurred). Burns should be commander in chief, and his headquarters should be recruited from UNTSO.[22]

Canadian objectives were similar. UNEF's purpose was, in the Canadian delegation's view, to supervise a ceasefire and an Israeli withdrawal;[23] transition to a long term ceasefire force to maintain peace and order during negotiations; and to try and dissuade an Anglo-French landing. This was to form the basis for a resolution establishing a UNEF. The Americans, led by Henry Cabot Lodge Jr., agreed but thought a simpler text should be used. Pearson asked Lodge if he could submit the draft in Canada's name, to which Lodge also agreed.[24] After canvassing the General Assembly, (which by and large supported the Canadian proposal informally), Resolution 1000(ES-1) went to the floor at 0945 hours on 4 November. It called for the establishment of a UN command, an "Emergency International Force" to supervise the cessation of hostilities. Directing that the Secretary General submit a plan for such a force within forty-eight hours, the resolution passed 57 to 0 with 12 abstentions.[25]

Dramatic events were unfolding in the Middle East as the diplomats in New York continued to talk. Transport aircraft dropped the 3rd Battalion, The Parachute Regiment on Port Said, while the 2e Regiment de Parachutistes Coloniaux landed on Port Faud, at the entrance to the Suez Canal. Not long afterward, the Soviet Union implied that it would use nuclear weapons against France and the United Kingdom directly if they did not withdraw; the Soviets also implied that they would send their own airborne forces to "peacekeep". President Eisenhower was told in a conference later that day that the oil supply for NATO forces in Europe would soon be endangered if there was not a quick resolution to the crisis. A bad situation had become worse.[26]

St. Laurent telephoned Eden on 5 November and expressed his dismay. Eden "appreciated Canadian good intentions but [the British] were going ahead with landings in Egypt".[27] The Americans proposed airlifting Canadian NATO troops in West Germany into the Canal Zone before British and French amphibious forces landed, but this was not feasible from a political point of view in Canada: an act of parliament was required for such a deployment and that would take time. Hammarskjöld was also unenthusiastic about inserting Canadian troops so abruptly. If the UN command was established before the Anglo-French forces landed but before UNEF troops arrived, UNEF could not, in Hammarskjöld's view, be introduced at all until those forces were withdrawn. The problem, he believed, was to get the Anglo-French forces out and replace them with UNEF before the Soviets sent their own "volunteers" to assist Egypt.[28]

On the morning of 6 November, British Buffalo amphibious tractors and Wessex helicopters headed for Port Said. Landing craft deposited French AMX-13 tanks and mechanized infantry in Port Faud and the airborne forces pressed on southward.[29] St. Laurent once again appealed to Eden to commit to a ceasefire.[30] In reply Eden reiterated that the Anglo-French force was deployed to intervene between the Egyptians and the Israelis, adding that if an international force had been in existence, they would not have had to resort to this action. The British were quite prepared to cease operations and hand over to a United Nations force if one was made ready and inserted.[31] Eisenhower followed up in the afternoon:

Eisenhower: [Hammarskjöld] is getting Canadian troops, lots of troops together... I would like to see none of the great nations in it [UNEF]. I am afraid the Red boy is going to demand the lion's share. I would rather make it no troops from the big five. I would say, "Mr. Hammarskjöld, we trust you. When we see you coming in with enough troops to take over, we go out."

Eden: That is not too easy unless they have a good force, you know.

Eisenhower: If [the Soviets] have enough, and they attack, they attack the UN and its whole prestige and force. Then everyone is on the thing. Then you are [not] alone.[32]

Meanwhile, at the UN in New York, Hammarskjöld had stayed up all night with Pearson to put together his second report on the UNEF for the General Assembly.[33] This report was the next step in determining what the UNEF was to accomplish. It established that the authority of the force was similar to that of UNTSO (to the Secretary General) as opposed to the other existing model, a unified command, as in Korea, run by a nation delegated by the UN. The UNEF's terms of reference were somewhat vague: it was to "secure and supervise the cessation of hostilities" in accordance with the 2 November ceasefire resolution. The UNEF was to be a temporary force and its duration "determined by needs arising from the present conflict." It would be established on Egyptian soil with the consent of the Egyptian government and it was specifically not established to enforce the withdrawal of forces from Port Said or back to the Armistice Demarcation Line and International Frontier.[34]

Beyond that, the report stated that "it is difficult in the present situation and without further study to discuss [functions] with any degree of precision" and that it would enter Egypt to "maintain quiet during and after withdrawal of non-Egyptian troops." As to organization, "the force should not have military forces exceeding those necessary to secure peaceful conditions...." Time was of the essence and the UN members had to place confidence in the Secretary General's hands to see this matter through.[35]

On 7 November 1956, the fighting stopped.

Hammarskjöld consulted General Burns extensively on the organization of the UNEF. Within the framework of the Secretary General's report and other information, Burns based his recommendations on four premises: 1) that Egypt would accept the concept of the UNEF and its deployment on Egyptian soil; 2) that sanctions could be used to get Israel to withdraw to the Armitice Demarcation line (ADL) and the International Frontier (IF); 3) that the Gaza

Strip would not remain in Israeli hands; and 4) that the Sinai would be, for all intents and purposes, a demilitarized zone. (see Figure 4) In Burns' view, the force "should be so strong that it would be in no danger of being thrust aside, pushed out, or ignored, as [UNTSO] had been." He therefore wanted a multi-national division with a tank brigade, a strong reconnaissance element, and fighter aircraft, "an operational force capable of fighting." National elements should be a battalion group in size and logistically self-supporting.[36]

Burns was unable to get what he wanted. The criteria for national eligibility for UNEF membership precluded most nations with developed forces from participating. This, combined with the impetus to get something, anything, on the ground in Egypt immediately precluded deployment of such a force.[37]

The time imperative to forestall the insertion of Soviet-bloc "Polish volunteers" drove Hammarskjöld and the Canadians to once again seriously examine an immediate deployment of Canadian troops from West Germany. (The Americans also thought this was a good idea so that it "would pull the rug out from under the Soviet psychological offensive.")[38] Hammarskjöld also thought that a public announcement by Canada that it was contributing to UNEF would spur on other nations. He was correct and on 7 November the UN also had firm troop offers from Canada, Columbia, Norway, Sweden, Finland, and Denmark.[39] After two days of preparation, Canada commenced Operation RAPID STEP, which was designed to move a Canadian battalion-group from Canada to Naples and then stage from Naples to Egypt. Canadian units in Germany were not considered for UNEF because of their vital deterrent role in NATO's Northern Army Group.[40]

Operation RAPID STEP stumbled, however, on 10 November. Hammarskjöld, in a telephone conversation with Nasser, discovered that Nasser would accept Colombian, Danish, Finnish, Norwegian and Swedish troops in UNEF but there may be problems with a Canadian component. There was the question of Egyptian public opinion "especially if Her Majesty's British troops were replaced with Her Majesty's Canadian troops."[41] Did Nasser understand that the Queen of Canada, though she was British, was "double hatted" as the separate Queen of both countries? The Canadian embassy in Cairo didn't think it was a misunderstanding. They believed Nasser was suspicious of UNEF.[42] The American ambassador met with Nasser to discuss this. What was wrong with Canadian participation in UNEF? Nasser stated that the similarity in uniforms and Canadian regimental titles like the "Queen's Own Rifles of Canada" (the Canadian battalion group earmarked for UNEF) could cause confusion amongst the population and result in incidents.[43]

Reluctantly, Hammarskjöld contacted Ottawa and asked that the Canadian advance party be delayed. After some discussion in New York, the Canadian delegation proposed that UNEF should wear UN arm bands, white helmets and white belts to distinguish themselves from the belligerent forces. This might alleviate the problem with Nasser.[44] Pearson sought out the Egyptian representative to the UN, Dr. Loutfi, to express his displeasure at this turn of events. The situation was "outrageous". Loutfi intimated that the reason was more political than "identificational". Nasser was now considering objecting to the inclusion of Denmark and Norway, since they were part of NATO. On the other hand, Loutfi explained, Nasser

Figure 4: United Nations Emergency Force, 1956-1957

really wanted General Burns to run UNEF because he was fair and impartial. Pearson then implied that if there were no Canadians in UNEF, there would be no Burns in UNEF.[45]

The seriousness of this situation should not be underestimated. The entire UNEF enterprise was an exceptionally fragile one. The Canadians had created a consensus in the UN (no mean feat) and had a military leader with the confidence of the belligerents. Burns even knew the commander of the Anglo-French landing force. Without these things, the Soviets would have been able to exploit the situation for their own ends, the Israelis would not have withdrawn, and there could have been a regional and possibly a global war. It was serious enough for Hammarskjöld to get on a plane to Cairo, for the Americans to apply diplomatic pressure on the Egyptians, and for the Canadians to ask the Indians to use their influence with Nasser.[46]

One part of the problem was of Hammarskjöld's making in the first place. Against Burns' advice, he had included the concept of consent in the UN resolution establishing UNEF. Now he was reaping what he had sown. In Burns' view, the Egyptians were actually very concerned that the whole UNEF project was a "soft" substitute for the Anglo-French force and that, once installed in Port Said, they would not leave. The Egyptians did understand that the stated aim of the force was to patrol the ADL/IF but had to be convinced that it was not UNEF's task to permanently occupy Port Said.[47]

Nasser acquiesced on the arrival of a UNEF advance party, as long as it did not have Canadians in it. As a result, 100 soldiers from the DANOR (Danish-Norwegian) Battalion wearing American helmet liners painted pale blue arrived in Egypt on 15 November.[48] According to Sir Brian Urquhart, the idea of equipping UNEF with blue berets was advanced at some point at UN headquarters in New York. There was no time to make them, so surplus U.S. Navy helmets from a depot in Italy were painted blue and issued. Other contingents acquired Canadian-made blue berets, blue soft caps and UN cap badges in December 1956.[49]

The details of the UNEF force structure and role still had to be worked out. Burns flew to New York on 15 November and met with Andrew Cordier, Ralph Bunche (special assistants to Hammarskjöld), and Major General A.E. Martola (Finnish Army). Despite the constraints imposed on the group as to specific mission and terms of reference, the group examined what forces had been offered and how to get them to the theatre of operations. India (a battalion), Canada (a battalion), Denmark and Norway (a composite battalion), Sweden (2 companies), Finland (one company), Indonesia and Brazil (a battalion each) pledged infantry units. Yugoslavia offered a reconnaissance battalion, Norway a medical company, and Canada a signals unit. Plans called for a composite military police unit drawn from all contingents. The Americans then allocated C-124 Globemaster transport aircraft and Canada a squadron of C-119's to move UNEF personnel by air. Heavy equipment would arrive by ship. Motor transport for UNEF was, surprisingly, offered by the withdrawing British forces.[50]

Burns was concerned about UNEF's organization and ability to carry out the tasks at hand:

The objective of the Secretary General and his advisors was to establish as quickly as possible an effective showing of the UNEF in view of the political situation, but they did not allow for administrative difficulties.[51]

He was also quite concerned about the force's terms of reference:

It is the practice, when a commander is sent out with a military expeditionary force, to provide him with a general instruction as to what he is expected to achieve, what his relations should be with his allies...and other guiding principles for his action... in the circumstances, it was impossible for such a document to be drawn up by the UN Secretariat since so many matters relating to UNEF were improvised and so much was dependent on political conditions which were fluid...I understood this but my difficulties were increased by the absence of a definite instruction as to how it was intended that the force would be constituted and function.[52]

Continuing problems with Nasser compounded the force structure situation. Nasser suddenly reversed himself and rejected the inclusion of Scandinavian troops in UNEF, to which those countries reacted as violently as Canada had earlier. This, according to a Canadian assessment, was the result of Soviet encouragement.[53] Burns, taking another approach, thought that Nasser wanted a force of neutrals that he could push around. It was vital that Canada be part of UNEF or it would not work.[54] There was a solution, however.

Burns met with Hammarskjöld, Pearson and Cordier to discuss the situation. Falling back on an idea generated in earlier conversations with Canada's Department of National Defence, Burns and Pearson proposed that, even though a Canadian battalion was essential, the UNEF had no support troops. Canada could provide air transport, administration, signals, transport, engineers and medical units first, wait for the situation with Nasser to cool off, and then bring in the infantry battalion later. Hammarskjöld agreed and flew off to Cairo.[55]

In what Hammarskjöld referred to as "the toughest situation he had ever had to face,"[56] the UN Secretary General rapidly perceived that Nasser had been in increased contact with the Soviets, who were influencing him on UNEF matters. Hammarskjöld portrayed the force structure matter to Nasser as a 'misunderstanding'. Nasser surely was concerned about what UNEF would do before he would allow the force into his country. Hammarskjöld was in Cairo to do just that. The objective of UNEF was to get Israel back to the ADL/IF and to guarantee an Anglo-French withdrawal. Nasser wondered if UNEF would be responsible for the Canal clearance (it was blocked by no less than 17 objects, including a railway bridge and a ship loaded with concrete). This was a possibility that required further study.[57]

Hammarskjöld was able to develop, with Nasser, a five point basis for UNEF in Egypt. In effect, the UNEF's area of operations after the Israeli withdrawal would be subject to UN-Egyptian agreement. UNEF would have no role in the Canal Zone after Anglo-French withdrawal. UNEF needed a staging area in Egypt; this would be done by mutual agreement. Any UNEF force structure changes would be discussed with Nasser first. Finally, UNEF would operate in Egyptian territory with Egyptian consent. Hammarskjöld informed Nasser that "The definitions of UNEF's task were extremely loose and in the event of a disagreement, have to be interpreted by the General Assembly."[58] In the end he secured Nasser's concurrence that Canada would provide service troops instead of a battalion and that Scandinavian nations could be part of UNEF.[59]

This agreement opened the Secretary General up to a wave of criticism. The British argued that UNEF was an "inadequate token force" for anything other that policing the ADL/IF between Egypt and Israel. It was incapable of securing the free operation of the Canal or its clearance. Winter was setting in and there was no oil flowing into Europe.[60] The Australians, left out of UNEF because they were "colonials", were equally scathing. Nasser, they said, was dictating terms as if he had won a war. The Soviets were expanding their influence in the region. UNEF had no "organization, training, equipment. prestige or strength." It was merely a "Swiss Guard for Nasser", in their view.[61] Pearson was violently opposed to Nasser possessing a veto over UNEF composition and operations. There was little that could be done at the time and Hammarskjöld chose not to justify his actions.[62]

On 19 November Eden had what is described as a physical breakdown. Harold Macmillan, speaking for Her Majesty's Government, confirmed that Anglo-French forces would withdraw. [63] This spurred the UN planners to get on with operations in the Port Said area. The DANOR battalion was in the process of landing between 21 and 25 November. The acting UNEF commander, Colonel Moo (Burns was negotiating with the Egyptians elsewhere), deployed a Danish company to Port Said from the build up area in Ismailia in response to local Egyptian complaints about ceasefire violations. By 28 November, the rest of the battalion was in Port Said protecting power stations and other utilities. Burns then inserted a Norwegian company between the Anglo-French forces and the Egyptian forces south of Port Said to create a buffer zone. As the Anglo-French forces withdrew up the causeway to the port, the Indian parachute battalion followed them north, while the DANOR battalion remained stationary facing the Egyptian forces.[64]

The Israelis unexpectedly announced on 1 December that they would withdraw 50 kilometers east of the Canal. Fortunately, the Yugoslav reconnaissance battalion was just off-loading in Port Said. Burns sent them with their armoured cars directly from their ships into the Sinai. Working with Canadian combat engineers, the Yugoslavs were able to clear some minefields on the east bank of the Canal, but were blocked by significant Israeli denial measures: the roads had been dug up with bulldozers, the rail lines torn up every 50 meters, and there were uncharted minefields everywhere.[65]

Meanwhile, back in Port Said, Burns issued his first operational instruction. UNEF was: to protect vital points; prevent Egyptian infiltration into Port Said; exchange prisoners of war; and establish liaison with all forces. Withdrawing British forces were concerned that the Egyptians would shoot Egyptian "'collaborators." UNEF established joint UNEF-Egyptian police patrols to prevent this.[66] Despite measures taken to maintain the ceasefire, there were still a number of serious incidents involving Egyptian military infiltration in the Port Fuad area; during one of these, the French employed tanks against snipers which produced 27 Egyptian dead and 40 wounded. The Egyptians shot up a Danish camp, while a Swedish patrol was fired on and returned fire.[67] Eventually the Anglo-French perimeter shrank, with UNEF maintaining a buffer zone between Egyptian forces and the Anglo-French landing force. By 2330 hours 22 December, the Anglo-French forces were gone and UNEF prepared to deploy to the Sinai.[68]

The Suez Canal was still not cleared yet. The Anglo-French naval force had brought a six-ship salvage force with them in their original deployment. The British government consequently offered its services. Nasser publicly interpreted this as an extension of the occupation and would not allow them to commence work. Another compromise was worked out whereby the ships would fly the UN flag, the crews would work in civilian clothes and all weapons aboard would be disabled. The British wanted a UNEF protective force on board each ship and also wanted a UNEF reaction force on shore covering each vessel while at work. Thus, UNEF also guarded the salvage fleet in addition to its other activities.[69]

The mechanics of the Israeli withdrawal from Sinai were, as usual, complicated by political factors. The Israelis were adamant that UNEF should be deployed into certain sensitive areas so that Egyptian or Palestinian forces could not use those areas against Israel. The first area was two islands in the Straits of Tiran and the ground overlooking them, the Sharm el Sheikh. Egyptian control over these effectively blockaded the Israeli port of Eilat. The second was the Gaza Strip. Israel was tired of Fedayeen raiding operations and could not afford to maintain an occupation force there. Israel also expressed the view that UNEF should actually use military force against Fedayeen units. Finally, Israel wanted the Sinai to become a demilitarized zone occupied at key points by UNEF. They did not want UNEF on the ADL/IF; rather, in the Israeli view UNEF should be deployed in depth throughout the area.[70]

In his talks with Abba Eban, the Israeli ambassador, Hammarskjöld deferred the Gaza matter but assured him that UNEF would occupy the Sharm el Sheikh and other

The first UNEF Canadian contingent arrives at Abu Suweir airbase near Ismailia, Egypt on 25 November 1956. The intransigent Egyptian President Nasser, possibly influenced by the Soviets, blocked the deployment of a Canadian infantry battalion. Service support troops as well as a recce squadron equipped with Ferret scout cars were brought in after much negotiation.

(CF Photo)

vital areas if the Israelis accelerated their withdrawn from Sinai. Eban suggested that UNEF establish a naval force to ensure the safety of Israeli shipping through the Straits, but Hammarskjöld also deferred this for further study.[71]

Burns had by this time established with the Israeli Defence Force a new withdrawal timetable. By 6 January 1957, the IDF was to be 10 kilometers west of El Arish and by 15 January, it was to have withdrawn 25 kilometers to the east. The IDF was to be on the International Frontier by 22 January and clear of the Gaza Strip by 6 March.[72]

Burns was, however, hampered by the slow build up of UNEF in the Canal Zone. He could employ what forces he had on the ground, but without the Canadian service support in-theatre, he could not sustain operations across the Sinai. Nasser's earlier obstruction delayed the departure of the Canadian contingent. HMCS *Magnificent*, a Royal Canadian Navy aircraft carrier finally sailed on 29 December bearing the rest of the Royal Canadian Engineers detachment, 56 Canadian Signal Squadron, 56 Canadian Transport Company, 56 Canadian Infantry Workshop, all in all 400 officers and men, 230 vehicles and four Otter aircraft.[73] The Colombian, DANOR, Indian and Swedish battalions were on the ground, as was the Yugoslavian reconnaissance battalion, the Norwegian medical company and a Finnish infantry company. The Indonesian and Brazilian battalions still had not arrived.[74]

The Yugoslav units, working with UNTSO military observers, maintained contact with their IDF counterparts at a separation distance of 5 kilometers. Burns positioned the Indian parachute battalion on the north road, the Columbians in the centre, and DANOR battalion on the south road, all in preparation for a move into the Sinai. The Swedes and Finns continued their protection operations in Port Said.[75]

HMCS *Magnificent* arrived on 10 January and her presence immediately caused consternation with the Egyptians. Canadian ships, including *Magnificent*, flew the White Ensign (Navy flag) and the Red Ensign (national flag). Royal Navy ships also flew the White Ensign, particularly those ships executing the shore bombardment and landing the landing force back in November! The Royal Navy ships participating in the salvage operation had UN flags by agreement and this confused the Egyptians. The exact status of the Canadian aircraft carrier was ambiguous for the time being and they protested to no avail.[76]

UNEF had reached the El Arish airfield two days earlier but had to wait until 15 January to occupy it. Egyptian Army forces also crossed the Canal but, in a local agreement with UNEF, did not advance more than 10 kilometers into Sinai. Egyptian Frontier Police followed UNEF units closely, intent on re-establishing civil control over the rural areas. Ominously, the Palestinian guerrilla organization al-Fatah re-constituted itself in the region. Burns directed his intelligence people to monitor their presence and he even established liaison with them.[77] Burns then flew (by RCN helicopter from *Magnificent*) to El Arish on the 15th to link up with the Yugoslav M-8 armoured cars entering the town. By the 18th, UNEF sent its advance headquarters there and prepared to follow up with its main later. A significant prisoner of war exchange occurred, brokered by UNTSO's and UNEF: four Israelis were traded for 6000 Egyptians.[78]

Up to this point UNEF had achieved its original aims. The Anglo-French landing force was gone and the Canal was being cleared. The Soviets had withdrawn their threats to intervene in the region and use nuclear weapons against the United Kingdom or France. The Israelis had committed to and were carrying out their withdrawal across the Sinai. The mere presence of 6000 men wearing blue helmets and berets provided the belligerents with an excuse to accomplish all of this. Yet UNEF's role in the region continued to expand until it reached the form and style consistent with the popular perception of UN peacekeeping operations.

One alternative not taken revolved around expanding UNEF to all of Israel's borders (the original ADL's) instead of just between Egypt and Israel. Jerusalem was another possible UNEF deployment area. In other words, UNEF would take over UNTSO's functions as well. Such an expansion necessitated having UNEF operate on Israeli territory, something Israel would not consent to. Another potential UNEF role (this one proposed by the British) was to have UNEF responsible for disarmament control for the region. This would involve stationing UNMOs at all airbases in the region, naval patrols in the Mediterranean and in the Red Sea, the creation of an expanded aerial surveillance capability for UNEF, and a larger land force. This, many believed, was too ambitious for the time being and it was shelved as well.[79]

The last major expansion of UNEF's mission occurred between January and March 1957. Hammarskjöld's earlier fears back in November regarding the Gaza Strip were now modified from fears of an Israeli massacre to fears of renewed Fedayeen raiding (by al Fatah and other groups), the maintenance of law and order, civil administration, and humanitarian relief. Back on 24 January, Hammarskjöld issued a report on future UNEF operations to the General Assembly. This report recommended that Egypt retain control of the Gaza Strip from an administrative and security point of view. Israel was to withdraw. UNEF was to move into Gaza and establish a buffer zone corresponding to the ADL and the IF. Any broader UNEF role, according to the report, was subject to the consent of the Egyptian government. UNEF would also move into the Sharm el Sheikh area (covering the Gulf of Aqaba) upon Israeli withdrawal.[80]

The Secretary General and his staff had specific aims in mind. By inserting UNEF into Gaza and situating them to prevent raiding activity, this would give Israel an excuse not to deploy military formations in the vicinity. If the Israelis did deploy heavy forces on the ADL and IF, this gave the Egyptians an excuse to deploy heavy forces to the Sinai. UNEF was not equipped or manned to sufficient levels to watch all such forces, particularly since it was not allowed to operate on the Israeli side of the ADL and IF.[81] The aim here was to eliminate one of the primary Israeli reasons for going to war in the first place: Fedayeen raids from Gaza.

After massive American pressure and threats of an Afro-Asian group proposal for UN sanctions, Israel announced that it would withdraw from Gaza and Sharm el Sheikh, if UNEF were permitted to replace their forces in these areas. On 4 March, Burns met with Moshe Dayan to make arrangements for UNEF occupation of the Gaza Strip.[82]

At 0400 hours 7 March, UNEF moved into Gaza and Sharm el Sheikh. The Indians, Colombians and DANOR established positions and check points in the Strip itself, the Swedish battalion secured Rafah Camp (UNEF's new Headquarters), while the Yugoslavs conducted mobile patrols on the ADL. The Indonesian battalion covered the IF, while the Finns went to Sharm el Sheikh. The Brazilians were the Force reserve for the operation.[83]

Burns' interpretation of UNEF's mandate in Gaza was twofold. With the consent of the Egyptian Government (which had not imposed significant diplomatic obstacles as they had in previous dealings with the UN force) UNEF was to maintain the quiet during and after the Israeli withdrawal from Gaza and to maintain civil affairs in Gaza for an indeterminate period or until arrangements could be made for Egyptian administration. Militarily, UNEF troops were to prevent any movement across the ADL and observe and report any incident. As the Israelis blew up the rail line between Gaza and Israel, the first significant incident between UNEF and the locals occurred. UNEF troops from an unknown contingent shot up a minaret thinking the Muezzin was inciting a riot. He was, in reality, only giving the call to prayer at that time of day.[84]

By the end of March 1957 UNEF was firmly established in what would become a ten-year routine. UNEF was situated on a linear buffer zone observing movements and investigating incidents. Israel consistently referred to UNEF as a tool of Nasser's, while the Egyptians were still extremely suspicious of having a UN army on its territory. Gaza's inhabitants did not appreciate being tear-gassed by UNEF whenever they harassed a United Nations Relief and Works Agency food convoy. Al-Fatah, for its part, did not like having its operations hindered by the UNEF on the ADL.

What, then, does the UNEF experience tell us? Was UNEF in fact an important aspect in resolving the Suez Crisis? Clearly UNEF was critical in resolving the immediate two crises, that is, the Soviet Union/NATO component and the US/Anglo-French component. UNEF also contributed significantly to clearing obstructions from the Suez Canal, which was a pre-condition to re-establishing oil flow to Europe. Whether UNEF was critical to the resolution of the long term Arab-Israeli situation is more problematic. Israel was withdrawing from the Canal under heavy American and Afro-Asian pressure anyway. Perhaps UNEF's presence allowed them to do this, but this is uncertain. Without UNEF's presence, it is probable that a larger regional war would have occurred, perhaps involving Syria. The nature, extent and willingness of the Soviets to intervene with military force remains unknown.

The UNEF experience also set the tone and form for future UN Peacekeeping operations: the Canadian media crowed that "The vision of Lester Pearson has been thoroughly vindicated" and that "Proving Rifle, Helmet Can Stop a Tank Is Triumph of Emergency Force in Gaza."[85] There would be more ad hoc operations mounted. There would be belligerent interference in UN force structuring in later operations. There would be disparity between a UN Force Commander's minimal requirements and what he is actually provided on the ground to work with. UN forces would remain light forces with vague enforcement mandates and minimal capabilities. Finally, and most importantly, UNEF was the first example of what is called "mission creep" in today's parlance: the mutation of a vague role into unforeseen things without altering the capability to carry such things out.

UNEF's original function was to prevent Anglo-French political humiliation in the UN and to stave off a major Soviet propaganda victory in the context of the Cold War. An additional function was to restore Anglo-American relations. Finally, UNEF became a vehicle to resolve the Arab-Israeli dispute in the short term. Eventually, UNEF handled Canal clearance protection duties, civil order in Port Said and Gaza Strip, the administration of the Gaza Strip, as well as maintaining and patrolling buffer zones and demilitarized areas.

It is clear that the credit for the creation of UNEF has been somewhat misplaced. Lester B. Pearson received the Nobel Peace Prize for his efforts during the Suez Crisis. Although Pearson got the credit, there were other significant contributors as well. Hammarskjöld had to be convinced that it was feasible, but once he was, he pursued it unflaggingly. Burns implemented a vague idea emanating from New York and produced a workable force on the ground, even though his suggestions for such a force had been rebuffed a year earlier. Bunche assisted in the massive organizational effort from New York. Dulles supported the UNEF efforts at all levels, including diplomatic maneuverings in the UN, with the Israelis, and with the British and French. Credit should also be extended to delegation and consular staffs in Cairo and in New York. It was, in sum, a team effort to prevent nuclear war and preserve NATO as an alliance.

Notes to Chapter 4

1. See Lester B. Pearson, *Mike: The Memoirs of the Rt. Hon. Lester B. Pearson* Vol II (Toronto: Toronto University Press, 1973), 230, 233, 237; *Foreign Relations of the United States [hereafter FRUS] Vol. XVI: The Suez Crisis: July 26-31 December 1956* (Washington: U.S. Government Printing Office, 1990), 639-645, (5 Oct 56) memcon Dulles-Lloyd-Pineau meeting in New York. In fact, Pineau noted that "the whole question of the existence of NATO is raised…." if the US and Canada did not support their allies in the Suez endeavor.

2. Pearson, 237.

3. See Keith Kyle's voluminous Suez (New York: St. Martin's Press, 1991) for a full examination of the British perspective on these events. As an aside, the US Joint Chiefs of Staff quietly ordered a USAF Air Task Group to Turkey "in order to be prepared to assist in carrying out any directives which may be issued by the United Nations." and to evacuate American citizens from the war zone. *FRUS Vol. XVI*, 864, (30 Oct 56) JCS meeting.

4. Pearson, 238-239, 244, National Archives of Canada [hereafter NAC] RG 2, Cabinet Conclusions, Vol. 5775, 3 Aug-3 Nov 56 folder.

5. *FRUS Vol. XVI* , 930-931, (1 Nov 56) msg US embassy Paris to State.

6. *FRUS Vol. XVI*, 924-925, (1 Nov 56) Eisenhower's instructions to Dulles.

7. NAC, Pearson Papers, MG 26 N1 vol 39 file Middle East: UNEF Pt. 1 Nov 1956, msg Moscow to Ottawa.

8. Urquhart, *Hammarskjöld*, 175-176.

9. Urquhart, *A Life in Peace and War,* 135; Pearson, 248-249.

10. This term appears throughout numerous examples of Canadian, American, and British diplomatic correspondence, as in "We must get the British off the hook before they are impaled on it."

11. *FRUS Vol. XVI*, 940-942, (2 Nov 56) Heeney meeting at the State Department; Pearson, 249.

12. Ibid., MG 26 N1 Vol. 39 Nov 1956 Pt.1, (3 Nov 56) msg Washington DC to Ottawa, "UN Assembly Action on Middle East."

13. *FRUS Vol. XVI*, 940-942, (2 Nov 56) Heeney meeting at the State Department; Pearson, 249; NAC MG 26 N1 Vol. 39 Nov 1956: Middle East-UNEF Pt. 1, (3 Nov 56) ADP Heeney, Memo for file: Middle East Crisis."

14. *FRUS Vol. XVI*, 946, (3 Nov 56) Eden Statement.

15. *FRUS Vol. XVI*, 947-8, (3 Nov 56) Memorandum of a Conference with the President.

16. NAC, MG 26 N1 Vol. 39 Nov 1956 Pt.1, (3 Nov 56) msg: Permanent Mission, NY to External Ottawa, "Palestine Emergency Assembly: Middle East Police Force."

17. *FRUS Vol. XVI*, 968-972, (3 Nov 56) JCS, "Analysis of Possible Soviet Courses of Action in the Middle East."

18. It was later expanded to seven members.

19. This advisory committee remained a permanent fixture of UNEF operations after the General Assembly established UNEF on 5 November.

20. NAC, MG 26 N1 Vol. 39 Nov 1956 Pt.1, (3 Nov 56) msg: Permanent Mission, NY to External Ottawa, "Palestine Emergency Assembly: Middle East Police Force."

21. Ibid., and NAC MG 26 N1 Vol. 39 Nov 1956: Middle East-UNEF Pt. 1, (3 Nov 56) ADP Heeney, Memo for file: Middle East Crisis."

22. NAC MG 26 N1 Vol 39 Nov 56 Pt. 1, (4 Nov 56) msg Permanent Mission, NY to External, Ottawa. "Middle East Crisis: Emergency UN Force."

23. Ibid., Pearson noted in his secret message traffic: "[the resolution] expresses the hope that not only could the Egyptian and Israeli forces be kept apart but that the Israelis could be rolled back to the Demarcation Line."

24. NAC MG 26 N1 vol 39 Nov 56 Pt. 1,(4 Nov 56) msg Permanent Mission, NY to External, Ottawa. "Middle East Crisis: Emergency Force."

25. *FRUS Vol. XVI*, 980-981, (4 Nov 56) 565th Plenary Session of the UN. UN resolutions, whether in the Security Council or in the General Assembly, carry no weight per se outside of the UN. They are the basis and authority for UN action and indicate the consensus of the SC or the GA if they pass. See H.G. Nichols, *The United Nations as a Political Institution* (London: Oxford University Press, 1967).

26. Roy Fullick and Geoffrey Powell, *Suez: The Double War* (London: Leo Cooper, 1990), 143; *FRUS Vol. XVI*, 993, (5 Nov 56) Letter from Bulganin to Eisenhower; 986- 988 (5 Nov 56) Conference with President Eisenhower; Pearson, 256.

27. *FRUS Vol. XVI*, 982-983 (5 Nov 56) US delegation UN to State.

28. *FRUS Vol. XVI*, 982-983 (5 Nov 56) US delegation UN to State; 981 (5 Nov 56) US delegation UN to State. Note that the Americans were already standing by with enough airlift in West Germany to move a Canadian force in first and follow it up with a Norwegian force immediately afterwards. American troops were not considered since there was a great concern all around that "there was a risk that the UN force might be given too much of an American aspect" for it to be credible.

29. Fullick and Powell, *Suez: The Double War*, Ch. 12 and 13.

30. NAC MG 26 N1 vol 39 Middle East-UNEF folder, Pt.1, (6 Nov 56) Heeney memo to file: Middle East Crisis.

31. NAC MG 26 N1 vol 39 Middle East-UNEF folder, Pt.1, (6 Nov 56) Msg to St Laurent from Eden.

32. *FRUS Vol. XVI*, 1025-1027 (6 Nov 56) telecon Eisenhower-Eden.

33. NAC MG 26 N1 vol 39 Middle East-UNEF folder, Pt.1, (6 Nov 56) Heeney memo to file: Middle East Crisis.

34. United Nations Archive, DAG-13/31100:4 OR 100 Formations and Plan folder, (6 Nov 56) full text of Secretary General's second and final report on plan for emergency international United Nations force.

35. Ibid.

36. Burns, *Between Arab and Israeli*, 188. Though not mentioned in any of the documents or memoirs, it is probable that Burns' request for armour and fighters ran counter to Pearson's and Hammarskjöld's conception of a lightly-armed police force.

37. Ibid., 189-190. Burns noted that "I still feel that a stronger and more coherently organized force might have been a better instrument for the execution of UN policies."

38. *FRUS Vol. XVI*, 1083 (8 Nov 56) NSC Meeting No. 303.

39. NAC MG 26 N1 vol 39 Middle East-UNEF folder, Pt. 1, (6 Nov 56) memo for acting minister, "Middle East: Canadian Contribution to Emergency UN Force."; Pearson, 257-258.

40. NATO was quite concerned about any more withdrawals: a number of British units participating in Operation MUSKE-TEER were withdrawn from I (British) Corps and this weakened the NATO Shield in NORTHAG. The Canadian brigade in NORTHAG, 2 Canadian Infantry Brigade Group, was a major component of I(British) Corps and could not be withdrawn as well. See NAC MG 26 N1 vol 39 Nov 1956 folder, Pt 1., (9 Nov 56) msg NATO Paris to External Ottawa, "Canadian Contribution to Emergency International UN Force." For material on Op RAPID STEP, see Department of National Defence Directorate of History 112.3M2.003 (D14) 9 Nov-19 Nov 56: Operation RAPID STEP.

41. *FRUS Vol. XVI*, 1096 (8 Nov 56) msg US Embassy Cairo to State.

42. NAC MG 26 N1 vol 39 Nov 1956 Pt. 1 (9 Nov 56) msg Cairo to Ottawa.

43. NAC MG 26 N1 vol 39 Nov 1956 Pt. 1 (10 Nov 56) msg Cairo to Ottawa.

44. NAC MG 26 N1 vol 39 Nov 1956 Pt. 1 (10 Nov 56) msg New York to Ottawa.

45. NAC MG 26 N1 vol 39 Nov 1956 Pt. 1 (10 Nov 56) J.W. Holmes memo to file: "Loutfi Conversation with Pearson."

46. NAC MG 26 N1 vol 39 Nov 1956 Pt. 1 (10 Nov 56) A.D.P. Heeney note to file: "Middle East Crisis"; (15 Nov 56) New York to New Delhi.

47. Burns, *Between Arab and Israeli*, 197.

48. NAC MG 26 N1 vol 39 Nov 1956 Pt. 1 (15 Nov 56) msg New York to Ottawa, "UN Emergency Force."

49. Urquhart, *A Life in Peace and War*, 134; NAC RG 25 vol 6101 file 50366-40 pt 5.1, (19 Dec 56) Canadian Army press release.

50. Burns, *Between Arab and Israeli*, 210-211.

51. Ibid., 226.

52. Ibid., 218.

53. NAC MG 26 N1 vol 39 Pt. 1, (16 Nov 56) ADP Heeney to Pearson, "Middle East: United Nations Force."

54. NAC MG 26 N1 vol 39 Pt. 1, (16 Nov 56) msg New York to Ottawa, "UNEF."

55. NAC MG 26 N1 vol 39 Pt. 1, (14 Nov 56) conversation between Pearson and Officers from the Department of National Defence; (17 Nov 56) msg New York to Ottawa, "UNEF"; (17 Nov 56) msg New York to Ottawa, "Canadian Contribution to the UNEF."

56. NAC MG 26 N1 vol 39 Pt. 1, (19 Nov 56) msg New York to Ottawa, "UNEF."

57. Urquhart, *Ralph Bunche: An American Life*, 270.

58. Urquhart, *Hammarskjöld*, 191-193.

59. NAC MG 26 N1 vol 39 Pt. 1, (18 Nov 56) msg New York to Ottawa, "UN Emergency Force."

60. *FRUS Vol. XVI*, 1150 (19 Nov 56) msg US Embassy UK to State.

61. NAC MG 26 N1 vol 39 Pt. 1, (18 Nov 56) msg For Casey from Menzies, to Eisenhower.

62. Urquhart, *Hammarskjöld*, 190.

63. *FRUS Vol. XVI*, 1163 (19 Nov 56) msg US Embassy UK to State. There was probably a mental component to this. Someone in the British Cabinet let slip to the Canadians that Eden was progressively neurotic as the crisis developed. See NAC MG 26 N1 vol 39 Pt. 1, memo (no date) from Arnold Smith to UK High Commissioner, Ottawa.

64. UN Archives, DAG 13 31100:4 OR 110I, (29 Sep 58) "Story of UNEF Given at Cultural Exchange Program."; DAG 1/2.2551:9 "Draft History of UNEF."

65. UN Archives, DAG 1/22551:9, "The Yugoslav Detachment To UNEF."; DAG 1/2.2551:9 "Draft History of UNEF."

66. UN Archives, DAG 1/2.2551:9 "Draft History of UNEF."; NAC RG 25 vol 6101 file 503366-40 Pt 3 (9 Dec 56) msg Cairo to Ottawa.

67. UNEF rules of engagement were 'loose': UNEF troops were authorized by Burns to "take whatever action they deem necessary for their own protection." See NAC RG 25 vol 6101 file 50366-40 pt. 4, (18 Dec 56) msg New York to Ottawa, "UNEF Responsibilities: Port Said."

68. UN Archives, DAG 1/2.2551:9 "Draft History of UNEF."

69. Urquhart, *Hammarskjöld*, 201; Burns, Between Arab and Israeli, 229; FRUS Vol. XVI, 1300-1302 (14 Dec 56) msg Dulles to State, (15 Dec 56) pp. 1311-1313 msg New York to State.

70. *FRUS Vol. XVI*, 1205 (27 Nov 56) USUN to State, "Conversation with Hammarskjöld."; 1198-1199 (26 Nov 56) "Conversation with Israeli Ambassador"; 1215-1217 (29 Nov 56) msg USUN to State; 1325-1326 (21 Dec 56) msg USUN to State, "Conversation with Israeli Ambassador."

71. *FRUS Vol. XVI*, 1325-1326 (21 Dec 56) msg USUN to State, "Conversation with Israeli Ambassador." No such naval force was ever established, even though there were several proposals from many sources recommending it. See NAC RG 25 vol. 6101 file 50366-40 pt. 6.1, (21 Feb 57) msg London to Ottawa; (21 Feb 57) memo for Acting Prime Minister, "The Use of Naval Forces on the Gulf of Aqaba."

72. Burns, *Between Arab and Israeli*, 240.

73. NAC RG 25 vol. 6101 file 50366-40 pt. 6.2, (14 Jan 57) Report by Captain Fraser- Harris RCN.

74. UN Archives, DAG 1/2.2551:9 "Draft History of UNEF."

75. UN Archives, DAG 1/2.2551:9 "Draft History of UNEF."

76. NAC RG 25 vol. 6101 file 50366-40 pt. 6.2, (14 Jan 57) Report by Captain Fraser- Harris RCN. Ambiguous with regards to the UN. The Canadian Government clearly stated in December that the *Magnificent* was provided to transport Canadian troops and equipment to the UNEF. It was not to come under UNEF command and was not required to fly the UN flag though it did fly the flag and its helicopters carried UN insignia. See (17 Dec 56) msg Ottawa to New York, "UNEF: Status of HMCS MAGNIFICENT."

77. UN Archives, DAG-13/31100:43 PO 137, (10 Jan 57) "UNEF Periodic Intelligence Report No. 1"; (28 Jan 57)"UNEF Periodic Intelligence Report No.2".

78. UN Archives,DAG 1/2.2551:9 "Draft History of UNEF."; NAC RG 25 vol. 6101 file 50366-40 pt. 5.2, (21 Jan 57) Report by Captain Fraser-Harris RCN; Burns, *Between Arab and Israeli*, 245.

79. NAC RG 25 vol 6101 file 50366.40 Pt. 6.2, (28 Feb 57) UN Division to Middle East Division, "UNEF and Disarmament Control."; vol 6101 file 50366.40 Pt. 3, (7 Dec 56) Secretary of State for Commonwealth relations to UK High Commissioner, Ottawa: "Middle East."; vol 6101 file 50366.40 Pt. 5.2, (17 Jan 57) memo for Pearson, "UNEF and Disarmament Control."

80. Urquhart, Hammarskjöld, 204; NAC RG 24 vol 6102 file 50366-40 pt. 8.2, (24 Apr 57) "Command Instructions for Commander, Canadian Contingent, UNEF."

81. Urquhart, Hammarskjöld, 204; NAC RG 24 vol 6102 file 50366-40 pt. 8.2, (24 Apr 57) "Command Instructions for Commander, Canadian Contingent, UNEF."

82. UN Archives,DAG 1/2.2551:9 "Draft History of UNEF."

83. Ibid.

84. Ibid.; Urquhart, A Life in Peace and War, 136.

85. "Proving Rifle, Helmet Can Stop a Tank Is Triumph of Emergency Force in Gaza," Toronto Telegram, 15 November 1957.

CHAPTER 5

THE POLITICS OF AMBITION: PEACEKEEPING AND THE DIEFENBAKER GOVERNMENT, 1957-1960

No one should think of letting down his guard at the present time; no prudent man can deny the need for defence insurance....I turn for a moment to the problem of Soviet activity in uncommitted neutral states. This is a serious and growing danger. How are they going? Are they going toward the Russians or toward the West? This cannot be ignored by NATO members, and yet NATO as such is perhaps not well equipped to deal with such a problem.

—Sidney E. Smith, House of Commons Speech, 26 November, 1957

The Diefenbaker Government placed greater emphasis on deploying small observer groups like UNOGIL in Lebanon and UNTEA/UNSF in West New Guinea, in addition to maintaining the existing Canadian presence in Laos, Cambodia, North and South Vietnam.

(CF Photo)

The Diefenbaker years produced a mixed contribution in Canadian peace operations. In numeric terms, three new missions were added to the ongoing four: the UN Observer Group in Lebanon (1958), United Nations Transition Executive Authority in West Iriya (1962) and the massive UN operation in the former Belgian Congo (1960-64). The total numbers of Canadian military personnel deployed, however, only increased from 1341 in 1957 to 1703 in 1962. Using qualitative criteria, two of the new missions used numbers of RCAF light aircraft involved in liaison work as opposed to using interpositionary peacekeeping troops on the ground. At first glance it appears as though the Diefenbaker government was following an "economy of force" path by deploying minor units to sideshow UN peace operations and keeping the main effort dedicated to operations which supported NATO, Canada's national security pillar.

This argument, perhaps, assumes far too much rationality on the part of the Diefenbaker national security policy process, although its unintended effects produced a similar result. One should, however, also keep in mind that Canadian diplomatic and military efforts were generally directed to dealing with a number of crises which had nuclear implications: West Iriya and the Congo were quite peripheral to problems in Laos in 1961, the Berlin Crisis of 1958-1962 and the Cuban Missile Crisis of 1962. Indeed, there were several planned but unexecuted UN peace operations contemplated during the Diefenbaker government's tenure, operations which were more numerous and just as ambitious as operations conducted by the previous two governments.

UNCLE LOUIS OUT, DIEF THE CHIEF IN

Fate did not allow St Laurent and Pearson to bask for long in the glory of the Suez affair. Within six months, the Liberal Party was defeated by the Conservatives, led by John G. Diefenbaker. The Saskatchewan-born garrulous prairie town lawyer "Dief The Chief" with his demagogue-like approach to campaigning was able to paint the Liberals as arrogant "Eastern Establishment" snobs flouting the traditional link between Canada and Great Britain. The Suez crisis appalled Diefenbaker, who believed that Canada should have backed the Anglo-French endeavour. The Americans, in his view, had back-stabbed Canada's closest ally, and Canada would be next. Pandering to Canadians' latent anti-Americanism paid off in the long run.

Diefenbaker's leadership style was somewhat chaotic. The Conservatives had not been in power for decades and had lost touch with how to govern a nation that was no longer a colony and one which had a serious and effective international role to play in the Cold War. The Ottawa bureaucracy as it existed in 1957 was essentially a Liberal Party creation which consisted of men of like mind. This frequently played itself out in the more paranoid chambers of Diefenbaker's mind. It probably was a factor in his decision to act as his own Secretary of State for External Affairs, not unlike Mackenzie King. Diefenbaker did not trust the Under Secretary of State for External Affairs, Norman Robertson, and preferred to deal with diplomat H. Basil Robinson. After the disastrous debates over the NORAD agreement in 1957, it became clear that the Chief could not also be an Indian. Sidney Smith took up the mantle until his untimely death in March 1959 and Diefenbaker resumed control of the position until he appointed Howard Green in June 1959.

Howard Green, a political opportunist masquerading as a non-drinking messianic peacemaker, had a conversion once he took over from the Prime Minister. In the fall of 1956, Green savaged the St Laurent government by referring to the UNEF operation as "the most disgraceful period for Canada" and that it "was high time Canada had a government which would not knife Canada's best friend in the back."[1] Green eventually came to believe that humanity was in such peril that only he and Canada could lead the way to peace. His chosen vehicle was nuclear disarmament (not arms control) fuzzily connected with the UN as the only global institution capable of carrying out such a project. This brought him into conflict with the defence team and Diefenbaker was loath to take sides.

This team included men like George Pearkes, the Minister of National Defence. A British Columbia native and a veteran of the First and Second World Wars, Major General Pearkes, VC, had been the Conservative defence critic. It was difficult for Pearkes to get up to speed on the myriad of defence issues dumped on his plate: Canada was involved in developing the Avro Arrow, the BOMARC missiles, and several other technologically-advanced air defence projects, while the Army and Royal Canadian Navy were about to incorporate nuclear weapons into their forces. Peace operations, therefore, took second place amidst this turmoil. Consequently, Pearkes relied on General Charles Foulkes, who remained Chairman of the Chiefs of Staff Committee until 1960, and Bud Drury, the Deputy Minister. In any event, Diefenbaker was highly suspicious of Foulkes and Drury and thought them to be Liberal sympathizers, thought at the same time he had a positive relationship with a very key man, Bob Bryce, the Clerk of the Privy Council Office.

In time, Pearkes stepped down as Defence Minister in part due to Machiavellian machinations directed at him by Howard Green after he became Secretary of State for External Affairs and announced his opposition to Canada's acquisition of nuclear weapons. Douglas Harkness former artillery officer, George Medal winner and Calgarian, took over National Defence in 1961 and placed a firm hand on the wheel. Harkness was a dedicated realist who understood the Cold War and what it entailed.

All of these personalities and the overarching problem of the nuclear threat produced a significant amount of turbulence as the Diefenbaker government struggled to define its national security policy and the role of UN peace operations within it. Lester Pearson, according to those in the media, "lapsed into the traditional opposition fault-finder, and in so doing is whittling away the statesmanlike reputation that once was his."[2]

PEACEKEEPING POLICY UNDER DIEFENBAKER

The Diefenbaker men were a very different breed from those who served in the Mackenzie King and St Laurent governments. The bulk of the Diefenbaker government leadership was from western Canada and were not products of Oxbridge or Harvard. They had been kept out of the policy-making loop (there were few venues for bi-partisan policymaking in Ottawa given the nature of the system and the proclivities of those in power) and were essentially involved in a reactionary, ad hoc policy making exercise from the start. It took time for some semblance of a coherent national security policy to emerge.

The government changed at a critical juncture in Canadian strategic policy formulation. This juncture consisted of two things: first, there was the NORAD agreement and all of the air defence projects which were in various stages of completion. The second was that the NATO strategic concept itself, which Canada used as a basis for her national security strategy, was evolving during and after the Suez Crisis. Emphasis on the first obscured the importance of the second throughout 1957 and 1958, a situation which was aggravated by Pearson's overly-informed attacks on the government's continental defence policy in the House of Commons. The Opposition's attacks distracted Diefenbaker personally and increased his level of paranoia when dealing with the people involved in the national security policy formulation machinery. His unwillingness to accept a detailed understanding of the existing basis for Canadian national security policy or to develop an alternative promoted a certain higher degree of entropy.[3]

Despite the entropy, Canada's national security strategy continued to be based on the evolving NATO strategic concept since NATO was trying to respond to a changing Cold War environment. Despite the success at extricating Britain and France from Suez and forestalling Soviet intervention which would have resulted in nuclear war, Hungary had been crushed under the Soviet jack boot. The Battle of Algiers was in full swing as the French fought to retain their largest colony, Algeria (territory which, incidentally, was recognized by NATO as constituting the NATO Area and thus subject to NATO planning). The British were still engaged in Malaya, Cyprus, and now Kenya, and Muscat and Oman in the vital Arabian Gulf.[4]

Coup after coup took place in Iraq and Syria generating even more instability, while the Shah of Iran consolidated the monarchist position (with British and American assistance) in the face of a Communist political movement. The first stirrings of Communist revolution in the Caribbean were occurring, with Fidel Castro taking the lead in that region. Psychologically, the West fell behind when the Soviets orbited Sputnik, the first artificial satellite. Viewed collectively, the Western powers were still awash in a world of Soviet-supported violence which was implicitly backed up with increasingly larger Soviet nuclear weapons tests, improved strategic nuclear delivery means and superior numbers of conventional forces in Eastern Europe.[5]

The situation remained relatively stable in the NATO Area. As with the previous NATO concepts, Canada had significant input into their formulation. In this case, the MC 48 concept was superseded by a document known as MC 14/2. MC 14/2 tends to confuse analysts studying this period. There were in fact two versions of MC 14/2, the first of which was tabled and accepted by the NATO Military Committee when the Suez Crisis broke out in the fall of 1956. The finalized version, known as MC 14/2 (revised), was significantly different when accepted by the North Atlantic Council in May 1957, just before the Diefenbaker government took over.

NATO strategy was ambiguous in two important areas: how a war would start so that the Phase I/Phase II pattern of conflict could be initiated and the role of crisis management in that process. The debate surrounding MC 14/2 and MC 14/2 (revised) revolved around the

British belief that MC 14/2 should be a "trip wire" strategy: any Soviet activity, left undefined, against the NATO Area or NATO members should be met with Phase I (nuclear warfighting phase) from the outset. The Canadian position as established by Charles Foulkes and Lester Pearson throughout 1956 was that the "trip wire" concept was unacceptable. West Germany was part of NATO and her political requirements relating to forward defence now needed to be considered. The British view was too ambiguous and in fact the British were pursuing such theories in order to reduce their hybrid conventional-tactical nuclear forces in West Germany and concentrate on their V-Bomber strategic nuclear force.[6]

The Canadian opposition to the British concept of MC 14/2 as expressed in NATO circles centred on the concern that conventional war outside the defined NATO Area could affect NATO and that NATO's strategy had to formally recognize this fact since MC 48 did not. Jules Leger, Canada's ambassador to NATO, was equally concerned that if this stance was integrated into a new NATO strategic concept, individual NATO nations with territory outside the NATO Area might initiate military operations against an adversary and then drag the rest of NATO into the conflict under Article 5. Note that Leger pointed this out in a NATO meeting held in October 1956, right before Suez.[7]

Foulkes also informed the Military Committee that, in his view, the nuclear-conventional hybrid force structure had kept the peace so far and that this remained the main effort for NATO. He was also concerned, however, that members remain "mindful that there are brushfires on the periphery of NATO which cannot be ignored, but we want to ensure that in dealing with such situations nothing is done to in any way weaken the determination to defend the NATO area."[8] This was Canada's view and it remained so throughout the MC 14/2 debate.

Once the Suez Crisis was resolved, NATO went back to the table to sort out MC 14/2 and by May 1957 the Council accepted the revised version. MC 14/2 (revised) retained the Phase I/Phase II pattern of war. Strategic nuclear, theatre nuclear, tactical nuclear and conventionally-armed forces were necessary to carry such missions out; that is, "This strategic concept is the foundation for the production of realistic, vital and constructive defence planning aimed at lessening the possibility of aggression and thereby securing peace." However, unlike earlier concepts, MC 14/2 (revised) pointed out that:

> In order to preserve peace and security in the NATO area, it is essential that, without disregarding the security of the NATO area, hostile Soviet influence in non-NATO regions is countered. Consequently, and insofar as practicable, it is desirable for certain NATO nations to retain sufficient military flexibility so that this policy may be implemented.[9]

MC 14/2 (revised) formally recognized, as Canadian national security policymakers had pointed out back in 1955, that nuclear and conventional forces would generate a stalemate in the NATO Central Region which would prompt the Soviets to use other methods to accomplish their aims, like "initiating military operations of a limited nature" which might trigger a larger war. These were termed "Alternative Threats" and warranted a separate discussion in the strategy document.

NATO planners thought that such alternative threats might consist of "infiltrations, incursions, or hostile local actions" which would be either "covertly or overtly" supported by the Soviet Union and its allies. These operations would be conducted "trusting that the Allies in their collective desire to prevent general conflict would either limit their reactions accordingly or not react at all." Therefore, NATO had to have the ability to respond to a wide variety of what we today would refer to as "asymmetrical threats" without recourse to nuclear weapons.[10]

What about outside the NATO Area? The Soviets could be expected to maneuver there by using "psychological, political and economic offensives; by arms deliveries; and perhaps even by setting up bases, hidden or not, in certain of these nations. This could lead to the outbreak of a local war with all its inherent dangers." MC 14/2 (revised) argued that the response to such activities should be conducted by individual NATO nations as necessary using NATO organization and equipment. The level and type of response was left ambiguous.[11]

MC 14/2 (revised) included a detailed geographic strategy section. The portion which concerns us here deals with the Mediterranean basin. The loss of NATO control over the Mediterranean in peacetime would drastically affect NATO's conduct of a war since the only means by which the southern flank nations (Turkey, Greece, Italy) could be supported was by sea. Similarly, NATO naval and air forces could use the Mediterranean for nuclear strikes against southern Soviet Union and the southernmost Warsaw Pact states. As MC 14/2 (revised) notes "The islands and southern shores of the Mediterranean provide a number of suitable sites in Allied or Friendly hands which are geographically well placed to provide bases both for offensive operations and for the protection of Allied air and sea lines of communication." A priority NATO task in the Mediterranean was the "defence of bases supporting the strategic air offensive."[12]

The NATO Area, in other words, was to remain the priority defence problem. This overlapped with the peripheral operation problem in that there was an increased emphasis in NATO on defending the northern and southern flanks as far forward as possible (known as the Forward Defence principle). Note that there remained a fair degree of ambiguity in how NATO expected to deal with peripheral and asymmetric threats. This would form the basis of a new strategy debate in the early 1960s, which, coupled with the flank problem, will be dealt with in Chapter 7.

Canada's diplomats and military leaders were integral to the process by which MC 14/2 (revised) was constructed and accepted within NATO. There can be no doubt that the tenets of MC 14/2 (revised), were the basis for Canadian national security policy after 1956 and evolved from those of MC 48.[13] The problem was with the elected officials of the Diefenbaker government, particularly the highest elected official. Diefenbaker wanted to be brought up to date with the defence program and a detailed briefing on MC 14/2 (revised) was conducted by Pearkes in September 1957. It appears as though Diefenbaker absorbed the briefing but did not proffer any detailed questions or dissent from the precepts of the established strategic concept.[14]

This is not really surprising given Diefenbaker's views on the Cold War and his disinterest in the details of how it was carried out—unless, of course, the details affected his domestic political agenda. Diefenbaker had been the Conservative external affairs critic for many years. He feared Communism and his support for NATO was strong, as was his support for the Commonwealth, given that he was a dedicated monarchist. In this regard Diefenbaker was also concerned about the emerging nations in the Third World and their relationship to the Cold War struggle. As for the UN, Diefenbaker retained a high level of disillusionment which was not unlike that possessed by Canadian diplomats in the early 1950s. To his credit, the Prime Minister did view Canadian involvement in NATO, the UN, and the Commonwealth as an interlocking arrangement to secure Canadian interests.[15]

Diefenbaker's vision fit with the critical 1957 NATO summit held in December. In that meeting NATO heads of government confirmed to each other that the peripheral areas were under threat since, as French delegate Gaillard noted, "NATO was politically and militarily immobile in situations where Soviets had turned Europe's flank." NATO's leaders were extremely concerned about the Middle East and increasingly concerned about Africa.

The Belgian delegation pushed for overt economic and social support to the underdeveloped areas to forestall Soviet influence: they felt that a "special mechanism inside or outside NATO" should be established to coordinate such tasks. The Turks focused on the loss of Syria and their belief that "if the Middle East fell, then Africa would follow and... Europe would become encircled." Diefenbaker's contribution to the discussion was to support means which would increase aid to underdeveloped areas in order to raise the standard of living and block Soviet propaganda.[16]

The 1957 election campaign and Diefenbaker's initial lack of interest in UN policy did not mean that deliberations on it were discontinued at External Affairs. The Suez Crisis had, like the Korean War, brought about an internal re-examination of Canada's role in that organization. This task was delegated to John Holmes, acting Undersecretary of State for External Affairs, who produced a cogent document on the matter in the spring of 1957. It is possible that this study was commissioned by Pearson to respond to the then-opposition leader John Diefenbaker's attacks on UN intervention in Suez "against" Britain, but the lengthy process of its completion spilled over into the new government's tenure.

Holmes was asked, for internal External Affairs consumption, to respond to both allied (European) and Canadian public criticism of the UN. The primary argument was that the UN was "increasingly dominated by a majority of African and Asian countries allied from time to time with the Soviet Bloc and Latin America, which is irresponsible in its attitude towards international relations [and is] dominated by an irrational hatred of Western countries, and unwilling to pay for the wide-ranging economic measures which it sponsors."[17]

Holmes believed that the situation was not that dire, although there were serious problems. The French and British wanted to boycott the UN. Holmes thought the UN was too valuable an institution in the Cold War fight to just throw away. He believed that "we and our allies must pursue policies which, without sacrificing essential interests, prevent the establishment of a malevolent majority" in the UN. Holmes did recognize, however, that there was "an anti-colonialist bias which is unjust." This bias promoted UN interference in French operations in Algeria and in matters relating to Cyprus since the British were fighting a guerrilla force to preserve this critical base area, and the Dutch were having problems with Indonesia in West New Guinea.[18]

The primary criticism that Holmes could not adequately address (although he tried) was the lack of positive UN action on the Soviet intervention in Hungary concurrent with the Suez Crisis. Holmes shifted focus to emphasize the success of UNMOGIP in the Kashmir, arguing that it "prevented a disastrous war in 1948." Similarly, there were successful non-UN diplomatic activities which assisted the creation of ICSC in Indochina.[19]

In sum, Holmes argued that the existence of the UN was an accomplished fact and had been so for a decade: "If we stick with the UN, then we should make the best of it." If Canada did not participate in a positive manner, the UN would "become an irresponsible body dominated by irresponsible countries hostile to the West and exploited by the Soviet Union." The UN had to be used in such a way that Western allied colonial countries in the process of decolonization were not overwhelmed by Soviet interference.[20]

It does not appear that the Holmes UN report was transmitted outside of External Affairs, so it is unlikely that it had any great effect on Diefenbaker when he was acting as Secretary of State for External Affairs. It does demonstrate that the intellectual basis for policy was transferable in the bureaucracy despite lack of interest on the part of the elected officials.

Meanwhile, in National Defence, George Pearkes commissioned a complete re-examination of all Canadian military commitments overseas. This was undertaken as part of a larger effort to effect savings so that the priority continental defence projects such as the DEW Line, Avro Arrow, BOMARC missiles, and SAGE computer systems could receive as much funding as possible.[21] Pearkes focused specifically on "peace making activity" since, in his view, "this sort of thing has no military value for the Canadian forces." External Affairs reacted with horror and set about producing briefings which highlighted the critical need for peace operations within Canadian national security policy. Influence, they argued, was disproportionate to the numbers involved.[22]

At the same time, External Affairs requested that National Defence increase the number of Canadian Military Observers serving with UNTSO. General Foulkes explained to Holmes that Pearkes believed that peace operations were "a heavy drain on [National Defence] and provide little benefit for the Services, and he wishes a review made of these commitments with a view of reducing them as early as possible." Increasing Canada's UNTSO contingent was out of the question for the time being, although it is clear that Foulkes saw UNTSO's value and was able to reverse the decision later on.[23]

Holmes then produced a detailed briefing paper for Diefenbaker with the aim of heading off Pearkes' project. Holmes forcibly argued that the UNEF commitment was "second only to NATO in political as well as military importance...Canada's participation in UNEF may be regarded as vital to the cause of peace....The collapse of UNEF would be likely to have very grave consequences in the Middle East, including a greatly increased risk of war." The same argument went for operations in Indochina since the ICSC was "of inestimable value in keeping the peace between the opposing parties." If Canada pulled out of the ICSC, "it might seriously disturb the uneasy status quo in Vietnam" and affect vital negotiations over Laos.[24]

In Holmes' view UNTSO and UNMOGIP were less vital but were necessary to maintain the credibility of the UN as an institution, a prime Canadian national security policy objective. UNMOs were "a useful form of insurance against minor incidents developing into hostilities on a large scale" in both regions. In larger terms, Canada was helping her allies by participating in these operations. If Canada pulled out, it would damage those relations, something not acceptable in the Cold War climate. Canadian participation in the UN and its operations was "very useful for political and intelligence purposes." In sum, continued participation "has preserved our international reputation and limited our [military] commitments to what is appropriate for a nation of Canada's size and place in the world."[25]

There were no cuts made to Canada's peace operations, although the written records do not reveal any in-depth debate on the issue. We may speculate as to why this is the case. The most likely reason was the awarding of the Nobel Peace Prize to Lester Pearson in the fall of 1957. This event boosted the leader of the Opposition's national and international prestige which, naturally, was interpreted by Diefenbaker to be at his and the Conservative Party's domestic political and personal expense.[26]

The Prime Minister was also in a bind. He could not disown or withdraw from UN operations to spite Pearson: it would cause too much damage to Canada's hard won position. Diefenbaker did two things. First, he attempted to take credit for inventing UNEF by having George Hees remind the press of a statement made by the Prime Minister when he was the leader of the Opposition in the House in January 1956:

> One of the things [Paul Martin, Canada's delegate to the UN] can do with his influence in the United Nations is to see to it that something in the nature of an international force is established to the end that this dangerous situation shall be obliterated. If it is not and war breaks out there (the Middle East) we shall have war all over the world.[27]

Pearson was forced to respond in a press statement in which he refuted the assertion by arguing that the idea was already in circulation at the UN before Diefenbaker made the statement in the House.[28] We have already seen that this was the case from E.L.M. Burns' trip to the United Kingdom that year. While the Opposition was tied up dealing with that issue throughout the fall and winter of 1957-58, Diefenbaker shifted positions and started to take a more active interest in Canadian UN activities. This new interest took many forms, including making plans to address to the UN General Assembly, and (once Sidney Smith was available as the new Secretary of State for External Affairs) developing pro-UN publicity lines within speeches and foreign policy forums.

Diefenbaker's speech to the UN General Assembly in September 1957 is an example. It is almost as although Diefenbaker was playing to a Canadian as much as an international audience. He announced that the UN was "the cornerstone of Canada's foreign policy" (technically true since NATO was based on the UN Charter) although he noted that "Another phase of Canada's policy is Canada's membership in NATO, which constitutes a major bulwark against the forces of aggression....without NATO world peace would be endangered." The Soviets, he asserted, were trying to use the UN as a vehicle to attain their objectives in the Cold War, particularly in the fields of disarmament and anti-colonialism, and that the UN must not allow that situation to occur.[29]

It is important to note that the Prime Minister reminded the General Assembly that it was he, and not Pearson, who proposed the idea of UNEF. He went even further and announced that the UN should "evolve a system by which [it] will have at its disposal appropriate forces for similar services wherever they may be required." In effect,

> The creation of UNEF, I repeat, has provided for tranquilization of the area in which it serves. The UNEF has provided a 'pilot project' for a permanent international police force. Malignant diseases, however, are not cured by tranquilizers, and for that reason, I still hold the view, which I have expressed many times in the past, that only by the establishment of a permanent UN force can many of the hopes of San Francisco be achieved.[30]

This was quite a turnabout from the notion of Canada stabbing Britain in the back over Suez using the UNEF as the weapon. Sidney Smith took up the cudgel in a long speech to the House of Commons in November 1957 which reiterated the same themes. He stated that the UN was "an imperfect instrument" but it was a necessary one. Smith amplified aspects of Dag Hammarskjöld's recently released annual report. The Secretary of State noted that "Small wars, small conflicts, expand into great wars" and a UNEF-like force could ensure that they did not. Although the UN was the centrepiece of the House speech, Smith was careful to devote a great deal of space to NATO. Canada's "participation in NATO is complementary to and not in conflict with our membership in the Commonwealth and the United Nations....Canada has a special reason for avoiding an absolutely rigid dependence on any one of these organizations as the sole instrument or channel of its foreign policy."[31]

Lest the reader believe that Diefenbaker and Smith were developing something new, it should be noted that UN Secretary General Dag Hammarskjöld had, throughout early 1957 and in the wake of the Suez Crisis, "steadily developed the idea of an active role for the United Nations through practical demonstrations of what the organization could do." In particular, Hammarskjöld was drawn to the idea of using the UN proactively as a preventive diplomatic tool, to forestall international crises and, if necessary, deploy existing "stand by" peacekeeping forces to stamp out the brushfires. The best nations, in the Secretary General's view, to carry this out were "middle powers" like Ireland, Norway, Tunisia, The Netherlands, and Canada, coupled with Great Power support. It was essentially a refined and more systematic approach that had started back in the late 1940s.[32] These ideas were known within the UN community and were known to Canadian diplomatic personnel and politicians in 1957.[33]

The Diefenbaker government's response was to take a December 1956 External Affairs study on establishing a permanent on-call multi-national UN Emergency Force and elevate it to policy. The government announced in early 1958 that a Canadian UN Stand By Force had been formed. It would take the Canadian Army another three years to actually work out how such a force would deploy and actually carry out its ambiguous task. It was not clear whether an entire brigade should be dedicated to the UN or a battalion group. The fact that the Canadian Army was already fully committed to its NATO and home defence tasks was not explored. What really mattered was that the Diefenbaker government announced the establishment of the force.[34]

Throughout 1959, the Army sorted out how it would meet the government-directed UN Standby force commitment. Lieutenant General "Fin" Clark, the Chief of the General Staff was operating in a vacuum; even General Charles Foulkes could not get more explicit political guidance on how big the commitment should be or what it was supposed to be able to do, although Pearkes told the Air Staff that Canada would be called on more and more to contribute to "peace preserving teams to prevent the outbreak of war in many parts of the world."[35] Therefore the original idea that the Standby Force would be a light infantry brigade with a recce squadron was discarded. Consequently, Army planners developed a number of assumptions. The Standby Force would be an infantry battalion or company. It was to be air transported by the RCAF and its role was to "carry out police-type duties" in a UNEF context. Its training would be normal infantry training. The unit was to be kept at 90 percent strength and be deployable in seven days.[36]

At the same time, elements within External Affairs initiated a propaganda campaign directed towards convincing George Pearkes and others at National Defence that peace operations were important aspects of national security policy. An example of this effort were External Affairs guest lecturers at the National Defence College (NDC) in Kingston, where networking between National Defence, External Affairs, and uniformed military leaders took place.

The External Affairs' point man was G.B. Summers. Addressing the NDC in the fall of 1957, Summers took great pains to distance External Affairs from the Prime Minister's remarks relating to the UN being "the cornerstone of Canadian foreign policy." He reminded his audience that the previous government had been queried in the House by the Conservatives (then in opposition) about which of the "four pillars" was the primary one and when an ambiguous reply was given, the Opposition asserted that the Commonwealth should be the centrepiece. Summers took great pains to explain that the current emphasis on the UN by the government did not in any way affect how Canada would do business in NATO, particularly in terms of self-defence. The real problem between the UN and NATO was the decolonization process currently underway. How did the NATO countries decolonize and prevent Communist influence from replacing colonial influence?[37]

External Affairs agreed with the British and American views that the UN was necessary as a bridge between the Communist Bloc and the Free World. World opinion as expressed in the UN was a critical ally in the Cold War. Similarly, Summers argued that the UN could also be used to prevent small wars from becoming big ones. This was in Canada's interest. The UN could also be used by Canada to pressure its allies if it was necessary to accomplish Canadian aims as well. Summers did emphasize, however, that although NATO operated under the UN Charter, "it is quite clear that our reliance on NATO as an instrument of security is greater than our reliance on the United Nations."[38]

Other pre-packaged briefings produced by External Affairs and approved for use by the UN Division for NDC and other National Defence visitors follow these themes. The most explicit statement of the factors which determine Canada's UN policy stated:

> One can say immediately that Canadian policy in the UN is, like that of other countries, firmly based on grounds of national self-interest....Consider for example such a basic interest as the preservation of our national security....it does not take much argument to show that insecurity far from our own borders can endanger our own security; that any serious threat to the peace in another part of the world contains danger for us.[39]

Canadian economic objectives were part of this as well:

> Consider secondly another obviously basic national interest-the advancement of our national wealth and prosperity. This is an objective which we can pursue on many planes, in various contexts...it is true today that we have a considerable and increasing self-interest in the progressive development of the economies of areas and countries which are relatively backward.[40]

In effect, the External Affairs view remained that NATO, the UN, the Canada-US relationship, and the Commonwealth/Canada-UK relationship were all part of a national security policy Gestalt. Attempts by ill-informed elected officials to place emphasis on any one of these elements was ridiculous, would be temporarily accommodated with public platitudes, and ignored. Canada had ongoing interests in all of these areas and those interests would be protected.

CONTINUING PROBLEMS IN THE MIDDLE EAST: UNOGIL IN LEBANON, 1958

As we have seen previously, Canada's Middle East UN commitments included UNTSO and UNEF. These missions remained in the public spotlight well into 1958, particularly since General E.L.M. Burns was adept at using media and international pressure as a tool in generating peaceful resolutions to ongoing incidents in the region. Coupled with this was the Canadian public's fascination with UNEF and the role it played in the Suez Crisis.[41]

The fact remained, however, that the Middle East was volatile. The Greek Cypriot guerrilla war against the British was reaching its climax and Soviet pressure was brought to bear in the UN to interfere with a resolution acceptable to western interests. Soviet-supported Syria then accused Turkey of massing troops and preparing to invade: this prompted a minor crisis which directly threatened a NATO ally. Even though the Suez Canal was open again, the fate of the Gaza Strip was still in question. A more disturbing development was the creation of the United Arab Republic (UAR) under that charismatic and forceful Egyptian Colonel, Gamal Abdel Nasser. The UAR merged Egypt and Syria into one political entity while The Yemen was a partially federated member. One possible purpose behind such a merger could be an anti-Israel purpose which did not bode well for the future of the Middle East.[42] (see Figure 5)

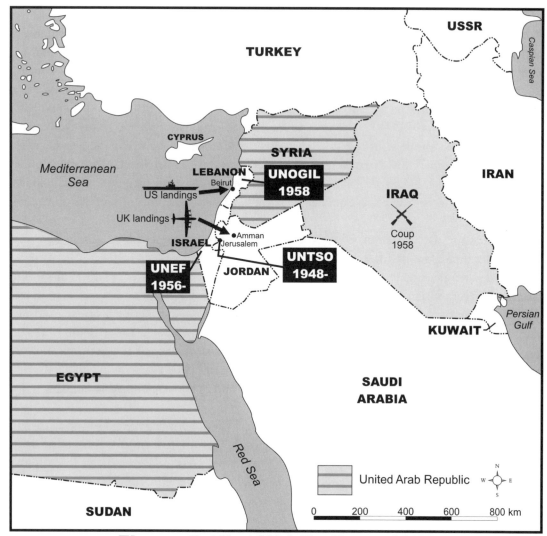

Figure 5: The Middle East, 1958

The volatility of the situation struck home for Canada in May 1958 when Canadian Army Lieutenant Colonel George Flint, an UNMO, was wantonly killed in Jerusalem. An Israeli patrol was taunting a Jordanian Army patrol on the Israeli-held enclave of Mount Scopus which resulted in a firefight, with the Jordanians firing first from their base against Mount Scopus. This firefight started to escalate into an Israeli infantry assault against the nearby Palestinian village when Flint intervened to arrange a truce and was killed by a sniper. It was unclear whose sniper it was, however, and External Affairs appears to have quashed serious speculation into the event at the time for reasons which today remain obscure.[43] In any event, George Flint's death, in an eerie parallel to Brigadier Angle's death in 1950, was overshadowed by an international crisis in Lebanon and Jordan.

In both the Lebanese Crisis of 1958 and the Suez Crisis of 1956 the Eisenhower Administration decided to publicly announce that any Soviet interference in the Middle East, in whatever form, would be met with American economic and military assistance to allies and US military intervention if necessary. The initiation of such a policy was prompted by the concern that Nasser was becoming too closely aligned with the USSR to the detriment of Western interests in the region. The coup in Syria, the subsequent Syrian-Turkish crisis in August 1957 and the inability of NATO to come to grips with military planning for the eastern Mediterranean/Middle East interface (as discussed in Chapter 3) bolstered the argument for additional containment measures. As a result, the US and the UK developed planning priorities (in line with MC 14/2 (revised)) to "Shield the NATO right flank, air base sites, Turkish Straits, eastern Mediterranean, the Cairo-Suez-Aden area, the Persian Gulf, and contiguous oil bearing areas" in late 1957.[44]

Throughout the winter of 1958, the Lebanese government led by Camille Sham'un came under increasing political attack by Arab nationalist and Islamic factions. Sham'un led a political party that was predominantly Maronite Christian and pro-West which made him a natural target. Syrian-Lebanese relations were poor, as were Egyptian-Lebanese relations. The formation of the UAR confirmed Sham'un's worst fears. Arab nationalism (also known as "Nasser-ism" since Nasser was its leading proponent) was hostile towards the Sham'un government because the latter backed the UN intervention in Suez back in 1956 and was actively considering membership in the Baghdad Pact (CENTO). The Syrian-Turkish dispute demonstrated to the Lebanese that the United States and Syria were antagonistic, which also added to improved American-Lebanese relations.[45]

In effect, there was an internal Lebanese political crises between the Maronite Christian and Muslim factions. An election was pending which prompted violent anti-government demonstrations. These flames were fanned by virulent propaganda emanating from Radio Cairo. A general strike was then proclaimed, violence spread into the hinterland, and all factions started to covertly arm themselves. Syrian sources supplied weapons to factions which they supported in southern Lebanon and rumours of a coup d'etat spread like wildfire. Sham'un sounded out the United States and the United Kingdom about military support in May 1958 after his Minister of Foreign Affairs, Dr. Charles Malik, publicly announced that the UAR was behind the violence and took the matter to the UN Security Council.[46]

The initial American reaction was caustic: "[Sham'un's] portrayal of himself as a lonely White Knight fighting battle against international powers of darkness is more Wagnerian than the situation warrants."[47] Some State Department observers were even concerned that the British were manipulating the situation so that pressure could be put on Syria to deter subversion directed against pro-Western Iraq and Jordan. The British denied this, of course.[48]

While the Americans and British examined military options, Canadian diplomats re-examined Canadian interests and UAR motives. Ambassador Paul Beaulieu told Sidney Smith in a message that the situation was "an inter-Arab dispute" but that Canada should:

...wish to voice support of any state exposed to comparable interference in its internal affairs. Moreover where countries involved is as notable for traditions of democratic tolerance and as vital to preservation of Western interest in strategic regions as is Lebanon, there can be no question that strongest stance consistent with tactical position of other friendly countries would be desirable.[49]

Charles Ritchie, Canada's Ambassador to the UN, agreed that the situation was an internal Lebanese matter, but that UAR motives were dangerous: "the UAR aim was...to bring into power in Lebanon a government which would be more in sympathy with UAR policies and in fact subservient to Nasser. Moreover the real and more sinister intent behind this move was to weaken the union of Iraq and Jordan and ultimately to isolate Iraq."[50] The Canadian government "informed the [American] embassy that Canadian support for the Lebanese case can be taken for granted" but it was up to the Lebanese to make a clear request of the Western powers and the UN before any action could be taken.[51]

In any event, a 10 June 1958 draft resolution presented to Hammarskjöld by the Americans and British prompted the Secretary General to send a three-man observation team plus ten UNTSO military observers equipped with jeeps to Lebanon. He made it perfectly clear publicly that these people were not a recce party for another UNEF, although plans were drawn up to provide 2000 UN troops to back them up if necessary.[52] The UNMOs, led by Galo Plaza (Ecuador), Rajeshal Dayal (India), and Major General Odd Bull (Norway) went about their business.

It was clear to Odd Bull that more observers, perhaps mounted in helicopters, were required: Lebanon is a hilly country and various factions were obstructing movement. This prompted Hammarskjöld to ask that a complete peace observation mission be formed and deployed: It would be called the United Nations Observer Group in Lebanon (UNOGIL). UNOGIL's mandate was "strictly limited to observation, to ascertain whether illegal infiltration of personnel, or supply of arms or other materiel across the Lebanese border was occurring."[53] The Secretary General immediately asked Canada to contribute military observers.[54]

George Pearkes consulted General Foulkes and plans were drawn up to send an initial observer contingent of ten men in 48 hours and an infantry battalion later if necessary. The Prime Minister went to the House of Commons to explain the Canadian position which, in effect, linked the preservation of peace in Lebanon with peace in the Middle East. This was a vague and uninspired but essentially accurate statement.[55]

How exactly Canadian policy was arrived at remains obscure. Diefenbaker's memoirs do not examine the Lebanese Crisis in any detail, although Basil Robinson stated that the Prime Minister "was pragmatic about it. He could see that to refuse a call from the United Nations would be far worse politically than to be blamed for following Pearson's tracks" which once again indicates that Diefenbaker's primary concern above all else was domestic political imaging. Caution was advised.[56] Other Canadian objectives are revealed in an 8 July 1958 meeting between Diefenbaker and Eisenhower. There was no disagreement between the two leaders and their advisors when the American President spoke of Soviet objectives in the region which were "to destroy the position of the West and in particular to deprive western Europe of Middle East oil on which it was dependent."[57]

Hammarskjöld's motives for creating UNOGIL were straightforward: the UN needed to know exactly what was happening in the Lebanon before it could pursue any other action like, for example, deploying a UNEF-like force. At the same time, however, Sham'un wanted whatever outside military assistance he could get and fast. The Americans and British were poised to intervene but were being held back because of their concerns about how the Soviets would react. It was in everybody's interests that UNOGIL get on the ground and find some answers. To what extent was there UAR interference with internal Lebanese political affairs? How far would they go? To what extent were the Soviets involved?

The possibility that the crisis might escalate was carefully considered by the Eisenhower administration. A CIA National Intelligence Estimate argued that, if the Sham'un government collapsed, "the governments of the Middle East disposed towards cooperation with the West would be strongly influenced to revise their policies" which in turn would increase Soviet influence in the vital region. The Director of Central Intelligence, Alan Dulles, argued that "what was at stake here was the whole periphery of the Soviet Union." American national security specialists developed a case that if Lebanon fell to UAR forces and there was no Western intervention, the hard-fought credibility the Western powers had built up in Turkey, Iraq, Iran, Pakistan, Thailand, Vietnam and Taiwan would be affected. This would be detrimental to Western interests, particularly in containing Communism within an area where there was no effective organization such as NATO. [58]

Dag Hammarskjöld, meanwhile, had arrived in the Middle East and was conducting shuttle diplomacy with Nasser and Sham'un. Galo Plaza, after a brief reconnaissance, told the Secretary General that "The world is being taken for a ride" by Sham'un. Hammarskjöld was not convinced that there was blatant UAR interference in Lebanon, but was able to have Nasser put pressure on the Syrian government to pledge that they were not supporting the rebel forces. Discussions with the Soviets then revealed that they were concerned about getting dragged into the conflict by Nasser and the UAR. Consequently, the Secretary General told the Americans, with regards to Sham'un's request for a UNEF, that he "could not really judge this question because the big powers would have to make up their minds in light of their own interests."[59]

If the Secretary General advocated a UN Charter Chapter 7 military force for Lebanon, Communist "volunteers" might arrive, as they had in Korea. Hammarskjöld's plan was to introduce a larger UN observation force to deliberately "lock the internal Lebanese situation into a stalemate," tell Nasser and the UAR to put a stop to subversive activities, and then have the Americans and British relent in their support for Sham'un.[60]

There was a problem determining exactly what was happening on the ground. The first UNOGIL report submitted by Galo Plaza did not find any evidence of UAR infiltration.[61] Several Canadian officers serving with UNOGIL who were debriefed by External Affairs gave a very different story, however. First, the observers were "not free to move as they wished. They indeed had access to most areas—but only by advance arrangement with rebel leaders who provided guides and usually on about forty-eight hours notice. Thus any evidence of infiltration and smuggling could easily be cleared away....the Observers still could see only what the rebels wished them to see." Night patrols were "quite out of the question" and if the UNMOs found an arms convoy "there was hardly a chance they would live to report." A Canadian UNMO, Captain A.S. Logan, had almost been shot one night poking around.[62]

In more specific cases, a Canadian UNMO team found rebels using heavy mortars against government forces:

> When asked by the Observers how they came to be in possession of mortars (which, unlike personal firearms, can hardly be regarded as a household standby, even in rugged Druze country) the local rebel leaders explained that they [were captured weapons] from the Lebanese Army. The observers could find no evidence that the Army had lost any mortars....As for the vast amounts of ammunition used by the various weapons employed by the insurgents, the explanation given to the Observers is that wealthy Druzes have made large cash contributions to rebel funds.[63]

Paul Beaulieu supported these reports in his recommendations to Sidney Smith. The view Ottawa was receiving from the field was that there was UAR support to the insurgency.[64]

At this point the already tenuous situation escalated into a crisis that held the possibility of nuclear weapons use. On the night of 14 July 1958, The pro-Western government in Iraq was overthrown in a coup led by General Abdul Karim Qassim, suspected of being pro-Soviet. Was the coup Soviet-backed? Was it UAR backed? Then violence started in Jordan and a plot to overthrow King Hussein was uncovered by the Jordanian secret police. Within 24 hours, Jordan and Lebanon requested Anglo-American military intervention to deter the UAR and the Soviet Union.[65]

The internal American debate revolved around the larger Cold War issues, not just the fate of Iraq or Lebanon. If there was no intervention, Dulles believed, the West would lose face with the Arabs again, American credibility elsewhere would be damaged, and "our bases throughout the area would be in jeopardy."[66] Eisenhower believed that the resulting loss of credibility "would be far worse than the loss of China because of the strategic position and resources of the Middle East."[67]

The one theme running through almost all American deliberations over intervention in Lebanon was the paramount concern that support by the UN was critical. Nobody wanted the Lebanese action to be equated with Anglo-French action over Suez, although Soviet and UAR propaganda would make the connection in any event.[68] When the US Marine Corps landed two battalions near Beirut, US Army troops flew into Beirut Airport on 16 July and the British 16 Parachute Brigade flew into Amman, Jordan on the 17th, it was by the formal invitation of the Sham'un and Hussein governments.[69]

The actions by British and American forces in those countries were orchestrated with other regional moves, which became necessary after Nasser flew to Moscow to ask Nikita Khrushchev for Soviet support. The British reinforced Bahrain, while the Americans moved a Marine battalion from the Pacific into the Persian Gulf. Coupled with these moves was a partial alerting of the Strategic Air Command nuclear bombers and NORAD air defence forces. The Soviets responded with a major land and air exercise on the Turkish border, naval exercises in the Black Sea, and the launch of Sputnik III.[70]

What, then, was UNOGIL's role now that the intervention forces were on the ground and what was Canada's policy towards it? The main problem was the relationship of UNOGIL to the landing forces. The Americans wanted a UNEF-like force to replace the landing force and thought UNOGIL should be expanded to do so. Hammarskjöld had already been thinking along those lines, but kept that plan in his hip pocket as a pressure tactic to moderate American movements elsewhere, particularly against Iraq. The Secretary General, however, was aware of Dulles' and Eisenhower's motives for the intervention and was motivated to help the Americans and the British if they kept the operations limited and withdrew as soon as feasible. These views were conveyed to Ambassador Ritchie at the UN and then back to Ottawa.[71]

UNOGIL could now serve multiple purposes. It could function as the UNEF in Egypt had, to allow the landing force to withdraw but still exert a Western-dominated but impartial presence. Information would be fed back through New York. A UN force could become a presence operation "not as a police force but a body which would guarantee UN commitment to preserve the independence or neutrality of [Lebanon.]"[72] As long as the Soviets and UAR stayed out, the Americans could leave.

As for Canadian policy, expanding the number of Canadian UNMOs for UNOGIL was not a problem and this action rapidly implemented in late July. Charles Ritchie hurriedly set about generating support from the non-aligned members of the UN in order to back the Anglo-American and Secretary General's initiatives.[73] The problem was that Prime Minister Diefenbaker did not seem to have any interest in the details of where UNOGIL fit in the larger aspects of Canadian objectives during the crisis or in the region. This is surprising given the key role Canada played in resolving Suez and Diefenbaker's ambition to match Pearson's accomplishments. Diefenbaker was aware of American and British objectives during the intervention and even received a phone call from Eisenhower a day before the forces went in. As Diefenabker stated in his memoirs, "I had considered that the urgent appeal from President [Sham'un] of Lebanon justified the US intervention."[74]

The SAC and NORAD alerts preoccupied Diefenbaker. SAC deployed tankers and nuclear bombers to and over Canada, with his concurrence. Diefenbaker felt that a clear signal had to made to Khrushchev to deter Soviet intervention. The joint Canadian-American NORAD command achieved an alert level commensurate with protecting SAC forces, but the Prime Minister had not been specifically asked to alert Canadian interceptors. This, in his view, was a gross breech of sovereignty despite Eisenhower's phone call. He was then attacked by the Opposition in the House of Commons, which was the latest in a series of such attacks dating back to the creation of NORAD. Diefenbaker allowed himself to be distracted with domestic political issues rather than playing an active role in the Middle East crisis of 1958.[75]

Despite this, Canadian participation bolstered UNOGIL's capability on the ground and went a long way to increasing its effectiveness and credibility. The second UNOGIL expansion authorized in the fall of 1958, which included more Canadian UNMOs, allowed American forces to re-deploy from the region and reduce the tension.[76] Clearly UNOGIL served multiple Western needs at a critical time. The American and British interventions were made to deter further UAR and Soviet actions in the region, American credibility elsewhere was maintained (for the time being), Sham'un remained in power, a NATO member (Turkey) remained secure from intimidation on three fronts, Hammarskjöld and the UN were viewed as making a positive contribution to crisis management, and Canada's regional and international interests were preserved. In time UNOGIL was disbanded and Lebanon remained at peace until the 1970s.

External Affairs' post-mortem of the crisis brought about calls for the expansion of Canadian diplomatic and other representation in the Middle East. A high priority was placed on gaining a foothold in Iraq primarily because "it is not possible to assess accurately the main social, economic, and political forces at work in the Middle East and therefore the adequacy of Western policies, on which we must continuously express views in NATO and in the United Nations." The secondary reason was that "Iraq also offers unusually attractive trade possibilities."[77] The overall problem was that the Qassim government had pro-Soviet leanings but was moderate and a more hard-line coup against him could cause further problems in the region. There was a great deal of concern expressed in Canadian, British and American national security circles that the oil flow would be shut off by either Nasser or Soviet puppets and this would affect NATO interests generally.[78]

In the end, it was clear that Canada's involvement in UNOGIL was intended to and did positively contribute to NATO interests in protecting the southern flank and access to Middle East oil, although Canadian decisionmakers did not explicitly state this perspective as publicly as they had during the Suez Crisis.

After the Lebanese Affair was concluded, Hammarskjöld remarked to John Holmes that "he had had enough of the Middle East and was now directing his attention to South-East Asia" to "prevent a clash between the Communists and Americans, whose policy in the area he considers dangerous"[79] a subject discussed further in Chapter 7.

ENTER HOWARD GREEN: PEACEKEEPING, DISARMAMENT, AND NEUTRALITY

Howard Green took over as Secretary of State for External Affairs immediately after the UNOGIL deployment. By this time Norman Robertson, an experienced External Affairs man who had been Undersecretary of State previously and had filled the highest diplomatic positions in London and Washington, became Undersecretary of State for External Affairs. Although Robertson did not have a good relationship with the Prime Minister, he got on well with Green, a man who had no experience in international affairs but felt compelled to become involved because he thought the world would end in a nuclear firestorm.[80]

Liberal Minister for Defence Production C.D. Howe once referred to Green as a "perambulating prognosticator of doom, stalking the halls of Parliament with a Bible in one hand and a stiletto in the other."[81] If Pearson was best described as "affable," Green was best described as "naive": he publicly stated that Canada had no enemies, only friends, this despite the fact that Canada had 12,000 soldiers and airmen deployed to West Germany to deter a Warsaw Pact attack and that Canada was spending billions of dollars for an air defence system to deter Soviet nuclear bomber attack.[82]

Robertson had by this time developed a fear of nuclear war which was fueled by a combination of factors. The issue of global fallout pollution and nuclear testing was a very public matter of the day. The development of hydrogen bombs in the multi-Megaton yield range brought with it serious debate about ecocide if they were ever used in quantity. Robertson apparently was personally affected after a classified SAC briefing in which the reality of nuclear war was brought home.[83]

The Green-Robertson combination in charge of External Affairs would attempt to alter the direction and character of Canadian national security policy which in turn affected Canadian NATO and UN peacekeeping policy. The flagship of Green's plan for Canadian national security policy was nuclear disarmament. Green's smiling visage could be seen regularly in the newspapers, on television, and in the UN General Assembly valiantly pushing for the elimination of nuclear weapons and the cessation of nuclear testing.

The annual External Affairs report now placed greater emphasis on disarmament than other activities. Where Sidney Smith remarked in the 1957 report that "the Soviet Government was seeking, not without success, to capture and could the forces of nationalism in the newly-emerging less-developed nations,"[84] Green would state in 1960 that "of the many subjects dealt with in the ensuing report none received more attention on the part of Canada during 1960 than disarmament."[85] Unfortunately, Green did not clear any of this with Cabinet so that Green's policies were not coordinated with either existing policies or future policies or with other government departments like National Defence.

It is important to distinguish between disarmament and arms control for they are two different concepts. Nuclear disarmament was a term used by those advocating the outright banning and elimination of all nuclear weapons globally. Arms control, on the other hand, was a Cold War diplomatic strategy designed to limit the opponent's military capability through diplomacy so as to achieve a favourable balance of forces in the event of war and/or to reduce the possibility of "hair trigger" actions involving nuclear weapons' use during a crisis. The first is utopian, the other pragmatic. Until this time, Canada's efforts in the arms control arena under the St Laurent government were specifically designed to support NATO power's efforts and to limit the Soviet Union's actions as much as possible.[86]

The forum in which arms control was carried out during the Cold War was complex. Arms control and disarmament efforts were conducted in the UN throughout the 1950s but it was apparent that other issues intruded in such discussions. In the UN, "disarmament problems often became confused with such issues as anti-colonialism, bases on foreign soil, nuclear free zones, disengagement. The tendency of the new nations to include criticism of Western disarmament policies in their general verbal assault on Western action in Africa or Asia, often while seeking arms themselves, has hardly advanced the possibilities of constructive negotiation."[87] In time a special negotiation body would be established in Geneva in 1960-61. Until that time, however, the UN remained the principle forum.

Disarmament and arms control proposals flew fast and furious in the UN General Assembly throughout the late 1950s. Green and Robertson entered this fray. They pushed for

Canadian involvement on as many committees and study groups as possible, so much so that General Foulkes contacted Robertson and questioned whether this was in Canada's best interests since Canada was part of NATO.[88] Green and Robertson wanted more and more low-level Canadian military participation on these committees, presumably to establish the veneer of military involvement.

It was inevitable that peacekeeping, disarmament, and arms control activities would become intertwined in the public mind. All three used the UN as a forum. The late 1940s discussions over establishing a UN army connected to discussions about giving the UN sole authority over all nuclear weapons were resurrected in the late 1950s. Interpositionary peacekeeping operations like Suez looked broadly similar to things like the Rapacki Plan which proposed a UN-controlled zone between NATO and the Warsaw Pact in central Europe. Arms control inspection plans like Open Skies and multinational observation teams looked remarkably like UNMOs going about their duties in the Kashmir and Middle East. Multi-national peacekeeping forces were elevated to the status of a single world police force. The belief among many that the UN was or should be a quasi one world neutral institution overrode the fact that the UN was just another Cold War battleground. To further confuse the issue, the now high profile General E.L.M. Burns was appointed by Green to be Canada's representative in Geneva. Canada's peacekeeper was now its disarmer.[89]

Behind the scenes, Robertson was trying to alter how Canada did business in NATO. Whereas External Affairs personnel involved in NATO activities "generally recognized that support for a politically outward-looking NATO had increased.... Certainly many countries believed outside problems should be studied within NATO, but without any decision bearing a NATO label being attempted." Robertson, on the other hand believed that "it was the duty of Canada to keep looking for diplomatic solutions and to discourage dramatic crisis making policies." Some Canadian diplomats thought Robertson was attempting to restrict Canadian action in NATO, but could not understand why.[90]

In essence, Green and Robertson were subtly shifting Canada's policies to reflect their agendas, which were not necessarily congruent with long-term Canadian Cold War aims, nor congruent with other elements comprising Canada's national security policy. Peace operations and arms control, which were vital Cold War concepts linked to the larger Canadian aims as expressed through NATO, were now in danger of becoming the focus of Canadian policy instead of NATO. A US State Department analysis of Green's activities concluded that he "is very nearly obsessed with the need to demonstrate 'Canadian initiatives' in the UN arena."[91]

For example, Green would lecture his American, British, and French counterparts in NATO forums "about their UN responsibilities." He continually stressed that the UN should be the main forum for "dealing with dangerous situations in peripheral areas." This was not something new, as we have seen in previous chapters. What was new was that Green thought NATO should support the UN, and not the other way around.[92]

Green's and Robertson's longer term objectives remain obscure, however. It appears as though they eventually desired a neutral Canada or at least a Canada that was an ineffective member of NATO and NORAD which in turn would be less reliant on the United States.

Individually, Robertson was motivated by fear of nuclear war, while we should entertain the possibility that Green, perhaps with tacit Diefenbaker concurrence, was searching for something else. American arms control negotiator Arthur Dean, once made a veiled reference to that "something else"—"too many statesmen, with an eye on the Nobel Prize, come forward with proposals that hit the front page but are both unrealistic and dangerous."[93]

Notes to Chapter 5

1. NAC MG 26 N2 vol. 89 file: External Affairs UN-General, 1958-61: Hon. Howard Green, Secretary of State for External Affairs speaking on "Press Conference" CBC-TV, 13 October 1959.

2. "A Falling Stature," *Victoria Daily Colonist* 28 October 1961.

3. This debate is covered in more detail in *Learning to Love The Bomb: Canada's Cold War Strategy and Nuclear Weapons 1951-1968*, soon to be published.

4. Louis J. Halle, *The Cold War as History* (New York: Harper Collins, 1991) Chapters 32 and 33; Anthony Clayton, *The Wars of French Decolonization* (New York: Longman, 1994) Chapters 7-9; Frank Kitson, *Bunch of Five* (London: Faber and Faber, 1977) Parts 1 and 4.

5. See Louis J. Halle, *The Cold War as History* and Mike Palmer, *Guardians of the Gulf.*

6. Ibid.

7. NAC RG 25 vol 4495 file 50030-E-1-40, (9 Oct 56) "Comments on IPT 131/20 of 15 Sep 56: Overall Strategic Concept for the Defence of the North Atlantic Treaty Organization Area," (5 Oct 56) memo Leger to Foulkes.

8. DHH, memo donated to DHH by Robert B. Bryce, "Statement by the Canadian Representative to the NATO Military Committee, 18 October 1956."

9. North Atlantic Military Committee, (23 May 57) "Final Decision on MC 14/2 (revised): Overall Strategic Concept for the Defense of the North Atlantic Treaty Organization Area."

10. Ibid.

11. Ibid.

12. Ibid.

13. Canadian MC 14/2 (revised) recipients included the three service chiefs and the chairman of the DRB (Zimmerman); the Deputy Minister (Drury), Undersecretary of State for External Affairs (Robertson); and the Secretary to the Cabinet (Bob Bryce). NAC RG 25 vol. 4495 file 50030-E-1-40 Pt. 1, (1 Aug 57) Joint Staff memo "Measures to Implement the Strategic Concept MC 14/2."

14. NAC RG 2 vol 1893 file 16 Aug-23 Sep 57, Cabinet Conclusions.

15. H. Basil Robinson, *Diefenbaker's World: A Populist in World Affairs* (Toronto: University of Toronto Press, 1989), 4-7.

16. National Security Archive, NATO Ministerial Meetings files, 917 Dec 57) message Paris to Secretary of State, "NATO Heads of Government meeting, 16 December 1957."

17. CIIA, Holmes Papers, file D II/2/a, "The Role of the United Nations."

18. Ibid.

19. Ibid.

20. Ibid.

21. The broad sweep of this activity is located in DHH, Raymont Collection, file 1332, 19 September 1957, Cabinet Defence Committee 115th Meeting and NAC RG 2, vol. 1893 file 16 August-23 September 1957, Cabinet Conclusions.

22. NAC RG 25 vol. 6948 file 5475-CX-2-40 pt. 7.1, (28 Jul 57) memo for DL(1) "Military Commitments Abroad," (6 Aug 57) memo Holmes to Miller.

23. NAC RG 25 vol. 6948 file 5475-CX-2-40 pt. 7.1, (15 Aug 57) memo Foulkes to Trembley, "Canadian Observers with UNTSO"; NAC RG 24 vol. 21482 file 2137-1 v.9, (4 Sep 57) letter Foulkes to Pearkes, "UNTSO-Additional Canadian Observers."

24. NAC RG 25 vol. 6948 file 5475-CX-2-40 pt. 7.1, (20 Aug 57) memo to the Minister, "Canadian Military Commitments Abroad, Excluding NATO."

25. Ibid.

26. Smith, *Rogue Tory* p. 274.

27. NAC MG 26 N2 vol. 89 file: External Affairs UN-General, 1958-61:"To Keep the Record Straight," *Winnipeg Tribune* 25 February 1958; "Hees Says Pearson 'Stole' UNEF Idea," *Victoria Daily Times*, 21 February 1958.

28. NAC MG 26 N2 vol. 89 file: External Affairs UN-General, 1958-61: "Liberals First to Suggest UNEF," *Ottawa Journal* 24 February 1958.

29. NAC RG 25 vol. 6976, file 5475-FA-40 pt. 4.2, (22 Sep 57) message PERMISNY to External, "Canadian Statement in the General Assembly."

30. Ibid.

31. NAC RG 25 vol. 6976, file 5475-FA-40 pt. 4.2, (26 Nov 57) "Aspects of Canadian Foreign Policy: Excerpts from a statement by Mr. Sidney E. Smith Secretary of State for External Affairs in the House of Commons."

32. Urquart, *Hammarskjöld*, pp. 255-258.

33. NAC MG 26 N6 vol. 10 file: UN Peacekeeping, (26 Jan 59) "A United Nations Peace Force-Standby Arrangements."

34. NAC RG 25 vol. 6101 file 50366-40 pt. 5.1, (20 Dec 56) "Forcible Measures to Enable the United Nations Effectively to Carry out Peace Supervision Functions"; NAC MG 26 N6 vol. 10 file: UN Peacekeeping, (26 Jan 59) memo DL(1) Div "A United Nations Peace Force—Standby Arrangements"; NAC RG 24 vol. 25 file 1200 pt. 2 v.9, (25 Feb 58) "General Staff Instruction 58/2: Preparation for Possible UN Commitment."

35. DHH, Raymont Collection, file 2002, Pearkes speech to the Air Officers Commanding Conference, 17-19 March 1959.

36. NAC RG 24 vol. 25 file 1200 pt. 2 v.5, (Apr 59) General Staff Instruction 59/, "Standby Battalion Group."

37. NAC RG 25 vol. 8143 file 5475-FA-40 pt. 6 FP, (25 Nov 57) "Talk to be given to the National Defence College by G.B. Summers."

38. Ibid.

39. NAC RG 25 vol. 6976 file 5475 FA-40 pt. 4.2, (21 Nov 57) UN Division, "Basic Factors which influence the formation of Canadian Policy toward issues in the United Nations."

40. Ibid.

41. See Burns, *Between Arab and Israeli* Chapters 18 and 19.

42. Arthur Goldschmidt Jr., *A Concise History of the Middle East* (3rd Ed.) (Boulder: Westview Press, 1988) Ch. 18; Alexander George and Richard Smoke, *Deterrence in American Foreign Policy: Theory and Practise* (New York: Columbia University Press, 1974) pp. 332-335.

43. Burns is less than cryptic in *Between Arab and Israeli* and a search of the External Affairs records at the National Archives of Canada produced an empty file folder. There is a hasty piece of message traffic based on American intelligence sources provided to Canadian diplomats in Washington which gives one account of the incident. See NAC RG 24 vol. 21482 file 2137.1 v.10, (30 May 58) message from Washington DC to External, "Death of Col Flint."

44. Palmer, *Guardians of the Gulf*, 78; George and Smoke, *Deterrence in American Foreign Policy: Theory and Practise*, 309, 332; and Barry Blechman and Stephen S. Kaplan, *Force Without War: U.S. Armed Forces as a Political Instrument* (Washington D.C." The Brookings Institution, 1978), 230.

45. Fahim I. Qubain, *Crisis in Lebanon* (Washington D.C.: The Middle East Institute, 1961), 28-29, 35-38, 44-45.

46. Qubain, *Crisis in Lebanon*, 53-60, 89; NAC RG 25 vol. 7700 file 11852-40, (22 Oct 59) memo for the Prime Minister, "Call by Lebanese Ambassador-Situation in Lebanon"; (17 Aug 59) Briefing package, "Lebanon and its Relations with Canada."

47. *FRUS 1958-1960 Volume XI: Lebanon and Jordan*, 23, (18 Apr 58) message McClintock to State.

48. *FRUS 1958-1960 Volume XI: Lebanon and Jordan*, p. 61, (18 May 58) memcon Dulles, Caccia, and Hood, "Lebanon"; p. 70 (21 May 58) memcon Dulles and Hood.

49. NAC RG 25 vol. 7700 file 11852-40 (20 May 58) message Beaulieu to Smith, "Lebanese Appeal to the Security Council."

50. NAC RG 25 vol. 7700 file 11852-40 (23 May 58) message Ritchie to External, "Lebanon."

51. NAC RG 25 vol. 7700 file 11852-40 (9 Jun 58) message External to PERMISNY, "Lebanon."

52. Urquart, *Hammarskjöld* p. 265.

53. United Nations Department of Public Information, *The Blue Helmets: A Review of United Nations Peace-keeping* (3rd ed.) (New York: UNDPI, 1996.), 116.

54. DHH, (27 Jul 66) "Report No. 9: Canada and Peace-keeping Operations in The Lebanon 1958."

55. NAC RG 25 vol. 7700 file 11852-40 (17 Jun 58) "House of Commons, Lebanon: Statement as to steps taken by the UN"; DHH Raymont Collection, file 459, (24 Jun 58) memo CGS to Minister; (24 Jun 58) memo CAS to Minister, "An Appreciation of the Problem of Airlifting a Canadian Army Force to Lebanon."

56. Robinson, *Diefenbaker's World*, 52.

57. DDEL, Ann Whitman File International Security file Canada(1), (8 Jul 58) memcon Eisenhower-Diefenbaker.

58. *FRUS 1958-1960 Volume XI: Lebanon and Jordan*, 93-98, (5 Jun 58) SNIE 36.4-58 "Consequences of Possible US Courses of Action Respecting Lebanon," and 166-167 (22 Jun 58) memcon Secretary of State, "Lebanon"; 171-175, (23 Jun 58) memcon, SECSTATE.

59. *FRUS 1958-1960 Volume XI: Lebanon and Jordan*, 175-180, (26 Jun 58) memcon Lodge and Hammarskjöld.

60. Ibid.

61. *The Blue Helmets*, 116.

62. NAC RG 25 file 12076-B-1-40 pt. 1.2, (24 Jul 58) message Canadian Delegation Lebanon to SSEA, "Views of Canadian Military Observers with UNOGIL."

63. NAC RG 25 file 12076-B-1-40 pt. 1.2, (10 Jul 58) message Canadian Delegation Lebanon to SSEA, "Conversation with Canadian Members of UNOGIL."

64. NAC RG 25 file 12076-B-1-40 pt. 1.2, (10 Jul 58) message Canadian Delegation Lebanon to SSEA, "Reaction to First Report of UNOGIL."

65. Qubain, *Crisis in Lebanon*, 92-93.

66. *FRUS 1958-1960 Volume XI: Lebanon and Jordan*, 209-211 (14 Jul 58) memcon State-JCS-CIA meeting.

67. *FRUS 1958-1960 Volume XI: Lebanon and Jordan*, 211-215, (14 Jul 58) memcon Presidential meeting.

68. Virtually every deliberation involving American diplomats, its allies, and the UN brought this matter up continuously. See *FRUS 1958-1960 Volume XI: Lebanon and Jordan*, section on the decision to deploy American troops and Urquart, *Hammarskjöld*, 278-279.

69. Nigel de Lee, "More Like Korea than Suez: British and American Intervention in the Levant in 1958," *Small Wars and Insurgencies* vol 8 No.2 (Autumn 1997), 1-24.

70. Bechman and Kaplan, *Force Without War*, 240-246; Stephen S. Kaplan, *Diplomacy of Power: Soviet Armed Forces as a Political Instrument* (Washington D.C.: The Brookings Institution, 1980), 158-159.

71. NAC RG 25 file 12076-B-1-40 pt. 1.2, (19 Jul 58) message PERMISNY to External, "Mideast."

72. Ibid.

73. NAC RG 24 file 12554-40 pt. 1.1, (6 Aug 58) message PERMISNY to External, "Emergency Session of the General Assembly."

74. Diefenbaker, *One Canada* Vol. II, 90. See also DDEL Anne Whitman File International Security file: Canada(1), (14 Jul 58) message President to US Embassy Ottawa.

75. See Maloney, *Learning to Love The Bomb*, Chapter 7.

76. NAC RG 25 file 12076-B-1-40 pt. 1.2, (11 Sep 58) message PERMISNY to External, "UNOGIL"; (7 Aug 58) message to SSEA from Canadian Legation, Beirut, "Second Report of UNOGIL"; DHH, (27 Jul 66) "Report No. 9: Canada and Peace-keeping Operations The Lebanon 1958."

77. NAC RG 25 file 12554-40 pt. 1.1, (9 Dec 58) Campbell to Matthews, "Proposed New Missions."

78. NAC RG 25 file 12554-40 pt. 1.1, (19 Dec 58) message from External to PERMISNY, NATOParis, WASHDC, "Developments in the Mideast."

79. NAC RG 25 vol. 6991 file 5475-6-40 pt. 4.2, (22 Apr 59) "Laos: Discussions with the Secretary General of the United Nations."

80. J.L. Granatstein, *A Man of Influence: Norman A. Robertson and Canadian Statecraft 1929-68* (Ottawa: Deneau Publishers, 1981), 325-326, 343.

81. NAC MG 32 B13 vol. 13 "Clipping file: 1961 file 2, William Stevenson, "Canada and the World," *Toronto Globe and Mail* 21 December 1961.

82. NAC MG 32 B13 vol. 13 "Clipping file: 1961 file 1, Peter C. Newman, "Howard Green: A Friendly peacemaker toughens up," *Macleans* (7 October 1961), 108.

83. Maloney, *Learning to Love The Bomb*, Ch. 7.

84. *Report of the Department of External Affairs 1957* (Ottawa: Queen's Printer, 1958)

85. *Report of the Department of External Affairs 1960* (Ottawa: Queen's Printer, 1961)

86. See Joseph Levitt, *Pearson and Canada's Role in Nuclear Disarmament and Arms Control Negotiations 1945-1957* (Kingston: McGill-Queen's University Press, 1993).

87. Arthur H. Dean, *Test Ban and Disarmament: The Path of Negotiation* (New York: Harper and Row, 1966), 12.

88. Albert Legault and Michel Fortmann, *A Diplomacy of Hope: Canada and Disarmament 1945-1988* (Kingston: McGill-Queen's University Press, 1992), 156.

89. NAC RG 25 vol. 5108 file 5475-6-40 pt. 6, (7 Apr 60) message External to DISARMDEL Geneva, "Canada's Role in Disarmament"; (7 Apr 60) External to DISARMDEL Geneva, "CDA's Role in Disarmament"; (7 Apr 60) PERMISNY to External, "Relationship Between the Proposed International Disarmament Organization and the UN-SECGEN's Views."

90. NAC RG 25 file 12554-40 pt. 1.1, "Meeting of Heads of European and Middle East Missions, Paris, October 26-29, 1959."

91. USNARA, RG 59 E3077 vol 250/62/30/3, file: Ottawa 1962 1/a, (21 Feb 62) letter Smith to Carlson.

92. USNARA, RG 59 E3077 vol 250/62/30/3, file: NATO 1959-62 3/a, (9 May 61) "Canadian External Affairs Minister Green's Remarks at Oslo."

93. Dean, *Test Ban and Disarmament*, 23.

CHAPTER 6

THE HORROR! THE HORROR! CANADA AND UN OPERATIONS IN THE CONGO, 1960-1963

"Mr. Kurtz has done more harm than good to the Company. He did not see that the time was not ripe for vigorous action. Cautiously. Cautiously, that's my principle....Look how precarious the position is—and why? Because the method is unsound." "Do you" said I looking at the shore, "call it unsound method?" "Without a doubt," he exclaimed hotly, "Don't you?" ... "No method at all," I murmured.

—Joseph Conrad, *Heart of Darkness*

"L'ONU? C'est quel tribu?"
[The UN? What tribe is that?]

—Congolese query to a UN peacekeeper in the Congo.

Nobel Peace Prize winner Ralph Bunche regularly represented the Secretary General in the field and worked closely with Canadian soldiers and diplomats on many missions. Criticized by the Soviets for being too pro-West, Bunche recused himself from the ONUC mission after labouring with General Von Horne to deploy UN forces before Soviet-supported elements could seize the Congo.

(CF Photo)

In 1960, Canada became enmeshed in a UN operation unparalleled in its complexity until the deployment of UNPROFOR to the former Yugoslavia from 1992 to 1995. The Arab-Israeli dispute appears straightforward and reasonable when compared to the conflict that gripped the former Belgian Congo. Congo operations encompassed plots within plots and wheels within wheels, from the Cold War grand strategic level contest between the West and the USSR, to the violent resolution of long-standing tribal disputes carried out under the guise of federalist legitimacy. Primal urges and their effects on man and society as described by Joseph Conrad in *Heart of Darkness* exploded into the sub-Saharan Africa scene and made a mockery of UN attempts to create a secure and stable member of the international community. The Congo would become a Manichean drama. There would be heroes: the Canadian, Swedish, Italian, and Irish soldiers and airmen serving with Operation des Nations Unies au Congo (ONUC), the UN military force sent into the middle of a steaming tropical hell. There would be anti-heroes: Patrice Lumumba and Moise Tshombe, each from opposing factions, each trying to assert personal power over the embattled region. There would also be a martyr: UN Secretary General Dag Hammarskjöld would die during the operation.

The Canadian role in this enterprise was, as in previous missions, related to Canadian NATO objectives. Although the Canadian force was not large compared to other UN contingents and was smaller than either UNEF or the later UN Cyprus mission in 1964, it was critical for the continued functioning of the UN force and for securing those Canadian objectives. ONUC was, however, different from previous UN peace operations like UNEF and, prefiguring the UN peacekeeping experiences in the 1990s, there was no peace to keep.

BACKGROUND AND CANADIAN INTERESTS TO 1960

The larger historical context for ONUC could be taken back to the late 1800s when Belgium explored, seized control, and then economically exploited the Western Europe-sized region north, south, and east of the River Congo and its tributaries. Joseph Conrad said it best: it was "the vilest scramble for loot that ever disfigured the history of human consciousness." The Belgian Congo was a vast, uncontrolled, wild territory with incredible mineral wealth: diamonds, copper, cobalt, tin, zinc, lead and that most important of all ores during the Cold War: uranium. Only the Belgian Congo and Canada had enough of this material, which in turn facilitated the expansion of the American nuclear stockpile during the 1950s.[1]

The Congo's Cold War context emerged in 1945 when Soviet Foreign Minister Molotov told British Foreign Secretary Ernest Bevin that the USSR was entitled to part of Italy's African colonies as reparations. If the USSR could not have Tripolitania, Molotov deadpanned, "we should be quite content to have the Belgian Congo." Bevin and American Secretary of State Byrnes were alarmed and thought the Soviets were after the uranium deposits for their atomic program.[2]

How were Canadian interests with Belgium and in the Congo defined prior to independence in 1960? Commercially, External Affairs was keeping an eye on several proposed African hydroelectric projects that could be used for uranium separation and aluminum production and thus compete with Canada's uranium and aluminum industries. Canada was at the time providing 50 percent of the nuclear material used in American bombs, while another portion came from the Belgian Congo: prudent observation of the competitor in this venture was just good business sense.[3]

In the defence sphere, the Royal Canadian Air Force and AVRO Canada had a close relationship with Belgium. Fifty-three of the sophisticated Canadian-built CF-100 Mk. V all-weather interceptors formed the backbone of the Royal Belgian Air Force's NATO-committed frontline fighter strength from 1957. These aircraft would eventually have to be replaced and the Belgians were looking at the Canadair CF-104 Starfighter. Lucrative spare parts and training contracts were in the offing throughout 1960.[4]

There was also Canadian concern, particularly in diplomatic and military circles, that the "Belgian politicians would go a long way to squirm out of their defence obligations."[5] The cost of operations in the Congo was cutting into Belgium's defence budget which affected the Belgian Army's ability to meet its commitments in the NATO Central Region. 4 Canadian Infantry Brigade Group had to take up the slack when I(Belgium) Corps was stripped of its infantry units for Congo duty: this affected the capabilities of the NATO deterrent force in West Germany and the deployment, safety and security of the Canadian brigade group.[6]

The role that western Africa and the Congo played in NATO strategic planning should also be counted among Canada's interests. (see Figure 6) Nasser's nationalization of the Suez Canal made that sea line of communication to Europe from the Arabian Gulf unreliable. Western Europe was dependent on Middle East oil. Therefore, in peace and wartime oil and other resources had to go around the Cape of Good Hope by ship. If the Soviets developed client states in western Africa prior to the outbreak of war, they could presumably base submarines and strike aircraft there which in turn would threaten NATO lines of communication in the southern Atlantic Ocean.

The Belgians had developed several bases in the Congo for the purposes of maintaining order and strategic reinforcement and projecting power in Africa. These included the huge airbase at Kamina in southern Katanga Province from which airborne forces could be sent anywhere in the region, and the naval and air facilities on the coast at Kitona and Banana where anti-submarine aircraft and destroyers could be based in wartime. The nearest NATO bases along the coast were the French naval and air bases at Dakar in Mali. In the wrong hands, the French and Belgian bases could be used against NATO shipping and cut off Europe from the Far East. Kamina had another important purpose: it was designed to house the Belgian government and Royal Family in the event of nuclear war in Europe.[7]

The NATO strategic planning factor was more or less subliminal in Canadian deliberations over involvement in ONUC. Canadian military planners in the NATO commands SACLANT, SACEUR and in the Canadian Joint Planning Committee would have been aware of the generalities of NATO's sea lines of communications problem, but such information was not always transmitted to or understood by higher levels because of the technical detail and information security implications inherent to military planning.[8]

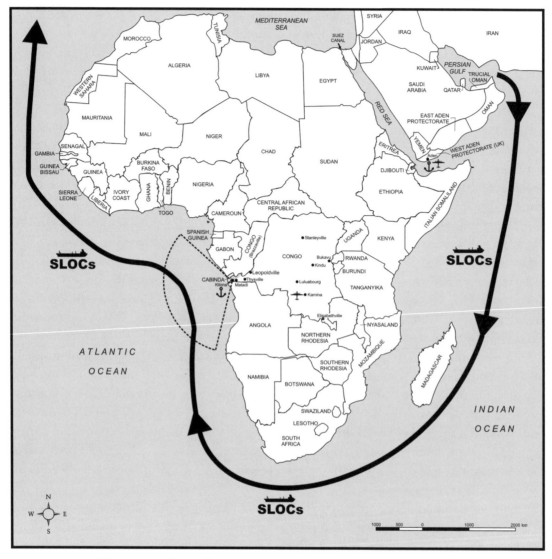

Figure 6: Africa and NATO Sea Lines of Communication

For multiple reasons, then, Africa had evolved into a Cold War battlefield by the late 1950s. The French war in Algeria influenced a number of Africa leaders, such as Kwame Nkrumah in Ghana, to make bids for independence. The French just walked away from Guinea, a vacuum which was rapidly filled by Soviet-backed supporters. In March 1960 seventy-eight blacks were killed in the Sharpville Massacre by South African security forces. South Africa was eventually barred from the Commonwealth (while Diefenbaker and Green valiantly tried to hold that organization together and moderate criticism of Western interests).

The combination of these events accelerated decolonization in Africa and consequently increased Soviet and even Chinese influence. The addition of seventeen new countries also contributed to the formation of an African-Asian power bloc in the UN, one which could compete with the West and/or the Soviet bloc.[9]

The Belgian Congo was not exactly tranquil. In 1958, the Belgians re-examined their engagement in the region and concluded that industrialization of the Congo should precede independence. The overall objective was to develop a Commonwealth or *Francophonie* kind of relationship, which was supported by Canada. That year, a young postal worker named Patrice Lumumba, leader of the *Movement National Congolese*, publicly called for independence. At the same time ABAKO, a cultural association, mutated into an independence political party led by Joseph Kasavabu, who then proceeded to develop a cult of personality among the large, uneducated portions of Congolese society. The Belgian administration promptly jailed Lumumba and banned ABAKO, which generated rioting in Leopoldville, the capital, throughout January 1959.[10]

In 1959 Canada's representative to Belgium, W. MacKenzie Wood, noted that violence in the Congo was discouraging Canadian investment. While keeping a watch on commercial developments, Wood picked up rumours as early as February that the powerful mining consortium, *Societe general de Belgique*, was prepared to "separate the Katanga province from the rest of the Congo" and hook up with Rhodesia if Belgium granted independence prematurely. Although the rumours were vehemently denied by the conglomerate's representatives,[11] they proved nearly prophetic.

On 16 October 1959, the Belgian Government announced that the Congo would be independent in four years. NATO Secretary General and later Belgian Foreign Minister Paul-Henri Spaak noted in retrospect that the decision to grant the Congo independence was "taken on the spur of the moment and it was made all the more dangerous by officially transpired optimism in Belgium and the joyful amazement of the Congolese."[12] The rapid move from an estimated twenty-five-year plan to a one-year time frame later in

"Everybody with a one way ticket to Hell, this way!" The deployment of 57 Canadian Signal Unit to the Congo abattoir in 1960 was in part designed to soothe the conscience of Cabinet members who didn't want "White Canadian troops killing Black Africans." Fortunately, they were permitted to carry submachineguns.

(CF photo)

1959 caught everyone by surprise. The main reason for this was that "the Belgian public's indifference to Africa was suddenly shaken by the nightmare of an Algerian-type war."[13]

According to Spaak, France's complex and squalid counterinsurgency war in Algeria was a "warning example to be avoided at all costs." The Belgian public was not prepared to have its troops and colonists killed in Leopoldville in the way the French *colons* and *pied noirs* had been in Algiers. Spaak noted that the abruptness of the announcement created a situation where "between them the idealists, the weaklings, and a few calculating individuals managed to put an end to the [Congo] venture." There was not even enough time for Spaak to generate NATO-member support and prepare the allies for it, although his objective was to have a stable, federalist neutral Congo that would respect Western interests.[14]

THE DESCENT: JANUARY-AUGUST 1960

After a whirlwind tour of Africa Dag Hammarskjöld increased his interest in that continent throughout February 1960 to the point where he and his staff conferred with Canada's UN representative Charles Ritchie several times about the future. The new African nations were going to need aid and lots of it. The Secretary General said during one of these confidential meetings that there was "a very grave problem raised by Russian aid." He hastened to note that acceptance of such aid by these nations did not mean they were pro-Communist: "the danger was that without desiring to become committed to Communist policies they would insensibly be drawn in this direction by increasing dependence on Soviet aid."[15] Hammarskjöld proposed that the UN fill the void and act as an honest broker for aid with special missions led by senior diplomats to "exercise a good influence in a wider sphere." This could work in most parts of Africa, unless there was anarchy when the colonial powers withdrew. Hammarskjöld was referring specifically to the Congo which he described as being in a "terrible state" that would become a "nightmare." He did not know what could be done in such a situation, but only that the UN was "not in a position to step into a country and run it for them."[16]

Canadian diplomats noted that "some bloodshed at least is expected from the tribal rivalries" as well as "from the struggle for personal power among the emerging leaders of the new nation." Further analysis suggested that "the Soviet Block [sic] may make inroads with the Congolese." The Belgian Prime Minister told a Canadian diplomat that some Congolese "have been flirting with many countries, including the Soviets and that the latter have special agents in Belgium" supporting an independent Congo through the trade union movements. Some External Affairs people thought that "the Belgians should raise the question in NATO, at least informally." Notably, "certain aspects of the problem might indeed warrant invoking the UN. The presence of UN observers might help ensure a fair election and at the same time keep the peace...some show of interest on our part might be worth considering."[17]

Hammarskjöld's special representative Ralph Bunche was dispatched to keep watch on the Congo and report. He found, on the eve of independence, that almost nothing had been done by the Belgians to prepare the Congolese for independence. Leopoldville was in a state of panic and the Western diplomatic corps was "obsessed with the possibility of a Communist takeover." The wife of an American diplomat asked Bunche if the "Reds" were coming, to which Bunch "replied mischievously and not untruthfully, 'my dear lady, they are already here.'"[18] The CIA was now predicting that Katanga would separate and join Rhodesia: the Katangese leader, Moise Tshombe, had already requested American military assistance if central government forces from Leopoldville occupied Katanga. The Americans were adamant that an avoidance of the "Guinean experience" was paramount to prevent Communist infiltration.[19]

On 30 June 1960, the Congo celebrated its independence. Former journalist President Joseph Kasavubu, former postal clerk Prime Minister Patrice Lumumba, and Vice Premier Antoine Gizenga were now nominally in charge of a country larger than France and West Germany combined. These men were in fact bitter political rivals. Kasavubu was "a nice, tired old man...completely dominated by Lumumba."[20] Lumumba, on the other hand, was "a highly articulate, sophisticated, subtle and unprincipled intelligence."[21] In conversations between Hammarskjöld and Lumumba, the Secretary General "was skillful and suave and used complicated arguments in scholarly language based on international law and practice. Lumumba was a revolutionary still fighting, unskilled in diplomacy...."[22] The gentle and reasonable Ralph Bunche himself believed that Lumumba was "crazy."[23] Gizenga was a "most singularly dangerous individual ...completely ruthless and untrustworthy."[24]

Under the terms of independence, the Belgians were entitled to garrison and use the Kitona and Kamina bases. Lumumba immediately incited the *Armee National Congolese* (ANC) to mutiny against its Belgian officers and harass Kamina and Kitona. On 5 July, the Leopoldville ANC garrison mutinied and committed rape and other atrocities against defenceless Belgian Army dependents. Regular Belgian troops stationed in the base areas were about to be called in. Bunche, already on the ground, was arrested and manhandled by ANC troops. On his release he told Hammarskjöld that if the Belgians intervened it might cause a backlash elsewhere against Western interests.[25]

Rioting and looting ANC troops rampaged through the capital and the violence spread elsewhere; Lumumbaist forces spread fear and alarm in the hinterland, claiming that the Belgians were sending troops to take away independence. Belgian nationals, the only people who could manage the electricity, telephones, gas stations, and transportation infrastructure, fled the country with their families. By 8 July French military forces in Brazzaville in the French Congo, just across the river from Leopoldville, conferred with Belgian and American diplomats: did they need French assistance? Their troops were being shot at by the ANC. At this meeting someone suggested that UN forces should be called in.[26]

As the main UN representative, Bunche was able to effect shuttle diplomacy. Bunche held back the Belgian ambassador, who wanted to call in Belgian airborne forces, while at the same time he asked US ambassador Clare Timberlake to pressure Kasavubu and Lumumba to accept a UN "stabilization force." Bunche eventually got everybody together in one room and convinced the Congolese to ask Hammarskjöld for UN help. Bunche suggested that the UN provide "technical assistance" which would involve a security component. Then, just to add more confusion, Kasavubu and Lumumba approached President Eisenhower with a request for direct American military aid: this was rebuffed and the men were instructed to deal with the UN. Eisenhower's advisors, however, argued that the "departure of the Belgians, which would be followed by practically all Europeans, would convert the modern Congo to jungle."[27]

The Americans did not want to be involved directly. They believed that the UN could play a role in restoring order and training the thuggish ANC as a proper paramilitary force, while UN technical assistance could be used to train the locals to run the infrastructure. The American agenda, similar to Hammarskjöld's and also in line with Canadian interests, was, in Timberlake's words, "to keep bears out of the Congo caviar." Kasavubu, however, had to decide on "his own initiative and not with a Belgian pistol to his head."[28]

Just when it looked as though an adequate response had been formulated, four Belgian airborne battalions staging from Kamina and Kitona intervened to protect Belgian nationals from ANC molestation. Belgium's allies were alerted before the mission was executed.[29] In a related move, Moise Tshombe declared that Katanga Province was a sovereign state on 11 July. The "clever, able and adroit" Tshombe, "always hospitable and friendly in manner," was Katanga's front man.[30] He was backed by the tall, well-built and aristocratic Minister of the Interior, Godefroid Munungo, who impressed UN force commander Carl Von Horn "as nothing more or less than a man drenched and impregnated with evil."[31] Their motives, not incidentally, revolved around maintaining "positive control" over Katanga's vast mineral deposits.

Hammarskjöld was concerned that the Soviets would block UN attempts to resolve the crisis in the Security Council. Consequently, all plans to insert UN forces into the Congo were referred to as "technical assistance in the field of security administration." While this action was deliberated in New York, Belgian forces protecting Belgian nationals clashed with the ANC and all economic activity in the Congo ground to a halt.[32]

The days of 11, 12 and 13 July 1960 were fateful ones for all concerned. The Congolese request for 2000 American troops to intervene under the UN flag (the Americans had a contingency plan to fly in a battalion from West Germany and land Marines from the aircraft carrier USS *Wasp* which was sailing just offshore) was turned down in Washington after US Secretary of State Christian Herter communicated with Howard Green and Hammarskjöld. Both men recommended that African troops be used instead. Kasavabu and Lumumba then went to the UN and asked for a UN force to expel the "imperialist interventionists" (the Belgian airborne forces who were protecting Belgian military dependents), a request very different from "technical assistance" to retrain the ANC.[33]

Concerned about the deteriorating situation in the Congo, Chief of the General Staff "Fin" Clark issued Operational Instruction 60/1 which instructed his staffs to review planning relating to the UN Standby Battalion Group. The instruction ordered preparations to commence for the deployment of a 1000-man infantry battalion, 2nd Battalion The Royal Canadian Regiment, which would be used for "policing duties." The RCAF alerted Air Transport Command to make similar preparations for the airlift of the battalion to the Congo.[34]

The situation continued to deteriorate as the placid Belgian colony was turned into a slaughterhouse. Belgian paratroopers re-took the ANC-held Leopoldville airport on 13 July.

Lumumba's response was to ask Kwame Nkrumah of Ghana for military assistance to fight the Belgians. Hammarskjöld's immediate plan was to "do something like Suez" and get UN troops on the ground immediately. This was to support the Belgians, prevent the complete breakdown of order and to prevent "various forms of outside intervention," specifically the Soviets and the Chinese or their surrogates. Eisenhower and Herter backed the Secretary General to the hilt: the UN would be used instead of American forces. Herter even noted that they "understood fully" if Hammarskjöld "wanted to play down American involvement." The best way the West could back the effort was, therefore, to provide the UN force with transport, communications, and logistics "like UNEF and UNOGIL."[35]

Hammarskjöld went to the Security Council that evening and proposed that the UN provide "technical assistance for security matters", humanitarian relief, and UN troops to protect the aid operation similar to how the UNEF was employed in Gaza. The objective of the exercise was to "create conditions in which the government could become capable of taking care of the situation itself." The force would have mostly African members and nobody from Security Council nations. The French representative, supported by Ambassador Lodge, suggested using Canadian troops that spoke French. Soviet representative Kunetzov then tried to use the forum to discredit the Belgians and get the UN to condemn their "aggression": this was blocked. China, France, and the British abstained, and the rest voted for the creation of ONUC.[36]

The Soviet moves worried Hammarskjöld and rightly so. Belgian UN representative, Luis Scheyver, approached Christian Herter and passed to him intelligence which demonstrated that Lumumba was communicating directly with Nikita Khrushchev. The Soviets were contemplating sending in "technicians", with Lumumba's consent, to infiltrate the UN humanitarian effort which would then allow them to send in forces by air. It was imperative that the Belgians not leave the Congo before ONUC fully deployed or the Soviets might get a foothold and reinforce it. The Americans concluded that "the situation in the Congo could lead to World War III." Herter then met with Hammarskjöld on 18 June 1960, who expressed grave concern and looked to getting more non-Communist nations in as part of ONUC as soon as possible to limit infiltration of the force.[37]

It is not a coincidence, then, that Hammarskjöld sounded out Canada to provide signals and logistics units to ONUC. Cabinet met to discuss the request. Green was not available, so Diefenbaker dealt directly with the Canadian UN delegation. The Prime Minister was vexed that Hammarskjöld used the wording "French-speaking units from a trans-Atlantic country" and demanded that it not appear in the Secretary General's public Congo report. The wording was removed. So far, Canada was contributing nothing to the UN effort in the Congo.[38]

The UN Standby Battalion was ready to go at a moment's notice, just as the government had demanded in 1958. There was a serious crisis that the unit had trained for: the Army's leadership was mystified as to why no decision had been made. Sources in New York then indicated that a request for a Canadian signals unit was under consideration. Clark and his staff were resistant. There were critical shortages in men and equipment: "The despatch of technical signal equipment particularly radio sets from Canada would reduce holdings in Canada to meet present military and national survival commitments to a dangerously low level."[39]

While Cabinet ignored the situation because of a seeming personal slight and 2 RCR stood by to board their North Star and Yukon transport aircraft and get going, the political situation was developing. UN representatives Bunche, Force Commander von Horn and his associated Ghanaian force commander British Major General Alexander met with Kasavubu and Lumumba. Lumumba threatened the UN men and demanded that UN troops expel the Belgians from the Congo. If not, he would ask the Soviets to send troops to do it. Bunche was blunt: either the Congolese leaders picked UN aid or Soviet aid. Which was it going to be? Kasavubu and Lumumba then backed down, claiming that they recognized "that the coming of Soviet troops could provoke a world nuclear war." UN aid was preferable, they decided.[40]

The problem was that the Belgians were willing to withdraw from all sites except Kitona and Kamina since they were permitted by treaty to garrison them. Lumumba was demanding that they both be evacuated. Kamina was in Katanga, which was controlled by Tshombe, who was no longer taking orders from the central government in Leopoldville. Belgian intelligence determined that the Belgian Communist Party (with Moscow funds), Antoine Gizenga and Minister of Information Kashamula were supporting Lumumba, which greatly concerned the Americans. The American ambassador to Belgium was convinced that Lumumba "threatened our vital interests in Congo and Africa...A principle objective of our [actions] therefore must be to destroy Lumumba's government as now constituted." A CIA briefing to Eisenhower concluded that Lumumba could be "Castro or worse"; they believed that Lumumba was receiving support from Nasser and the UAR which when combined with a Lumumba-run Congo would produce "a formidable salient into Africa."[41]

Army HQ in Ottawa was in the process of exploring the deployment of a French-speaking battalion from the Royal 22nd Regiment when UN requests for one North Star transport aircraft and some Military Observers came in. These requests were granted by George Pearkes since these resources were already committed to supporting UNEF and UNTSO in the Sinai and thus already part of the UN. With regard to other forces, Pearkes told Clark that the government "did not want to send troops until we know the situation."[42] Meanwhile, troops from ten nations, as diverse as Sweden and Ethiopia or Morocco and Indonesia, were on their way to the Congo. UNEF HQ was stripped and re-deployed to Leopoldville.

Cabinet met again on 19 July and, again, its members could not determine whether or not Canadian troops would join ONUC. In his memoir Finance Minister Donald Fleming summed up the underlying government concern that the Congo might become another Ghana based on his recent trip to Africa: "there was deep seated uneasiness in Ghana. Prime Minister Nkrumah was exhibiting totalitarian tendencies, flirting with Moscow and accepting Russian aid. Planes containing men purporting to be technical experts were frequently arriving from Russia."[43]

It was clear that Green was supportive but Pearkes thought that there was not enough detailed information emanating from the UN regarding the specifics of a signal unit. How large was the UN force? Over what distances would it be operating?[44] The problem must be put into perspective. The haste with which Hammarskjöld and Bunche were moving was motivated to get a UN *presence* on the ground in the Congo to forestall Soviet intervention, not necessarily deploy an operational military force. There was no time for them to consider the detailed military aspects of the problem and, in any event, there was mass confusion within ONUC HQ as to who was really in command: Bunche, Alexander, von Horn, or some combination. Bunche parceled out the national ONUC contingents throughout the Congo by air to flood the more remote urban areas but he did it without setting up communications or a logistics system.[45] (see Figure 7) It was left to von Horn and Alexander to sort things out after the initial objective was achieved. The fact that these two men were not in agreement did not help the efficiency of the UN operation. A Canadian assessment of von Horn noted that "If he has a fault it is his quick mind which at times runs away with his tongue but it is thought that he is intelligent enough to control himself when the circumstances really require it."[46]

Unlike their Canadian counterparts, the American national security policy decisionmakers were far beyond toying with language. The Soviets had flown in two TU-114 strategic jet transports non-stop from the Odessa in the USSR to Leopoldville, while eight shorter-ranged IL-18 transports refueled at a Greek air base and then staged through Khartoum in the Sudan bound for Stanleyville, Lumumba's political stronghold.[47] Although carrying "relief supplies" and "technicians", the message was clear: Moscow had the ability to intervene. Missionary sources fed back information that strangers were in the outlying areas stirring up trouble, with the Czech embassy acting as the focal point for such activity. The Secretary of State sent a priority message to all US missions: "Denial of Katanga assets to Soviet influence through Communist oriented central government extremely important.

On arrival, most ONUC contingents were in the dark about their mandate in the Congo, as the details of the brewing superpower crisis remained obscure to all but a few. RCAF and RC Sigs personnel "somewhere in the Congo."

(CF photo)

Much depends on eventual political outcome of the UN intervention." If Belgium was not allowed to save face in the Congo "this could cause a serious split among NATO powers."[48]

The American plan was to "encourage" the UN to control ports, harbours, and airfields with UN forces to ensure that Lumumbaist ANC forces could not secure them for the Soviets. If necessary, the USS *Wasp* could land Marines by helicopter in some areas on the coast, but the aircraft did not have the range to get inland. Therefore, it was a race to get the UN forces onto every airfield and urban area in the interior. Thirty-three US Air Force C-130

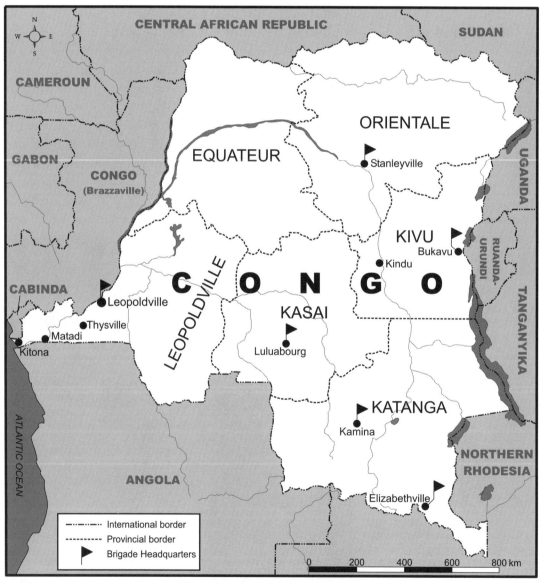

Figure 7: ONUC in the Congo, 1960

Hercules and C-124 Globemaster transport aircraft were allocated to von Horn and Ralph Bunche to expedite the airlift of ONUC forces to the Congo from as far away as Indonesia, and then deploy them in-country.[49]

While troops for ONUC were pouring into the Congo to forestall Soviet intervention, Cabinet met again on 21 June. Under pressure from his man on the ground in Leopoldville, Howard Green asked for the use of four RCAF North Star transports to distribute food. He also reminded Cabinet that there was still an outstanding request for signalers. Green noted that the UN force would be ineffective without signalers because the bulk of ONUC was made up of African nations without technical skills. Pearkes explained the problems in mounting the operation: most importantly, there was the need for inoculation and the subsequent delay of three weeks before deployment. The UN Standby Battalion was already inoculated and could go immediately. Cabinet decided that immunization could go ahead but no commitment was made to the Secretary General at this time. The North Stars could go, but only if the UN accepted a senior RCAF officer in its air headquarters so that Canadian resources would not be misused.[50]

We must examine Cabinet's seeming reticence to send Canadian forces to ONUC. Analysis of Cabinet documents indicates that Howard Green did not explain to the Prime Minister or Cabinet at the start of the crisis the nature of the strategic situation and the role that Canada might play in preventing Soviet infiltration. The delay occurred because he was away at a conference at Montebello and Diefenbaker was acting in his place. Norman Robertson was urging Canadian involvement and Diefenbaker did not trust his analysis, which may not have had a full analysis of Soviet interference and the actual reasons for UN involvement.[51] Basil Robinson, Diefenbaker's advisor, noted that the Prime Minister's main concern was that he simply didn't want to have white European troops killing black African people.[52] Diefenbaker was shaken by the Sharpville Massacre in South Africa and the destructive effects it had on the Commonwealth, an organization he treasured more than the UN. It is probable he did not want to see Canadian troops, particularly the men of the UN Standby Battalion, put in a situation where they would be shooting Black Africans.

Cabinet met again on 28 July after Christian Herter contacted Howard Green to consult about UN operations in the Congo. Lumumba was about to visit the UN, Ottawa, and Washington. Herter had just received an angry Luis Sheyver who, upon hearing about the Soviet airlift, wondered "what would happen if Belgium invited Fidel Castro to Brussels and accorded him a great reception!" Herter and Green agreed that Lumumba might be on a "shopping expedition to play us off against the Soviets" and that Canada and the United States could "use UN aid to undercut this." Notably, Green and Herter had a mutual understanding that any aid money from North America would be funneled through the UN to maintain the appearance of impartiality, disallow Lumumba a diplomatic coup, and then highlight Soviet machinations when they provided aid to the Congo.[53]

Green had also heard from Jules Leger at NATO. The British and French were backing the Belgians and basing their line on the need to retain Kamina and Kitona, although they were wavering and thought the UN might play a role in preserving NATO's capability in the region. There were moves afoot within NATO to suggest to the Belgians that the bases were not critical to NATO planning when compared to the larger issues of global peace. Andre de Staercke, Belgium's NATO representative, warned Leger that "if conditions [in NATO] continue to 'rot'...a neutralist sentiment will develop in [Belgium]. This would be coupled with a complete acceptance of General de Gaulle's leadership." The consequences of a neutral Belgium aligned with a quasi-neutral France would destroy NATO. Leger noted with alarm that "during the last few weeks Belgium has become a small, weak, and politically unstable country." If Lumumba visited Ottawa, Leger recommended that he "get the Profumo Treatment, not the Herter Treatment."[54]

This did indeed happen. After a day of talks Lumumba asked Howard Green for some women. The pious and devout Howard Green thought the Congolese leader wanted stenographers so that he could get caught up on paperwork. Stenographers apparently showed up at his hotel, to Lumumba's chagrin. Green was called in the middle of the night and "arrangements were made to meet the wishes of the Congolese Prime Minister the following night." External Affairs apparently wrote the prostitute's fee off under the flower account.[55]

In communications with Robertson, Canada's man in Brussels played down the danger of a NATO split but noted that there was still serious concern on the part of the RCAF and Canadair. Canadair was producing the CF-104 nuclear strike aircraft for RCAF use and agreements had been made to sell spares and training equipment to the Belgian Air Force, who were also re-equipping with this aircraft which would then become part of SACEUR's nuclear deterrent force. There was concern that the whole Belgian F-104 project would fall apart with resulting economic consequences for Canadian companies. A greater burden would fall on the Canadian RCAF forces in Europe's contribution to deterrence if the Belgians did not deploy F-104 squadrons.[56]

There was some opposition in Cabinet since some members "expressed serious reservations about sending Canadian troops into such a chaotic situation." Green explained to Cabinet that Canada should not become as directly involved as other UN members. He was particularly concerned about Katanga: Canada should side with Belgium over maintaining an independent Katanga because it was "friendly to the West" but that worked at cross purposes to the UN efforts. Green wanted to support the UN since, in his view, the ONUC deployment "meant the exclusion of Soviet and United States forces from the area thus preventing what would probably have been a very tense and difficult situation. Much had been made of Canada's support of the United Nations." If Canada did not deploy with ONUC, it "would be a mistake"[57] and Canada's credibility in the UN (and presumably Green's credibility in nuclear disarmament efforts) would be damaged. Green obviously was not getting the hint that the UN was acting as a Western surrogate in the Congo matter.

Green did, however, make at least one astute move. He told Andrew Cordier through Charles Ritchie that RCAF transports were no longer to be used for the inter-Congo airlift and could only be used for transport missions to and from the Congo. There was serious concern that Canadian aircraft would be used to repatriate Belgian airborne forces from outlying areas back to Kamina base in Katanga: this could be twisted in the Congo kaleidoscope to make it appear as though Canada was supporting Katangese succession by flying in Belgian troops.[58] Whether Green knew it or not, Soviet aircraft, ostensibly committed to the ONUC airlift, were in fact not under UN control and had been used by Lumumba to ferry ANC troops to Kasai Province to brutally suppress a Ba-luba tribal rebellion there. Canadian military forces were not to become similarly involved in someone else's genocidal operation.

Two days later Cabinet convened. The Prime Minister was in a better frame of mind about Canadian participation in ONUC. This time the debate centered around whether or not Parliament should be consulted. Many Cabinet ministers thought it should not, but others were concerned that if there were "serious casualties" then the government would be put at risk by the Opposition. There was further concern that Pearson would demand that a *larger* Canadian force be sent and make the government look foolish if 150 men were sent. Therefore, they recommended that the Prime Minister not announce the size of the force.[59] Diefenbaker then told Parliament that the size of the Canadian force would be 500 men, as opposed to the 150 that the UN asked for, the Army had planned to deploy, and the number that Pearkes had been told could be sent without affecting other commitments.[60]

While Canada was dealing with numbers, Hammarskjöld and Bunche were struggling with the thorny Katanga issue. Katanga, as they saw it, was the *schwerpunkt* of the crisis. The problem areas now were the UAR, Guinea, and Ghana, all of which sent troops to ONUC, troops which would probably act for Lumumba and Gizenga without UN consent if the Belgians didn't leave Kamina base. The Soviets were carrying on a vociferous diplomatic and propaganda offensive[61] in the UN in which "all of these elements working to stymie efforts favourable to the UN." Word got back to the Americans through Lodge that Hammarskjöld's moves were now "influenced by news which reached him of systematic action by Soviet agents to sabotage [ONUC]...Hammarskjöld had to act in order to avoid 'a kind of Korea'."[62]

The only solution, as Bunche and Hammarskjöld saw it, was that ONUC forces had to move into Katanga and take over Kamina base from the Belgians. This of course would aggravate the pro-Western Tshombe, who would see the UN occupation as a tool of the Lumumbaist central government designed to overthrow Katanga. Another problem was that ONUC's terms of reference were such that force could only be used in self defence. Hammarskjöld would have to go back to the Security Council and get authorization for ONUC to do so. It would be better, however, to have ONUC peacefully inserted into Katanga. When he approached the Belgians, they would not cooperate. The Secretary General was exasperated and privately suggested that "the diplomatic and political complications and the risks experienced on previous UN operations...[were] nothing compared to this."[63]

Kunetsov viciously attacked the Secretary General's integrity in the Security Council and declared that ONUC was "a cover for the continued occupation by Belgian forces of Katanga." Dag Hammarskjöld decided that the stakes were so high that he would personally accompany the ONUC forces into Katanga. Charles Ritchie was shown "in strict confidence" the plan of action which involved flying part of the Swedish Battalion into

Katanga's capital, Elisabethville. Canada had no objections.[64] Indeed, Canadian diplomats understood that

> whether the UN likes it or not, it will probably prove extremely difficult to avoid involvement in the domestic affairs of the Congo. there is not only the question of relations between Katanga and the Central government but also the relations among conflicting political and tribal elements....By its very presence the UN is likely to favour certain political developments and discourage others; and there is a risk that UN officials, however, well meaning, may let their personnel views colour too overtly their relations with the Congolese.[65]

With the Secretary General embarked in General Von Horn's white Convair transport followed by four DC-4s full of Swedish troops, Hammarskjöld negotiated with Tshombe via aircraft radio while the aircraft were circling the city. These negotiations eventually succeeded and the troops were brought in. ONUC now had a presence in Elisabethville and negotiations were underway to remove Belgian troops stationed at Kamina airbase. Hammarskjöld's gamble paid off, but this did not stop Soviet-bloc criticism in the UN, nor did it stop Lumumba's efforts to destabilize ONUC. Charles Ritchie noted that the Soviets were "playing a tricky game at the moment, lending Lumumba out and out support for whatever mischief he can make while at the same time appearing to support action by the Security Council and the Secretary General."[66]

ONUC's success in Katanga may have stimulated Canadian policymakers in a positive way. Operation MALLARD got underway and the first Canadian transports finally started to arrive in the Congo on 11 August, bringing in the much-needed ONUC signals unit's personnel, followed by American C-124 Globemaster aircraft carrying the Canadian signals equipment. Canada lacked strategic lift and had to rely on the Americans since Canada's Yukon and Northstar transports were not large enough to accept the large signals vehicles.[67]

While this operation was in progress, the Soviets attacked Canada both publicly and in the Security Council. Behaving as though Canada was a criminal nation, Kunetsov declared that "Canada is known to be a member of the NATO military bloc, as well as Belgium, which has committed aggression against the Independent Republic of the Congo." For many minutes the Soviet representative droned on about Canadian imperial aggression. External Affairs' rational explanation of the need for ONUC to have adequate signals communications was drowned out.[68]

Not coincidentally, Patrice Lumumba publicly called for the replacement of non-African ONUC forces with forces from Soviet-backed countries like Ghana and that "western" ONUC forces in Katanga be replaced with ANC troops. He then demanded that ONUC provide his military forces with transport aircraft so that he could "restore order" himself and to turn over Belgian military equipment to the ANC. It is clear that there was a coordinated attack on the ONUC in progress. The propaganda attack was about to become physical.[69]

At this point Lumumbaist elements targeted the Canadian ONUC signals contingent as it landed at dispersed sites around the country. Between 18 and 27 August, there was a series of six incidents in which Canadian soldiers were detained and beaten. The first occurred on 18 August when the ANC disarmed, assaulted, and threatened to kill fourteen Canadians at Ndjili airport. Ghanaian ONUC troops led by Indian Brigadier Indar Jit Rikyhe intervened. Two days later, a Canadian and an Indian ONUC officer received the same treatment.[70]

Ralph Bunche tried to reach Lumumba to protest the first incidents, but was blocked from entering the Prime Minister's residence by ANC troops and was subsequently abused by them. Hammarskjöld and Bunche informed Canadian representatives that they were "fully convinced that Fomin [Soviet Ambassador] in Leopoldville is having the worst influence on Lumumba, who in any event has shown himself [to be] arrogant, excitable and completely unpredictable."[71]

On 21 August, ONUC's Stanleyville advance party, which included a Canadian officer, was beaten by troops loyal to Lumumba. Six days later, the worst incident to date occurred when four Canadian signalers and five USAF personnel were dragged off a Globemaster at Stanleyville and beaten, while seven more Canadians were thrashed by a mob and paraded shoe-less through the streets.[72] Finally, on 29 August, two Canadians and eight Americans were attacked and beaten by a mob while Lumumba was giving a speech at Stanleyville airport. He made no move to intervene in the city which was his political stronghold.

In all incidents, Canadian troops were accused by Lumumbaists of being Belgian paratroopers in disguise. One work on Canadian peacekeeping states that it was all a case of "mistaken identity."[73] Canadian intelligence analysis, however, noted that the incidents were part of a larger strategy to discredit ONUC. Targeting the Canadian contribution was the crucial *schwerpunkt* since, due to geography and space, signals were so critical to the UN operation in the Congo.[74] Lumumba "is personally involved in 'witch hunts' and does not give centralized control or direction" so that the spontaneous incidents could also" be attributed to the stupidity of the Congolese."[75] The Americans subsequently learned that, in addition to Fomin, a bevy of Nkrumah's Ghanaian advisors and an Algerian FLN agent were advising Lumumba on how to expel the UN forces from the Congo.[76]

Diefenbaker was publicly outraged at this series of incidents, but in private he told Cabinet that this underscored his earlier view that "the presence of white troops in darkest Africa might have an inflammatory effect." Furthermore, Diefenbaker said, "Canada had no grounds to protest the recent detentions of Canadians in the Congo to check their credentials because any sovereign state was entitled to check the certificates of aliens." In his view, these were Canadians serving with the UN and therefore only the UN could protest. Clearly, the Prime Minister did not want to get involved and in fact championed withdrawing the Canadian contingent if the situation deteriorated. Indeed, the next batch of Army personnel preparing to deploy were held back.[77]

Fortunately there were no strenuous calls by Pearson in Opposition for the withdrawal of Canadian troops from ONUC. Canada refused to be pushed around and intimidated. Indeed, UN requests for Canadian military technical assistance beyond the signals unit was examined. External Affairs believed that the "provision of Canadian personnel under contract to Congo if handled carefully may help to some extent to ward off the risk of large infusion of Soviet bloc personnel. The success of the operation depends of course on Congo government becoming reasonably stable...."[78]

Lumumba, meanwhile, accepted a Soviet "offer" of strategic lift aircraft which were subsequently used to transport ANC forces (which had been re-equipped with Belgian weapons at Ralph Bunche's prompting so that the ANC could start to train and learn to behave like a real army) to put down an uprising of Ba-luba tribesmen. With support from covert Czech advisors, Lumumba's forces killed thousands. The Katangese thought they would be next, which prompted increased covert Belgian support for Moise Tshombe's people.[79]

The further deterioration of the Congo situation prompted the Americans to examine more drastic measures. Hammarskjöld's views were relayed to the National Security Council. The UN Secretary General thought Lumumba was "an impossible person" and that one "explanation for his up and down behaviour may be that he takes dope." Hammarskjöld was also "worried about Nkrumah" working too closely with Lumumba. The US Joint Chiefs of Staff, on the other hand, considered "it essential that the airfield at Kitona and the port of Banana and the Kamina base complex...remain in friendly hands and that they be denied to the military forces of the Soviet Bloc" since "the protection of shipping is a major task vital to any war effort." ONUC counted as a "friendly force" and the Lumumbaist elements of the ANC did not qualify.[80]

By the end of August 1960, after the latest beatings of Canadian and American servicemen, the National Security Council Special Group Subcommittee for Covert Operations concluded that Patrice Lumumba's "removal must be an urgent and prime objective" of any American activity in the region.[81] American policymakers agreed with Hammarskjöld: the Congo could not be sorted out until "Lumumba was broken." Lumumba was repeatedly referred to as "another Castro."[82]

INTO THE ABYSS: SEPTEMBER 1960-JANUARY 1961

The situation as it stood in the Congo throughout August and early September was fluid. The main issue for Lumumba was the continued presence of Belgian troops at Kamina and Kitona. The Belgians insisted that the treaty permitted these forces, while Lumumba declared that aspect of the treaty null and void because of Belgium's use of the bases to intervene to protect her citizens from the ANC. Attempts by the UN and American leadership to develop alternatives like stationing UN forces at these sites were undermined by the assault on ONUC's legitimacy and Soviet suggestions that national ONUC contingents from Soviet client states could or would be used to secure them.

A debate started between the US State Department and the Joint Chiefs of Staff and NATO as to the actual strategic importance of the bases to NATO. The Canadian position developed in External Affairs and National Defence was that ONUC was an acceptable method to accomplish Canadian and NATO objectives, namely filling the power vacuum before the Soviets could, building the emerging state, and then protecting it from subversion. The base issue was now secondary to that effort. The fact that one of the bases was in the secessionist and mineral rich Katanga province did, however, complicate the matter.[83]

Patrice Lumumba issued more and more public threats to invite the Soviets in if the UN would not do his bidding. As if to anticipate what was to come, Hammarskjöld cautioned Christian Herter not to have Lumumba killed since the Secretary General didn't "want him to become a martyr."[84] Kasavubu, long dormant, met with Andrew Cordier on 3 September and asked him if ONUC forces would arrest some dissidents for him. Cordier said no but did prevent dissident forces from using the UN-controlled radio station for propaganda purposes. Street-level intrigue continued in Leopoldville as the UN held its breath. Kasavubu then dismissed Lumumba as Prime Minister. Lumumbaist coup plotters were then arrested as Lumumba himself went on the radio and called for a revolution. On 6 September, ANC forces led by Colonel Joseph Mobutu seized power and then retained Kasavubu as President. The UN was now in a quandary. ONUC was in the country to support the central government. Which government had legitimacy now? ONUC troops were even guarding Lumumba's residence![85]

The situation was equally precarious in the UN Security Council. It was quite possible that pro-Lumumba elements would demand ONUC's withdrawal. This would accomplish Soviet objectives since it would allow Lumumbaist forces supported with Soviet airlift to challenge Mobutu's forces. The situation would probably escalate from there and the Belgians would intervene again, which in turn would draw in pro-Soviet ONUC units. It was conceivable that the United States would then intervene with military forces; there was even concern that the Indonesian, Ghanaian and Guinean ONUC units would support Lumumba, and affect the delicate game being played out in the Pacific between the Netherlands, Indonesia, and the United States as well as the French and British relations with their former colonies (see Chapter 7).[86] The UAR airborne battalion even ignored von Horn's orders and moved into Leopoldville to protect the Soviet embassy.[87]

Mobutu then ordered the Soviet Union to withdraw its 400 "technicians" and aircraft, which they did with profuse protestations. A Canadian estimate indicated that a further 600 Soviets were inbound and turned around in Khartoum.[88] Soviet and supporting bloc diplomats were also expelled, while Guinea, Morocco and Indonesia pulled their troops out of ONUC.[89]

The Soviet response was to increase its attacks on ONUC in the UN General Assembly and the Security Council by mobilizing its allies. Although the diplomatic moves and countermoves in those arenas are detailed and complex, they were essentially attempts by the Soviets to alter ONUC's mandate, modify the Secretary General's terms of reference, and undermine funding to ONUC. It was a concerted assault on the confidence of the UN as an institution and was quickly cast as "the UN crisis" by Canadian diplomats in New York, once personal attacks were made against Dag Hammarskjöld by Soviet representatives.[90]

As Charles Ritchie pointed out, Soviet tactics were to "delay, divide, and confuse the issue." Canada's objective in this conflict was to generate support for Hammarskjöld and ONUC in every way possible. It was an election year in the United States and the Americans "may be tempted to overplay their hand" which might exacerbate the Western effort in the UN.[91]

The Americans were now supporting proposals to recognize Kasavubu, Mobuto, and company as the legitimate government in the Congo. Initially, Lumumba had been temporarily neutralized during the coup when he was placed under house arrest. When his residence was raided by Mobutu's forces, however, a briefcase was found which contained a series of letters from Kwame Nkrumah to Lumumba which detailed how to set up and run a dictatorship. Other materials included secret appeals to Moscow and Beijing for assistance, and documentation on how to use torture as a political weapon.[92] These men demanded that ONUC arrest Lumumba and turn him over to them. Ralph Bunche's replacement, Rejeshwar Dayal of India, resisted this demand.[93]

While the debate raged throughout September over what was to happen to Lumumba, new rounds of intertribal violence rocked the Congo. Mobutu planned to attack Katanga through Kasai province and eliminate the Tshombe regime under the noses of ONUC. Lumumba's campaign against the Ba-lubas in Kasai paved the way, but in turn generated a backlash against the Ba-lubas by the Lulu tribal administration in Luluabourg, who had suffered at the Ba-lubas' hands. ONUC forces dissuaded Mobutu's ANC from attacking in Katanga, but could not stop the Ba-luba-Lulu massacres. The Katangese,led by European mercenaries, backed the Ba-lubas and were moving into Kasai province to engage the Lulus. The ANC was preparing to enter Katanga in response. ONUC Force Commander General von Horn wanted the Secretary General to beef up ONUC so that it included tanks, artillery, and air support. This was, in von Horn's view, the only way to control the Congo. Hammarskjöld dismissed this as akin to "starting an armaments race."[94]

ONUC forces were then employed to generate a ceasefire in the region. During the course of these operations, eleven Irish UN soldiers were massacred in a particularly brutal fashion by forces operating on the Katanga border. This incident prompted the Diefenbaker Cabinet to re-examine the terms of reference for the Canadian ONUC forces and greater controls were put in place to prevent their possible misemployment.[95]

The situation in the Congo remained tense. Von Horn was relieved as Force Commander after ongoing differences of opinion with Hammarskjöld were made public. There was also significant friction generated between the Indian ONUC contingent and von Horn's staff when they did an "end run" to appeal to Dayal on several occasions. The Canadian policy on ONUC at this point remained one of supporting ONUC diplomatically while at the same time using Canadian ONUC staff officers like Colonel J.A. Berthiaume to improve the formation's operational effectiveness. These measures included the creation of a Canadian-like staff system, regular and accurate reports and returns, the placement of Canadian signals detachments in key locations to facilitate information flow, and the improvement of the UN intelligence system. External Affairs wanted Berthiaume to remain in ONUC HQ in order to "maintain both Canadian and Western influence."[96]

The diplomatic situation in the UN General Assembly was deadlocked. Then, on 27 November 1960, Patrice Lumumba disappeared. Mobutuist ANC forces pursued and eventually arrested him on 1 December which triggered rioting in Stanleyville and throughout Orientale Province. (ONUC forces, not understanding that Lumumba was on the run, assisted him which prompted demonstrations in Leopoldville against the UN). Even while imprisoned in Thysville, Lumumba continued to exert influence in certain ANC quarters. Rumours spread that Antoine Gizenga and ANC forces loyal to him would attempt a coup against Mobutu and Kasavubu and perhaps release Lumumba. A 13 January 1961 mutiny of ANC forces appears to have forced Mobutu's hand (Ghanaian ONUC forces were incapable of dealing with it since *they* were mutinying among themselves over housing). Arrangements were made between the Leopoldville government and Tshombe in Katanga: Lumumba was transferred to Elisabethville. He was then murdered in the presence of Godefroid Munungo and Moise Tshombe on either 17 or 18 January 1961.[97]

Once it was known that the Katangese had killed Lumumba, there was a backlash at the UN in New York. A number of initially pro-ONUC members from the Afro-Asia bloc withdrew their support when the Soviets and their allies claimed that Lumumba was murdered by the Belgians and/or the CIA. Then Antoine Gizenga started agitating in Stanleyville to form a separate state. Consequently, the Congo was in the process of splitting into a secessionist Katanga (which was oriented towards the Belgians and the French), a semi-legitimate government in Leopoldville backed by the United States, and several burgeoning independence movements in practically every province. The United Nations favoured a federalist state controlled by Leopoldville. Canada backed the United States and the United Nations.

FLOUNDERING AROUND THE DEEP END: 1961-1962

Gizengaist forces operating from Stanleyville now moved against ANC forces based in Kasai Province, to which ONUC was unable to respond effectively. Mobutu then initiated a purge of Lumumbaist, now Gizengaist, elements of the ANC and government. The violent incidents increased between ONUC forces and the Leopoldville ANC. Tshombe now saw that it was time for Katanga to take advantage of the confused situation and once again make an attempt at full independence. This move even plunged the Congo deeper into the abyss.

Paul Henri Spaak, former NATO Secretary General and now Belgian Prime Minister, appealed for Congo unification. His argument, which now had more and more credibility, was that Gizenga was developing Orientale Province into a pro-Soviet stronghold to be used as a springboard to take over the whole Congo.[98] Spaak believed that Katanga had to remain part of the Congo to set the example. Tshombe, however, was making plans to expel potential Gizengaist supporters from northern Katanga which bordered on Orientale Province: he was even developing a mercenary-led army capable of doing so. Similarly, Tshombe had problems with the so-called "Province of Luluaba" led by Jason Sendwe in Luluabourg. Sendwe's people thought Tshombe had not done enough to stop Lumumba's forces from killing Ba-lubas back in 1960. Sendwe initiated a campaign to drive out pro-

Katanga supporters from eastern Kasai Province. Their favoured method was to flog such people to death with bicycle chains. Tshombe responded with military force.[99]

Over time, the Leopoldville government pressured the UN into conducting what amounted to a counterinsurgency operation in Katanga throughout 1961, in part to pre-empt war between Orientale and Katanga. The details of these operations are covered elsewhere.[100] In essence, UN forces were not operating as peace observation forces (like UNTSO or UNMOGIIP) nor were they patrolling an established interpositionary demarcation line as they were with UNEF. In the Congo, ONUC was using mobile columns, light bombers, and attack aircraft, supported with a comprehensive intelligence system which included signals intelligence and photo-reconnaissance, to keep the peace. In essence, ONUC was operating more like UNPROFOR in Bosnia during the 1990s or KFOR in Kosovo in the 2000s than the so-called "classic" interpositionary peacekeeping model like UNEF.[101]

From a Canadian context, the problems in the Congo required re-examination of Canadian objectives and interests throughout 1961. Canadian diplomats agreed with Andrew Cordier who feared that if ONUC was forced out of the Congo, "something in the nature of a Spanish Civil War situation would ensue." References were also made to Korea. That was just on the ground in Africa. Even if war did not ensue, the UN's credibility as an international institution would also be severely damaged if it had to withdraw ONUC. The international organization would then be unable to perform the role Canada had envisioned.[102]

British analysis on Africa which was passed onto Canada through the ABC intelligence relationship noted that "The Satellites are at present helping to consolidate Communist influence in the bridgeheads already won, and reconnoitering the possibilities of further penetration." Those bridgeheads were Mali, Guinea, and Ghana.[103] External Affairs requested further analysis. The expulsion of Soviet bloc advisors had seriously crippled their efforts in the Congo. Opportunism was the watchword as the Soviets sought means to re-insert themselves into the region. Meanwhile, the continent would continue "to play an important part in the Soviet Union's grandiose plan to harry the West, in the United Nations and elsewhere, on the issues of disarmament, anti-colonialism and the overhaul of UN machinery."[104]

The matter was studied carefully within External Affairs throughout 1961. External analysis coined a term, "competitive co-existence," to describe what was happening: the Soviets were employing "a variety of instruments of which the most important are its diplomatic activities, economic aid, propaganda, direct political action, and guerrilla warfare." Communist theory was "irrelevant" since "great political power can be built on intellectual trash."[105] The Soviets would continue trying to gain power in the Congo and even if they failed, there were still opportunities to embarrass the West.

The Diefenbaker Government, however, was distracted with other events throughout 1961. The Cold War crisis of the day, Berlin, was foremost, along with the increasingly public debate over nuclear armament for Canada's NATO and NORAD forces. The Congo crisis was secondary for quite some time and its management left to External Affairs specialists (who were members of the UN's newly-formed Congo Committee) and the officers and men of 57 Canadian Signal Unit. Even the mass execution, mutilation, and cannibalization of thirteen Italian Air Force personnel by an enraged mob at Kindu in November 1961 attracted little attention in Ottawa: it was just one more massacre in the Congo abattoir. There were minor discussions on providing two C-119 transports to ONUC or RCAF ground personnel, requests which were routinely granted.[106]

The use of ONUC forces to expel foreign mercenaries from Katanga remained questionable under the rather hazy UN mandate and was roundly criticized in the UN forums and by the press. The situation reached the point where the more extreme Katangese and their supporters seriously believed that the UN was doing the bidding of the Soviet Union. Paul Henri Spaak was even referred to as a Communist in Katangese propaganda broadcasts. The hatred of Dag Hammarskjöld reached such a fever pitch that, as some believed, the French *Organization Armee Secret* (OAS) members (people who thought French President Charles de Gaulle was a communist sympathizer for abandoning Algeria) were brought in to sabotage Hammarskjöld's aircraft, *Albertina*. Who paid for them to do so may never be known: some say Godefroid Munungo, some say British, Rhodesian, or Belgian operatives. In any event, on 17 September 1961, the UN Secretary General left for Ndola, Rhodesia to meet with Tshombe and arrange peace in Katanga. The DC-6B crashed on approach and Hammarskjöld and his staff were all killed.[107]

As Dag Hammarskjöld's body lay in state, confusion reigned. The Soviets attempted to immediately push their agenda for UN leadership (called the "troika" concept: essentially the creation of three Secretary Generals) which would have increased Soviet control over vital elements of the UN headquarters in New York. These efforts were resisted and the Burmese Ambassador replaced Hammarskjöld as Secretary General. The cigar-smoking man from Burma was neutral, and the very relaxed "warm, humorous and serene" U Thant had no apparent enemies.[108]

In December 1961 there was continuing criticism within the UN over ONUC counterinsurgency operations in Katanga. The British were more deeply involved and attempting to block or limit these efforts. On one level, there was a British belief that Katanga was a bulwark against communist infiltration in the region. At another level, British motives related to possible threats to Rhodesian stability and the fact that the Katangese were prepared to grant British mining companies concessions in return for political support.[109]

Diefenbaker and Green were caught in a dilemma. The Canadian media proclaimed that there was a "Failure in the Congo."[110] Canada had supported the UN throughout the Congo affair, but now UN interests might not coincide with those of Britain which Diefenbaker held so dear. Cabinet met and considered the situation late in December. There was a prevailing belief that the UN perhaps "had gone too far in attempting to force the Congolese into one federated nation, disregarding the tribal background and the varying degrees of development in the different sectors." Canada could not, however, just withdraw from the effort since ONUC was completely dependent on 57 Canadian Signals Unit. Canada would attempt to moderate ONUC behavior through the UN itself instead of making such a radical move.[111]

The American perspective had to be considered as well. Eisenhower was succeeded by John F. Kennedy in 1961. In the Kennedy administration, the Congo was viewed as another Laos. The problem was one of appearances: ONUC operations against Katanga came in the wake of the Bay of Pigs and Kennedy was skittish about anything which might be labeled as "American involvement" by the Soviets or the press. Unlike Eisenhower, Kennedy was more sensitive to the British and Belgian perspectives on the situation, particularly during the Berlin Crisis and the need for NATO unity. The Americans were divided on what to do, but finally chose to support Cyrille Adoula.[112]

Tshombe was persuaded to meet with Adoula, the man who replaced Kasavubu and Mobutu as the elected head of the Congo (with American backing: he was coerced into attending talks with the Katangese by the Kennedy administration). Mobutu remained as head of the ANC. Negotiations between the central government and Katanga were conducted throughout 1962. Tshombe eventually signed the Kitona Declaration whereby he recognized the existence of the federal government, but he reneged and ONUC had to be used with some vigor in Katanga in 1962 and again in 1963.[113]

In the background, there were other factors affecting Canadian policy in the Congo. In effect,

> the prime objective [of the Soviets] is to establish Soviet control over the Secretariat. The Congo operation has demonstrated the independent authority of the Secretary General and the inability of the Soviet Government, once it had agreed to UN involvement in the Congo, to influence the Secretary General's policy.[114]

If the Secretary General decided to move in other spheres, such as disarmament or arms control, External Affairs analysts thought that the Congo operations gave him a precedent if he chose to establish an international force to implement such a policy. In other words, there might be a precedent to establish a UN force to force one country or another to give up its nuclear weapons, for example. This Canadian analysis was provided to Howard Green. Consequently, precipitous Canadian action on the Congo matter might jeopardize Green's nuclear disarmament agenda.

When combined, all of these elements contributed to Diefenbaker's policy of maintaining the UN status quo. As things settled down in Europe and Asia, attention was gradually directed towards the Congo in 1962. Over time a plan emerged (based on a 1960 UN concept) by which the ANC would be trained by Western military personnel and ultimately its professionalism improved. This was seen as a critical step in the creation of a federal Congolese state. Joseph Mobutu continuously asked Canada to contribute francophone officers and NCOs to this effort. The Diefenbaker government was slow to act on this and other requests to strengthen ONUC with Canadian intelligence personnel. The Army did not have the additional personnel resources and was stretched thin globally. Until the Katanga succession issue was solved, Canada would not contribute training personnel.[115]

By the end of 1962, the dangerous Cuban Missile Crisis overshadowed all other crises. The Diefenbaker government's behaviour during that crisis contributed to its downfall in the spring of 1963 and the Congo problem was passed on to the new government led by Nobel Peace Prize winner, Lester B. "Mike" Pearson.

WHAT DID CANADA ACHIEVE BY CONTRIBUTING TO ONUC?

At the height of the UN crisis of 1961, External Affairs continued its campaign to explain Canadian participation in the UN to the public. The head of External Affairs' UN Division, G.S. Murray, emphasized the view that UN peacekeeping operations were effective at "preventing brushfire wars from becoming a nuclear holocaust." ONUC apparently fit into this category. For the realists in the audience, Murray pointed out that "Canadian support for the United Nations would not continue for long if we came to believe that this Organization did not serve the national interests of Canada."[116]

Despite Howard Green's protestations that Canada operated independently from the rest of NATO in UN circles,[117] it is evident that Canadian actions during the Congo crisis were in line with Canadian NATO interests at several levels. First, the matter of denying base areas critical in global war to hostile entities was important. Second, keeping a fragmenting NATO together was equally important. Third, preventing the Congo from exploding into a civil war which in turn would have been exploited by those hostile to Canadian interests was achieved. Finally, by subtly backing the UN in New York and in the field, Canada contributed to maintaining the UN as a credible international institution during the Cold War and prevented the organization's domination by Soviet puppets. This in turn prevented the discrediting of peace operations as an instrument for global stability: if the Congo crisis had had a different outcome, it is likely that UN operations in Cyprus, which was more critical to Canadian and NATO interests, would have been impossible to conduct.

Notes to Chapter 6

1. See Joseph Conrad, *Heart of Darkness* (New York: W.W. Norton and Co, 1988); Patrick Manning, *Francophone Sub-Saharan Africa 1880-1995* (Cambridge: Cambridge University Press, 1998); Adam Hochschild, *King Leopold's Ghost: A Story of Greed, Terror, and Heroism in Colonial Africa* (New York: Mariner Books, 1999) and Ieuan Ll. Griffiths, *The Atlas of African Affairs (2nd Ed)* (London: Routledge, 1993).

2. J.D. Hargreaves, *Decolonization in Africa* (New York: Longman, 1988), 88.

3. NAC RG 25 vol. 7034 file 6386-A-40 pt. 1, (13 May 57) message Economic Div to Commonwealth Div, "Hydroelectric Projects in Africa South of the Sahara," (7 Mar 58) message Embassy Brussels to SSEA, "Kouilou and Inga," (8 Oct 58) "Confidential Memorandum on Inga."

4. Larry Milberry, *The AVRO CF-100* (Toronto: CANAV Books, 1981), 151-153; NAC RG 24 vol. C280 file 1038-110 F-104G, (16 Dec 60) message Bonn to External Affairs, "Proposed Special Mission to Europe on Cooperation on the F-104G Program"; (13 Jul 60) message Bonn to External Affairs, "F-104 Program."

5. NAC RG 25 vol. 5869 file 50161-40 pt. 1.2, (9 Jul 58) message Canadian Ambassador, Brussels to SSEA, "Belgian Foreign Policy."

6. Maloney, *War Without Battles* Ch. 3 and 4.; NAC RG 25 vol. 7034 file 6386-A-40 pt. 1, (22 Oct 59) message Air Attaché to CANAIRHED, "Belgian Defence Budget."

7. Henri Anrys et al, *La Force Naval: De l'amiraute de Flandre a la Force Naval Belge* (Tielt: lannoo, 1992), 216-226; Robert J. Hanks, *The Cape Route: Imperiled Western Lifeline* (Washington D.C.: Institute for Foreign Policy Analysis, 1981); FRUS 1958- 1960: Africa, 425-427 (18 Aug 60) Twining to Gates, "Kamina and Kitona-Banana Bases"; Conor Cruise O'Brien, *To Katanga and Back: A UN Case History* (New York: Simon and Shuster 1962), 73; Ted Gup, *The Book of Honor: Covert Lives and Classified Deaths at the CIA* (New York: Doubleday, 2000), 146.

8. See, however, an External Affairs message RG 25 vol. 6991 file 5475-6-40 pt. 5, (12 Feb 60) PERMISNY to External Affairs Ottawa, "Africa and the United Nations" in which basing is discussed.

9. D.A. Low, *Eclipse of Empire* (Cambridge: Cambridge University Press, 1993), 215; Hargreaves, *Decolonization in Africa*, 148; Denis Smith, Rogue Tory, 353-366; Manning, *Francophone Sub-Saharan Africa*, 146-147.

10. Hargreaves, *Decolonization in Africa*, 177-178; Low, *Eclipse of Empire*, 223; FRUS 1958-1960: Africa, 251 (8 Oct 58) Herter-Wigny conversation, "Belgian Congo"; NAC RG 25 vol. 5869 file 50161-40 pt. 1.2, (16 Oct 58) USS to External Affairs, "Visit of Belgian Foreign Minister to USA."

11. NAC RG 25 vol. 7034 file 6386-A-40 pt. 1, (20 Feb 59) message Canadian Ambassador, Brussels to SSEA, "Belgian Investment in the Congo."

12. Paul-Henri Spaak, *The Continuing Battle: Memoirs of a European 1936-1966* (Toronto: Little Brown and Co., 1971), 357.

13. Hargreaves, *Decolonization in Africa*, 178

14. Spaak, *The Continuing Battle*, 358-362.

15. NAC RG 25 vol. 6991 file 5475-6-40 pt. 5, (26 Feb 60) message PERMISNY to External Affairs, "Africa."

16. NAC RG 25 vol. 6991 file 5475-6-40 pt. 5, (26 Feb 60) (17 Feb 60) PERMISNY to External Affairs, "Africa and the UN."

17. NAC RG 25 vol. 7034 file 6386-A-40 pt. 1.2, (19 Feb 60) message Brussels to External Affairs, "The Congo Round Table Conference."

18. Urquart, *Ralph Bunche: An American Life*, 307.

19. *FRUS 1958-1960: Africa*, 262 (18 Feb 60) memcon Burden and Dillon; p. 274 (5 May 60) NSC special meeting; p. 277 (23 Jun 60) message State to Leopoldville.

20. NAC RG 24 vol. 21485 file 2137.3 v.2, (30 Aug 60) Directorate of Military Intelligence, "Situation in the Congo Republic."

21. *FRUS 1958-1960: Africa*, 262-266 (25 Feb 60) memcon Burden and Lumumba.

22. Indar Jit Rikhye, *Military Adviser to the Secretary General: UN Peacekeeping and the Congo Crisis* (New York: St. Martin's Press, 1993), 22.

23. *FRUS 1958-1960: Africa*, 353-354 (25 Jul 60) NSC Meeting #453.

24. NAC RG 24 vol. 21485 file 2137.3 v.2, (30 Aug 60) Directorate of Military Intelligence, "Situation in the Congo Republic."

25. Urquart, *Hammarskjöld*, 392-394.

26. *FRUS 1958-1960: Africa*, 282, (8 Jul 60) message Embassy France to State.

27. Rikhye, *Military Adviser to the Secretary General*, 5; Urquart, *Hammarskjöld*, 393- 394; *FRUS 1958-1960: Africa*, 286-288 (10 Jul 60) message Embassy Belgium to State.

28. *FRUS 1958-1960: Africa*, 286-288 (10 Jul 60) message Embassy Belgium to State.

29. DDEL, Staff Secretariat International Security, Box 3 file: Congo (1),(9 Jul 60) message Brussels to SECSTATE.

30. O'Brien, *To Katanga and Back*, 118; von Horn, *Soldiering for Peace*, 190.

31. von Horn, *Soldiering for Peace*, 190.

32. Urquart, *Hammarskjöld*, 394.

33. *FRUS 1958-1960: Africa*, 293-295 (12 Jul 60) Eisenhower-Goodpaster conversation; (12 Jul 60) memcon Eisenhower and Herter; Rikhye, *Military Adviser to the Secretary General*, 6.

34. NAC RG 24 vol. 21484 file 2137.3 v.1, (11 Jul 60) AHQ, "Operational Instruction 60/1: Standby Battalion Group."

35. Urquart, *Hammarskjöld*, 396; *FRUS 1958-1960: Africa*, 300-301 (13 Jul 60) memcon Eisenhower and Herter; pp. 303-304, (13 Jul 60) message State to USUN."

36. Urquart, *Hammarskjöld*, 398; *FRUS 1958-1960: Africa*, 306-307, (14 Jul 60) memcon Herter-Lodge.

37. *FRUS 1958-1960: Africa*, 314-317 (15 Jul 60) memcon Herter and Schyver; 320-322 (18 Jul 60) message USUN to State.

38. NAC RG 2, vol. 2747, Cabinet Conclusions, 14 Jul 60.

39. DHH, file 73/297 (17 Jul 60) "United Nations Force: Congo Republic Canadian Contribution."

40. Urquart, *Hammarskjöld*, 405; Rikhye, *Military Adviser to the Secretary General*, 11.

41. *FRUS 1958-1960: Africa*, 330-332 (19 Jul 60) message Burden to State; 338-342 (21 Jul 60) NSC Meeting #452.

42. DHH, file 73/297 (18 Jul 60) Minutes of a Special Meeting of the Army Council"; NAC RG 24 vol. 21484 file 2137.3 v.1, (19 Jul 60) "Possible Canadian Contribution to UN forces in the Congo Republic Synopsis No. 1."

43. Donald M. Fleming, *So Very Near: The Political Memoirs of the Honourable Donald M. Fleming Vol. Two: The Summit Years* (Toronto: McClelland and Stewart, 1985), 236.

44. NAC RG 2, vol. 2747, Cabinet Conclusions, 19 July 1960.

45. von Horn, *Soldiering for Peace*, 148-153.

46. NAC RG 24 vol. 21482 file 2137.1.v.10 (4 Feb 58) message from Canadian Ambassador, Stockhom to SSEA, "Head of UN Truce Supervisory Commission in Palestine (UNTSO)."

47. The matter of Greek support to this operation became a minor cause celebre when Senator John F. Kennedy went public with this information. There has been no adequate explanation for this NATO member's behaviour during the Congo affair. See DDEL, Herter Papers, box 13 file: CAH Telecons 8/31/60 (3) (dtg obscured) telecon Herter-Kennedy.

48. *FRUS 1958-1960: Africa*, 338-342 (21 Jul 60) NSC Meeting #452; pp. 344-345, (21 Jul 60) Herter to all missions.

49. Tarleton H. Watkins, "Operation NEW TAPE: The Congo Airlift," Air University Quarterly Review , Vol. XIII No. 1 (Summer 1961), 18-35.

50. NAC RG 2, vol. 2747, Cabinet Conclusions, 21 July 1960.

51. Granatstein, *A Man of Influence*, 334.

52. Robinson, *Diefenbaker's World*, 148.

53. *FRUS 1958-1960: Africa*, 367-370 (28 Jul 60) memcon Schyver, Herter and Herter, Green; DDEL, Herter Papers, box 13, file: CAH Telecons 7/1/60 to 8/31/60 Box 2, (28 Jul 60) memcon Green-Herter.

54. NAC RG 24 vol. 21484 file 2137.3 v.1, (28 Jul 6) message NATO Paris to External, "Congo: Withdrawal of Belgian Troops." These views regarding NATO fragmentation were supported by SACEUR, General Lauris Norstad. See *FRUS 1958-1960: Africa*, 384-385 (4 Aug 60) memcon Burden and Herter. The reference to disgraced British Defence Minister Profumo is intriguing but obscure.

55. George Ignatieff, *The Making of a Peacemonger: The Memoirs of George Ignatieff* (Toronto: University of Toronto Press, 1985), 191.

56. NAC RG 24 vol. 21484 file 2137.3 v.1, (9 Aug 60) message Brussels to External Affairs, "Congo-NATO"; (2 Aug 60) message Brussels to External, Congo: Situation in Bru."

57. NAC RG 2, vol. 2747, Cabinet Conclusions, 28 July 1960.

58. NAC RG 24 vol. 21484 file 2137.3 v.1, (23 Jul 60) message PERMISNY to External Affairs, "Congo: Use of RCAF Aircraft"; (23 Jul 60) message External Affairs to PERMISNY,"Congo: Use of RCAF Aircraft."

59. NAC RG 2, vol. 2747, Cabinet Conclusions, 30 July 1960.

60. NAC RG 24 vol. 21484 file 2137.3 v.1, (27 Jul 60) message PERMISNY to External Affairs, "Congo-UN Force"; DHH, file 73/297 (4 Aug 60) Minutes of a Special Meeting of the Army Council"; (8 Aug 60) message External Affairs to PERMISNY "Congo: Canadian Contingent for UN Force."

61. NAC RG 25 vol. 5108 file 5475-6-40 pt. 6, (15 Aug 60) message Moscow to External Affairs Ottawa, "Congo"; (8 Aug 60) message Moscow to External Affairs Ottawa, "Congo."

62. *FRUS 1958-1960: Africa*, 395-399 (7 Aug 60) message USUN to State.

63. NAC RG 24 vol. 21484 file 2137.3 v.1, (3 Aug 60) message Bru to External Affairs, "Congo-Katanga"; Urquart, *Hammarskjöld*, 413.

64. NAC RG 24 vol. 21484 file 2137.3.v.1, (4 Aug 60) message PERMISNY to External Affairs Ottawa, "Congo."

65. NAC RG 25 vol. 5108 file 5475-6-40 pt. 6, (15 Aug 60) message PERMISNY to External Affairs Ottawa, "Congo."

66. NAC RG 25 vol. 5108 file 5475-6-40 pt. 6, (15 Aug 60) message PERMISNY to External Affairs Ottawa, "Congo."

67. DHH, (16 Jul 66) "Report No. 8: Canada and Peace-keeping Operations in the Congo."

68. NAC RG 24 vol. 21484 file 2137.3.v.1, (8 Aug 60) message PERMISNY to External Affairs Ottawa, "Congo."

69. NAC RG 24 vol. 21484 file 2137.3.v.1, (18 Aug 60) message CANARMY to distribution list, "Intelligence Summary: Congo Situation."

70. NAC RG 24 vol. 21484 file 2137.3.v.1, (18 Aug 60) message Brussels to External Affairs Ottawa, "Congo"; (18 Aug 60) message PERMISNY to distribution list, "Congo ."

71. NAC RG 24 vol. 21484 file 2137.3.v.1, (19 Aug 60) message PERMISNY to External Affairs Ottawa, "Congo."

72. NAC RG 24 vol. 21484 file 2137.3.v.2 (19 Aug 60) report to Lt Col J.A. Berthiame from S/S D.K. Johnson; (20 Aug 60) Consulate General, Leopoldville to USSEA, "Incident Between Congolese Army and Canadian Troops"; (27 Aug 60) message Leo to External Affairs Ottawa, "Emergency from Wood."

73. See Fred Gaffen, *In The Eye of the Storm*.

74. The same technique was used in the 1990s in Somalia, Bosnia, and, more horrifyingly, in Rwanda when ten members of the Belgian Army contingent were butchered by one faction so as to deliberately generate calls by the Belgian population to withdraw from UNAMIR, making that formation less effective in carrying out its duties. A similar action occurred in Somalia in 1993 when an entire platoon of Pakistani peacekeeping troops were targeted and slaughtered.

75. NAC RG 24 vol. 21484 file 2137.3.v.2 (30 Aug 60) Directorate of Military Intelligence, "Situation in the Congo Republic." See also (18 Aug 60) letter Wood to Green, "Congo-UN Relations."

76. *FRUS 1958-1960: Africa*, 419-421 (17 Aug 60) message Timberlake to State.

77. NAC RG 2, Cabinet Minutes, 17 August 1960.

78. NAC RG 25 vol. 7034 file: 6386-A-40 pt. 1.2, (21 Aug 60) message External Affairs Ottawa to PERMISNY, "Congo-Technical Assistance."

79. Urquart, *Hammarskjöld*, 435; von Horn, *Soldiering for Peace*, 205-206; DDEL Staff Secretariat International Security Box 3 file: Congo Sitrep (7), (26 Aug 60) JCS Situation Report 42-60; (28 Aug 60) JCS Situation Report.

80. *FRUS 1958-1960: Africa*, 421-424 (18 Aug 60) 456th Meeting of the NSC; pp. 425- 427 (18 Aug 60) Chairman of the JCS to SECDEF, "Kitona-Banana and Kamina Bases."

81. *FRUS 1958-1960: Africa*, 443 (25 Aug 60) NSC Special Group Subcommittee for Covert Operations.

82. *FRUS 1958-1960: Africa*, 444-446 (26 Aug 60) message USUN to State; pp. 448-449 (29 Aug 60) message Embassy Congo to State.

83. DDEL, NSC Series, Box 1 file: Africa-US Policy (1), (1 Aug 60) US Policy Towards the Congo (NSC 6001); DDEL, Staff Secretariat International Security, Box 2 file: Canada (4) (20 Sep 60) memcon Green, Heeney, Herter, Merchant, "Exchange of Views: UN Matters"; DDEL, Staff Secretariat International Security, Box 2 file: Congo (2) (2 Aug 60) message State to distribution list.

84. DDEL, Herter Papers, box 13, file: CAH Telecons 7/1/60 to 8/31/60 (1), (15 Aug 60) telecon Hammarskjöld-Herter.

85. Urquart, *Hammarskjöld*, 444; see also NAC RG 24 vol. 21484 file 2137.3.v.2 (6 Sep 60) message Brussels to External Affairs Ottawa, "UN and Congo Crisis."

86. DDEL, Herter papers box 10, File: Miscellaneous Memoranda 1960/61 (1) (26 Sep 60) memcon Hammarskjöld-Herter; NAC RG 24 vol. 21484 file 2137.3.v.2 (9 Sep 60) message PERMISNY to External Affairs Ottawa, "Congo-Security Council Meeting."

87. von Horn, *Soldiering for Peace,* 213.

88. NAC RG 24 vol. 21484 file 2137.3.v.2, (17 Sep 60) message Leo to External Affairs Ottawa, "Congo-Soviet Technicians."

89. O'Brien, *To Katanga and Back*, 96.

90. NAC RG 25 vol. 6460 file 5475-FA-40 pt. 3, (25 Jan 61) Statement by G.S. Murray to CIIA, "Canada and the United Nations."

91. NAC RG 24 vol. 21484 file 2137.3.v.3, (18 Sep 60) message PERMISNY to External Affairs Ottawa, "Congo: Special Emergency Session of the UNGA."

92. von Horn, *Soldiering for Peace*, 211.

93. Bunche was withdrawn after the Soviets accused him of being a CIA agent of influence. The fact that Bunche was ex-OSS didn't help matters.

94. von Horn, *Soldiering for Peace*, 191, 214-215.

95. NAC, RG 2, (10 Nov 60) Cabinet Conclusions.

96. See von Horn, *Soldiering for Peace*; NAC RG 24 vol. 21484 file 2137.3.v.3, (29 Dec 60) message Green to PERMISNY, "Congo: Canadian Views about Current UN Operations"; NAC RG 24 vol. 21484 file 2137.3.v. 4 (18 Jan 61) message External Affairs Ottawa to PERMISNY, "Col Berthiaume-Transfer from ONUC to UNTSO."

97. O'Brien, *To Katanga and Back*, 97-103; Urquart, *Hammarskjöld*, 501-505; Dayal, *Mission for Hammarshkold: The Congo Crisis*, 190.

98. Canadian reports indicate that there were several Soviet "journalists" and at least twelve UAR officers in Stanleyville providing training and intelligence support to Gizengaist factions. See NAC RG 25 vol. 7034 file 6386-A-40 pt. 1.3 (27 Mar 61) message External Affairs Ottawa to distribution list, "Congo: Situation in Orientale."

99. See O'Brien, *To Katanga and Back* ; NAC RG 25 vol. 7034 file 6386-A-40 pt. 1.3 (17 Mar 61) message London to External Ottawa, "Congo Situation in Orientale Province."

100. See Rikhye, *Military Adviser to the Secretary General*, Dayal, *Mission for Hammarskjöld* and O'Brien, *To Katanga and Back*.

101. See Rikhye, *Military Advisor to the Secretary General*; Ernest W. Lefever, *Crisis in the Congo: A UN Force in Action* (New York: The Brookings Institution, 1965); Michael Harbottle, *The Blue Berets: The Story of The United Nations Peacekeeping Forces* (Harrisburg: Stackpole Books, 1972).

102. NAC RG 25 vol. 7034 file 6386-A-40 pt. 1.3 (27 Jan 61) message External Affairs Ottawa to distribution list, "Congo."

103. NAC RG 25 vol. 5560 file 12774-40 pt. 2, (20 Feb 61) No. 24 INTEL "Communist Satellite Activities in Africa (excluding Egypt, Sudan, and Libya)."

104. NAC RG 25 vol. 5560 file 12774-40 pt. 2, (16 Mar 61) Research Department Memorandum," Communist Bloc Interests in Africa No. 6: September to December 1960."

105. NAC RG 25 vol. 5560 file 12774-40 pt. 2, (11 Oct 61) "Soviet Non-Military Strategy in Underdeveloped Areas."

106. NAC RG 2 (23 Sep 61) (23 Oct 61) Cabinet Conclusions.

107. Attempting to figure out who had the UN Secretary General killed is like trying to determine who killed John F. Kennedy. See O'Brien, To Katanga and Back and Arthur L. Gavshon, *The Mysterious Death of Dag Hammarskjöld* (New York: Walker and Co., 1962).

108. June Bingham, *U Thant: The Search for Peace* (New York: Alfred Knopf, 1966) Ch. 14; U Thant, *View from the UN* (New York: Doubleday, 1978) Ch. 1.

109. Peyton Lyon, *Canada in World Affairs 1961-1963* (Toronto: Oxford University Press, 1968), 321-326; NAC RG 25 vol. 7034 file 6386-A-40 pt. 1.3 (21 May 61) message London to External Ottawa, "Congo Situation in Katanga"; NAC RG 2 (7 Dec 61) Cabinet Conclusions.

110. "Failure in the Congo," *Globe and Mail*, 5 December 1961.

111. NAC RG 2 (7 Dec 61) Cabinet Conclusions.

112. Thomas J. Noer, "Africa," Thomas G. Paterson (ed) *Kennedy's Quest for Victory: American Foreign Policy 1961-1963* (New York: Oxford University Press, 1989), 263- 270; NAC RG 25 vol. 6460 file 5475-FA-40 pt. 5, (15 Apr 61) "Crisis at the United Nations: Talking Points for Mr. Robinson."

113. Ibid.; *Report of the Department of External Affairs 1962* (Ottawa: Crown Printers, 1963).

114. NAC RG 25 vol 6976 file 5475-FA-40 Pt 5.2 (30 Aug 61) Sixteenth Session Supplementary Item, "Prevention of the Wider Dissemination of Nuclear Weapons."

115. NAC RG 2 (28 Dec 61) Cabinet Conclusions; (26 Jan 62) Cabinet Conclusions; NAC RG 24 vol. 21484 file 2137.3.v.6, (29 Nov 61) letter Miller to Robertson, "Assistance for the UN in the Congo"; (15 Nov 61) letter CGS to Minister, "Instructors for the Congo"; NAC RG 25 vol. 6460 file 5475-FA-40 pt. 5, (15 Apr 61) "Crisis at the United Nations: Talking Points for Mr. Robinson."

116. NAC RG 25 vol. 6460 file 5475-FA-40 pt. 3, (25 Jan 61) Statement by G.S. Murray to CIIA, "Canada and the United Nations."

117. Ibid.

CHAPTER 7

UNREALIZED AMBITIONS: PITFALLS, SIDESHOWS AND NON-STARTERS, 1960-1963

When there was a dispute between two small powers, the dispute eventually disappeared.

If there was a dispute between a small power and a great power, the small power disappeared.

And if there was a dispute between two great powers, the Security Council disappeared.

—Arsene Usher, *Ivory Coast Ambassador to the UN*

Elements within the Diefenbaker government did their best to commit Canada to several unrealistic peacekeeping endeavours which forced Canadian personnel to put on brave faces under politically and physically adverse conditions.

(CF Photo)

During the last three years of its tenure, the Diefenbaker government was involved in several futile attempts to use UN peace operations machinery to solve international crises. There were several major opportunities available to Diefenbaker's men to "make their bones" in international crisis resolution and perhaps be awarded a Nobel Peace Prize. Intervention by UN military forces was discussed in all of these crises. Yet none of the opportunities were successful for Diefenbaker and Green. Canadian participation by default revolved around supporting NATO allies in efforts to contain Communism inside and outside the NATO Area. The agenda based on Canada leading a more activist and neutral UN in between the superpowers simply could not be activated. The only mission which prompted the deployment of Canadian forces was in indirect support of NATO objectives under the UN flag and once again it was in a place far removed from the NATO Area: West New Guinea in the Pacific. (see Figure 3, pg 47) Trouble was also brewing elsewhere in the Pacific and Canada was slowly drawn into the quagmire.

CANADA AND THE INTERNATIONAL CONTROL COMMISSION, LAOS 1959-61

The kingdom of Laos, tucked between Communist North Vietnam and China on one side and SEATO-member Thailand on the other, devolved into an Asian version of Lebanon throughout 1959. Vietnam specialist Bernard Fall once stated that "Laos is nether a geographical nor an ethnic or social entity, but merely a political convenience" in which the family loyalties and clans dominated specific regions delineated by artificial boundaries. A nation of two million people, Laos was a French colonial backwater until the Indochina War when outnumbered French and Laotian forces held back the Communist Viet Minh and their Laotian Communist surrogates, the Pathet Lao, in the face of total collapse of the French effort after Dienbienphu. The 1954 Geneva Accords generated a situation in which Laos became independent, although two provinces were under tacit Pathet Lao political control. The French were allowed to retain an airbase complex at Xieng-Khouang, but it was never fully occupied by French military forces. The Geneva Accords also set limits on the numbers of military forces and equipment for both sides. An International Control Commission with Indian, Polish, and Canadian members was installed to monitor the situation.[1]

The ICSC organization, ICC Laos, was not really effective. The biggest impediment was the terrain: Laos is covered in jungle, is very mountainous, and its transportation network remained undeveloped. There were static and mobile ICSC teams: the mobile teams were deemed ineffective and pulled out in 1955. As with the other ICSC groups in Southeast Asia, the reporting chain for sending incident reports was unclear, since there was no UN type body to receive them. Finally, the "troika" nature of ICC decisionmaking usually resulted in the Poles vetoing anything that was not in Communist interests.[2]

In 1957, China started making demands for the removal of the French air base since it "feared SEATO aggression." The Americans diplomatically backed France in the UN, and the Chinese covertly supported the Pathet Lao. The North Vietnamese then interfered with Laotian elections, while the Soviets backed their Communist allies in a UN diplomatic offensive.[3] A US Military Assistance Advisory Group (MAAG) was established and covert French military support started to flow to the Laotian government.[4] Eisenhower's decision to back such measures was not taken lightly: his advisors did not believe it would be in American interests to build up the Laotian army "at the expense of creating serious difficulties with our relations with Canada, France, India." Canada should be encouraged to help, since the ICC was a useful vehicle "towards the prevention of a resumption of hostilities while exercising our influence to prevent the Communists from exploiting it to extend their domination over Laos."[5]

A pro-Western government led by Phoui Sanaikone won the 1958 elections, with help from the CIA and the French Dieuxieme Bureau. A portion of the Royal Lao Army, specifically the battalions dominated by the Pathet Lao, headed for the hills and started a rebellion. Sanaikone promptly ordered the disbandment of ICC Laos. Why he did so is unknown. It may have been due to American and French pressure since covert support could have been exposed by ICC Laos inspection activity. The Laotian government also distrusted ICC Laos because North Vietnam was a signatory of Geneva and presumably had access to its information: North Vietnam was not a member of the UN.[6]

Phoui Sanaikone went to the UN on 4 September 1959 and requested that a force similar to UNEF be sent to Laos to protect it from North Vietnamese aggression. The American military commander in the Pacific informed Washington that he was prepared to fly in a US Marine Corps brigade to Laos under the guise of a SEATO peacekeeping force.[7] China and North Vietnam responded that they wanted ICC Laos re-established, not a UN force. Dag Hammarskjöld was extremely wary of the entire situation and felt the UN should stay out of it. He was aware of American covert support and did not want the UN used as a Western proxy in the region. He petitioned Nehru and the Indians for help in backing the ICC solution. Nehru told the Secretary General that Canada had to be involved if such a solution was to be effective.[8]

Canadian interests under the St Laurent government were related to supporting American and allied efforts to stabilize the region so that military operations similar to Korea could be avoided (and thus scarce Canadian troops not be committed) and the threat of escalation into global war could be averted in Asia and in Europe. Canadian interests in the ICSC remained part of that "economy of effort" strategy into the late 1950s despite a complete lack of interest displayed by the Diefenbaker government. External Affairs did, however, keep a wary eye on events. External Affairs' "Trends of Communist Policy" for October 1959 noted that the Laotian "rebels have been concentrating on propaganda, recruitment and the collection of arms," clearly in preparation for some future activity.[9] Still, the Diefenbaker government remained uninvolved for the time being, although Howard Green cautioned Secretary of State Herter in 1959 that American military support for the French, who were training the Laotian army, might be in contravention to the Geneva accords.[10]

In the larger context of the Cold War, instability in Laos could affect Thailand. This nation was a close American ally which had numerous USAF bases. Laos was also adjacent to South Vietnam. Holding Laos or at the very least denying it to Communist forces prevented it from being used as a base (by the Chinese and North Vietnamese) against Thailand, South

Vietnam, and then Malaya. Once again, the West was engaged in a chess game in which secure base areas and the ability to project military, economic and political power were the prize. Covert action to sustain a pro-West Laos ensured that a buffer zone against Communism was maintained in Southeast Asia.[11]

The Eisenhower administration then decided to support Laos in developing a UN-based solution rather than an ICSC-based one. The matter went before the Security Council with predictable results. The Soviets manoeuvered to block Hammarskjöld from sending a delegation to report on the situation. The Soviets then argued that ICC Laos should be re-established and cautioned the Americans and French to stop using the UN to "interfere."[12]

Despite Soviet protestations, the UN Secretary General sent a commission (called a "subcommittee" of the Security Council to circumvent the Soviet objections) to Laos consisting of representatives from Italy, Tunisia, Japan and Argentina. Hammarskjöld, who went to Vientiane in November 1959, suspected that Laos was fabricating and magnifying foreign interference in the same way he suspected the Lebanese of doing so in 1958. The "subcommittee" found no evidence of massive infiltration but that North Vietnam did send arms to the Pathet Lao. Educated observers on the ground knew that the real threat was "internal chaos aided and abetted by pro-Communist movements supported from the outside" which would then be used as a springboard for further overt military action, but the UN was unwilling to openly speculate on that.[13]

By this time, Howard Green was running External Affairs and Canadian interest became stronger. Canada opposed the re-activation of ICC Laos since this would interfere with Laotian sovereignty. At the same time, however, Green publicly stated that "the United Nations had an important role to play in supplementing the arrangements made at Geneva for the stability of the area" so that "world peace and security" could be maintained.[14] This amounted to an exercise in neutrality. The Laotians, French, and Americans wanted a UN solution while the UN Secretary General, the Pathet Lao, North Vietnamese, China, and the Soviets wanted an ICSC solution!

Hammarskjöld left a pseudo-official UN "presence" in Laos to avoid Soviet accusations of interference. He told the Laotians that they should stay neutral or the situation would deteriorate and that the UN would not tolerate "crying wolf." The small UN mission in Laos tried to mediate during the first of a series of six coup d'etats conducted by the armed forces against the government. UN representatives failed to have any impact and the UN was pushed into the background in Laos. In was made clear to the Americans by Hammarskjöld that he favoured letting SEATO handle the matter.[15]

The Soviets increased their activity by providing heavy weapons and armoured vehicles to the Pathet Lao through North Vietnam. Soviet "civilian" IL-14 cargo flights even dropped supplies in broad daylight to Pathet Lao forces. American Special Forces were introduced to train anti-Communist tribes in the mountains, while the CIA-owned Air America flew helicopters in support of "economic aid efforts." The Cold War proxy fight was heating up: Laos entered a state of "chaotic neutrality."[16] Canadian policy at the time was that the ICC's were structured for 1954 Geneva Accord enforcement, with the three ICCs to effect a ceasefire like a UN force. In a whirl of diplomatic doubletalk, an External Affairs report in 1960 noted that "Canada sought to ensure that the means adopted would be those that would give the best promise of success in the new situation."[17]

By 1961, however, several events affected the plight of Laos. John F. Kennedy was elected President of the United States and altered the American policy line towards the region. Eisenhower told Kennedy that "if the Communists establish a strong position in Laos, the West is finished in the whole South-East Asia area."[18] A neutral Laos might work, but only a truly neutral Laos. Kennedy favoured a neutral Laos over Eisenhower's existing pro-West bastion policy. This shift came as a result of the failure of the Bay of Pigs "covert" operation, Kennedy's questioning the competence of the CIA to run a war, and probably the more important ongoing Berlin crisis which would bring the world to the brink of war. Neutralization in Laos was an American "economy of effort" exercise. What was unclear to the Kennedy administration was the best venue to affect neutralization: the UN or ICC Laos.[19] ICC Laos was favoured by some after Kennedy's State Department people talked to their counterparts in External Affairs: the Canadian view, however, was that it would take some time to re-establish ICC Laos and only if the Laotian government agreed with such a move. British support also may have provided additional incentive for the Americans to go with the ICC.[20]

In his memoirs, Secretary General U Thant (who had by that time succeeded Hammarskjöld) notes that he became convinced that "the United Nations could not play a major role in the Indo-Chinese situation." His reasoning was that the Chinese "ostracized by the international community, had been denouncing the United Nations as a stooge of Washington. Moscow and Paris did not favor United Nations involvement in the Vietnam War because Hanoi did not want it." This situation applied to Laos too since it was all part of the same problem. In U Thant's view, there was no great power consensus on looking for a UN solution, so he did not offer one.[21]

Kennedy met with Diefenbaker in February 1961 and discussed Laos with Green, Dean Rusk, Livingston Merchant and A.D.P. Heeney present. Diefenbaker was told that American policy was "to achieve a genuinely independent neutral Laos which would not be pro-Western to a degree to disturb its Communist neighbors." That was why they had been following the UN option. The UN did not want to cooperate. Green told the Americans that "Canada had not been enthusiastic over the restoration of the ICC but was willing to do its duty" if the UN route was not feasible.[22]

The French, British, and Americans, concerned about the deterioration of the Western position on the whole international scene, convened in Geneva and invited Canada to participate in discussions. Howard Green shifted position again, declined to send Canadian representatives and told Canada's closest allies that "he did not think it appropriate to attend a 'Western caucus' since Canada is a member of the ICC." American representative Dean Rusk was taken aback and asked Green whether the ICC had lost its Western representative: did the ICC now have two neutrals and a Communist? Rusk was so perturbed he sent an "eyes only" message to Kennedy which stated that "Green is obviously bemused by the great peace-making role which Canada (obviously fully) plays in such situations as Suez, Congo and other affairs on which they have been asked to participate."[23] This shift in the Canadian position took the Americans by surprise and influenced them to examine the ICC Laos solution as a real option.[24]

Norman Robertson's assistant, George Ignatieff, then started to send out signals to his American colleagues vis-a-vis ICC Laos and ICC Vietnam. Ignatieff told an American diplomat that "you Americans seem to think our task on the ICC is to represent the West and not to be an impartial objective agent." Ignatieff lectured his American colleague at length about them "underestimating Canadian sensitivities about appearing to be an American satellite,"[25] a theme which was starting to resonate more and more with Diefenbaker personally since he and the younger, brasher, more secure Kennedy did not get along.

Negotiations between the Chinese, Soviets, and the United States started in Geneva in May 1961. Canada's decision to continue as part of ICC Laos may have been influenced in part by an External Affairs analysis of Communist activity in Southeast Asia conducted during these talks. Canadian analysts correctly noted that there were several Communist parties in the region, but they were not under Moscow's central control. In fact North Vietnam had the closest relations with the Pathet Lao and both organization's "aggressive moves...seem to have been inspired by the Communist Chinese [and] pursued over the objections of the Soviet Union." Communist moves "in the future" would "be strongly influenced by the outcome of the current Geneva Conference on Laos." If Communist forces in Laos appeared successful they would "resume their nibbling at the remainder of the Indo-Chinese peninsula."[26]

One of the first agreements made in Geneva was that ICC Laos would be re-established, which was a major Communist propaganda victory that, incidentally, had Green's support. In December a pro-Western coup led by General Phoumi Nosavam seized control in Vientiane: the "neutralist" faction led by Souvanna Phouma asked for Soviet assistance and the "neutralists" sided with the Pathet Lao. The "neutralists" were then slowly absorbed by the Pathet Lao and became a "front organization." By July 1962, an agreement was reached between the superpowers: Laos would be neutral with a coalition government. All foreign forces were to leave and the ICC Laos would monitor the withdrawal. The ICC was then blocked from carrying out its mandate by the Pathet Lao and Polish observers. The Indians and Canadians ignored the Poles and started to patrol in Pathet Lao territory. ICC Laos was able to confirm that 40 of the estimated 10 000 North Vietnamese troops in Laos had left.[27]

The Green-Robertson-Ignatieff axis's agenda in External Affairs was now in full operation. Despite what Diefenbaker and the Canadian people desired in the Cold War fight against the Soviets, these men wanted Canada to be regarded as neutral in a general sense and now the ICC Laos issue gave them another opportunity to prove it. These three men were at the same time deliberately hindering Canada's acquisition of nuclear weapons and thus her ability to meet her long-standing NATO and NORAD obligations. They were also in the forefront of the Canadian disarmament effort. Thus if Canada was going to "do its duty" on the ICC, Green and Robertson would portray it as a grudging activity resulting from American pressure. Canada would indeed become the second neutral on the ICC and not act as the West's representative.

For example, the Americans noted that the "attitude of the Canadian and Indian members of the ICC is...distressing." ICC Laos, once deployed, generated a situation where "no one believes that the ICC is capable of evicting the Viet Minh from Pathet Lao territory." The ICC personnel were hopelessly bogged down in bureaucratic procedure and the Canadian representative, General Brindle, "has on occasions been less than forceful than his Indian colleague." Observers knew that there was a staged withdrawal in progress, but were unable to investigate since they did not have the mobility to get into the remote areas: the only helicopters available were Air America machines which were liable to be shot at. The CIA prevented ICC Laos from receiving raw or processed intelligence which could have allowed the ICC teams to investigate areas still controlled by North Vietnamese forces.[28]

It has been suggested by some historians that the neutralization of Laos directly contributed to the loss of South Vietnam. By not making a stand in Laos and adopting a policy which allowed the pro-Western Laotian forces to be kept unarmed and away from the supply and sanctuary routes from North Vietnam to the South, the ability of the Communist insurgency to subvert the South was sustained. Selecting the ICC as the instrument of the West's "economy of effort" strategy failed, which then prompted the United States to initiate a covert war in Laos with a series of fragmented operations designed to deny North Vietnam access to South Vietnam.[29] Green's backing of the ICC solution instead of using Canada's influence to push for a UN solution should be seen in this light, although there is plenty of blame to go around, particularly when Kennedy's Laos policy is scrutinized.

BERLIN AND CUBA, 1961-1962

Berlin and Cuba are two of the most important, intricate and best-known crises of the Cold War. It is therefore necessary to compress the intricate detail for the purposes of our discussion since this section is limited to the proposed peacekeeping aspects of the Berlin and Cuba events.

The Berlin problem dates back to the start of the Cold War. Berlin was controlled by a four-power agreement established by the victorious Allies at the end of the Second World War. The UN did not have any jurisdiction over the arrangements. The Berlin Blockade of 1948-49 and the resultant airlift merely formalized the painted lines drawn on the cobblestones and in the U-Bahn. West Berlin had three sectors: French, British, and American, all of which were garrisoned by their respective occupation troops. The largest zone in the East was controlled by the Soviets with their associated military forces. Three air and land corridors connected West Berlin with West Germany. These corridors were the only means by which West Berlin could survive surrounded by the hostile Deustche Democratische Republik (DDR) better known as East Germany. The corridors were subject to periodic harassment by Communist forces after the 1948-49 blockade was called off.[30]

In NATO circles, there were continuing discussions as to whether Berlin was part of the NATO Area or not. Prior to 1959, the matter was deliberately left in an ambiguous state since Berlin was considered indefensible. However, Nikita Khrushchev did not like the fact that West Germany was now part of NATO and wanted closer political ties with Berlin. When NATO forces re-equipped with American-supplied nuclear weapons in 1958, it included West German forces as well. This was completely unacceptable to Khrushchev. A coordinated propaganda, political, and subversive attack was directed against West Germany and veiled threats were made regarding nuclear weapons use.[31]

By 1959, NATO leaders had altered their stance on Berlin. Berlin, already critical as a Western showpiece and intelligence outpost deep in Communist territory, now became a vital propaganda tool during the Cold War. If the Soviets put pressure on Berlin, at what point would NATO use nuclear weapons? The West, including Canada, responded with a relatively coordinated propaganda and diplomatic campaign to signal Khrushchev that interference with Berlin would not be tolerated.[32]

Canadian policy towards the Berlin situation was driven by Norman Robertson who had been interested in finding a diplomatic solution to the "Berlin problem" for years, a solution in which Canada (and presumably Robertson) would play a key role. He had successfully lobbied Sidney Smith to support such an exercise, but Diefenbaker was lukewarm. Then Smith died, the Berlin Crisis intensified and new opportunities abounded.[33]

Alarmed by the prospect of nuclear war, British Prime Minister Harold Macmillan flew to Moscow in February 1959 with Diefenbaker's blessing. Macmillan had a vague notion that one solution could involve UN peacekeeping forces situated in Berlin. On his return trip through NATO capitals, Macmillan consulted with Diefenbaker, who indicated that he was inclined to let Macmillan, De Gaulle, and Eisenhower handle the crisis. Robertson and his ideas were left behind.[34]

During the meeting, it was clear that Diefenbaker did not favour a solution which would turn Germany into a neutral zone leading "to the departure of USA and Canadian troops from Europe, the last thing Western European governments wanted." A UN solution should be studied, although the British were thinking that some UN agencies or even the whole General Assembly should relocate to Berlin, as opposed to introducing a peacekeeping force. The UN should "underwrite" a four-power settlement to give it legitimacy, but not control it.[35]

The Americans were thinking of a UN solution as well. When they approached Hammarskjöld, he told them that UN action over Berlin could take two forms: either "as constructive forum" or "as a kind of a cloak for action already determined on which could, as an abuse of the UN, both mark the beginning of the end for the UN itself and neither lessen present tension or contribute to any real solution."[36] On the other hand, the French view towards any UN presence in Berlin was "positively psychopathic."[37]

Then Lester Pearson, who was now leading the Opposition in the House of Commons, told the CBC that a UN force should be sent into Berlin. A CBC reporter presented this to Dag Hammarskjöld in New York who replied "I leave that proposal to Mr. Pearson to develop more in detail. I do not know enough about it to comment on it." The Secretary General did not really think that a UNEF solution for Berlin was "practical," however:

> What would be the functions of a UN force in Berlin? It would be something very different from what it has been in the case where a UN force has been used. Which parties would such a force separate....What kind of military functions, in a more general sense, would such a force have? Against whom would they protect whom?[38]

Hammarskjöld concluded that the concept was "unsound." Norman Robertson would have to allow NATO to solve this crisis. In 1961 the world went to the nuclear brink over Berlin. NATO's graduated response strategy, championed by Canada's NATO diplomats and National Defence, contributed to preventing escalation without sacrificing the free world's position in Berlin.

We now turn to the matter of Cuba. Fidel Castro seized power in 1959 and installed a Communist regime which had Soviet support. The geographical proximity between Cuba and the United States (70 miles) alone was enough to make the Americans nervous and the CIA was tasked with altering this new status quo. The climax of their effort was the disastrous Bay of Pigs operation of 17 April 1961, the details of which are covered elsewhere. The affair was a serious propaganda and credibility blow to the West's position in the Cold War.

The Diefenbaker government's policy towards the Castro regime was coloured by the fact that Eisenhower's replacement, President John F. Kennedy, did not have a good relationship with Diefenbaker. Diefenbaker saw Kennedy as a young American upstart pushing Canada around. The Prime Minister was concerned about Cuban-supported Communist revolution in Latin America, but this was overshadowed by the more personal aspects of American assumptions about Canadian support for the American position.[39]

It is not clear from available records to what extent the UN was involved in the Bay of Pigs situation. The Cuban exile landing force encountered significant opposition and fought a losing battle to maintain a salient, waiting to be reinforced or supported by US forces. A Royal Canadian Navy task group was apparently ordered to prepare a destroyer to participate in a naval version of UNEF, so that the Cuban exile landing force could be extracted in the same way the Anglo-French force had withdrawn from Suez in 1956. How this decision was arrived at and why it was never implemented is unknown.

The next opportunity for UN involvement came during the Cuban Missile Crisis in October 1962. The invitation by Castro to Khrushchev to station nuclear-armed medium and intermediate-range ballistic missiles in Cuba provoked a massive American response which included a blockade to cut off further Soviet support. Canada's involvement with the crisis was, in the main, focused on sovereignty issues related to alerting Canadian-committed NORAD and naval forces for the defence of North America. Diefenbaker hesitated for several days before allowing a NORAD alert in the face of the obvious Soviet nuclear threat. During the crisis Howard Green made contradictory public statements which indicated he wished the Canadian people to believe that Canada was not involved in the crisis and was a neutral party. This flew in the face of Canada's NORAD and NATO political and military commitments and produced a great deal of confusion within NATO ranks.[40]

While Canadian policymakers were distracted over whether or not Canada's nuclear forces should be prepared to defend the country, the Americans in the State Department were exploring how to get the UN aligned against Castro and Khrushchev. U-2 spy plane imagery used in the UN forum contributed greatly in this regard. Kennedy's people thought that having the UN handle the inspection and removal of Soviet missiles and warheads from Cuba would provide highly effective propaganda.[41]

At the same time Secretary General U Thant suggested that a UN Observation Group (UNOG) be formed "consisting of eminent personalities from non-aligned countries, the primary task of which would be to verify, on the ground, the dismantling and return to the USSR of the missiles systems in Cuba."[42] Extensive discussions between UN representative General Rihkje and American ambassador Adelai Stevenson suggested that UNOG be allowed to visit Cuban exile training camps in Florida as a reciprocal arrangement.[43]

Howard Green, after consulting Norman Robertson, contacted Diefenbaker with a similar UN observation and verification proposal and then passed it on the American ambassador to Canada, Livingston Merchant. Analogies to Suez were being made in media and External Affairs circles. Pearson was about to be consulted to give the veneer of bipartisan resolve. As Basil Robinson recalled "It is not hard to imagine the lights that must have flashed on in Diefenbaker's mind at this reminder of an occasion on which Pearson himself had gilded his reputation and been rewarded with the Nobel Peace Prize."[44] In interviews with the CBC, a confident Howard Green crowed that Canadian supported UN observers would go to Cuba since "When its decided at the United Nations that observers should go in generally speaking the result is that they go in....I don't think any nation in the world large or small today is prepared to defy world opinion and world opinion is expressed at the United Nations."[45]

The whole operation came to a crashing halt when Castro would not permit UNOG to operate on Cuban soil. Then CIA director John McCone balked at allowing the UN access to U-2 aircraft and American photo interpreters because he did not trust U Thant. A plan was then put together in the UN to use civilian aircraft equipped with surveillance systems to monitor the withdrawal once an agreement was reached. The UN contacted Hunting Aviation in Canada to supply these aircraft: Douglas Harkness approved the request. At the same time, the UN was dealing directly with the US Air Force in an effort to borrow several C-130 transport aircraft which would be equipped with surveillance systems. Canada was asked to provide the pilots. The Americans then agreed that an entire wing of RB-66 strategic reconnaissance aircraft would handle UN verification imagery requests. These aircraft had their USAF insignia painted out and UN insignia put on, although they used USAF pilots for the missions. Canada had no role to play in the operation.[46]

In the end, a Canadian Chiefs of Staff analysis concluded that "the solution reached is in no sense a UN solution; it is a Great Power solution. The fact that the UN has served as a focus of negotiations and that a role was found for the Secretary General has...served to strengthen the UN. However, the organization which has been strengthened is the Security Council [not] the General Assembly or...'quiet diplomacy.'"[47]

NATO's inaction forced Dutch Foreign Minister Josef Luns to deal directly with Kennedy. The President pressured Luns to give up West New Guinea. Luns argument was that "we don't want another Congo" and that the Netherlands would not behave as Belgium had in Africa. Kennedy, in Luns' view, was opposing the self-determination of the Papuan population of West New Guinea who did not want to be part of Indonesia. He attacked Kennedy for the American policy of sending weapons to Sukarno: this, he said, was the equivalent of the Netherlands sending weapons to Castro.[59]

Secretary of State Rusk and Luns agreed that a UN solution was preferable. The problem would be how to prevent Indonesian infiltration and interference with a plebiscite. Would the UN control the plebiscite? Would the US issue a warning to Sukarno on the Netherlands' behalf? Rusk told Luns that the use of the US Navy's Seventh Fleet was not acceptable: As with Berlin, the Congo, and Laos, threats to use force had to be backed up. The West could no longer afford to bluff, which is what would happen if this course were taken.[60]

The Dutch and Americans started work on a plan throughout 1961 and early 1962 to involve the UN. What is extremely puzzling is Dutch unwillingness to involve Canada in assisting them in these forums. The close connections between Canada and the Netherlands established in part on Canada's liberation and economic support during the Second World War appear to have been ignored. Such a course of action did not make sense given Canada's reputation in NATO and in the UN. It is possible that the Dutch correctly perceived the serious decline in Canadian influence with the Americans throughout 1961. Green and Robertson were behaving as though Canada was quasi-neutral and the rest of NATO could see that Canadian intransigence on the nuclear weapons issue was interfering with the Diefenbaker-Kennedy relationship.

In January 1962 Indonesian forces shot at a Dutch transport plane. In a brief but furious naval action, two Royal Netherlands Navy destroyers sank two Indonesian torpedo boats and damaged a third: 53 Indonesian prisoners were taken. Indonesian landing forces dropped onto Biak Island, another Dutch-controlled territory, and were repelled.[61] NATO members started putting pressure on the Kennedy administration to support the Netherlands when the Dutch requested that a Dutch Marine battalion be allowed to fly through North America and stage from Hawaii to reinforce the West New Guinea garrison. The Americans were caught unprepared:

> Failure to [honor our commitments] can have serious consequences for US/Dutch relations with repercussions in NATO....to deny the Dutch request will also cause serious misgivings among our NATO partners who are already suspicious of our ability to preserve Western positions outside of Europe.[62]

A Dutch task group of two destroyers and two submarines was on its way through the Panama Canal and requests to release patrol aircraft purchased by their government from the US were received. American intelligence sources then discovered that Indonesia planned to sink a Dutch troop ship in order to produce massive casualties and force negotiations. In March, 2000 Indonesian airborne troops were inserted into West New Guinea and fighting broke out. Things were heating up over that piece of "mountain and swampland."[63]

In May the Dutch went to U Thant and requested UN help to stop the aggression. They wanted a UNEF type force or, barring that, a UN observer mission. U Thant believed that "no resolution was possible" in the Security Council or the General Assembly, even though the situation "became a genuine threat to peace when the Netherlands sent reinforcements and [Sukarno] received Soviet military aid."[64] Ellsworth Bunker, former American ambassador, was asked to be the Secretary General's special representative to investigate the feasibility of a UN solution.

Bunker and his team came up with a scheme whereby the UN would establish a 'Temporary Executive Authority" under the Secretary General's control. Such an arrangement would ensure that there was a temporal separation of forces, as opposed to a physical-linear separation similar to UNEF in Egypt. After the transition period was over, a plebiscite would be held amongst the Papuan population to see if they wanted to join Indonesia. While Bunker's negotiations were underway, the Indonesians dropped more paratroopers into West New Guinea which accelerated the process.[65]

The Dutch and Indonesians signed off on the Bunker Plan on 15 August 1962. The United Nations Transitional Executive Authority (UNTEA) would deploy a UN Security Force (UNSF) to West New Guinea. The transition to Indonesian control, something which the Dutch understood would be accomplished around 1969, was stepped up to 1963, much to their displeasure.

The UN now had to form UNTEA. There was still residual disarray within the UN in the wake of the death of Dag Hammarskjöld (see Congo chapter). Unlike other UN missions, UNTEA had no formal UN mandate and was not passed through the Security Council or the General Assembly. U Thant maintained a hands- off approach and allowed the principle parties to negotiate through American mediation. The Soviet Union, smelling an exploitable success against the Netherlands, backed American efforts in the endeavour.[66]

In the end, U Thant was able to muster a 21-man observer group which deployed almost immediately in August 1962. The UNSF consisted mainly of 1500 Pakistani troops, four USAF DC-3's and six helicopters, plus the Canadian contingent.[67]

Canadian UNTEA decisionmaking was influenced, finally, by the Dutch who, in diplomatic traffic to External Affairs, requested Canadian support since there was "no more acceptable source from Dutch standpoint for personnel and equipment for UN force than Canada."[68] Green recommended to Cabinet that the UN request for the aircraft be fulfilled. There was practically no Cabinet discussion on the matter and the Otters were loaded onto RCAF C-130 transports for their long trip to the South Pacific.[69]

UNTEA has been described as a "farce" by interested observers of the day. Indonesia gained a major propaganda victory, Josef Luns publicly attacked the American President which produced a rift in Dutch-American-NATO relations, the Indonesians had no intention of conducting a fair plebiscite, and UNTEA was incapable of preventing Indonesian intimidation of the Papuan population to side with Sukarno. The Australians were not mollified: TU-16 bombers could be based closer to them.[70] In the end, after UNTEA ceased in May 1963, Sukarno was emboldened to initiate "The Confrontation" against British interests in Brunei and Malaysia. This war lasted until 1966 and proved equally divisive in NATO circles, this time between the Americans and British. The British were wary of UN "solutions" and carried out successful military operations to stop Sukarno which in turn sent a message to China and the Soviets that the West could fight and win "brushfire wars."[71]

Canada's small role in the UNTEA enterprise does not cast a positive light on the Diefenbaker government's peacekeeping efforts. The lack of Canadian interest, initiative, and understanding ensured that a lackluster solution was found and shoddily implemented, with dire results for the liberty of the population of West New Guinea. Although UNTEA helped get the Dutch out of a serious situation, the half-hearted deployment of two float planes can only be considered minimal in a crisis which exacerbated the serious ruptures within NATO in the early 1960s.

The Diefenbaker government's handling of these crises was uneven and unsuccessful. By focusing on "big" crises politics and overestimating Canada's ability to influence those situations, Diefenbaker and Green missed opportunities to expand Canadian influence in areas where it might have had a positive effect, particularly with the Dutch in the Pacific or by exploiting nearly a six years worth of experience and credibility in Indochina. It is clear Green believed that Canada was much more independent than was really the case and forgot that Canada's influence was based on participation in NATO, the bi-lateral relationship with the US, and the tripartite relationship in the ABC arrangement. Behaving as a quasi-neutral exposed the limits of Canadian power outside of the West's fold.

Notes to Chapter 7

1. Bernard B. Fall, *Anatomy of a Crisis: The Story of the Laotian Crisis of 1960-61* (New York: Doubleday, 1969), 23-24, 43-44, 58-61.

2. Ibid., 66-69; Martin Stuart-Fox, A History of Laos (Cambridge: Cambridge University Press, 1997), 86-89.

3. Ibid., 81-83.

4. Timothy N. Castle, *At War in the Shadow of Vietnam: US Military Aid to the Royal Lao Government 1955-1975* (New York: Columbia University Press, 1997) Chapters 1 and 2.

5. *FRUS 1958-1960 Vol. XVI: Asia,* 475-477, (20 Aug 58) memo Dillon to Sprague.

6. Stuart-Fox, *A History of Laos,* Chapter 4; Fall, *Anatomy of a Crisis,* 96-106, 139; Urquart, *Hammarskjöld,* 330-331; *FRUS 1958-1960 Vol. XVI: Asia,* 552-553 (6 Aug 59) 416th Meeting of the NSC.

7. DDEL, Office of Staff Secretary International Security File: Laos (1) (19 Sep 59) message JCS to distribution list.

8. Urquart, *Hammarskjöld,* 330-334.

9. NAC RG 25 vol. 4767, file 50072-40 pt. 2, "Trends in Communist Policy October 1959."

10. DDEL, Office of Staff Secretary International Security File: Canada(1), (11 Jul 59) memcon Herter, Diefenbaker, "Military Training Program in Laos."

11. Castle, *At War in the Shadow of Vietnam,* 12-13; see also Norman B. Hannah, *The Key to Failure: Laos and the Vietnam War* (London: Madison Books, 1987).

12. Urquart, *Hammarskjöld,* 340, 343, 348, 352; Fall, *Anatomy of a Crisis,* 143. See also DDEL, Office of Staff Secretary International Security File: Laos (1), (15 Sep 59) memorandum to the President.

13. Fall, *Anatomy of a Crisis,* 144-147.

14. Report of the Department of External Affairs 1959 (Ottawa: Queen's Printer, 1960), 38-39.

15. Fall, *Anatomy of a Crisis*, 174, 177, 180; Urquart, *Hammarskjöld*, 348; DDEL, Office of Staff Secretary International Security File: Laos (3) (2 Jan 61) memcon with President.

16. See Castle, *At War in the Shadow of Vietnam*; Fall, *Anatomy of a Crisis*, 204-209.

17. Report of the Department of External Affairs 1960 (Ottawa: Queen's Printer, 1961), 18.

18. *FRUS 1961-1963 Vol. XXIV Laos Crisis,* 5 (3 Jan 61) Eisenhower-Kennedy conference.

19. Hannah, *The Key to Failure*, Chapter 2; *FRUS 1961-1963 Vol. XXIV Laos Crisis*, 9- 10 (17 Jan 61) State-CIA-JCS meeting. Note that a SEATO option was on the table as well: the French and British (members of SEATO) did not favour this since it would mean deploying regular troops *back* to Indochina. This was impossible for the French to do given the events of 1954 and in Algeria in 1960. The British were overextended elsewhere: Kenya, Cyprus, and Malaya.

20. *FRUS 1961-1963 Vol. XXIV Laos Crisis*, 9-10 (17 Jan 61) State-CIA-JCS meeting; Stuart-Fox, *A History of Laos*, 119.

21. U. Thant, *View From the UN*, 56.

22. *FRUS 1961-1963 Vol XIII: West Europe and Canada, 1140-1141* (20 Feb 61), visit of Canadian Prime Minister Diefenbaker.

23. *FRUS 1961-1963 Vol XIII: West Europe and Canada, 1152-1153* (14 May 61), message Rusk to Kennedy.

24. *FRUS 1961-1963 Vol. XXIV Laos Crisis*, 322-326 (28 Jul 61), memcon President and his advisors.

25. USNARA RG 59 E3077 box 1, 250/62/30/3 file: Nationalism, Neutralism, Anti- Americanism 1960-62 1.14, (26 May 61) memcon Igantieff/Smith, "Canadian Attitudes Towards the Cold War."

26. NAC RG 25 vol. 4767 file 50072-40 pt. 3, (30 Jun 61) draft intelligence study for Far Eastern Division.

27. Peyton Lyon, *Canada in World Affairs 1961-1963* (Toronto: Oxford University Press, 1968), 313-315; Richard H. Schultz Jr., *The Secret War Against Hanoi: Kennedy's and Johnson's use of Spies, Saboteurs, and Covert Warriors in North Vietnam* (New York: Harper Collins, 1999), 27-28; Thomas J. Shoenbaum, *Waging Peace and War: Dean Rusk in the Truman, Kennedy, and Johnson Years* (New York: Simon and Shuster, 1988), 391.

28. *FRUS 1961-1963 Vol. XXIV Laos Crisis*, 930-931, "State Department Bureau of Intelligence and National Security Council Report on Laos", 893-895 (29 Aug 62) Cabinet meeting with Kennedy.

29. See Hannah, *The Key to Failure* and Schultz, *The Secret War Against Hanoi*.

30. See Ann Tusa, *The Last Division: A History of Berlin, 1945-1989* (London: Hodder and Stoughton, 1997)

31. Jack Schick, *The Berlin Crisis 1958-1962* (Philadelphia: University of Pennsylvania Press, 1971).

32. Sean M. Maloney, "Notfallplanung fur Berlin: Vorlaufer der Flexible Response 1958- 1963," *Militargeschichte* Heft 1.1 Quartal 1997 7 Jahrgang.

33. Robinson, *Diefenbaker's World*, 87-91.

34. Ibid.

35. NAC RG 25 vol. 6089 file 50346-4-40 pt. 1, (23 Mar 59) message External Affairs to NATOPARIS, "Germany and Berlin: UK Discussions."

36. *FRUS 1958-1960 Vol. VIII: Berlin Crisis 1958-1959*, 388, (24 Feb 59) message USUN to State, "Berlin."

37. *FRUS 1958-1960 Vol. VIII: Berlin Crisis 1958-1959*, 631, (23 Apr 59) NSC Special Meeting.

38. NAC RG 25 fol. 6991 file 5475-6-40 pt. 4.2, (26 May 59) PERMISNY to External Affairs, "SECGEN Comments on a UN force and the Presence of UN Military Forces in Berlin."

39. Robinson, *Diefenbaker's World*, 192-193, 200-201.

40. See Maloney, *Learning to Love The Bomb*.

41. *FRUS 1961-1963: Cuban Missile Crisis and Aftermath*, 232-235, (26 Oct 62) "Cuba: Talks with U Thant."

42. U Thant, *View from the UN* (New York: Doubleday Boks, 1977) p. 192.

43. *FRUS 1961-1963: Cuban Missile Crisis and Aftermath*, 242-244, (26 Oct 62) message US UN to State, "Cuba."

44. Robinson, *Diefenbaker's World*, 287.

45. NAC MG 32 B13, vol. 12 file 45, "Text of a television interview with the Secretary of State for External Affairs on the CBC, October 22, 1962."

46. DHH Raymont Collection file 2503, (23 Apr 70) "Cuba-Canadian Action."; Dino Brugioni, *Eyeball to Eyeball: The Inside Story of the Cuban Missile Crisis* (New York: Random House, 1991), 510.

47. DHH Raymont Collection file 2503, (5 Nov 62) memo for the COSC, "The Lessons of the Cuban Crisis."

48. Frederica M. Bunge, ed. *Indonesia: A Country Study* (Washington D.C.: Department of the Army, 1983), 42-43.

49. Ibid.; Arnold C. Brackman, *Southeast Asia's Second Front: The Power Struggle in the Malay Archipelago* (London: Frederick A. Praeger, 1966), 91-92.

50. Harold Crouch, *The Army and Politics in Indonesia* (Ithaca: Cornell University Press, 1978), 44-46.

51. Brackman, *Southeast Asia's Second Front, 94-95*;
Hal Kosut, ed. Indonesia: The Sukarno Years (New York:
Facts on File Interim History, 1967), 49, 51, 53.

52. Brackman, *Southeast Asia's Second Front*, 97-98.

53. Crouch, *The Army and Politics in Indonesia*, 47;
Brackman, Southeast Asia's Second Front, 101-102.

54. *FRUS 1961-63 Vol. XXIII: Southeast Asia*, 302-304,
(25 Jan 61) US Embassy in Indonesia to State.

55. *FRUS 1961-63 Vol. XXIII: Southeast Asia*, 336-338
(3 Apr 61) Rusk to Kennedy, "Proposal for Dealing with
Dutch-Indonesian dispute over West New Guinea (West Irian)."

56. *FRUS 1961-63 Vol. XXIII: Southeast Asia*, 328-333, (27
Mar 61) Bissell to Bundy.

57. NAC RG 25 vol. 4767 file 50072-40 pt. 2, (25 Feb 57) Far
Eastern Division, "Communism in the Far East"; (7 Jun 60
message Embassy Djakarta, "Fortieth Anniversary of the PKI";
NAC RG 25 vol. 4767 file 50072-40 pt. 3, (20 Feb 61)
Canadian Embassy, Djakarta, "The Policy of the Communist
Bloc in Indonesia."

58. Paul-Henri Spaak, *The Continuing Battle: Memoirs of
a European* (Toronto: Little- Brown and Company, 1971)
Chapter 39.

59. *FRUS 1961-63 Vol. XXIII: Southeast Asia*, 345-352
(10 Apr 61) Luns-Kennedy meeting; 352-360, (10 Apr 61)
Luns-Rusk meeting.

60. *FRUS 1961-63 Vol. XXIII: Southeast Asia*, 352-360,
(10 Apr 61) Luns-Rusk meeting.

61. Kosut, *Indonesia: The Sukarno Years*, 55-56.

62. *FRUS 1961-63 Vol. XXIII: Southeast Asia*, 542-543
(27 Feb 62) Tyler to Rusk.

63. *FRUS 1961-63 Vol. XXIII: Southeast Asia*, 558-559
(14 Mar 62) State to US Embassy, Indonesia; 595-596,
(22 May 62) memo to DCI; Kosut, *Indonesia: The Sukarno
Years*, 55-56.

64. U. Thant, *View from the UN*, 48.

65. DHH, (9 Dec 66) "Report No. 12: Canada and
Peace-keeping Operations: West New Guinea (West Irian)."

66. Durch, *The Evolution of UN Peacekeeping*, 288.

67. Ibid, 290.

68. As quoted in DHH, (9 Dec 66) "Report No. 12: Canada
and Peace-keeping Operations: West New Guinea (West Irian)."

69. NAC RG 2 Cabinet Conclusions, 29 August 1962.

70. DHH, (9 Dec 66) "Report No. 12: Canada and
Peace-keeping Operations: West New Guinea (West Irian)";
Brackman, *Southeast Asia's Second Front*, 108-113.

71. Michael Carver, *War Since 1945* (New York: Putnam and
Sons, 1981) Chapter 6.

CHAPTER 8

PEACEKEEPING
AS LOW INTENSITY CONFLICT?
THE ARMED FORCES, PEACE OPERATIONS
AND BRUSHFIRE WARS,1960-1963

Although peace-keeping is a fundamentally different occupation to the countering of subversion, there is a surprising similarity in the outward forms of many of the techniques involved....It is also important that those involved in countering subversion should realize that they are involved in this activity and not peace-keeping. It is not difficult to become confused in this respect.

—Frank Kitson, *Low Intensity Operations*

After the ONUC experience in the Congo, more and more questions emerged: was UN peacekeeping a form of counterinsurgency? Airmobile operations in a non-linear environment in Cyprus demonstrated that not all UN operations were of a "thin blue line" nature like UNEF.

(CF Photo)

Canadian operations in the Congo and elsewhere highlighted serious deficiencies in Canada's approach to UN peace operations: Canada's military forces were not structured or trained, nor were they equipped to carry out protracted peace operations in the UN context. It was all very well for a government to develop peace operations policy; it was something quite different to be able to implement it both quickly and effectively.

UNTSO, UNMOGIP, UNOGIL and the ICSC missions were conducted by individual Canadian soldiers, sailors, and airmen seconded to those bodies. They carried their own personal kit and were integrated into international teams living off the economy of the regions in which they were deployed. UNEF was the first example of formed Canadian units deploying on UN missions, but these were ad hoc composite units pulled out of the Canadian Army and RCAF's existing force structure. Could or should Canada multi-task its armed forces to handle both NATO "hot war" and peripheral area Cold War tasks?

NATO military and political leaders were attempting to understand the role of low intensity conflict within the NATO Area itself and its relationship to conventional and nuclear war. The focal point was, in 1960, the crisis over the city of Berlin which had implications for NATO activities on the peripheries and influenced Canada's attempts to create a military force structure able to conduct operations across the spectrum of conflict. Problems in force structure and application from 1960 to 1963 laid the ground work for more radical peacekeeping concepts implemented by the Pearson government after 1963, and further blurred the distinction between NATO and UN interests.

PROTO-FLEXIBLE RESPONSE, BRUSHFIRE WARS AND PEACEKEEPING

The establishment of the Canadian UN Standby Battalion in 1958 appears to be the first concrete step taken by the armed services towards accepting that a permanent peace operations capability would exist as part of Canada's force structure. Previous responses, including Operation RAPID STEP in 1956, were all ad hoc affairs. There was no peace operations doctrine. From 1958 onward, a great deal of effort would be spent on formalizing the new capability. This effort, however, did not occur in a Canadian vacuum. It was part and parcel of larger trends in NATO circles relating to revolutionary warfare.

Military theorists of the day recognized that Communist-inspired revolutionary warfare existed long before the Cold War, but the term became ubiquitous throughout the 1950s as the French and British armies fought their decolonization campaigns. Like the term "peacekeeping," the West's response to revolutionary warfare had a myriad of terms, such as "counter-revolutionary warfare," "counterinsurgency," and "low intensity warfare," which obfuscated doctrinal matters.

Revolutionary warfare, in essence, included some or all of the following activities: political subversion; black and white propaganda; the supplying of arms and training by proxy; political assassination; sabotage; ambushes; and small sub-unit activity. In short, revolutionary warfare consisted of any combination of methods, perhaps in conjunction with traditional military engagements, between formed bodies of identifiable soldiers directed towards achieving political objectives. The process by which Western armies identified and responded to this type of warfare was an arduous one and was in progress throughout the 1950s.[1]

Cold War conflict in the Third World can be categorized in a number of ways. There were the long term insurgencies in larger colonies such as Algeria. There were conflicts of smaller scale and shorter duration as in Kenya. There were crisis flashpoints in both Suez and Lebanon. Some had Communist support, others did not. At the time, however, such fine distinctions were not made because Western theorists lacked the vocabulary and means to measure them. They were all lumped together and placed within the Cold War strategic framework.

As we saw in Chapter 4, NATO debated and accepted that revolutionary warfare techniques might in fact be applied against the NATO Area as well as the Third World. The MC 14/2 (revised) strategic concept recognized this in 1957. Thus, when the Berlin Crisis started in 1958-59, NATO Supreme Allied Commander Europe, General Lauris Norstad, had some agreed-on strategic basis from which to formulate a response to low-level Soviet military and political activity. This related to the larger problems of linking Western nuclear response to Soviet activity either inside or outside the NATO Area. NATO's strategy was ambiguous and deliberately so. The problem was, should NATO use nuclear weapons in response to a border incident involving Warsaw Pact and NATO forces? If the Soviets blockaded Berlin? If Soviet naval forces interfered with Norwegian sovereignty? If Syrian forces crossed the Turkish border near Iskendrun? Employing a small conventional NATO force to contain such a situation was similar in concept to the employment of UNEF at Suez, although the specifics of the method differed.[2]

To forestall the possibility of Armageddon, Norstad formed a special contingency planning group called LIVE OAK in 1959. It was not a NATO organization: it was a tripartite French-British-American body strictly designed to deal with low level Soviet military activity related to Berlin. It used forces committed to NATO in West Germany by those three powers and was capable of providing a conventional Western military response from platoon to brigade in size. LIVE OAK allowed the West a flexible, graduated response and crisis management tool for situations in and around Berlin.[3]

Norstad initially wanted to re-organize the Canadian Army NATO commitment, 4 Canadian Infantry Brigade Group, as an airportable and airmobile light infantry formation to handle what were referred to as "fire brigade tasks" throughout the Allied Command Europe (ACE) area. He wanted a force that could "strengthen his deterrent power in the event of a border incident" since only a single nation force which "was not suspect by the Warsaw Pact peoples" could do the job. Conceptually, such a force would deploy to a border area to demonstrate NATO will and prevent escalation to nuclear weapons use over a minor incident involving the Warsaw Pact. This plan was not implemented for a variety of political reasons relating to French and British intransigence over NATO strategy evolution.[4]

Again, as we have seen with MC 14/2 (revised), the principle of Forward Defence of the NATO Area took concrete form. This meant that the Central Region was no longer viewed in isolation from the Northern Flank (Norway, Denmark) and the Southern Flank (Mediterranean). The Soviets might employ a diplomatic offensive combined with threatening gestures (exercises) and political subversion in attempts to isolate and wear down the political will of flank countries to resist. Norstad again looked to the Canadian NATO forces to provide a brigade-sized airportable force which could rapidly deploy to the flanks when a crisis started to escalate in order to signal the Warsaw Pact or the UAR that NATO meant business. This force was to be capable of dealing with low-level military activity as well as being a deterrent. Although it would take several years, the ACE Mobile Force concept would become a reality in 1964, even though it was multi-national in composition and not strictly Canadian.[5]

LIVE OAK and ACE Mobile Force demonstrate that NATO was seriously engaged in examining military crisis management options that overlapped with peace operations and counterinsurgency. The fact that Canada was frequently consulted on such activity and its similarity to the planning underway for Canada's UN Standby force is critical in the development of Canadian conceptualization for low intensity operations.

This development accelerated when Douglas Harkness replaced George Pearkes as Minister of National Defence in 1960. That same year, General Charles Foulkes handed over the reins of the Chiefs of Staff Committee to Air Vice Marshal Frank Miller.

A whirlwind series of Senate hearings in 1960 on defence expenditures forced the Diefenbaker government to articulate some of its more ambiguous defence policies. The Privy Council Office consulted with External Affairs and produced an analysis called "The Defence Problem." Although the bulk of the study dealt with NATO, disarmament and nuclear weapons, it also suggested that "limited wars may well occur around the peripheries of the Soviet and Western Blocs....the provision of suitable standby forces in Canada for such wars should be one of the objectives of Canadian policy." It went so far as to suggest that:

> Indeed it may be that practically all branches of the Canadian forces may make their greatest contribution to the defence of the West and Canada if they concentrate on preparation for limited wars....our forces should be trained and equipped to protect themselves against the effects of [nuclear weapons] for fear that limited wars in which they are engaged should spread and the great powers, using nuclear weapons, should intervene.[6]

This study suggested that intervention forces, some of which might be naval forces, would eventually be needed in the Caribbean, Gaza Strip, and "elsewhere in the Middle East." There was acknowledged overlap between peace operations and counterinsurgency since "the conventional forces needed as a standby in Canada for duties in limited wars should also be capable of performing police or inspection duties as non-combatants."[7] The anti-nuclear components of the study suggest strong influence from Green and Robertson. Nevertheless, Frank Miller provided it to Douglas Harkness as a background paper. The limited war themes resonated in ongoing National Defence examinations of a rapidly deployable force.

Canada's rapid deployment force development was, however, driven less by post-Congo analysis than by the Diefenbaker government's prodding. The unwillingness of the Diefenbaker government to deploy an infantry battalion to the Congo forced the Army to re-assess the standby force concept. In 1960 the CGS General "Fin" Clark directed that a second standby force concept be examined, one which would consist of administrative and signal troops as opposed to combat arms. In the course of this study, several important issues became clear.

First, "the nature and extent of any United Nations request for Canadian contribution cannot be anticipated in detail." Second, the Canadian Army's priority was NATO, followed by national survival operations and the defence of North America. There were simply not enough troops to cover all of the commitments and create a separate UN Standby force. An existing unit would have to be "dual hatted" in the role. The problem of strategic lift was not examined in detail.[8]

An entirely separate study was needed to determine exactly what the force was to do. In general terms, the first time the Army actually defined peacekeeping operations was when the Director General for Planning and Operations commissioned an operational research study in 1961. The terms of reference generated by Army HQ indicated that the following missions were likely for "the Canadian Army in the UN Police Role":

a. Supervisory Organizations—the supervision of truce or other agreements.
b. Border-watching—The separation of forces and the identification of transgressors.
c. Occupation—The positioning of a force in a country to fill a political vacuum during an interregnum; the conduct of a plebiscite as was done in the Saar in 1936 by the League of Nations.
d. Suppression of a para-military force—An example of, and a precedent for, this type of task is the employment of Commonwealth forces in the independent state of Malaya.
e. Limited War.[9]

Creating a Canadian force structure that was strategically mobile yet able to fight and defend itself was a problem facing planners in the early 1960s. Ferret scout cars and Yukon transports represented one solution, but the question remained: how light was too light?

(CF Photo)

Clearly peacekeeping meant more to the Canadian Army than interpositionary operations. Other supporting studies amplified the idea that peacekeeping was not just Kashmir or Suez: "maintaining internal order" also appeared alongside "policing a demarcation line."[10]

The Strategic Studies Group (SSG) was commissioned by the Chiefs of Staff Committee on UN military operations in March 1961. In its report, the SSG noted that "The term 'UN Police Force' has been applied indiscriminately to all three types of forces" that is, observer commissions, UNEFs in Egypt and the Congo, and Korean War operations. This tended to blur the political objectives of each mission. Observer missions and the Suez operation were more straight forward than the ONUC in the Congo. The SSG argued that "the UN has acquired many of the responsibilities of a colonial power" since UN forces were involved in economic matters "in the face of the inability of the Congo government to do"[11] while at the same time it could not replace the Congolese government.

The Congo would be the model for a new type of UN peacekeeping operation:

There is a potential role for further UNEFs elsewhere in Africa, Berlin, Formosa, and in other disputed areas. It is probable, however, that a UNEF can only be deployed if there is at least tacit agreement between the two super-powers to neutralize the area concerned. The role of the UNEFs is therefore influenced by the realities of power politics.[12]

The SSG staff were quite cognizant of how future situations would evolve in the context of the Cold War:

Despite the efforts of the UN, it seems likely that limited warfare will continue to occur in a variety of forms, including civil war aided and abetted by unofficially sponsored volunteers and military supplies from outside countries, boundary incidents and outright aggression. Countries initiating future international incidents are likely to so endeavour to arrange matters that the UN cannot readily become militarily involved...they can draw from past UN experience and avoid the mistakes of their predecessors. Thus each future UN incident may be expected to be as unique as its perpetrators can make it.[13]

Consequently, maximum flexibility on Canada's part was required, particularly with the type of forces Canada established. They had to be capable of fighting their way out of a situation. They could not be based on a previous model like Suez. Each mission would be unique.[14] The chiefs of Staff Committee accepted the SSG study as the basis for UN force planning. When the study was distributed to External Affairs, it "caused considerable anguish" because of its brutally realistic approach to the conditions of the Cold War world. Norman Robertson and Howard Green were, however, in no position to dictate to Douglas Harkness how National Defence should organize and prepare its forces to meet the vague but established government policy that Canada would have a UN Standby force ready to deploy globally.[15]

By mid-1961, the Joint Planning Committee was brought in to clarify inter-service aspects of where the armed services stood on matters relating to UN military operations. In essence operations similar to Kashmir, Suez, and the Congo would be the norm rather than operations like the Korean War. Earmarking existing Canadian forces for UN operations would detract from the main force structure dedicated to NATO commitments. Therefore, dual-tasking existing forces was the only answer, barring additional government funds. Notably, "Limited war might occur outside UN auspices and we must retain the capability of taking part."[16] External Affairs was kept fully informed of military developments in this field, but its personnel rarely commented on them.[17]

The Army's view in 1961 then, was that UN operations were not high priority since "the meeting of these commitments inevitably detracts from the Army's ability to fulfill its wartime tasks....it is not considered feasible to make any reasonably accurate forecast of [additional commitments]." The best that could be done was to earmark forces and hold them at a higher state of readiness.[18] Lieutenant General Geoffrey Walsh, the new Chief of the General Staff, believed that "there is a tendency to underestimate the extent to which the [UN] commitments which this government has undertaken have an impact on the Army."[19]

What of the Royal Canadian Navy? The Chief of the Naval Service, Vice-Admiral Herbert Rayner, and his staff were proficient in limited warfare trends. At the time the RCN was preparing to re-organize the fleet. As early as January 1959, the Naval Board incorporated a "General Purpose Destroyer" into future ship acquisition plans. By 1960 the Naval Board recommended that "the RCN must be prepared to assist United Nations police force actions....the RCN must assume it will be required to provide escorts and appropriate logistics support."[20]

A 1961 RCN study group, the Ad Hoc Committee on Naval Objectives, examined the problem of fitting a limited warfare capability into the fleet to support UN operations. The report to the Chief of the Naval Staff, called the Brock Report, acknowledged that Canadian participation in UN operations was secondary to NATO and continental defence and thus geared to "stabilize situations that threaten to lead to wider conflict." It also recognized that "Canadian troops assigned to these duties have been given virtually no special training. Guerrilla warfare, equipment handling, and inter-service training which would enable our services to co-operate effectively in other than a European-type war have played very little part in high level Canadian defence planning."[21]

The Brock Report identified a spectrum of conflict that included no-warning nuclear attack and unlimited war as a result of escalation. Another type was limited war, or "a number of situations involving national forces from one or more countries in the immediate area of the origin of hostilities." The next type was "sporadic hostilities in trouble spots" particularly Asia, Latin America, and Africa, where the methods were "internal disorder, subversion or infiltration and involving intervention forces from outside countries for stabilizing the situation."[22]

As with Army thinking, there was overlap between peace operations and counterinsurgency. For economic purposes, Canada's force structure had to accommodate all contingencies with the same force structure for "limited war and 'brush fire' situations." Speed was of the essence, the study group argued and Canada had to "possess highly mobile and flexible and versatile forces trained to prevent disorder rather than to inflame passions by the application of more force than is needed. The best police forces are equipped with motor cars and side arms, rather than tanks and mortars."[23]

As for a naval force structure,

> For limited war, intervention or policing action the basic maritime requirement is for general purpose, versatile forces which can co-operate with the other services.... a capability is needed for escorting and transporting army units to almost any area in the world where trouble might develop and support them.[24]

The primary platform for such activity, as envisioned by the Navy in 1961, was the General Purpose Frigate (GPF). The eight planned GPFs would be structured for brushfire wars but had the additional capability to conduct anti-submarine operations. The GPF was to carry a helicopter, an anti-aircraft missile system, and a gun capable of supporting landing operations. Each GPF could carry 200 troops and put them ashore by landing craft.[25]

The Royal Canadian Air Force leadership were also keen to keep abreast of Army and Navy efforts. Like the Navy, there had been high-level musings throughout 1959 by Air Marshal Larry Dunlap and his senior staff. They debated the distinctions between "limited war" and "policing" operations and concluded that there was a difference: UN operations involved "a police force in military uniform, transported by the Air Force," and the Air Force "subscribed to the 'police concept'" without further definition.[26]

In 1960, however, the annual high-level Air Force meetings brought Air Commodore Fred Carpenter into the limelight on "brushfire war" issues. Carpenter was head of Air Transport Command and about to work with the UN on Operation MALLARD in the Congo. He advocated a radical idea: there should be one service instead of three and it should "be a kind of combat police force. This means inaugurating a body to operate in a disarmament inspection role." Canada should have a mobile force afloat with two or three "commando carriers" to serve "as bases in moving in police forces." Others did not agree with Carpenter's thinking, particularly the Chief of the Air Staff, since the bulk of discussion was directed toward providing air defence forces in North America and nuclear strike forces for NATO in Europe.[27]

By the time the Army and Navy were refining their thinking in 1961, however, there was less discussion in Air Force circles on brushfire wars. Carpenter admonished his boss for not doing enough to support the UN. Air Vice Marshal Campbell took issue with this: "We are quite willing to do things willingly vis-a-vis the Congo. Originally the government was very keen to get in there with all four feet. Well, the attitude of the coloured man to the white man quickly changed that. The treatment meted out to some of the troops makes the government wonder whether white troops should be in there."[28]

International events accelerated the armed forces' interest in rapid deployment forces. The most important was the Berlin Crisis in August-September 1961. Canada planned to send 3 Canadian Infantry Brigade Group to reinforce 4 Brigade in West Germany as part of NATO's deterrent maneuver at the height of the crisis. The problems were a lack of strategic lift to move the force quickly, and the high costs involved in doing so. Similar problems affected American and British forces which prompted changes to their force structures.[29] How could the two NATO reinforcement brigades in Canada be lightened for rapid deployment?

Canadian aspirations in the development of a rapid reaction UN standby capability should, therefore, be put in the context of Allied developments. British thinking on the use of a strategically air portable reserve dated back to 1953 when proposals were made to develop a rapid reinforcement capability for operations East of Suez. By 1957, the Royal Navy deployed one of four available aircraft carrier battle groups in the Indian Ocean to support a strategic air troop deployment. The 1958 Lebanese Crisis and the 1961 Kuwait Crisis highlighted the need for more systematic planning; by 1961 the British Army Central Strategic Reserve was reorganized into the 3rd Division (two brigades) and the 16th Independent Parachute Brigade. The RAF's 38 Group consisting of two ground attack squadrons, two helicopter squadrons, and a variety of strategic transports worked closely with the Central Strategic Reserve. Missions for the force tended to be low intensity conflicts in existing and former British colonies East of Suez and in Africa.[30]

The United States formed a joint organization called Strike Command in January 1962. STRICOM consisted of the US Army Strategic Army Corps (STRAC) which had been formed in the 1950s, and the USAF's Tactical Air Command (40 squadrons). STRAC consisted of two airborne divisions and two infantry divisions, the bulk of which were air-deployable. A 250-man company was on one hours' notice to move, followed by an 1800-man battle group at four hours' notice to move. The motives underlying STRICOM's creation related to problems with rapidly mobilizing and reinforcing NATO Europe during the 1961 round of the Berlin Crisis as much as developing a global limited war capability, although the Kennedy Administration strongly and publicly advocated the development of such a capability.[31]

The Canadian Army's post-Berlin assessment concluded that a rapid deployment capability would contribute to reinforcing Europe more efficiently and the matter of a UN Standby Force could be solved simultaneously. In early 1962 the Army looked at establishing 3 Brigade as a dual-tasked NATO reinforcement and UN Standby brigade group.[32] One battalion in 3 Brigade was the designated UN Standby Battalion Group on seven days' notice to move. Its training tasks were defined as "supervising UN-sponsored political and military arrangements; to maintain order; and to create a situation in which it is cannot be defied without creating an overt incident."[33] This last role was inserted to cover the projected NATO Mobile Force requirements that SACEUR was currently working on.

Then the Joint Planning Committee got involved since strategic lift and sustainment was a joint task with the other services. The Navy and Air Force identified the areas in which they thought they could provide such support without seriously affecting Canada's priority NATO commitments. Matters did not proceed much beyond this brief identification and no in-depth joint planning was conducted at this time.[34]

This did not prevent the Army from fine-tuning its views on UN operations. In his five-year program initiated in 1962, General Walsh stated that "UN military intervention, as a result of Communist influence or infiltration, could be expected in the under-developed nations. Additionally the UN may be asked to intervene militarily should clashes develop between Western and Communist-supported nations." Once again, the Canadian conceptual link between intervention and UN "police actions" was maintained.[35]

Notes to Chapter 8

1. See Roger Trinquier, *Modern Warfare: The French View of Counterinsurgency* (New York: Praeger, 1964); Robert Thompson, *Defeating Communist Insurgency* (London: Chatto and Windus, 1966); Douglas S. Blaufarb, *The Counter-Insurgency Era: US Doctrine 1950 to Present* (New York: The Free Press, 1977); Frank Kitson, *Low Intensity Operations: Subversion, Insurgency, Peace-Keeping* (Harrisburg: Stackpole Books, 1971); Michael A. Hennessy, *Strategy in Vietnam: The Marines and Revolutionary Warfare in I Corps, 1965-1972* (London: Praeger, 1997).

2. The "Flank Debate" also known as "Flank O' Mania" was a public one: see D.J. Gordon, "Guarding the Right Flank," *The Royal Air Forces Quarterly* Vol. 1 No. 1 (Feb 1961), 19-23; William H. Hessler, "Norway's Role in US Defence," *US Naval Institute Proceedings* July 1960, 31-37; E.H. Wyndham, "NATO: The Flanks," *Brassey's Annual 1960*, 149-162.

3. Gregory W. Pedlow, "Multinational Contingency Planning During the Second Berlin Crisis: The LIVE OAK Organization, 1959-1963," Nuclear History Program Third Study and Review Conference, Ebenhause, 26-29 June 1991.

4. DHH file 112.1.003 (D13) (23 Nov 59) message CCJS(L) to COSC Ottawa. See also Sean M. Maloney, "Fire Brigade or Tocsin? ACE Mobile Force and Flexible Response, 1958-1993," unpublished paper.

5. Sean M. Maloney, "Fire Brigade or Tocsin? ACE Mobile Force and Flexible Response, 1958-1993," unpublished paper.

6. DHH, Raymont Collection, file 767 (22 Oct 60) Miller to Harkness, "Brief on Canadian Defence Thinking."

7. Ibid.

8. NAC RG 24 acc 83-84/215 vol. 26 file 1200 pt. 4.2 vol. 16, (12 Sep 60) "Standby Force for the United Nations: first report of the APCC Sub-Committee."

9. NAC RG 24 acc 83-84/215 vol. 26 file 1200 pt. 2 vol. 15, DGPO, "Proposed CAORE Project."

10. NAC RG 24 acc 83-84/215 vol. 26 file 1200 pt. 2 vol. 15, (23 Feb 61) "United Nations Standby Administrative and Support Force."

11. DHH, Raymont Collection, file 1082, (1 Mar 61) Joint Staff, "The Role of United Nations Sponsored Military Forces."

12. Ibid.

13. Ibid.

14. Ibid.

15. DHH, Raymont Collection, file 1082, (17 Aug 67) memo Waldcock to Allard.

16. NAC RG 25 vol. 6104 file 50366-40 pt. 18.1, (31 Jan 61) JPC, "Canadian Military Support of the United Nations."

17. NAC RG 25 vol. 6104 file 50366-40 pt. 18.1, (20 Jun 61) DEA "Summary of paper entitled The Role of United Nations Sponsored Military Forces."

18. NAC RG 24 acc 83-84/215 vol. 26 file 1200 pt 2 vol. 18, APCC, "Tasks and Aims of the Army 1961-1963."

19. DHH, file 81/674 vol. 2, "The Tasks and Problems of the Canadian Army: CGS' Talk to National Defence College, 12 Jul 61."

20. Peter Haydon, *When Military Plans and Policies Collide: The Case of Canada's General Purpose Frigate Problems* (Toronto: Canadian Institute for Strategic Studies, 1991), 38.

21. DHH, (July 1961) "The Report of the Ad Hoc Committee on Naval Objectives."

22. Ibid.

23. Ibid.

24. Ibid.

25. Ibid., see also Haydon, *When Military Plans and Policies Collide*.

26. DHH, Raymont Collection file 2002, "Minutes of a Conference of Air Officers Commanding, 17-19 March 1959."

27. DHH, Raymont Collection file 2007, "Minutes of a Conference of Air Officers Commanding, 17-19 March 1960."

28. DHH, Raymont Collection file 2008, "Minutes of a Conference of Air Officers Commanding, 20-21 March 1961."

29. DHH file 114.3Q1 (D14) (12 Aug 61) memo D Movements to DQOP, "Brigade Movement-NWE"; (12 Aug 61) CGS to MND, "Despatch of a Second Brigade Group to Germany."

30. William Jackson, *Britain's Defence Dilemma: An Inside View* (London: B.T. Batsford, 1990), 42, 59, 81-82; Neville Brown,

Strategic Mobility (London: Chatto-Windus, 1963), 54-55.

31. Brown, *Strategic Mobility*, 50-53; The History of the Unified Command Plan 1946-1993 (Washington D.C.: Joint History Office, Office of the Chairman of the Joint Chiefs of Staff, 1995), 32-33.

32. NAC RG 24 acc 83-84/215 file S1200 pt. 2 vol. 18, (14 Feb 62) "Pre-Planning the Despatch of a UN Standby Force."

33. NAC RG 24 acc 83-84/215 file S1200 pt. 2 vol. 18, (14 Mar 62) "Standby Force: General Policy."

34. NAC RG 25 vol. 6104 file 20366-40 pt. 18.1, (26 Jun 62) JPC, "Canadian Military Support of the United Nations"; (6 Nov 62) JPC, "Guidance on Types of Forces Canada can most Readily Provide for use when dealing with requests for Support of the UN."

35. NAC RG 24 acc 83/84/215 vol. 26 file 1200 pt. 2 vol. 21, APCC, "The Canadian Army Programme 1963-1968."

BLUE AND WHITE KNIGHT: PEACEKEEPING AND THE PEARSON GOVERNMENT, 1963-1964

There is a widely held view that Canada can most appropriately contribute to world security through the agency of the United Nations. Viewed in the abstract, this proposition cannot be challenged. As a practical matter.... the prospects that the UN will during the next quarter century be capable of functioning as a global system of collective security are dim. The opposition which some Canadians have detected between NATO and the UN is fictitious. In fact, any prospect there may be that the UN can eventually develop into a true instrument of global security depends on the maintenance of a strong, stable North Atlantic community.

—Report of the Ad Hoc Committee on Defence Policy, 1963

The controversial Minister of National Defence, Paul Hellyer, drops by UNFICYP. The rapid deployment of Brigadier Jim Tedlie's 2 Brigade headquarters, the Royal Canadian Dragoon recce squadron and 1st Battalion, R22eR to dampen ethnic unrest in 1964 reinforced the case for creating a Canadian rapid deployment force called Mobile Command.

(CF photo)

The demise of John Diefenbaker's government was in part due to the 1963 federal election in which a majority of Canadians disagreed with the Government's nuclear disarmament agenda and emphasis on the UN over NATO and NORAD. Canada's failure to act responsibly during the Cuban Missile Crisis severely damaged relations with the United States at a crucial juncture of the Cold War. In the end, Lester B. Pearson was elected on a platform which promised a complete review of Canadian national security policy.[1]

The Diefenbaker government's foreign policy apparatus, led by Howard Green, reacted with little consistency every time a crisis with the possibility of UN force deployment emerged. There were no large Canadian UN deployments equal to UNEF: instead there were a series of small deployments in which the Canadian military and diplomatic contributions were obscured. When Pearson took office, the character of Canadian UN activity changed. Canadian troops would be used only in selected cases related to Canadian national interests and not deployed just because the UN requested Canadian participation. Once again Canada was back on course. The largest Canadian peacekeeping deployment of the time was Cyprus and that issue was directly linked to NATO. Yemen in 1963-64 and the slight expansion of the India-Pakistan mission in 1965-66 were sideshows but still related to important Western interests.

Another important aspect of Canadian UN operations under the Pearson government was the greater importance placed on institutionalizing such operations within the armed forces. Prior to 1964, Canadian UN operations were ad hoc. After 1964 changes to the armed forces incorporated a new low intensity conflict capability to conduct both counterinsurgency and peacekeeping, basing it on the foundation laid in 1961.

This chapter will examine the evolution of Pearson's peacekeeping policy from 1963 to 1965. It is important to note that Pearson's government remained committed to existing operations which included UNTSO, ONUC, and UNEF I. These three operations will be discussed in Chapter 11.

PEARSON'S NATIONAL SECURITY POLICY TEAM

The primary players in the formulation of Canadian national security policy during this period included Lester Pearson, Secretary of State for External Affairs Paul Martin, and Minister of National Defence Paul Hellyer. Air Marshal Frank Miller remained at the helm of the three services until they were merged to form the Canadian Armed Forces in 1964. Miller would then become the first Chief of the Defence Staff (CDS) from 1964 to 1966.

Paul Martin had been Secretary of State and Minister for Health and Welfare in the St. Laurent Government. An experienced Liberal Party powerbroker, Martin lacked foreign policy experience. He made up for it however with an unbounding enthusiasm and energy: he was not afraid to ask hard questions. Martin was ambitious and sought to succeed Pearson as head of the Liberal Party and Prime Minister. His relationship with the Undersecretary of State for External Affairs, Norman Robertson, was strained somewhat since Robertson was opposed to Canadian nuclear weapons acquisition. By late 1964, however, Robertson was diagnosed with cancer and had been replaced with Marcel Cadieux, a "staunch opponent of Communism" who had served with the ICC in Indochina and in NATO.[2]

Paul Hellyer's interest in defence matters went back to 1955 when he served as Associate Minister of National Defence under Ralph Campney. As Opposition defence critic during the Diefenbaker years, Hellyer was quite adept at hounding George Pearkes (but less adept getting at Douglas Harkness) particularly over nuclear weapons issues and NATO strategy. It was Hellyer and future Minister of Health and Welfare Judy LaMarsh who convinced Pearson to flip-flop on the nuclear aspects of the Liberal defence platform after the two secretly met with NATO Supreme Allied Commander Europe, General Lauris Norstad, in 1962. Hellyer had definite ideas about the future of Canada's defence forces and set about implementing them.[3]

The conduct of foreign policy during the Pearson years was generally left to Pearson and Martin, with little Cabinet input, according to Minister of Finance Walter Gordon.[4] In the early days, Pearson was an enthusiastic participant but as more and more domestic crises arose, he turned over greater control to Martin.[5] That said, Pearson's defence policy platform for the 1963 election was valid and formed the basis of future action. Its essential pillars were to defend the peace, have Canada do her part in the Western alliance, strengthen mobile defence forces, prevent nuclear proliferation, and ensure flexibility. Part of the platform stated that "[the Canadian forces] will be available for United Nations or other assignments to keep the peace. A new Liberal government will press for the formation of a permanent UN police force."[6] Many columnists and pundits latched on to the last statement and declared that Canada would take the lead in this area.

Pearson and Martin determined immediately after the 1963 election that the foreign policy priority was the repairing of the Canadian-United States relationship, so badly damaged during the Cuban Missile Crisis and the nuclear weapons issue. The bulk of Canadian diplomatic activity was therefore directed towards this end and included negotiations over acceptance of nuclear weapons for Canadian military forces and the development of trade relationships through mediums such as the Auto Pact.[7]

Secretary of State Paul Martin and Ambassador Robert Ford firmly believed that NATO was the cornerstone of Canadian national security and global influence. The UN, they maintained, was a tool to be used if NATO could not be implemented. Here Martin and Ford ask Soviet Premier Alexi Kosygin some hard questions at a meeting in the Kremlin.

(CIIA Photo)

Martin's second priority was NATO. NATO was undergoing a significant period of turmoil. The debate over who would control theatre nuclear weapons (such as the Multi-Lateral Force and Allied Nuclear Force projects) and Charles de Gaulle's intransigence over American domination of the release system affected Canadian interests. Canada had nuclear strike fighters based in France and West Germany and had made nuclear commitments to NATO. This was linked in turn to the problems of the Canada-US nuclear relationship in NORAD. The future of NATO strategy and France's role in it was of concern as well. Commonwealth affairs took a back seat to these problems, although Martin became involved in the Rhodesia question and British deliberations over whether or not a blockade should be placed on that colony. [8]

Martin formulated five Canadian foreign policy objectives which built on but essentially echoed Louis St Laurent's 1948 basis for Canadian Cold War national security policy:

1) Canada must have military security.
2) Canada must have expanding economic strength.
3) Canada must be able to exert influence on others.
4) Canada must be able and willing to play a creative role in international affairs.
5) Canada must maintain national unity at home.[9]

Martin believed that the cornerstone was item 1, expressed through NATO and NORAD. Without this foundation, the rest were impossible to achieve.

Where, then, did the United Nations fit in Martin's vision? In effect, the UN was supposed to act as a mechanism to maintain peaceful co-existence between the superpowers and to mediate crises which might affect this status quo. Secondly, the UN was a means for middle powers to influence the great powers. As for UN peace operations, Martin believed that they demonstrated a willingness for action, not just empty diplomatic words in a stagnant international forum. Consequently, Martin's Canadian UN policy was to use every means to affirm UN peacekeeping capability and to provide that international organization with the ability to act. This entailed ensuring that finances, forces, and constitutional mechanisms within the UN were functioning. UN peacekeeping allowed Canada the ability to act, and act independently if necessary, which contributed to maintaining an independent Canadian identity.[10]

Martin's emphasis on action is not surprising given the deadlocked atmosphere surrounding UN matters in 1963-64. Martin was most concerned with peacekeeping financing, the entry of the People's Republic of China into the UN, and the Middle East and Cyprus crises.[11]

The relationship between Canadian diplomats and the UN Secretary General during the Pearson years was almost in direct contrast with the previously close relationship with Dag Hammarskjöld. U Thant appears rarely to have consulted Canada on major issues prior to the 1967 evacuation of UNEF. The sole exception was a meeting between Thant and Martin relating to the war in Vietnam and the ICC. Martin's memoirs rarely mention Thant and imply that the two men continuously disagreed over America's handling of Vietnam. It is probable that Thant deliberately distanced himself from Western countries, including

Canada, to deflect criticism directed at the UN Secretariat during the continuing Soviet propaganda offensive in the wake of the Congo crisis.[12]

THE FINANCIAL CRISIS AT THE UN CONTINUES

While the Pearson government was debating the nuclear weapons issue with the Americans, External Affairs and National Defence continued to handle UN matters internally and concurrently throughout 1963. The primary issue was the ongoing financial crisis over who would pay for UN peacekeeping operations. When the UN deployed small numbers of UNMOs on missions like UNTSO or UNMOGIIP, the costs could generally be borne by the contributing countries. Even the costs for UNEF could be distributed and absorbed. With the proliferation of protracted UN peace operations like ONUC, however, the UN was incapable of supporting them without some form of formalized cost sharing. Essentially, one option was to have the contributing nations each make voluntary cash contributions in addition to turning over their military forces "free" of charge to the UN commands. Another option was to have all UN members contribute to a pooled fund from which all operations would be funded, with each member contributing on a sliding scale.[13]

The pitfalls of these approaches were obvious in light of Cold War intrigue within UN headquarters in New York. Who would decide which formula would be used for what mission? An obvious tactic, employed by the Soviets and the Belgians against ONUC, was to not pay into the communal pot and force contributors to pay more than their fair share, putting economic pressure on the force contributors. The so-called "Article XIX" debate broke out during this time: Once invoked, Article XIX would have prevented any nation from voting in the General Assembly if it had not paid its UN dues for that year. The problems of implementing such an article against a superpower were immense, and perhaps insurmountable.[14]

U Thant and his people struggled with these problems throughout 1963. Canada's interest was obvious, as a major troop contributor to both UNEF and ONUC. The Canadian position was to push for robust long-term financial arrangements to fund peacekeeping operations.[15] In the short term, however, the Pearson government favoured scaling back existing Canadian commitments to UN operations in small ways to save money. For example, the recce squadron committed to UNEF was equipped with Ferret scout cars. These were relatively expensive to maintain and less suited to desert recce operations. They were replaced with jeeps and the number of personnel committed to UNEF decreased. The Canadian ONUC signals unit was slowly reduced in numbers, as was the committed RCAF air lift to the Congo. There was no immediate solution to the long-term financing problem, however.

U Thant noted in early 1963 to insiders that a review of UN peacekeeping was imminent. The Honduran and Indian delegations were preparing a resolution to that effect, and there were similar public pronouncements by American and British senior diplomatic personnel. These developments prompted External Affairs to conduct its own study. G.S. Murray of the UN Division was dismayed about the "tendency in the thinking on United Nations peace-keeping methods to concentrate unduly on developing permanent or 'stand-by' arrangements for an international military force under United Nations command." Murray observed that UN peace operations encompassed a spectrum of activity, all of which involved peacekeeping. These included the establishment of UN commissions, the creation of watch dog committees, supervision groups for ceasefires (i.e., UNTSO), observation groups to report to the Secretary General (UNOGIL), the deployment of a Special Representative of the Secretary General or appointment of a distinguished personality (Ralph Bunche in the Middle East), and finally the direct personal intervention of the Secretary General (Dag Hammarskjöld in the Congo).[16]

According to Murray, the UN had changed, but the evolution was not going well. Peacekeeping, prior to Hammarskjöld's missions in the late 1950s, was the preserve of the Security Council and, when there was too much Soviet interference, the General Assembly became involved. The Security Council set the mandate for the operation. Over time, the Secretary General "was generally recognized as the only agent enjoying sufficient confidence to conduct the essential negotiations....his inventions and formulations served to bridge the gap created largely by the loss of confidence."[17]

The period 1956 to 1961 was unique, as Murray noted, "while Dag Hammarskjöld occupied the post, the Western powers could be reasonably assured that, although they might disagree with [his] decisions or with some of the details of his political philosophy, he would generally follow a policy line which could be supported by the West." Now, in 1963, Murray was alarmed that "in present circumstances, U Thant cannot be expected to react in the same way and he is more likely to be affected by advice from non-Western advisors." Murray recommended, therefore, that "the Western powers would be well advised to establish, for peace-keeping operations of the future, a form of political control which will ensure...that Western views are taken into account."[18] This was to ensure that Canadian UN forces and Canadian money were not misused for purposes which contradicted Canadian interests. Unfortunately, this was not evident to media outlets which ran headlines like "Canada: UN's Financial Patsy?"[19]

THE FIRST TEST: UNYOM IN THE YEMEN, 1963-1964

Pearson's first peace operation since becoming Prime Minister was lackluster when compared with the triumph of Suez. The Yemen, a decayed remainder of the Ottoman Empire, was a poverty-stricken, mediaeval Islamic state controlled throughout the 1950s by the equally decayed and violent Imam Ahmed. Ahmed had coveted the southern end of the Arabian peninsula, including British-controlled Aden, since the 1920s. It was no surprise, therefore, when he courted both the Soviets and the Chinese in the 1950s: the Soviets sent tanks, aircraft, and a military training mission while the Chinese built the ports, roads and airfields. Ahmed, concerned about a coup, would not allow his army to train on the Soviet-supplied equipment, which rusted away in open air storage areas. Western attempts to match guns with aid failed in this harsh regime that encouraged judicial amputations of extremities.[20]

By 1959, Ahmed was ill and his Crown Prince, a more moderate man, took power temporarily. Mohammad al-Badr asked for Egyptian assistance and before long a United Arab Republic army team was in-country training the decrepit Yemeni army. On Ahmed's return, however, the Egyptians were expelled. Throughout 1960 and 1962, UAR-trained Yemeni officers plotted a coup. Ahmed died in September 1962 and al-Badr took over again. Colonel Abdullah as-Sallal, with the assistance of UAR forces, finally staged a successful coup that month, declared that Yemen was now a republic, and joined Egypt and Syria as part of the UAR. The Soviet Union immediately declared that "any act of aggression against The Yemeni Arab Republic would be an act of aggression against the USSR."[21] Soviet engineers, East German agricultural specialists, and almost 30,000 Egyptian troops poured into the country.

Soviet interest in The Yemen was immediately obvious to any trained military observer. The territory adjacent to The Yemen included Aden Protectorate and Aden Colony, British-controlled areas. The British administered the colony portion and provided the defence for both. Aden had been a Royal Navy coaling facility since the 1800's and, with the advent of oil-fueled ships, a bunkering facility. During the Second World War, however, Aden's base facilities took on critical importance. Aden's geographical location at the base of the Arabian Peninsula commanded the entrance to the Red Sea and thus the Suez Canal. Its proximity to the Indian Ocean allowed the British to project power into that body of water and protect the sea lines of communications which connected the Red Sea to the Persian Gulf. It was also a vital supply line to India, Malaya, Hong Kong, and Singapore.

The closure of the Suez Canal in 1956 did not lessen Aden's importance. In the event of war with the Soviet Union, shipping still had to move from the Persian Gulf around the Cape of Good Hope, past the Congo and onward to Europe. The basing facilities at Aden, including the British Petroleum oil refinery constructed in 1957, the port which handled 5000 ships every year, and the RAF's Khormaksar airfield, were important elements in projecting Western power outside the NATO Area (see Chapters 3 and 4). Aden retained its importance in the 1960s when Sukarno initiated his confrontation with the British over Borneo and Brunei and force had to be employed to contain Indonesia (see Chapter 7). In 1960, the entire British Middle East Command joint headquarters was moved to Aden.[22] (see Figure 8)

Khormaksar airfield, however, had a special importance. In addition to handling the large air transports of the UK Army's Strategic Reserve, it was a staging base for Far East deployments of the RAF's Vulcan and Valiant nuclear bomber force. Starting in 1959, the PROFITEER exercise series demonstrated that rapid deployment of nuclear bombers through Aden was feasible. As a member of CENTO, Britain had nuclear commitments that assisted in containing overt Soviet, Chinese, and other activity in the region and protecting NATO's flank. The PROFITEER exercises were also useful signals to Sukarno in Indonesia, perhaps deterring him from having designs on Singapore or Australia.[23]

Al-Badr was less concerned about Cold War geopolitics and, in 1962, initiated a counter-revolution using the fierce tribes to the north and east of Sana'a, the capital. The bulk of the fighting was between the Egyptian Expeditionary Force and the Monarchist tribes since

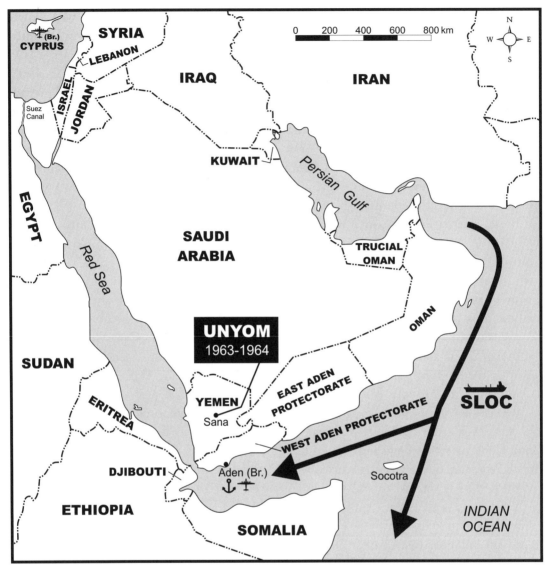

Figure 8: The Yemen and Aden, 1962-1966

Colonel as-Sallal's forces were laughably unreliable on the battlefield. As-Sallal himself was never more than a cut-rate Nasser replica in any event.

As-Sallal fell in with Nasser on matters that were far outside his purview. Nasser was irritated by Jordanian and Saudi Arabian criticism of Cairo's activities in the Yemen. He encouraged as-Sallal to initiate military operations against Saudi Arabia. Egyptian and Soviet piloted airplanes and helicopters attacked Saudi settlements in early 1963. The Saudis then covertly sent weapons to al-Badr's Monarchist forces, but one such flight defected to Egypt.[24]

As-Sallal then called for revolution in the British-controlled Aden Protectorate, which had about 20,000 ethnic Yemenis. These people were pro-Republican and sought to merge Aden Protectorate and Aden Colony with the YAR. Egypt backed the forming of a revolutionary organization, the National Liberation Front, which was supported by as-Sallal through the YAR. Infiltration of the Aden-YAR border started and before too long mines were blowing up British vehicles in Aden Colony. As-Sallal then armed the Radfan tribes in Aden Protectorate and they started harassing British facilities.[25]

U Thant's memoirs, like Pearson's and Martin's memoirs, hardly deal with The Yemen and off-handedly state that "the conflict threatened to split the Arab world."[26] Ralph Bunche, who acted as U Thant's representative to The Yemen, understood that the stakes were even higher: there were American policymakers who would perceive this to be the Soviet's use of two proxies to undermine American economic and thus security interests in the Persian Gulf, with all of the obvious implications.[27] Indeed, Israel was providing arms and training to the Monarchists with the express purpose of tying down large parts of the Egyptian Army in a place far removed from the Armistace Demarcation Line and the International Frontier in the Sinai.[28]

Canadian interest in The Yemen and Aden went back to 1958. Arnold Smith, Canada's representative in Cairo, noted that,

> The factors which determine Canada's concern with the UAR are both general and particular...arising out of our vital interests in helping maintain peace, the security and influence of Western civilization against Communist expansion, and support for the UN are much the more important; and a variety of circumstances give Canada...
> a significant opportunity and hence responsibility for contributing to support the common interests in this area which we share with our allies.[29]

This view was accepted wisdom in External Affairs and National Defence. The importance of the Aden base facilities was recognized by External Affairs and there were even Canadian concerns of Soviet involvement in The Yemen as early as 1958: "Yemen can be expected to make an intensive effort to dislodge the United Kingdom from its last military foothold in the Middle East". Concerns were also raised in NATO circles over the security of Aden at this time.[30]

The events of 1962 and 1963 concerned External Affairs greatly. Sympathies were with Saudi Arabia and the British[31]: "[The] determination of Saud to stamp out Yemeni revolution is understandable because it implies grave menace to his own regime." Nasser "would not let Yemen Republic to fail" although apparently Nasser privately let it be known that "if the Saudis did not publicly intervene, but confined themselves to smuggling arms to counter revolution, the UAR would not intervene" on a massive scale and involve the Soviets.[32]

In any event, the Kennedy Administration had forestalled all this by recognizing the as-Sallal regime in the UN. This needlessly irritated the Jordanians and Saudis, not to mention the British. This blunder, on par with American support for Indonesia against the Netherlands over West Iriya, was rectified in time and Kennedy nominated Ellsworth Bunker to conduct shuttle diplomacy in concert with Ralph Bunche, representing the UN. U Thant had a vague plan for disengaging the Saudi-YAR border and establishing a small UN military observer presence in that region.[33]

Bunche then flew to Sana'a to meet with as-Sallal, who promptly told the UN representative that he would attack Aden if something was not done about the Monarchists. Bunche told U Thant that "Yemen could become the Cuba of the Near East." His plan was to develop a Yemeni-British *rapprochement*, provide UN technical support to the YAR, and get Bunker to restrain the Saudis. Bunche recommended against a UN peace force. The problem was that Bunker had just talked the Saudis into accepting a phased withdrawal of Egyptian forces in return for ceasing support to the Monarchists, to be overseen by UN military observers.[34]

U Thant was now forced to accept the fact that the UN would deploy a peace observation force to The Yemen. He sent Major General von Horn to conduct a reconnaissance, and the foundation of the United Nations Yemen Observer Mission (UNYOM) was formulated. The Secretary General ran into the financing problem as the Soviets continued to interfere with the costing mechanisms. Third World troops contributors were out of the question unless they could get American financing, which in turn would be attacked by the Soviets as "imperialist interference." Consultations between American and Canadian diplomats highlighted the American plight: Canadian assistance was required.[35]

Paul Martin and Norman Robertson discussed the matter. Robertson's position was that the primary objective was to maintain the prestige of the UN and that UNYOM was a vehicle to do so. He did understand, however, that deploying UNYOM quickly was necessary "in order to forestall obstruction by the Soviet Union." Robertson warned, however, that there "is no assurance that the intended operation will achieve its objectives" and this might damage Canadian prestige.[36] It was clear that Robertson's subordinates believed that participation in UNYOM was a good move and similar to UNOGIL and UNTEA in that they "provided cover for disengagement" since "certain outside states, notably the USA...could be embarrassed if the process of disengagement were not carried out smoothly."[37]

"The most dangerous, worst equipped and least politically realistic UN mission." UNYOM's UN flag acted as a fig leaf for the cringing international community in Saa'na, Yemen, while Nasser's Soviet-backed UAR troops used chemical weapons and napalm against poorly armed monarchist guerilla forces.

(CF Photo)

The Soviets reacted with predictable venom in the UN, particularly when Thant proposed using UNTSO, ONUC, and UNEF personnel to work around the financing problem. Ambassador Robert Ford's view from Cairo was that the Soviets were behaving poorly "because disengagement from Yemen favours USA by diminishing likelihood of early overthrow of Saudi Arabian monarchy."[38]

It was rapidly becoming clear to observers that UNYOM was essentially a fig leaf. Von Horn reported that the terrain was extremely forbidding and would have to be monitored by helicopters and light planes, not the jeep-mounted patrols originally proposed. Such units were more costly, and they could not be seconded permanently from UNEF or ONUC since they were national assets dedicated to those operations. The UAR troop commander in Yemen decided that the UN plan lacked credibility and demanded that the UN extend its disengagement line to cover the YAR-Aden border too. These factors were passed on to New York. Canadian analysis confirmed von Horn's concerns: UNYOM was going to be a "diplomatic umbrella." Robertson changed his mind, and now thought that Canada "should not be in too much of a hurry.... We shall not be doing ourselves any service, nor the United Nations, if we press forward with a proposal that has no real meaning either in political or military terms."[39]

Canadian analysis indicated that the Egyptian Expeditionary Force would not withdraw and that it would leave "substantial number of troops in Yemen in guise of a training mission." UNYOM, as presently conceived, would be a "token" observer mission that could verify but not actually monitor disengagement.[40] Canada was then asked by the UN to provide a composite light aircraft/helicopter unit to UNYOM. Air Marshal Miller indicated to Norman Robertson that the UN mission in The Yemen was "a highly dubious one" and he strongly recommended against "even limited Canadian participation."[41] Hellyer, when told about Miller's objection, overruled him on principle and told Martin that the armed forces would participate.[42] Miller proceeded to drag his feet. When Ralph Bunche asked Canada for a Caribou aircraft to transport him to the YAR, Miller denied the request, citing logistics problems and suggested to Robertson that the matter be referred to Cabinet for consideration.[43] After Paul Hellyer got involved, the aircraft was released. Then it was shot at and damaged enroute to Sana'a. Robertson sheepishly requested National Defence to ask the RCAF air advisor to the UNYOM advance party "not to expose their aircraft to undue risks."[44] Given the chaotic environment on the ground and the nature of the mission, Robertson was clearly out of his depth.

U Thant, meanwhile, was able to get the Security Council to go along with the creation of UNYOM, but not fund it. Alternative methods were used by which the UAR and Saudi Arabia agreed to fund the limited UNYOM force equally, but not a force which was actually capable of closely monitoring the disengagement line nor the forces behind it. The American diplomats were "extremely relieved."[45]

Canadian consideration of UNYOM participation was handled rapidly in mid-June 1963. Martin backed involvement, while Hellyer was concerned that Canada would get too involved, that there was no clearly defined duration of the operation (what we would refer to today as an "exit strategy") and that it would cost too much. Furthermore, it would mean reducing Canadian contributions to UNTSO and UNEF. Which was more important strategically? Maintaining the peace opposite Israel where Canada was already established, or launching a new mission which was contrived? Martin's argument was that the mission had to appear to succeed since it would bolster the position of the Secretary General and the Security Council in the larger debate over UN peacekeeping. Hellyer continued to dissent, but Pearson closed the argument stating that "Canada was almost bound to participate." An RCAF light air unit partially composed of aircraft and personnel dedicated to UNEF was authorized and dispatched to The Yemen.[46]

Although the situation appeared to be resolved at the political level, prospects for a successful mission in-theatre were less promising. The Disengagement Agreement established a forty-kilometre-wide zone on the northern border with Saudi Arabia. Robert Ford in Cairo noted that "UAR Air Force has almost certainly used phosphorus bombs against Saudi towns. This will not help create that atmosphere of confidence between Saudis and Egyptians which....is essential if the disengagement is to work."[47] Ford noted that the UNYOM venture was in serious trouble since "UNYOM cannot and was not intended to stop hostilities between Republicans and Royalists inside Yemen" since the "aim of the operation is to provide a face-saving cover for this Saudi-UAR disengagement which would prevent a direct confrontation possibly engulfing [the] whole Mideast in war."[48]

No one asked al-Badr and the Monarchists for their opinions on peace and they continued their operations against the YAR and UAR forces elsewhere. Von Horn's disgust was privately passed on to Canada: he was "very pessimistic and thought that [UNYOM was] the most dangerous, worst equipped and least politically realistic" UN mission he had participated in. In his view, "only the presence of a symbolic mission had been accepted."[49] Von Horn's comments were widely distributed within External Affairs. This prompted External Affairs to ask the American State Department for their opinion.

The Americans confirmed that they were taking action to pressure Saudi Arabia and had in fact sent a USAF air defence squadron to Dhahran, Saudi Arabia as a sign that the United States would not allow further cross-border UAR air operations. If the Saudis violated the Disengagement Agreement or interfered with UNYOM, the squadron would be withdrawn with the obvious implications. This had a calming effect on things in Riyadh. They confirmed that they viewed UNYOM as a "face saving exercise" for both the UAR and the Saudis.[50]

None of the actions taken by the UN, Canada, or the United States had a noticeable effect on the guerrilla war inside the YAR. In some instances, UAR fighter-bombers carrying napalm reportedly closely followed the UN's RCAF aircraft, which were conducting aerial observation related to the Disengagement Agreement, and then peeled off to attack Monarchist villages on the ground. It appeared to the Monarchists that the UN was supporting the UAR.[51]

More importantly, UNYOM had no impact on the UAR-sponsored subversion and infiltration of Aden Protectorate. Indeed, British covert operations in support of the Monarchists designed to draw fire away from Aden were seriously curtailed. In legitimately focusing on the possible conflagration that might result if Saudi Arabia went to war with the UAR, an opportunity by Canada and the United States to employ UNYOM to limit the damage to Aden was, perhaps deliberately, overlooked. Von Horn, for example, thought the Kennedy administration had sold the British out over Aden to protect Saudi Arabia, while other observers noted that the American policy in the region was uncoordinated.[52] It does not appear as though the United Kingdom asked Canada for assistance in using UNYOM to act as a buffer for Aden. Why so, given the agreed-upon importance of the bases?

The British government changed in 1964 and, with the winding down of the confrontation with Indonesia, considered Aden to be less important (despite the opinions of the military leadership). The UAR-supported insurgency against British forces in Aden Protectorate was increasingly nasty and posed public relations problems for the British in other, more important, oil-bearing countries in the Gulf, like Muscat and Oman. It is probable that Aden was sacrificed. In time Soviet naval vessels and patrol-bomber aircraft were using Aden as a base for their operations in the Indian Ocean, which posed an even greater threat to the vital Persian Gulf shipping lanes.[53]

An internal account of Canadian operations in The Yemen noted that "a more ill-conceived or disorganized mission than that in Yemen cannot be visualized....Whether or not the existence of UNYOM averted a major conflict, it certainly did not succeed in attaining any degree of peace in Yemen."[54]

THE 1964 WHITE PAPER ON DEFENCE AND UN PEACEKEEPING OPERATIONS

While Canadian troops and aircraft observed developments in The Yemen, Pearson launched the promised defence review and Paul Hellyer set out almost immediately to make it happen. The product was the *1964 White Paper on Defence* released in March. The process by which the 1964 White Paper was formulated, however, provides significant insight into the continuing Canadian conceptual overlap between counterinsurgency and peacekeeping operations (see chapter 8) and the means by which such operations were to be carried out. Essentially, Hellyer held open hearings in the House of Commons Special Committee on Defence (SCOD). At the same time, Hellyer formed the closed Ad Hoc Committee on Defence which consisted of military and civilian analytical personnel from the three services. In addition to these forums, several tri-service committees were struck to examine specific military problems. All of these inputs flowed back to Hellyer and the White Paper was derived from this data by the Minister himself.

Held in June 1963, SCOD was designed so that a variety of views could be aired and trial balloons launched: it was essentially a politically antagonistic brainstorming session so that the Pearson government could claim it was involved in bi-partisan defence policy formulation, which was new to the Canadian political process. Many influential ideas, however, gained saliency.

Hellyer's presentation to SCOD subordinated UN peacekeeping to NATO operations. His view was that "from time to time suggestions have been made that we should turn over part of our armed forces to the UN. To date there has been no inclination on the part of the UN to accept this kind of offer and the maintenance of a standby battalion...seems to be the best alternative in these circumstances."[55] In fact, the bulk of discussion on Hellyer's presentation related to nuclear weapons and NATO strategy.

Each service presented its current establishment and deployment. The Navy ignored UN operations in its presentation. The Army explained that UN operations provided the variety that was necessary to offset the boredom of garrison life in Canada. SCOD members also learned that the standby battalion had, in fact, been alerted for service in Lebanon and in the Congo and that the designated unit exercised regularly. In one case, "last month we moved the battalion from Valcartier (Quebec) to Wainwright (Alberta) and on landing it carried out an exercise to restore law and order."[56] No eyebrows were raised among the SCOD members. The Air Force presentation noted the number of UN airlift operations it had participated in, but as with previous presentations, the question and answer period revolved around NATO and nuclear weapons.[57]

SCOD also heard from Secretary of State for External Affairs, Paul Martin. Building on his existing foundation, Martin told the committee:

> We have been living under a massive threat from militant communism in circumstances of cold war which robbed the United Nations of its ability to perform its main peace-keeping operations under article 43 of the charter. Clearly our first duty has been to help maintain the peace through collective security arrangements, and this we have done through playing our full part in NATO and NORAD consistent with our resources. It represents our contribution to the deterrent which has successfully kept a precarious peace.[58]

Martin also noted that,

> At the same time and in the same period, there has been an urgent need to improve the international means of dealing with limited wars and regional disputes and otherwise developing the means for a peaceful settlement of potentially dangerous conflicts. Here our support for the United Nations both in its mediation functions and its peace-keeping roles has been the main vehicle for Canadian action.[59]

The main problem for Canada now was where to put her military resources. Martin believed that there should be more focus on developing means to deal with limited conflict, but did not specifically refer to UN peacekeeping as the mechanism to do so.[60] As before, NATO and nuclear weapons dominated the discussions.

It is fair to state that the parliamentarians were overly fascinated with the minutiae and mechanics of nuclear warfighting in the NATO and NORAD contexts and less so with how conflict could be prevented through deterrence and peacekeeping interventions. This is not surprising given the fact the previous governments had denied them access to such information and the last government had fallen because of it. There was a distinct lack of interest directed at the grand strategic themes they were meant to discuss.

A retired Navy Commodore, James Plomer, leveled a series of public accusations against the Navy leadership. Plomer's attack was comprehensive and he noted that there was a lack of strategic sea lift. Plomer cited a plan to rent a Canadian Steamship Lines freighter for the sum of one dollar so that Canada's ONUC contingent could deploy.[61] Opposition members in SCOD pursued this, perhaps as a means of embarrassing the government, and implied that the government was not doing enough to support the UN with naval forces. The Chief of the Naval Staff, Herbert Rayner, pointed out that there were no standing UN naval commitments and that "Our present ships are adaptable to the peace-keeping or policing operations. If there was going to be more emphasis placed on that role then we would move to a certain type of ship." The Navy's priority was, however, homeland defence—hunting Soviet nuclear missile submarines in the North Atlantic.[62]

SCOD also heard from the now-retired Lieutenant General Guy Simonds, former Chief of the General Staff, and General Charles Foulkes, the former Chairman of the Chiefs of Staff Committee. Simonds had definite ideas on the future of the Canadian armed forces:

> I believe that a role which is suited to a country of our size and having regard to the financial burdens possible to be borne out over a lengthy term, would be a tri-service force whose main objective was peace-keeping. I believe its organization should be very much like that of the United States Marine Corps which is a mobile force complete with all its ancillaries and able to meet what are commonly called brushfire situations.[63]

Simonds thought Canada should move away from nuclear commitments in the NATO Central Region and focus on making "a contribution to preventing a situation developing which would lead to thermonuclear exchange."[64] It is unclear exactly what Simonds was referring to. It appears to have been a hybrid between NATO's ACE Mobile Force and a UN peacekeeping force, rapidly deployable and either capable of fighting a low intensity war to generate a peaceful environment or a force to be inserted after peace had been made through the UN. He did indicate that it should be the size of a division and equipped with strategic air transport.[65]

Charles Foulkes was then questioned on the possibility of a Canadian mobile force for peacekeeping. Foulkes had originally suggested in 1959 that the brigade group committed to NATO in West Germany should be re-equipped as an airportable formation capable of nuclear and conventional operations. The committee members, not being military men, were clearly confused and tended to lump all conflicts short of nuclear war together. They thought Foulkes had been referring to a concept similar to Simonds'.[66]

Foulkes chose to address the idea voiced in the press and in SCOD about turning over the entire Canadian armed forces to the UN. Essentially, this idea emerged after Pearson, the hero of Suez, was elected Prime Minister and there was still a wave of public optimism about the role of the UN in world affairs. The former Chairman noted that Canada had played critical roles in UN peace operations and that the UN should have some permanent stand-by arrangement with member countries, but turning the Canadian forces into such a force was ridiculous. Foulkes pointed out that even Dag Hammarskjöld did not think this was feasible since each emergency situation demanded a different type of response:

> To suggest that Canada should put all of its forces at the disposal of the United Nations is not a sound proposition.... it should be constant Canadian policy to make our armed forces available for United Nations service as required. This does not mean, however,

that Canada or any other country is expected to turn over its forces to the direction of a non-existent United Nations command to be used in accordance with the will of any fleeting majority in the Security Council or assembly.[67]

Eventually, SCOD called back General Geoffrey Walsh, the Chief of the General Staff, for more extensive discussions about strategic lift for a mobile force. Walsh had to explain in great detail that there was one brigade group deployed in West Germany and two more in Canada dedicated to NATO as a strategic reserve force. There was an additional brigade group for operations in North America. There was not enough shipping to move the two Canada-based brigades with their tanks, vehicles, ammunition and artillery to Europe in an emergency: this had been tested during the 1961 Berlin Crisis but the previous government chose not to do anything about it.[68]

After SCOD, Hellyer formed several internal National Defence committees to explore the ideas in more detail. One of these was the Mobile Force Committee, which met from August to November 1963. Hellyer's instructions were rather specific: determine what such a force would look like and how much would it cost.

> The type of mobile force I have in mind is basically an air transportable fighting unit which could be airlifted with its equipment for quick deployment anywhere in the world. The force should be mechanized and have a high fire power and great flexibility which would make it adaptable to varying circumstances. It should be flexible enough that it could form part of the mobile reserve of the Supreme Allied Commander in Europe or serve in a United Nations operation or other circumstances as required to meet national policy. It may be desirable that some units be air-droppable, but the principle criterion is air-portability of the entire force.[69]

The Minister thought that the force should be the size of a division with its own air transport and close air support capability. Thought was to be given to the ability to transport and land the force by sea.

The Joint Planning Committee set about fulfilling the Minister's direction but there was some confusion. When Hellyer used the term "mobile force", was he referring to NATO's ACE Mobile Force (Land), the multinational brigade group of which Canada was not yet a member? This would not make sense, since AMF(L) was to act as a "show of force" deterrent manoeuvre on NATO's flanks. AMF(L) had special deployment criteria in a crisis situation with the Soviets so that this manoeuvre could be made. How was the Canadian mobile force to interface with this? There was also the question of a force having a high volume of firepower and at the same time being light and airportable. Was that firepower to be nuclear, conventional, or both?[70] There was no further direction and the committee went off on its own to deliberate.

The mobile force committee concluded that such a Canadian force could fulfill the defence of Canada and NATO ACE Mobile Force tasks, but that the UN task was "more difficult as it could range from a UN police-type effort similar to the Congo or UNEF force to the Korean-type conflict."[71] The existing models examined by the committee included the US Marine Corps, the US Army Strike Command, the UK Strategic Reserve force and UNEF. Essentially, the planners were looking for a division which could take on whatever role was needed at the time, an early concept where there was a brigade group dedicated to NATO AMF(L) missions, an airborne brigade group and an amphibious brigade group for UN tasks.[72]

More clarification was required. Air Marshal Miller, the Chairman of the Chiefs of Staff Committee elaborated where he thought he should. The problem was one of nuclear armament. If the mobile force was going to participate in NATO operations either alongside the AMF(L) or other NATO formations, it had to have a nuclear capability to function within NATO's strategic framework. Miller thought that the Canadian mobile force should be nuclear-capable and "possess equipment which was nuclear adaptable" like the airportable Little John nuclear rocket that could be carried by transport helicopter.[73]

All those involved noted the serious obstacles to the creation of such a force. No companion study on strategic air or sea lift had been conducted, so that if the Canadian mobile force was created from the existing Army units, nothing would really change. Secondly, the structure for the planned mobile force was dependent on equipment and technologies which did not exist or were unavailable at the time. Fielding this force would be an expensive proposition. Finally, such a force would be light on the ground in the NATO context. This was unacceptable since the enemy forces were heavily mechanized with tanks, APCs and self-propelled artillery. Such a force might be able to function in a UN context, but not a NATO one and therefore was incapable of meeting the Minister's requirements.[74]

Hellyer finally redefined the committee's terms of reference. Could the West Germany-based heavy mechanized brigade co-exist with the mobile force? This would solve the NATO problem. The mobile force could then come from the three brigade groups based in Canada.[75] A Joint Service Study Group was also formed to look at strategic lift. Their report was quite pessimistic: there was barely enough airlift to move one battalion, let alone nine.[76] Hellyer's demand that the mobile force have its own close air support capability caused a certain amount of difficulty for the Air Force, which was not used to joint operations. In any event, the Air Force members thought that a squadron of F-4C Phantom II should be acquired for recce and interdiction, while two squadrons of A-6 Intruders or A-4D Skyhawks could provide close air support to the mobile force. All three aircraft types were dual capable, conventional-nuclear delivery platforms.[77]

In their final analysis the mobile force planners were never able to reconcile the need for mechanization and the requirement that the force be light and airportable. They were frustrated in their attempts to design a formation which had three brigades which were homogeneous. The strategic lift issue was one that needed to be addressed jointly at a higher level. Hellyer's insistence that the formation be capable of instantaneous deployment into an incredibly varied set of scenarios proved too much for the committee to handle, although they were intellectually honest in their approach to the problem.

Hellyer formed the Ad Hoc Committee on Defence Policy, which carried out its deliberations concurrent with the mobile force and other committees. Since the final product of this committee seriously influenced the 1964 White Paper, it is useful to examine its conclusions on the role of the UN and UN peacekeeping in Canadian national security policy.

Led by Dr. R.J. Sutherland of the Defence Research Board, the five-man tri-service committee explored where Canadian defence and foreign policy had been since 1945 and where it was going well into the 1970s. Hellyer's terms of reference for the committee included the development of alternatives to the status quo. The primary focus was on the NATO commitments, whether or not Canada could or should disengage from them, and to what degree was this possible or even desirable.[78]

The report concluded that "the purpose of Canadian defence programmes and activities is to support an alliance policy. In terms of Canadian national interests, the rationale of Canadian defence is to maintain influence with our allies. The immediate purpose of Canadian defence is to serve as an effective support of Canada's intra-alliance diplomacy." Therefore, was the UN a more effective agent than NATO, the Commonwealth, or the Canada-US relationship in the achievement of these objectives?

Essentially, there were two predominant public views on the future of the UN. Either the UN would become a "functioning world government" or it would cease to exist. If the UN were to change from the status quo of 1963, it would through uncontrolled international forces, not through "the proliferation of ingenious schemes by persons who, being unable to reform the world, believe they can reform the United Nations." The Security Council was "impotent" and the probable trend was "more effective Great Power diplomacy pursued of the UN." The UN General Assembly was a "world debating forum which reflects neither the realities of power nor a political consensus." That said, however, "the UN will continue to serve as the focus of a non-public multilateral diplomacy."[79]

What about UN peacekeeping? The members thought that there was a trend by interested parties towards delving into the minutiae of UN operations to the detriment of more fundamental issues. The three existing control bodies of the UN, the Security Council, General Assembly, and Secretary General, were in varying degrees incapable of positive sustained action. The possibility of a new controlling body for peace operations existed but "any organ of the UN which does not reflect the realities of power cannot make effective use of force. To ignore this is probably the one sure means of destroying the UN."[80]

The report also tackled the "UN Army" concept:

It is worth noticing that the enthusiastic support for a permanent UN military force which is felt by certain Western nations such as Canada, the Scandinavian countries and Ireland, is not shared by the great majority of Afro-Asian, including such important nations as India. The reasons are not hard to find. Few Canadians would welcome the idea that the UN should interest itself in the grievances of the North American Indian, the rights of the Sons of Freedom or the Columbia River Treaty. The majority of Afro-Asians regards a permanent UN military force as a potential instrument of intervention in matters which they consider with equal definiteness to be their own business.[81]

Canada should not, however, shy away from participating in UN peace operations. The problem was a preoccupation in the media and in academia that Canada should re-orient the armed forces strictly for UN operations: "Such proposals have tended to be conceived in the abstract and without much regard to the tangible circumstances of the UN or for Canadian national interest. In some cases political innocence has been carried to rather excessive lengths."[82]

The committee looked askance at these ideas since "it is quite possible that Canada would be instructed to make war on South Africa or to defend Cuba against the United States." Therefore, the most likely Canadian employment of force under the UN umbrella was the provision of "technical troops not readily available from other sources," airlift and light aircraft, and staff officers since "it is unlikely that Canadian combatant forces would be acceptable." This was not just because Canada was part of NATO, as alleged by many detractors, since "Canada is a white nation. Canada is too powerful a nation to be innocuous and Canada's interests are too clearly identified with those of the North Atlantic community to qualify as a neutral."[83]

The drafting of the new defence policy continued throughout late 1963 and early 1964. Hellyer himself wrote the first draft, which was then circulated to External Affairs for comment. There were two major differences of opinion between the two departments: Hellyer's views on NATO strategy and on UN peacekeeping.

Hellyer wanted to explain to the public that massive retaliation and trip wire nuclear defence concepts were obsolete in the 1960s. He took pains in the draft to explain that Canada's forces had to be able to operate or respond flexibly across the whole spectrum of military force (from peace observation to nuclear warfare) in order to deter as well as fight if necessary. This was in accordance with the direction of NATO strategy in 1963 (see chapter 8). The External Affairs personnel altered this to emphasize that flexibility in Canadian force structure was necessary so that the majority of Canadian forces at home would be available for UN duty. Hellyer was, in effect, skeptical about the future utility of UN peacekeeping. Similarly, his section on UN peacekeeping was far more critical than the final version which was influenced by External Affairs. Hellyer was quite critical of UN operations, of the Afro-Asian bloc, and the validity of UN stand-by forces. All of this was removed and replaced with a list of operations which had a smug tone.[84] The modifications to the 1964 White Paper appear to reflect Norman Robertson's views more than Paul Martin's.

The final version of the 1964 White Paper was a departure from previous defence statements: it was explicit, clear, and public. NATO deterrence operations were clearly ascendant; the objective of Canadian defence policy was "to preserve the peace by supporting collective defence measures to deter military aggression" and then "support Canadian foreign policy including that arising out of our participation in international organizations."[85]

The main threat to Canadian interests was still the Soviet nuclear and conventional forces directed against the NATO Area. Notably, however, the policy now recognized that "Communist countries can be expected to continue to promote expansionist aims by measures short of all-out war." Canadian defence policy formally recognized a spectrum of conflict and formally set out to institutionalize its force structure to operate within it. Canada anticipated having NATO forces to hold the line and UN peace operations to handle crises which might affect superpower peace.[86]

The controversy over the White Paper did not involve strategy or objectives. It was the section on the future shape of the Canadian forces which overshadowed all else. Hellyer proposed the merger of all three services into a single service, essentially one big "triphibious" mobile force which was interoperable. The details of that controversy are beyond the scope of this work.[87] Within the new structure, one Army brigade group was to remain in Europe for service with NATO, while two of the Canadian-based brigade groups would be retrained and re-equipped "to permit their effective deployment in circumstances ranging from service [with NATO] to United Nations peace-keeping operations." The fourth brigade group was to be modified into an airportable formation for rapid deployment.[88]

The White Paper fell short on the question of strategic lift. A small section noted that a modest capability should be acquired, but there were no specifics. There was a lot of detail about the need for mobility and flexibility but none on how to achieve it.

The Army was not idle during the 1964 White Paper process and was engaged in anticipatory planning throughout 1963. Army planners believed that the main front was still NATO's Central Region. Army appreciations of the future world situation, however, placed some emphasis on preparing for "Peripheral Wars" which were "local in scale and will probably involve the Western powers in peace-keeping rather than fighting roles." In addition to maintaining a capability to react to those, Army planners assumed that a global capability be retained by the smaller Western powers "so that a confrontation of the major powers can be avoided." In other words, pro-NATO middle powers should be able to take on peripheral conflicts as surrogates.[89]

For the 1960s, Army planners thought there would be continuing moves toward the creation of a standing international UN force, but the more probable type of UN operations would be similar to the Suez, Lebanon, and Congo variants. The participation of Army combat units was "unlikely to be accepted...from a nation so firmly in the Western camp as Canada." The deployment of technical units as in the UNEF and ONUC cases was more likely.[90]

The main problem was training and organization to operate across a spectrum of conflict which included nuclear war, conventional mechanized war, counterinsurgency, and peacekeeping. Consequently, the forces required to fight in the main battle area in NATO's Central Region "are neither organized nor equipped for the type of role Canada is likely to assume in UN operations." To do so would necessitate having two sets of equipment and two training syllabi. There would have to be two armies.[91]

To be fair, by 1963 many in the Army were skeptical about the UN standby battalion role. In their view "at no time has the demanded or agreed upon Canadian contribution for a UN operation matched the Canadian Army units assigned to the UN standby role." Maintaining forces, which would not be sent, at such a high readiness level placed great strains on the personnel.[92]

Paul Hellyer thought the Army was dragging its feet. In early 1964 he committed Canada to providing two infantry battalions to NATO's ACE Mobile Force (Land). He was interested in

> pressuring the Canadian military into beefing up the capability of our land forces and giving that capability higher priority vis-a-vis the nuclear concept than they had been willing to do. I felt that a well-equipped, well-trained 'bird in the hand' was of greater potential use than a non-existent division to be mobilized over some ill-defined period.[93]

Chief of the General Staff Geoffrey Walsh then converted 2 Canadian Infantry Brigade Group (2 CIBG) to "a Special Service Force with an emphasis on airportability" on 26 March 1964.[94] By November, 2 CIBG was the repository of the AMF(L) commitments and the existing UN Standby Battalion role.[95] Therefore, Canada had a mechanized brigade group in West Germany as part of NATO, this new, barely airportable Special Service Force, and two other brigade groups which were supposed to handle defence of Canada operations and serve as reinforcements to the Germany-based brigade group. In effect, 2 Brigade became the Army's low intensity conflict rapid deployment force.[96]

The 1964 White Paper was released in March 1964. Over the next year, the Army, Royal Canadian Navy, and Royal Canadian Air Force and their associated headquarters ceased to exist in an exercise referred to as "integration" or more commonly "unification." The replacement organization was the Canadian Armed Forces led by a Chief of the Defence Staff who commanded Canadian Forces Headquarters (CFHQ). It consisted of several functional commands which reported directly to CFHQ including Maritime Command (Atlantic) and Maritime Command (Pacific) which incorporated the naval and maritime anti-submarine forces on each coast; Air Defence Command; Air Transport Command; 1 Air Division (the NATO-committed nuclear strike force in Europe); 4 Canadian Mechanized Brigade Group (the NATO-committed land force in Europe) and Mobile Command.[97]

The obstacles to this vast project were incredible, in that it necessitated severe cultural shifts which took years to implement. There was no Army or Army headquarters, so much corporate knowledge was in danger of being lost in the interim. Continuity of operations overseas was also in danger of disruption. Mobile Command was now responsible for peacekeeping and low intensity operations, while the rest of the command handled the deterrent forces in North America and Europe. The matter of deployability for Mobile Command became a secondary issue for the time being: the dangerous Cyprus Crisis loomed in the eastern Mediterranean and threatened to fling NATO into the abyss.

Notes to Chapter 9

1. Maloney, *Learning to Love The Bomb*.

2. John Hilliker and Donld Barry, *Canada's Department of External Affairs Volume II: Coming of Age, 1946-1968* (Kingston: McGill-Queens University Press, 1995) 250-255, 260

3. See Maloney, *Learning to Love The Bomb*.

4. Walter Gordon, *A Political Memoir* (Toronto: McClelland and Stewart, 1977), 279- 280.

5. See *Mike: The Memoirs of the Rt. Hon. Lester B. Pearson Volume Three 1957-1968* (Toronto: University of Toronto Press, 1975)

6. NAC MG 26 N6 file: Defence Memoranda 1962-1965 (n/d) "Responsibility in Defence."

7. Paul Martin, *A Very Public Life Volume 2* (Toronto: Deneau Publishers, 1985) Chapter XII.

8. Ibid.; see also David N. Schwartz, *NATO's Nuclear Dilemmas* (Washington D.C.: The Brookings Institution, 1983) and Jane E. Stromseth, *The Origins of Flexible Response: NATO's Debate over Strategy in the 1960s* (Oxford: Macmillan Press, 1988).

9. Paul Martin, *Paul Martin Speaks for Canada: A Selection of Speeches on Foreign Policy, 1964-67* (Toronto: McClelland and Stewart, 1967), 17.

10. Ibid., 19-20, 29-30.

11. Martin, *A Very Public Life Vol. 2*, 529.

12. U Thant, *View from the UN*, 64-65; Martin, *A Very Public Life Vol. 2*, 432.

13. Norman J. Padelford, "Financing Peacekeeping: Politics and Crisis," in Norman J. Padelford and Leland M. Goodrich, eds., *The United Nations in the Balance: Accomplishments and Prospects* (New York: Praeger Books, 1965), 80-98.

14. DHH, Raymont Collection, file 847, (n/d) "Background Paper on United Nations Finances: Fourth Special Session of the United Nations General Assembly."

15. DHH, Raymont Collection, file 847, (8 May 1963) memorandum to Cabinet, "Fourth Session of General Assembly on Financing Peacekeeping Operations."

16. DHH, file 653.003 (D 28) (n/d) UN Division, G.S. Murray, "United Nations Peace- keeping Machinery."

17. Ibid.

18. Ibid.

19. Arron R. Einfrank, "Canada: UN's Financial Patsy?" in *Montreal Daily Star*, 22 July 1964.

20. Edgar O'Ballance, *The War in Yemen* (London: Faber and Faber, 1971), 54-58.

21. Ibid., 73.

22. Tom Pocock, *East and West of Suez: the Retreat from Empire* (London: The Bodley Head, 1986), 64; Eric J. Grove, *Vanguard to Trident: British Naval Policy Since World War Two* (Annapolis: Naval Institute Press, 1987), 256, 265-266.

23. Humphrey Wynn, *RAF Nuclear Deterrent Forces* (London: HMSO, 1994), 311, 443- 444; Pocock, *East and West of Suez*, 64.

24. Ibid., Chapter 4.

25. Julian Paget, *Last Post: Aden 1964-1967* (London: Faber and Faber, 1969), 34-40.

26. U Thant, *View from the UN*, 49.

27. Urquart, *Ralph Bunche*, 362.

28. Tony Geraghty, *Who Dares Wins: The Special Air Service 1950 to the Gulf War* (revised edition) (New York: Warner Books, 1997), 384; NAC RG 25 vol. 5438 file 11282-B-40 pt. 1, (5 Jul 63) message Tel Aviv to External Affairs, "Yemen."

29. NAC RG 25 (volume obscured) file 12554-40 pt. 1.1, (6 Oct 59) message Cairo to External Affairs Ottawa, "CDA-UAR Relations."

30. NAC RG 25 vol. 6146 file: 50406-B-40, (12 May 58) Summary report No. 32 "Aden: The United Kingdom-Yemeni Dispute"; (16 Jul 58) message NATO Paris to External Affairs Ottawa.

31. NAC RG 25 vol. 6146 file: 50406-B-40, (1 Mar 63) message London to External Affairs Ottawa, "Yemeni Incursion in Aden Federal Territory."

32. NAC RG 25 vol. 6146 file: 50406-D-40, (3 Oct 62) message Cairo to External Affairs Ottawa, "Yemen."

33. U Thant, *View from the UN*, 49.

34. Urquart, *Ralph Bunche*, 364-365; NAC RG 25 vol. 5438 file 11282-B-40 pt. 1, (30 Apr 63) message PERMISNY to External Affairs Ottawa, "Yemen."

35. NAC RG 25 vol. 5438 file 11282-B-40 pt. 1, (30 Apr 63) message PERMISNY to External Affairs Ottawa, "Yemen."

36. NAC RG 25 vol. 5438 file 11282-B-40 pt. 1, (1 May 63) memo for Minister, "Request for Canadian Participation in UN Operations in Yemen."

37. NAC RG 25 vol. 5438 file 11282-B-40 pt. 1, (2 May 63) message External Affairs Ottawa to distribution list, "UN Presence in Yemen."

38. NAC RG 25 vol. 5438 file 11282-B-40 pt. 1, (8 May 63) message London to External Affairs Ottawa, "UN Presence in Yemen."

39. Von Horn, *Fighting for Peace*, 315-319; NAC RG 25 vol. 5438 file 11282-B-40 pt. 1, (13 May 63) memo USSEA to UN Division, "United Nations and Yemen."

40. NAC RG 25 vol. 5438 file 11282-B-40 pt. 1, (16 May 63) message External Affairs Ottawa to Washington D.C. "UN Presence in Yemen."

41. NAC RG 25 vol. 5438 file 11282-B-40 pt. 1, (31 May 63) memo Robertson to Martin, "Canadian Participation in United Nations Observer Group in Yemen."

42. NAC RG 25 vol. 5438 file 11282-B-40 pt. 1, (4 Jun 63) memo SSEA to distribution list, "United Nations Observer Group in Yemen."

43. NAC RG 25 vol. 5438 file 11282-B-40 pt. 1, (7 Jun 63) memo Robertson to Martin, "Yemen Operation."

44. NAC RG 25 vol. 5438 file 11282-B-40 pt. 1, (18 Jun 63) message PERMISNY to External Affairs, "Yemen: UN Operation"; (19 Jun 63) memo for Minister, "Yemen-Canadian Participation."

45. NAC RG 25 vol. 5438 file 11282-B-40 pt. 1, (12 Jun 63) message PERMISNY to External Affairs Ottawa, "Yemen."

46. NAC RG 2 (11 Jun 63) Cabinet Conclusions; DHH, Raymont Collection, file 847, (4 Jun 63) memo to Cabinet, "Canadian Participation in United Nations Observation Group in Yemen."

47. NAC RG 25 vol. 5438 file 11282-B-40 pt. 1, (25 Jun 63) message London to External Affairs Ottawa, "Yemen."

48. NAC RG 25 vol. 5438 file 11282-B-40 pt. 1, (21 Jun 63) message Cairo to External Affairs Ottawa, "Yemen."

49. NAC RG 25 vol. 5438 file 11282-B-40 pt. 1, (26 Jun 63) message London to distribution list, "Yemen-UNYOM."

50. NAC RG 25 vol. 5438 file 11282-B-40 pt. 1, (29 Jun 63) message Washington D.C. to distribution list, "UNYOM."

51. NAC RG 25 vol. 5438 file 11282-B-40 pt. 1, (19 Jul 63) memo for SSEA, "UN Operation in Yemen"; (22 JUl 63) memo DL(2) to DL(1) "UN Operation-Yemen."

52. Von Horn, *Soldiering for Peace*, 314; Grove, *From Vanguard to Trident*, 249.

53. Palmer, *Guardians of the Gulf*, 86.

54. DHH, (19 Dec 66) "Report No. 13: Canada and Peace-keeping Operations Yemen- UNYOM."

55. House of Commons, *1963 Special Committee on Defence: Minutes of Proceedings and Evidence Tuesday, June 18 1963 and Thursday June 27 1963*, 18.

56. House of Commons, *1963 Special Committee on Defence: Minutes of Proceedings and Evidence, Thursday July 11 1963*, 147.

57. House of Commons, *1963 Special Committee on Defence: Minutes of Proceedings and Evidence, Thursday July 16 1963*, 172.

58. House of Commons, *1963 Special Committee on Defence: Minutes of Proceedings and Evidence, Thursday July 25 1963*, 241.

59. Ibid.

60. Ibid.

61. House of Commons, *1963 Special Committee on Defence: Minutes of Proceedings and Evidence, Thursday October 10, 1963*, 386.

62. House of Commons, *1963 Special Committee on Defence: Minutes of Proceedings and Evidence, October 15 1963*, 424-425.

63. House of Commons, *1963 Special Committee on Defence: Minutes of Proceedings and Evidence, Thursday October 17 1963*, 439.

64. Ibid.

65. Ibid., 477.

66. House of Commons, *1963 Special Committee on Defence: Minutes of Proceedings and Evidence, Tuesday October 22 1963*, 498.

67. Ibid., 505.

68. House of Commons, *1963 Special Committee on Defence: Minutes of Proceedings and Evidence, Tuesday October 29 1963*, 593-594.

69. NAC RG 24 vol. 22 file 1200.M4, (27 Aug 63) memo from MND to CCOS.

70. NAC RG 24 vol. 22 file 1200.M4, (27 Sep 63) Allan to DGPO, "Mobile Force."

71. Ibid.

72. Ibid.

73. NAC RG 24 vol. 22 file 1200.M4, (25 Sep 63) "First Report of the Ad Hoc Mobile Force Study Group"; (27 Sep 63) memo Miller to Love, "Report of the Ad Hoc Mobile Force Study Group."

74. NAC RG 24 vol. 22 file 1200.M4, (4 Oct 63) "Army Component of Mobile Force."

75. NAC RG 24 vol. 22 file 1200.M4, (24 Oct 63) memo to Planning Group, "Army Division-Mobile Force."

76. NAC RG 24 vol. 22 file 1200.M4, (4 Nov 63) Minutes of the 30th Meeting of the Joint Service Study Group.

77. NAC RG 24 vol. 22 file 1200.M4, (1 Nov 63) Minutes of the 29th Meeting of the Joint Service Study Group.

78. DHH, file 72/153 (30 Sep 63) "Report of the Ad Hoc Committee on Defence Policy."

79. Ibid.

80. Ibid.

81. Ibid. The Sons of Freedom were a Doukhobor terrorist group which operated in British Columbia in the 1960s.

82. Ibid.

83. Ibid.

84. DHH, Raymont Collection, file 759, (15 Jan 64) memo to CCOS, "Comments on the Views of External Affairs on the Draft White Paper on Defence Policy"; (30 Dec 63) memo to CCOs from MND, Draft of 1964 White Paper on Defence; *White Paper on Defence: March 1964* (Ottawa: Queen's Printer and Controller of Stationary, 1964).

85. *White Paper on Defence: March 1964* (Ottawa: Queen's Printer and Controller of Stationary, 1964).

86. Ibid.

87. See Douglas L. Bland, *Chiefs of Defence* (Toronto: CISS, 1995) and Paul Hellyer, *Damn the Torpedoes: My Fight to Unify Canada's Armed Forces* (Toronto: McClelland and Stewart, 1990).

88. *White Paper on Defence: March 1964* (Ottawa: Queen's Printer and Controller of Stationary, 1964).

89. NAC RG 24 acc 83-84/215 vol. 26 file S1200, 4.2 vol. 23, APCC "Statement of Canadian Army Objectives 1964."

90. Ibid.

91. Ibid.

92. NAC RG 24 acc 83-84/215 vol. 26 file S1200, 4.2 vol. 23, (6 Apr 64) memo VCGS to DGPO, "Standby Force."

93. Letter Hellyer to Maloney, 16 August 1995.

94. DHH file 112.1.009 (D39), (26 Mar 64) message CANARMY to all commands.

95. DHH file 112.1.009 (D39), (30 Nov 64) "Special Service Force: Organization and Employment."

96. Note that the 1963-65 Special Service Force should not be confused with the 1970s incarnation of the same name. The 1960s SSF consisted of HQ 2 Canadian Infantry Brigade Group, 4 Royal Canadian Horse Artillery (to be converted to a light artillery regiment), 1st Battalion, Canadian Guards, 2nd Battalion, Royal Highland Regiment of Canada, and 1st Battalion, Queen's Own Rifles. A light armoured regiment was added later on. See DHH, Raymont Collection file 3284 , (2 Apr 65) "Special Service Force Establishments."

97. Bland, *Chiefs of Defence*, 83.

CHAPTER 10

YOU'VE GOTTA KEEP 'EM SEPARATED: CANADA, NATO AND THE UNITED NATIONS FORCES IN CYPRUS, 1964-1965

The capacity of most people on this island for self-deception is staggering.

—Arthur Andrew, Canadian High Commissioner for Cyprus, 1964

Unlike Diefenbaker's Congo operation, the Pearson government was not afraid to deploy Canadian combat troops to stamp out a burgeoning brushfire war. The situation in Nicosia calmed down when the Canadian contingent repeatedly demonstrated that it would not be pushed around by the opposing forces.

(CF photo)

Canada's involvement with the United Nations Forces in Cyprus (UNFICYP) lasted from 1964 to 1993. It has been Canada's longest peace operation to date, with an average of 800 to 1000 Canadian soldiers deployed in any given year. The situation even reached the point where an entire second generation of Canadians manned observation posts their fathers had manned in the past. The explanations for this lengthy commitment to the so-called "Island of Love" have remained obscure. The imperatives driving Canadian UN peacekeeping policy throughout the Cold War, as established in previous chapters, remained the same in the Cyprus dispute; that is, to prevent an increasingly violent and anarchic situation in a former British colony from developing to the state where it could be exploited by the Soviets to deny a vital region to NATO and its deterrent forces. At another level, the Cyprus dispute cut straight into the heart of the NATO alliance as two members faced off with each other and prepared for a limited war. The Alliance was already under strain as a result of John F. Kennedy's poor treatment of France, the Netherlands, Belgium and Canada over various NATO-related issues. What was the best way to defuse the situation and maintain the common front against Soviet expansionism? Any wrong move would destroy NATO and possibly lead to an American withdrawal from Europe, with disastrous consequences.

From a Canadian perspective, the resolution of the 1956 Suez Crisis has always been held up as the single shining moment in Canadian diplomatic history and crisis management. Clearly Suez was important, but Canada's role in the Cyprus peace process was of equal importance, even though it was less dramatic in its execution and more convoluted in its *modus operandi*.

BACKGROUND TO THE CONFLICT IN CYPRUS 1560-1960

The situation in Cyprus was, as in other parts of the Middle East and the Balkans, related to the long term effects of ethnic and strategic policies established by the Ottoman Empire seven hundred years ago. Cyprus was settled by the Venetians and Greeks until 1570 when, after a long siege by the Ottomans led by Lala Mustafa, Venetian forces capitulated. The valiant but outgunned garrison commander, Marc Antonio Bragadino, was flayed alive, mutilated, and his straw-stuffed body put on display. The population was subjugated and assimilated into the Ottoman Empire through a combination of depopulation and enforced servitude in either Ottoman brothels or the Janissaries.[1] The situation would remain static until the 1800s, when Greece gained her independence and looked to isolated Mediterranean Greek communities to unify with the mainland. Mainland Greeks brought to Cyprus to teach transmitted this doctrine, called *enosis*, to the Greek Cypriots. During the First World War, however, the British annexed the island at the expense of the defeated Ottoman Empire. Greek refugees from other Ottoman-controlled areas in the Middle East made their way to the island. By the 1950s, the island had half a million residents of which 80 percent were of Greek descent while a further 18 percent were Turks.[2]

Cyprus was subsequently incorporated in the British empire. Despite the fact that Greece and Great Britain fought together against the Ottomans during the war, there was more and more agitation on Cyprus among the Greek population for *enosis*. This agitation resulted in severe rioting in 1931. The Second World War put a damper on violence while the Italian and German offensives raged through the Balkans and into mainland Greece. The Greek Civil War from 1944 to 1949 also distracted Greek nationalists until the mid-1950s as the Greek polity defended itself from Soviet-backed Bulgarian and Albanian communist forces.[3]

British policy against *enosis* in the 1950s was dictated by the belief that the movement could be exploited by the Soviet-backed Communist AKEL party on the island. The Turkish government was also anti-*enosis* for the same reason: in the event of a Third World War they did not want to fight on three fronts if Cyprus shifted into the Soviet sphere of influence. The pro-*enosis* Greek Cypriots, however, had other ideas. Led by Colonel George Grivas and the Greek Ethnarch, Archbishop Makarios III, the National Organization of Cypriot Fighters (EOKA) and a number of political front organizations were formed between 1953 and 1955 (note that there was no initial connection between EOKA and AKEL: EOKA was nationalist but not communist). Violence erupted against the British forces on the island in March 1955: by the winter of 1956, EOKA terrorist activity was stimulated further by the failure of the Anglo-French expedition to Suez.[4]

On the international front, a September 1955 bomb attack by unknown perpetrators against the Turkish consulate in Thessalonika provoked rioting in western Turkey. Thousands of Greeks fled. Intercommunal violence started on Cyprus, although it was of a comparatively minor nature. The Eisenhower Administration then dispatched several strongly worded letters to Athens and Ankara. The Greeks reacted poorly to the American missives as "they were seen as putting the victims on the same level as the assailant."[5] NATO Commander in Chief Allied Forces South (CinAFSOUTH), Admiral William Fechteler, met with both Greek and Turk military authorities to ensure that peace was maintained on the Bosporus.[6]

By 1958, however, EOKA guerrilla warfare against British forces on Cyprus and Turk Cypriot communities escalated into massive unrest and chaos. One observer noted that "it was impossible to know whether the day would be one for riots, shootings, bombings or arson or any combination of these."[7] Nine Greek Cypriots were killed by Turk Cypriots and the tension level on the island increased. The EOKA campaign was having some success at convincing British authorities that Cyprus was becoming yet another colonial liability. This perception was promoted by the Americans who had determined "that Greece and Turkey should not renew their ancient feud and so jeopardize the security of NATO's southern flank."[8] Economic pressure was applied to bring the antagonists to the bargaining table in late 1958.

The negotiating table was located in Paris and was arranged through NATO channels. An earlier plan championed by the British government two years previously was once again brought forward by Paul Henri Spaak in NATO circles. In essence, it postulated a seven year period in which there would be two legislative assemblies on the island: one Greek and the other Turk, while the British determined the specifics of independence. In December 1958, the Turks accepted the concept, but the Greeks rejected it. The British told the Greeks they would implement the plan with or without their consent. Makarios then rejected *enosis* (although Grivas did not agree) as a tactical move to keep the talks going. The British conceded that the island could become independent earlier but only if the military bases remained under British control. These concessions led to further talks in 1959.[9]

The Zurich and London agreements of 1959 between Ankara, Athens, and London were "intended to provide a formula whereby the Greek and Turkish Cypriots could live together in peace."[10] The long political process which would culminate in the 1964 crisis was now set in motion. The February talks produced agreement that there would be a Cypriot republic with a Greek Cypriot President and a Turkish Cypriot Vice President. The next steps, taken over the next year, were to formulate a constitution and work out the language of three treaties: the treaties of Guarantee, Establishment, and Alliance.[11]

The Treaty of Establishment permitted the creation of the British Sovereign Base Areas (SBAs, discussed in the next section), while the Treaty of Guarantee established that there would be no *enosis*, and no ethnic partition. There would be bi-national independence and the rights and equality of both ethnic groups would be enshrined. The Treaty of Alliance was the basis for the creation of a bi-ethnic joint military headquarters for the Greek and Turkish military contingents on the island.[12]

It would, however, take some time before all three agreements were hammered out. Canadian observers of the process noted early on that one means to solve the situation would be to make Cyprus a member of the Commonwealth, since it was a former colony. Other ideas under consideration in early 1960 also included allowing a united Cyprus to join NATO. An initial assessment by External Affairs concluded, however, that such a drastic step might not prove necessary if the Treaty of Establishment was accepted by all parties "since the West's defence interests in the island will be secured by the United Kingdom's retention" of the bases.[13] Indeed, Athens would probably "welcome the admission of Cyprus to NATO" but there were no initiatives planned. Athens intended to leave the decision to the Greek Cypriots if the matter was raised formally.[14] The Turkish position was:

> For public consumption the Turks argue that their southern flank can never be secure unless the strategic area of Cyprus is included in NATO's regional defence planning, but there is obviously more to it than that. The Turks seem to feel that Cypriot membership in NATO would be one more useful guarantee against future trouble from the Greek Cypriots and that if Cyprus became a clearcut NATO responsibility it could never be allowed to fall under control of the Greek Cypriot communists. It also seems possible that in supporting Cypriot membership, Turkey (and perhaps Greece) have in mind increasing the importance of the South-Eastern area of NATO and adding a new voting member which could be expected to loyally support their view.[15]

There were, however, recurrent concerns throughout this period in NATO and Canadian venues that "there is a real danger that [the] USSR will make a play for Cyprus as soon as the republic is established." There was a related concern that NATO membership would invite undue Soviet attention and that the Commonwealth route remained the best one since the security of the bases would be retained in that eventuality anyway.[16]

CANADIAN INTEREST IN CYPRUS 1960-1963

It is clear that in the early manifestations of the Cyprus crisis, Canadian and NATO interest in Cyprus revolved around the critical Sovereign Base Areas (SBAs). Why exactly were they so important? The importance is readily apparent when the geographical position of the island and its relationship to the Middle East and the Soviet Union is considered (see Figure 9).

As discussed in previous chapters, the provision for and maintenance of bases for Western forces involved in nuclear deterrence was paramount. The British SBAs on Cyprus were extremely critical in that effort. British Valiant, Vulcan, and Victor nuclear bombers operating from Cyprus could conduct an "end run" on strong Soviet air defences situated in the Warsaw Pact countries. Western Russia was home to more than 700 intermediate-range ballistic missiles aimed at NATO's European members. Only a pre-emptive strike by a combination of V-Force bombers and Greek and Turkish air forces equipped with nuclear strike aircraft could damage this force. RAF Akrotiri acted as one of many world-wide "shell game" dispersion bases in the event of war and thus complicated Soviet attempts to target V-Force and destroy it.[17] Notably, there were also plans to use Cyprus as a British intermediate range ballistic missile base equipped with the planned Black Knight and Blue Streak rockets.[18]

The United Kingdom also had nuclear commitments to CENTO so that the oil fields in the Persian Gulf which lay outside of NATO's protective umbrella could be defended. Consequently, six squadrons of Canberra bombers and recce aircraft of the Near East Air Force (NEAF) were based on Cyprus. From 1961 to 1965 some of these aircraft were equipped with a LABS capability which allowed them to drop nuclear weapons. The NEAF strike squadrons also were committed to deterring attacks against Jordan, and Kuwait.[19] It should come as no surprise, therefore, that British strategic and tactical nuclear weapons were stored at RAF Akrotiri.[20]

The SBAs also acted as staging bases so that conventional land and air forces could be rapidly deployed to hot spots in the Middle East. A prime example occurred in 1961 when Iraq threatened to invade Kuwait. The UK Army's Strategic reserve deployed through Cyprus on its way to the Persian Gulf, as did several fighter and light bomber squadrons. The rapid deployment of British forces, impossible without the Cyprus bases, staved off a serious conflict in that region which would have affected the West's oil supply.[21]

Covert intelligence gathering was critical to the deterrent effort directed against the Soviet Union, in which Cyprus also played a role. Numerous British signals intelligence sites were located on the island prior to independence and some remained in the SBAs after 1960. American CIA U-2 reconnaissance aircraft operated from Akrotiri, as did Royal Air Force-manned U-2s, throughout the 1960s.[22]

Any crisis over Cyprus would seriously disrupt NATO's ability to deter and defend itself in other areas. For example, various American military and civilian intelligence agencies maintained no less that seven large signals and electronic intelligence gathering sites in Turkey. These resources were directed primarily at the Soviet space launch and ICBM test centre at Tyuratam and also collected strategic early warning intelligence. "Ferret" missions using USAF EC-130 and CIA U-2 aircraft were also conducted from Turkish soil. There were no less than eleven American nuclear storage sites in Turkey, many of which provided nuclear weapons to the Turkish military forces. The Greek contribution to the deterrent effort was smaller since Greece did not directly abut the Soviet Union. Nevertheless, there were eleven more nuclear storage sites located in Greece, as well as ten critical communication facilities, one of which "talked" to American ballistic missile submarines committed to NATO's nuclear strike plan.[23]

Indeed, the base issue was central to the Cyprus debate throughout 1960 while the constitutional arrangements were devised. Makarios and his principle advisor and UN ambassador, Zenon Rossides, delved into the minutiae of how many square hectares the SBAs would include. Rossides followed a course of outright obstructionism until the Greek government agreed to the British position because of the importance of the bases to NATO efforts and put pressure on the Cypriots.[24] There was some internal UK debate over the need for the bases, elements of which were communicated to Canadian sources, which tended to accept that "the bases are extremely useful, both for the communications and air facilities they provide."[25] The Turkish position was a non-issue: "they are anxious to see the United Kingdom maintain strong military installations on the island," although Dr. Fazil Kuchuk, the Turkish Cypriot Vice-President, supported Makarios.[26]

American policy regarding Cyprus during this period consisted of retaining Cyprus as part of the West in the worldwide anti-Soviet effort. The SBAs were "inviolate" and the United States "should enjoy unrestricted use of [the] communications facilities on the island."[27]

External Affairs convened a rare interdepartmental meeting on the Cyprus issue in February 1960 so that the basis for a Canadian policy could be formed. Essentially the Canadian debate revolved around the acceptance of Cyprus into the Commonwealth and NATO. The members concluded, however, that no detailed policy could be made without a military appreciation of the need for the SBAs. The Chairman of the Chiefs of Staff Committee, Air Chief Marshal Miller, was asked to provide such an appreciation.[28]

Miller's staff unearthed similar paperwork which had been requested by External Affairs in June 1956, in which then-Chairman of the Chiefs of Staff Committee General Charles Foulkes concluded that "these bases are particularly valuable in cold or local wars, and their retention by the British is a significant contribution to the overall deterrent to war."[29] Was this still valid for the 1960s? It appeared at the time that alternative oil sources might be available from Libya and Algeria and, since Iraq had become hostile to Western interests, that the British need for a deployment base may have lessened. Obviously, the External Affairs analysis could not have foreseen that the pro-West Libyan government would be toppled in a coup in 1969 or that the French would give up Algeria in 1961. The 1956 military appreciation still held in 1960: the Cyprus bases were still important.[30]

As for admitting Cyprus into NATO, Makarios decided by late 1960 that he wanted Cyprus to be non-aligned. Both External Affairs and National Defence also noted in their analysis that NATO membership was not in the best interests of the organization: the SBA formula was an acceptable mechanism to protect NATO interests.[31]

Unexpectedly, the Turkish government was overthrown by military coup on 27 May 1960. The 38-member army council led by General Gursel then took charge. In time the

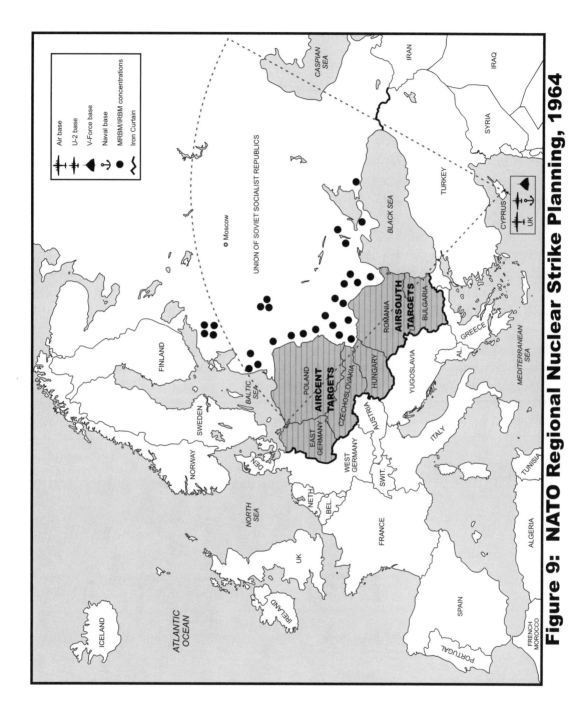

Figure 9: NATO Regional Nuclear Strike Planning, 1964

Karamanlis government in Greece would also fall, this time in an election, which left the Cyprus issue in the hands of governments which had not signed the original agreements.[32] Gursel announced that a specially-trained Turkish Army battalion would be sent to Cyprus for independence day celebrations to guarantee the protection of the Turkish Cypriots and maintain peace between the two ethnic communities. This move did not bode well for future relations.[33]

Cypriot independence occurred in August 1960 and one month later it joined the United Nations. By February 1961, Makarios assented and Cyprus became a member of the Commonwealth. The three treaties came into effect: the only one that was fully implemented without controversy, however, was the Treaty of Establishment. The flawed implementation of the Treaties of Alliance and the constitutional arrangements were the primary catalysts to the 1963 Christmas Crisis which in turn precipitated the 1964 wave of violence which resulted in the deployment of UN forces.

The President was Greek Cypriot, while the Vice-President was Turkish Cypriot. The legislative assembly was 70 percent Greek Cypriot and 30 percent Turkish Cypriot. The problems with this state of affairs is obvious: the Turkish Cypriot population was approximately 18 percent, not 30 percent, which engendered negative feelings in the Greek community about Turkish over-representation. The Treaty of Alliance also got off to a rocky start: the bulk of the police forces were drawn from the Greek Cypriot communities, which produced some overcompensation by the Turkish Army in the numbers of troops it wanted to station on the island.[34]

Independence demanded that Canada develop diplomatic representation on the island and in time Margaret Meaher was selected to be the Canadian High Commissioner. The accreditation of a military "Service Advisor" for her, suggested by the Director of Military Intelligence, was also approved: this individual was authorized to liaise with the British intelligence services on Cyprus with the aim of developing information on the Arab world and Israel. The service advisor's primary role, however, "was to make his principle interest what goes on in Cyprus outside of the bases."[35]

Canadian officers like Colonel Ned Amy were called upon time and again to mediate complex diplomatic and political tasks in volatile situations. Colonel Amy, representing UNFICYP, meets Archbishop Makarios III in Nicosia, Cyprus.

(CF photo)

High Commissioner Meaher's briefing on Canadian interests is instructive. In general, Meaher was sent to Cyprus since the island was "of undeniable importance in the complex of Middle Eastern politics, and both the internal political situation and the development of Cypriot external relations will need to be watched." Meaher was warned that the demand for *enosis* was still strong in the Greek Cypriot population and that the complex constitutional arrangements would produce instability. She was also asked to keep a careful eye on AKEL developments, as well as watch for Communist infiltration. AKEL "was biding its time, it is well-organized and could easily pose a threat to the present political structure of the island." Soviet and Chinese activity were also targeted for analysis.[36]

Meaher was told that "Canada's primary interest in Cyprus is that country's membership in the Commonwealth." As for the Sovereign Base Areas:

> It is understood that during the initial months of independence the bases have been operating smoothly. Any interruption in the peaceful operation of the bases would have implications not only for Anglo-Cypriot relations, but also for the Commonwealth as a whole, and we would be most anxious to receive early news of it.[37]

In her first report Meaher confirmed to External Affairs that the British had nuclear weapons on Cyprus and that the bases were vulnerable to low level labour agitation since their water supplies came from outside the territory controlled by the British parachute brigade and RAF forces. As for Communist activities, there appeared to be no penetration of the Turkish Cypriot communities, but on the Greek Cypriot side, "it seems clear that the Cypriot Communists are playing their hand cleverly and that their goal is to win over the country by legitimate means." They would exploit the Greek-Turk split at every opportunity and were developing closer ties with Makarios, even though the Archbishop denied this to the Canadian High Commissioner. Meaher was convinced that the Soviets backed AKEL and that the overly-large 28-man Soviet embassy staff "are certainly not all fully engaged in normal Embassy activities."[38] Ambassador Pavel Ermoshin was "pleasant, friendly, mild, and apparently harmless. Clearly, as the head of the Soviet mission which numbers far more staff than its normal diplomatic duties could possibly justify, in a country where communism had made substantial headway, Ermoshin is unlikely to be the innocuous, simple fellow he appears."[39]

Canadian observers in Turkey noted with alarm that Makarios appeared to be developing closer ties with Nasser, which, combined with growing Turkish concerns about Communism in Cyprus, was generating increasing paranoia in Ankara. Gunsel's advisors believed that AKEL extremists would generate conflict between EOKA hold-outs and the Turkish community. In the Canadian ambassador's words, "an attempted *coup de force* on the island could not be excluded." If that happened, the Turkish military would invade to stabilize the situation.[40] Canadian and American personnel in Ankara conferred and concluded that the Turkish government was in fact inclined to view Cyprus as a potential Cuba and that using such terminology in private with other NATO allies was significant.[41]

Toward the end of 1961, Archbishop Makarios signed a trade pact with the Soviet Union, while General Gunsel was elected in Turkey. Canada was increasingly agitated about Cyprus and even considered sending a Royal Canadian Navy squadron to the eastern Mediterranean for a goodwill tour to remind Greece, Turkey, and Cyprus that NATO's other North American member was concerned about developments in the region. The British and Germans initiated an economic aid scheme to counteract Soviet penetration and Canada considered adding to it on High Commissioner Meaher's recommendation.[42]

In terms of internal Cypriot politics, the 70-30 representation ratio and the dual-chambered legislature was generating unforeseen problems relating to income tax, who collected it, and how it was administered by the executive level. The Turkish Cypriots were threatening to collect and hold their contribution if certain alterations were not made to the bureaucracy to reflect the 70-30 ratio, as Makarios had not fully implemented the agreement. The British conveyed a sense of concern to Canadian representatives since "the Cyprus situation was endemically so full of political dynamite (and large supplies of hidden arms owned by both communities) that British attitude remained one of watchful anxiety."[43]

Arthur Andrew replaced Margaret Meaher as High Commissioner in 1962. His briefing on Canadian interests relating to Cyprus reflected updated Canadian concerns. The 70-30 ratio was of paramount interest since "any interruption in the operation of these complicated communal government institutions poses a threat to the inter-relationship upon which Cyprus rests." AKEL was still considered to be "another source of instability." Although Canadian-Cypriot trade was minimal, Canada's concern remained the connections to NATO and the Commonwealth.[44]

Andrew discovered in his travels that Makarios' foreign policy was a complex balancing act. At a conference in Belgrade the Archbishop announced that Cyprus would be part of the non-aligned movement in the UN, which produced some concern in NATO circles and raised eyebrows in London and Washington. Andrew believed, however, "how effectively this policy could be applied in a crisis can be gauged from the fact that the armed forces of three NATO powers are stationed in strength on the island." The prevailing view was that Makarios "adopted this policy as a cheap way of showing the Cypriots that Cyprus was really independent. He did not for a moment believe that Cyprus was neutral between East and West." As for Communist activity, the Soviet embassy remained overly large and there were "frequent suggestions of improper activities by Soviet diplos who are now said to be extending their operations to the countryside. Their influence on Government foreign policy appears to be slight."[45]

On 25 March 1962, Greek Independence Day, a series of bombs were set off in Nicosia: two mosques were targeted and a monument venerated by the Turkish Cypriots was seriously damaged. The Greek Cypriot Minister of the Interior suggested publicly that the attacks were conducted by the Turks themselves, which generated a wave of agitation. Memories of the 1955 violence were re-kindled and Canadian and British sources sought to discover whether the bombings were the work of EOKA or AKEL. They were unable to do so. Then two editors of a Turkish Cypriot newspaper were gunned down. Both men, it transpired, had Communist connections and used their paper as a vehicle to attack Kuchuk, the Turkish Cypriot Deputy President. Rauf Denktas, the leader of the Turkish Cypriot chamber, was asked by an American diplomat in the wake of the killings what was going on and wondered how Communism could be countered in Cyprus. Denktas "said confidently, 'we have ways.'"[46]

The possibility of a Communist takeover in Cyprus deeply concerned the Turkish government and, when Archbishop Makarios paid a visit to Ankara late in 1962, he was told that Turkey would "not intervene in Cyprus except in case of violent abrogation of the agreements by extremists."[47] Makarios pledged that he would do his utmost to replace Communist influence by facilitating more Western foreign aid to the rural areas. Indeed, British money, American Peace Corps and German aid efforts, as well as Israel's assistance in organizing non-Communist labour unions, had a noticeable effect by the end of 1962. Arthur Andrew noted that the impression was that the Soviets originally saw Cyprus as a "Middle East Cuba" but had changed their minds when confronted with these techniques.[48]

THE CHRISTMAS CRISIS: 1963-1964

Despite the bombing of a mosque in January 1963, the situation remained relatively calm. Backroom diplomacy conducted by the British Ambassador, the Turkish Ambassador and the Canadian High Commissioner seemed to be working. In April 1963, however, Canadian diplomats in Ankara identified the problem: "what Makarios visualizes as minor modifications [to the constitution] may to Turks seem major." This view was reinforced by the arrival in Cyprus of a high-level Turkish military delegation. The perception held by all was that "it was more of a warning to Makarios that Turkey would not put up with any nonsense." A noted Turkish naval planner was present (there were no Turkish Navy units based in Cyprus) which indicated that this was actually a reconnaissance mission for an amphibious landing. When Canadian, American, and British diplomats talked privately, the Americans agreed to handle the Greeks, while the British suggested that a NATO meeting in Ottawa should be used as a vehicle to pressure the Turks to back off if intercommunal violence got out of hand.[49]

Greek-Turkish relations outside of Cyprus, however, worsened in the summer of 1963. Turkey announced that she would extend her territorial waters and establish a fishing zone at the twelve-mile limit. The obvious problems with such a move revolved around who controlled various parts of the island-cluttered Aegean Sea. The Greeks, on the other hand, were interfering in the developing European Common Market and Turkey's preferential relationship to it. The Soviets created some agitation by trying to get Makarios to incorporate Cyprus into a Mediterranean Nuclear Free Zone, with obvious consequences for the SBAs. This aroused Turkey's ire for some weeks.[50]

Those who have analysed Cyprus generally conclude that by the end of 1963 a combination of factors produced nearly uncontrollable intercommunal violence. The constitutional problem had at its heart the unbalanced ratio and the convoluted political system. There was perceived Greek and Turkish interference by the Cypriots, that the London and Zurich agreements had been made without due consideration of the Cypriot peoples. More significant, however, was the fact that Britain's withdrawal "removed the buffer of external authority and brought the two communities face to face" and that "violence and popular emotions eventually overtook long range considerations." The fact that the police were Greek Cypriot-dominated and that the Turkish Cypriot minority created secret armed militias to counter the police force only caused the situation to escalate.[51]

Makarios offered the Turkish Cypriots a series of constitutional amendments in the fall of 1963. These amendments explored the possibility of dissolving separate ethnic enclaves to facilitate taxation and services as well as redressing the ratio problem.[52] When these were rejected, "violence was therefore provoked by an incident apparently planned by Makarios" in which two Turkish Cypriots were gunned down by Greek Cypriot police.[53] The Turkish Cypriots claim that this was the first stage of something called the "Akritas Plan" which had as its objective "to dissolve the Republic of Cyprus in predetermined stages and methods to being about [*enosis*]." The ultimate aim of the Akritas Plan was the ethnic cleansing of the Turkish minority from the island.[54] The Greek view was that the Turks provoked the incident so that the Turkish military would intervene and partition the island in a way unfavourable to the majority Greek Cypriots.[55]

By 24 December 1963, fighting had broken out between both communities in Nicosia and spread to Larnaca. EOKA members materialized, as did their Turkish Cypriot counterparts. Towns were fortified, roadblocks set up, and a long no-mans land called the "Green Line" established through central Nicosia. Makarios then requested British assistance to achieve a cease-fire. British land forces led by Major General Peter Young intervened from the SBAs into Larnaca and then Nicosia to protect British and Commonwealth dependents, facilities and diplomats: they also uncovered evidence of local massacres of both Greek and Turkish Cypriots. Through ad hoc measures, these troops were able to temporarily calm down the situation and establish communications between both sides. This did not stop the fighting in the hills north of Nicosia or the "Mexican stand-offs" which threatened to block the important Kyrenia road. To make matters worse, the Turkish Air Force overflew Nicosia on several occasions at low level. At the same time, the Turkish Navy deployed a destroyer flotilla in the direction of Cyprus. The Greek government warned that if Turkey intervened, so would Greece. As Brigadier Frank Kitson of the British Army noted, "there was a very real danger of major war breaking out in the Eastern Mediterranean."[56]

American involvement up to this point had been practically non-existent. This was probably in part due to John F. Kennedy's assassination in November 1963. To highlight American concern over the rise in fighting, the new President, Lyndon Baines Johnson, sent diplomatic missives to both Makarios and Kuchuk to encourage them to find a solution to intercommunal tension. This was backed up by the dispatch and maintenance of a United States Navy guided missile destroyer on station near Cyprus. It is possible that word of Soviet offers of military aid to Makarios may have prompted this manoeuvre.[57]

Makarios then intimated that he would renounce the London and Zurich agreements, upon which Duncan Sandys flew in and forced him to recant. The result was a secret meeting between Sandys, Denktas and Glafkos Clerides, who was Denktas's Greek Cypriot counterpart. This meeting took place in London on 15 January 1964 and was instrumental in producing several concepts for an international peacekeeping force for the island. The UN option was rejected by the British who believed that the ongoing problems with the Soviets and the Security Council would prevent the introduction of a force like UNEF or ONUC. Perhaps a NATO peacekeeping force could be employed?[58]

Preliminary back room diplomacy in Paris indicated that the United States, Turkey and Greece thought this was acceptable, although the French did not, and the West Germans were ambivalent. General Lyman Lemnitzer, NATO SACEUR, was then dispatched as an envoy to both the Greek and Turkish governments. He outlined the proposed NATO peacekeeping force plan which was to have consisted of 1200 American troops and an estimated 8800 from other NATO countries deployed to the island for up to three months. The London Conference was punctuated by another spate of fighting late in January: this time, President Johnson deployed a US Navy amphibious squadron from the 6th Fleet in addition to the destroyer so that dependents could be evacuated if necessary.[59]

The question was, should the peace force come from NATO or the UN? Before this could be sorted out in detail, British Prime Minister Sir Alec Douglas-Home asked U Thant to send a UN observer in case a UN solution was developed. General Gyani from India left for Cyprus to monitor events. At the same time, Johnson sent American diplomat George Ball to Athens and Ankara. Douglas-Home and "Rab" Butler, his Foreign Secretary, and Dean Rusk, US Secretary of State, then approached the Pearson Government. Paul Martin noted: "Aware of the dangers of involving the United Nations while the uneasy ceasefire lasted, I treaded warily. The possibility of a Soviet presence in so strategic a part of the eastern Mediterranean deterred me from acting peremptorily." In his memoirs Martin states that non-European NATO members and the British were acceptable, but that the deployment of other forces would be inflammatory. He was probably referring to the problems with employing West German troops as part of the NATO peacekeeping force, a move which would have endless propaganda value for the Soviets who would denounce it as a "renewal of Nazi aggression"in the Mediterranean.[60]

The preservation of British bases supporting nuclear deterrence was paramount in the decision to deploy Canadian forces to Cyprus in 1964. Here an RCAF Yukon taxis past bombed up RAF strike aircraft at RAF Akrotiri.

(CF photo)

One of the attractive aspects of the NATO peacekeeping force plan was that "NATO could mount a peacekeeping force much more quickly than the United Nations." A special meeting held in Ottawa on 20 January with American, British and Canadian representatives concluded that a 10 000-man force could be in place by 4 February: 4000 British, 1000 Americans, 1000 Canadians, and 4000 other NATO forces. Although Martin does not state it directly, this probably referred to the employment of the NATO ACE Mobile Force (Land) as a peacekeeping force. Such a move would have been controversial since, as we have seen in Chapter 8, ACE Mobile Force was designed as a deterrence and signaling device to indicate to the Soviets that NATO meant business. Note that ACE Mobile Force also included a West German airborne battalion. The Canadian position at the meeting, after Paul Hellyer was consulted, was that Canada would contribute a unit from the Special Service Force if the Cypriot government agreed to the NATO peacekeeping force proposal.[61]

Makarios rejected the NATO proposal on 31 January.

The backup plan was to get the UN to accept a NATO or NATO-led peacekeeping mission for Cyprus and then convince the belligerents that this was an acceptable move under the UN Charter. If this did not work, representations would be made for a purely UN force. In Ottawa, Cabinet discussions revolved around detaching a battalion from the NATO-committed 4 Canadian Infantry Brigade Group in West Germany for service in Cyprus. If a NATO force was deployed, this posed no problem. If, however, a UN solution was found, some Cabinet members thought that deploying an obviously NATO-tasked unit might cause propaganda problems with the Soviets. It was better that a Canada-based battalion be used, preferably one from the Special Service Force on UN Standby duty.[62]

Cabinet was also concerned with domestic repercussions in two areas. First, the Pearson government wanted to limit the numbers to 500 troops which would only have been half a battalion. There was concern about getting Parliamentary approval and they believed that Diefenbaker's announcement to deploy a 500-man contingent for the Congo without such approval constituted a precedent. This would, however, limit the effectiveness of the unit and in any event Diefenbaker (now in Opposition) approved of using forces to peacekeep in Cyprus. The second problem was with Pearson's Quebec cabinet ministers who did not want the designated UN standby battalion (drawn from a French-speaking regiment) deployed for "English purposes" since this would cause an outcry in the separatist press. Hellyer suggested that a Canadian Guards battalion assume the duty instead. Pearson disagreed and insisted that the French-speaking battalion remain on standby.[63]

Claude Roquet, Canada's ambassador in Ankara, told Paul Martin that "the Anglo-American proposals have put Makarios in a nutcracker between Western wishes and the feeling of a large section of the Greek Cypriot community. Our Turkish Foreign Ministry colleagues here have admitted that the Cypriot, whether Turkish or Greek, is a rather xenophobic type who cannot be expected to welcome foreign forces of any kind." Therefore, if pressed, "It is no use for the Turks winning the first match sixty-love if Makarios then refuses to go on playing."[64]

On 11 February, External Affairs and National Defence representatives met to coordinate a possible Canadian military response to the Cyprus crisis. In their deliberations, British pleas for an armoured reconnaissance unit were explored and the group concluded that any Canadian contribution to the planned NATO International Force for the island would consist of an infantry battalion group and a Ferret armoured-car-equipped recce squadron. Terms of reference for the force were to be similar to those employed by ONUC in the Congo: it was not planned to be a UNEF type of interpositionary operation. The idea that the Canadian contingent to the NATO International Force would report to 4 Brigade in West Germany was ruled out. In the Canadian Army's concept of operations, the planners noted that

> The concrete duties of the contingent could hardly be spelled out in advance. The situation would probably be fluid for a while. It seemed clear, however, that the force would not land in Cyprus until both communities agreed to the maintenance of the cease-fire. Any fighting, therefore, should be ascribed to terrorists and irregular forces which would not be controlled by the responsible leaders in each community. It should be possible to obtain undisputed authority to deal with them. The [Canadian Army] will have received instructions on irregular warfare based on British defence papers and the Canadian experience gained in the Middle East and the Congo.[65]

Such tactics would be needed: in addition to taking hostages and conducting five minor operations by 11 February, Greek Cypriot forces engaged in a 24-hour battle in Limassol against Turkish militias. It was "the first incident which demonstrated the command and control organization...in action"[66] and marked an escalation in the sophistication of the fighting. Roquet in Ankara warned that "if the killings continue at the present level, it is doubtful how long the Turks can pursue Byzantine negotiations with Makarios." Denktas flew to Ankara "pressing for decisive action" but was put on hold because American representative George Ball was conducting shuttle diplomacy.[67]

As for Ball's mission, he had allowed himself to be manipulated into a debate with Makarios and the Greeks over the control and constituent elements of the International Force. Makarios now suggested that the force be a Commonwealth force with a Swedish contribution. U Thant was now involved at Makarios' urging and more and more concepts emerged to muddy the waters. Every possible variant was explored: NATO-Commonwealth under NATO command, NATO-Commonwealth under UN command, even NATO under NATO command.[68]

It was evident to Canadian and British observers that Makarios was playing for time. As the world would see thirty years later, using negotiations to delay international intervention while the civilian populations of the belligerents were driven from their homes by military forces was not invented in the former Yugoslavia. Kuchuk and the Turkish Cypriot leaders were in a "mood reminiscent of a small military headquarters in wartime" and they were utterly convinced that "the Greek community was pursuing a policy of genocide." The situation was further complicated by the fact that there were 14,000 British military dependents on the island and the British were concerned that both sides might take hostages. Thus, "if the Turks invade the results would be horrible."[69]

The British High Commissioner was then targeted by a bomb at his hotel, but was unharmed. Makarios was in the process of negotiating with Nasser for arms, some of which had already arrived by ship, and the Archbishop had gone so far to distribute weapons to the AKEL. The potential for even more chaos was confirmed when Makarios told Andrew that this was a mistake and "it was not difficult to imagine EOKA taking on the task of liquidating AKEL which they themselves had armed." There were now an estimated 24,000 displaced Turkish Cypriots: what was to be done with them? Kuchuk told the Canadian High Commissioner that his people were being "slowly liquidated" and that he had to call in Turkish military forces "or face extinction." Partition was the only answer, in his view, and only an international force equipped to use force could be effective in combating what UN representative Gyani called "the thousands of armed men mostly labeled 'police'" which were not under any control. Andrew pointed out that such men were from both communities and Greeks were not entirely to blame.[70]

Paul Martin, Dean Rusk, and Rab Butler continued to coordinate efforts to establish a peacekeeping force. Martin started pushing for a UN force which, as it was becoming clearer, would be the only solution that would work at all levels. Rusk apparently clung to the belief that a non-UN mission was still feasible. Martin believed that UN legitimacy was critical and that anything less than a UN solution would be publicly attacked by the Soviets. Domestic political manouevring by the Johnson administration relating to the possibility of China joining the United Nations forced the American negotiators to push more for non-UN force solutions, which complicated the three allies' attempts to reach agreement. Martin relented for the time being.[71]

In the UN forums, the British, American, and Canadian representatives were trying desperately to get Cyprus onto the Security Council agenda. The Turks had had enough. On the night of 14 February, the Turkish 39th Infantry Division was assault-loaded onto amphibious ships at the port of Iskendrun and left port that night. The 39th Division, Canadian intelligence sources noted, was a Pentomic division structured and equipped for nuclear warfare, although it did not have nuclear weapons. The invasion fleet returned to port the next day, possibly as a result of American diplomatic pressure and assurances that the UN could make headway. Indeed, the Turkish Navy recalled 12 mothballed landing craft and loaded them with troops from the 39th Division after the first sortie. Seven Turkish submarines were deployed between Iskendrun and Cyprus to protect the convoy. Intelligence reports to Ottawa direly warned that "Turkish naval and military units remained poised in a high state of readiness."[72] The Greeks were not idle while the Turks were making ready. The Greek 508th infantry battalion was flown into Crete, as was the Greek Special Raiding Force (Commandos) which moved onto the island of Rhodes. Landing craft sailed to both locations ready to deploy both units to Cyprus. The British then reinforced with 2000 men brought in by air to the SBAs on the night of 18 February.[73]

The UN Security Council finally met on 18 February. The British delegation presented a plan for a NATO peacekeeping force for Cyprus operating under UN concurrence. U Thant was unable to get the Council to agree on structure and financing of the operation. The Soviets attacked the resolution, arguing that "discord in Cyprus was fomented from abroad to justify intervention so that NATO influence could be extended to Cyprus." The matter was deferred.[74]

When asked by UN representatives as to what force composition was acceptable, Makarios insisted that the peacekeeping force not have any "Americans or Moslems in it" although a Commonwealth force expanded to include Swedes and Irishmen was feasible. The State Department and the Foreign Office quickly realized that "various restrictions and pre-occupations limited Commonwealth possibilities virtually to Britain and Canada."[75]

Lester Pearson was under increasing scrutiny in Parliament and decided to state Canada's position in that forum. Canada, he said, had certain criteria for sending troops. First, he had to be convinced that "the composition and terms of reference of the force were such as to contribute to peace and stability." Prophetically, Pearson also insisted that Canada "would not wish the commitment of the force to be of indefinite duration," an ironic statement given the fact that Cyprus would become Canada's longest peacekeeping commitment. Another important condition which the Prime Minister wanted the UN to accept was that Canada wanted a say in how the force was controlled on a day-to-day basis, which meant the placement of Canadians high up in the force hierarchy. If these conditions were met, the final condition was that there be Parliamentary approval. It is clear that the audience for this announcement was located in Washington, London, and New York, as well as Ottawa.[76]

By 2 March, discussions in NATO circles resulted in a tacit policy that NATO members would keep a low profile and exercises in the Mediterranean would be toned down or postponed while the UN mechanisms were explored. On 4 March, the Security Council approved in principle the creation of a United Nations peacekeeping force for Cyprus. Galo Plaza became the main UN mediator, after a previously nominated Finn had succumbed to a heart attack.[77]

Cabinet held a lengthy meeting the next day to determine a Canadian approach to the crisis. This meeting was driven by the need to initiate sealift preparations. The standby battalion group could deploy by air, but its heavy equipment needed to move by sea and that would take time. Pearson was critical of U Thant, who was "taking Canada's participation for granted" even though the financial arrangements were still sketchy, as were the command arrangements. The Prime Minister was in no hurry. If other troop contributors committed, however, "it would be difficult not to accept" the fact that Canada would go.[78]

Another matter for concern was that Pearson and Martin were cognizant that UN operations in Cyprus could involve combat operations against the belligerents and they believed that U Thant was shying away from admitting this publicly by not incorporating it into the force's terms of reference. Pearson was particularly critical of this. In effect, Pearson was withholding Canadian participation to force the Secretary General to develop a more detailed plan and not repeat the ONUC experience.[79]

Arthur Andrew, meanwhile, successfully insinuated himself into a high-level meeting in Nicosia which included Makarios, Kuchuk, Gyani, the British High Commissioner, and the

American chargé d'affaires. These men were discussing how a peacekeeping force would be physically introduced to the island. "The question of Canadian participation in the Force was uppermost in the minds of everyone," he noted. Makarios particularly was impressed with Canadian discipline and impartiality as displayed elsewhere in the Middle East, as was Kuchuck. Word of this discussion made its way back to New York, with Makarios practically demanding that the force include one thousand Canadians.[80]

Paul Tremblay in New York used the opportunity to question U Thant on the terms of reference and command issues. The Secretary General admitted that troop contributors were entitled to a have a say in how their forces were used.[81] Paul Martin then arrived on the scene and met with U Thant. Canada was committed to the operation and successfully persuaded the Irish, Swedish, and Finnish ambassadors in Ottawa to get their respective governments to commit. Finland had done so, the Irish and Swedish had, surprisingly, not done so, probably because of their negative experiences in the Congo (although they would join later on). If U Thant could get replacements for those powers, then Canada would publicly commit now that the Secretary General had clarified the command issue.[82]

The Turkish government, meanwhile, was getting impatient. Greek Cypriot forces had moved into the Kyrenia mountains and were engaging Turkish Cypriot towns and villages. Turkey's NATO representative in the NAC blasted the delays in the UN which "tends to make matters worse and [gives] Makarios time to create a fait accompli." NATO Secretary General Dirk Stikker concluded that with the delay between the UN resolution and the actually deployment of UN forces, "the situation has become worse and may become explosive."[83] In effect, Turkey sent an ultimatum to Makarios: stop the atrocities against the Turkish Cypriots and stop obstructing the establishment of a UN force, or military force would be employed against the Greek Cypriots.[84]

Twenty-one Turkish naval vessels sortied from Iskendrun on the night of 10 March, while Turkish air force aircraft overflew the island. The Greek Navy readied nine Landing Ship Tanks, a Landing Ship Dock and three destroyers in Salamis Bay. President Lyndon Johnson dispatched the USS *Enterprise* nuclear carrier task group to stand by 250 miles off Cyprus. Pressure was applied to the Greeks not to deploy their amphibious forces: they stood down after a volatile discussion in the North Atlantic Council which the British and Americans used to ask for more NATO-member contributions for the UN force.[85]

There was great anxiety in the Johnson White House over the latest and most serious situation. The slow pace of establishing the UN peacekeeping force was seen as contributing to deaths and de-stablizing the south-eastern flank. Johnson called Pearson on 12 March, asking for his assistance. Johnson thought that if Canadian troops were deployed before formal action was taken, it would act as a catalyst and force the issue, which at this point was stalled on two possible contributing nations debating whether they would go or not. Pearson said that if they committed publicly, "not to worry; we knew our duty to the UN; we knew the danger of war....the President seemed reassured and very grateful."[86]

That day Paul Hellyer approved the airlift and it got under way as Cabinet met to approve its departure (Pearson noted that he would have recalled them if it had been necessary).

Lieutenant General Geoffrey Walsh allocated the code name Operation SNOW GOOSE to the Canadian Cyprus contingent. Snow Goose forces were to "prevent a recurrence of fighting and, as necessary, contribute to the maintenance and restoration of law and order and a return to normal conditions."[87] Contingent commander Colonel Ned Amy proceeded to Cyprus to conduct a reconnaissance and liaise with the British and the Cypriots prior to the arrival of the main body. Cabinet then met and essentially approved the operation without debate.[88] Johnson called Pearson later and told the Prime Minister "You'll never know what this has meant, having those Canadians off to Cyprus and being there tomorrow. You'll never know what this may have prevented."[89]

Indeed, Arthur Andrew was able to report that the British overflew the Turkish naval bases and forces and determined they were headed home: "tonight might have been more likely time but with UN and Canadian action situation has eased."[90]

As RCAF Yukon and Hercules transports departed in droves from Trenton, Quebec City, and Montreal for Cyprus, the aircraft carrier HMCS *Bonaventure* was modified to carry the Canadian contingent's heavy equipment and vehicles. She set sail on 18 March. Diplomatic efforts, however, did not cease with the dispatch of the UN Standby Battalion Group. The Pearson government developed a multi-faceted approach for the next phase of the crisis. Andrew, Amy, and the Canadian contingent were the authority in Cyprus, while Claude Roquet and the Canadian Military Attaché in Ankara reported on Turkish military movements, and Martin handled the discussions with Rusk and Butler.

A coercive tool was also employed. Under the terms of the NATO military force structure plan which all NATO members agreed to, Turkey was to acquire and equip a number of squadrons so that they could conduct nuclear strike operations against the Soviet Union in the event of war. The aircraft selected by the Greek and Turkish air forces was the F-104 Starfighter. This aircraft was built by Lockheed in California, but there was a Canadian variant called the CF-104 built in Montreal by Canadair. In essence, Canada was instrumental in convincing many NATO nations to acquire and operate the F-104 primarily because this standardized the NATO strike force. Their ulterior motive was to sell spare parts, training simulators, and other support equipment throughout NATO.[91]

Some of the aircraft were in the process of delivery to both countries when the crisis erupted. Initially, there was concern that Canada's impartial role in a peacekeeping operation would be compromised if it were discovered that the aircraft came from Canadair. Arrangements were made to conceal the origins of the aircraft and claim they came from Lockheed. At the same time, it was pointed out that even though the aircraft were configured for nuclear weapons delivery, they could be modified to deliver conventional weapons. It would be embarrassing to have Canadian-built aircraft attacking one belligerent or the other on the island with Canadian troops on the ground also subject to attack. To prevent undue problems, External Affairs considered delaying the delivery and then using it to pressure both Greece and Turkey. This move was held in reserve.[92]

Paul Martin was active in maintaining the shaky diplomatic peace throughout March. His public pronouncements were mostly directed against the convoluted UN approach to peace operations in New York and, when carefully examined, constituted a warning to the UN that Canadian participation should not be taken for granted.[93]

In a private meeting with the Secretary General, an enthusiastic U Thant told Martin that "Canada had saved the situation." Martin's concern, however, was that it was not clear how much force UNFICYP could use. Why could the Secretary General not be more specific in public? Martin also told the Secretary General that "we were anxious to ensure adequate Canadian representation in senior posts and to get command of the zone in which Canadian troops would be operating." In time this request would emerge and U Thant would ask for a Canadian brigade group headquarters to control the vital Nicosia-Kyrenia zone. It is clear that Martin was deeply concerned about the welfare of Canadian troops on the ground, determined that they would not be misused, and he pushed for the mechanisms to protect them. Canada's continued participation was, therefore, conditional.[94]

Martin then met with Ball and Erkin. Erkin was concerned about UNFICYP's mandate and wanted Martin to know that someone needed to be able to disarm Greek Cypriot irregular forces. Gyani was weak and not up to the task, he believed. Martin had to cajole Erkin to give UNFICYP a chance. In doing so he conceded the mandate was hazy, but emphasized that flexibility was a good thing. One solution was to have all armed forces in Cyprus come under UN command: the feasibility of this was questioned, however, by all concerned and the matter held in abeyance.[95]

U Thant's man, Piero Spinelli, was also questioned at length by Martin. The irregular force issue had taken a strange turn: Makarios incorporated his irregulars into the Greek Cypriot armed forces and claimed the only irregulars were Turkish Cypriots. Therefore, UNFICYP would only have to fight Turkish irregulars. Both sides indicated that if UNFICYP attempted to disarm them, "it would lead to a fight."[96]

Consequently, Paul Hellyer to instructed Air Chief Marshal Miller to develop a contingency plan for a unilateral evacuation of the Canadian contingent. Miller initiated this process. Despite the official optimism, he also asked Walsh to develop a plan for maintaining the Canadian UNFICYP contingent beyond the three month limit.[97]

TWICE MORE TO THE BRINK OF WAR IN THE SUMMER OF '64

By the end of April 1964 UNFICYP had expanded to nine infantry battalions and four armoured car squadrons. (see Figure 10) The main problem during this time was the constant probing by both factions against UN patrols and the continuing efforts by the belligerents to push them into using force. The Green Line and the Kyrenia road were the two main areas of disturbance: UNFICYP was permitted freedom of movement under the agreement, and Turkish Cypriot irregulars kept blocking the entry points into the Kyrenias. UNFICYP's concept of operations at the time was to provide a UN presence in areas of mixed ethnicity, to rapidly respond with a show of force to deter violent activity, and to mediate disputes with UN civilian police. At the same time, UNFICYP was responsible for maintaining freedom of movement for all Cypriots and to support measures necessary for the return of the island to

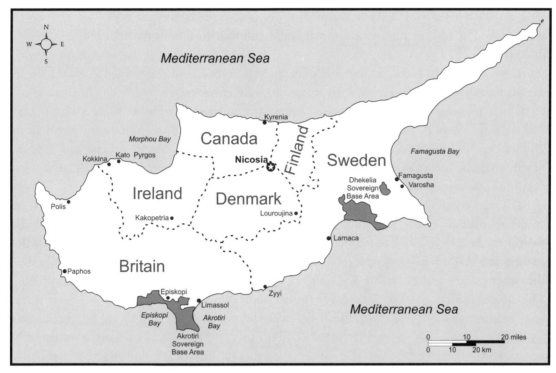

Figure 10: UNFICYP Dispositions in Cyprus, 1964

normal living conditions. The only area that resembled UNEF was the Green Line in Nicosia, where UNFICYP patrolled between the now easily-defined community split.[98]

The "honeymoon period for UNFICYP" came to an end, however. Sporadic fighting on the Green Line escalated and a bridge was blown up. The British contingent was drawn into a huge riot in Nicosia which distracted them from a Greek Cypriot offensive against the Turkish-held entrance of the Kyrenia Pass. The Canadian contingent deployed to interpose themselves with some force between the two sides. There were several other tinderboxes just waiting to blow up in UNFICYP's face at any time. Canadian media outlets started to question Canada's role in Cyprus and headlines like "UN Force has Little to Show for Month's Effort in Cyprus" appeared.[99]

Canadian analysis was that "the calming influence which the introduction of the UN Force had initially introduced into the Cyprus situation has since been dissipated." The Greek Cypriots initiated an "incipient campaign" against the British presence in UNFICYP which was compounded by Makarios' "unscrupulous attempts" to "alter the status quo before the [UN] Mediator has begun his task." By making small incursions against Turkish areas, Makarios could gain more ground and then conduct final negotiations in his favour. Unfortunately, this produced a backlash in Turkey against people of Greek descent, leading to a situation where "The Greek and Turkish governments seemed to be caught in an uncontrolled, divergent movement which could still lead to the ultimate tragedy of Turkish intervention."[100]

Time was running out, External Affairs analysts agreed, and they urged Paul Martin to use his initiative immediately. Martin would do so over the next three weeks in three areas. First, he would use his influence with the Americans to "exert maximum influence in Ankara and Athens." Second, he would deal directly with the Turkish and Greek ambassadors in Ottawa and use the Canadian ambassadors in a coordinated fashion in Athens and Ankara. Finally, Martin intended to bring NATO into play: he would also urge Dirk Stikker to pressure Greece and Turkey in the military field.[101]

U Thant and Ralph Bunche met with Martin, but did not concur with the Canadian view of the seriousness of the situation. This was contrary to other detailed Canadian analysis. Arthur Andrew laconically noted that "UNFICYP's method of peace-keeping starts with the assumption that the parties concerned want the peace kept. This is sometimes true of one or the other parties and even, on occasion with both, but it is not always true everywhere." The normalization process "has made some steps forward and some back." UNFICYP was "increasingly unpopular with the Turks" who did not trust General Gyani because he was an Indian Hindu (recall the Indo-Pakistani dispute). There was still no effective UN negotiation process on between the parties, even though UNFICYP was effective at reacting to lower level events.[102]

What were the medium and long term UN strategies for Cyprus? Martin seemed to have one, but U Thant and Bunche did not, even after a serious Greek attack against the Turkish positions on the Kyrenia Pass. Martin was distressed: "vigorous action was required to overcome the public impression that the UN was a passive bystander." Bunche was not in favour of having UNFICYP conduct Congo type operations, but the situation did not warrant operations like UNEF. It was a unique situation and UNFICYP would have to adapt to it over time.[103]

Exasperated, Martin called on Secretary of State Dean Rusk during a meeting between Prime Minister Pearson and President Johnson on 30 April. Pearson told Johnson that "developments on this island were a depressing example of a small and somewhat dirty tail wagging a big dog." Martin and Pearson wanted Johnson and Rusk to crack down on Makarios and pressure the Turks into not invading. This would give Canada time to explore other avenues and pressure the UN to deploy an effective negotiator, to allow UNFICYP more freedom of action, and to get UNFICYP to disarm the irregular forces.

Rusk thought American influence with Makarios was spent, but agreed to pressure the Turks. This was not easy since "the Turks had shown remarkable restraint. They could not, however, remain idle when Turkish Cypriots were being murdered." Pearson raised the problem of the continuing existence of NATO. Rusk agreed, but there were limitations on American activity since "the USA is not prepared to shoot Turks to prevent them from landing on Cyprus where [American] interests were secondary....The US had 17,000 men and vital communications facilities in Turkey. In the view of the United States, the only way to stop the Turks was to get the job going in Cyprus."[104]

The Kyrenia fighting prompted Dirk Stikker to travel to Ankara where he found President Inonu "in a desperate frame of mind." Inonu told Stikker he would invade unless UNFICYP increased its effectiveness immediately. The NATO Secretary General pleaded with Inonu for restraint and flew to Athens, where he was rebuffed by a disorganized President George Papandreou. Stikker found him "difficult to pin down" but reached a point where there was an admission from the Greek President that "there were Greeks on Cyprus who were not under the control of Makarios." Papandreou thought the 1960 agreements were null and void since there was no longer any hope of "establishing a Greek government in Cyprus,"a statement which "rather shocked Stikker" since that was not the objective of the London and Zurich arrangements at all. NATO's leader came way highly disturbed and convinced that "even more pressure needs to be applied to both governments to prevent the situation from slipping irreparably into war." There was a "dangerous fatalism" in both countries.[105]

Stikker convened a Saturday meeting of the North Atlantic Council on 2 May. Both the Greek and Turkish governments were informed that the consequences of their dispute would only benefit the "Soviet bloc including Bulgaria that might take action to gain an outlet to the Aegean." Stikker had to cut off both delegations from talking past each other on matters irrelevant to the situation. Nothing was accomplished. Not even the threat of leaving Greece open to Warsaw Pact attack was enough to deter the Greek leadership from supporting what amounted to ethnic cleansing operations in Cyprus.[106]

Even an emotional NATO Ministerial Meeting held on 14 May failed to gain headway. Spaak (representing Belgium) and Butler pushed for a clarified UNFICYP mandate which would allow it intervention powers. Rusk reiterate the Soviet threat, while Martin did some backroom negotiating with the antagonists. What emerged was an agreement to disagree between Turkey and Greece and a pledge that events in Cyprus would not trigger any further deterioration between Greco-Turkish relations.[107]

It fell to UNFICYP's soldiers to make sense of the vague UN mandate and avert war in an increasingly hostile environment. In an eerie parallel to the situation in the former Yugoslavia in the 1990s, no one in UN headquarters wanted to expand UNFICYP's ability or legal basis to use greater force to prevent intercommunal violence despite what the situation on the ground in Cyprus demanded. There was fear of Soviet criticism in the UN and elsewhere, there was fear of a repeat of the Congo situation, there was also concern that UN peacekeeping financing would be jeopardized by the Afro-Asia or non-aligned blocs (bodies with which Makarios was making serious and effective inroads).

Arthur Andrew, in one of his cogent dispatches to Ottawa, agreed that stronger measures were necessary to keep the situation under control:

> but before this decision can be taken intelligently UNFICYP must know what it
> is here to do. The activities of the last month have shown that "peacekeeping" and
> "normalization" are not concepts that a soldier can be expected to interpret and

carry out. The UNFICYP soldier must therefore be given a conception of peacekeeping that is intelligible, clear, and within his power to enforce. I submit that to give him more weapons or greater freedom in using them without first telling him to what achievable end the new power is to be used will merely increase the flow of blood, some of it Canadian, without helping the Cyprus situation.[108]

Andrews realized that "the total cessation of all shooting on the island is completely unattainable" and that if a stronger mandate was achieved "it should be presented to the contending parties and not negotiated with them."[109]

Dirk Stikker brought pressure to bear on U Thant to strengthen the mandate, although he had to be careful not to portray a situation where NATO and the UN appeared to be competing for control of the peacekeeping mission in Cyprus. U Thant told Stikker that one problem was the import of more arms to the island. Could NATO pressure its members not to do so? The UN's hands were tied but "agreement in the NATO council to refrain from shipping arms would not only materially assist the task of UN peacekeeping force but would also be a manifestation of confidence in the role of the UN." Martin and Rusk were concerned that Turkey would escalate the quantity and sophistication of arms to the Turkish Cypriots which could trigger an arms race and force the Greek Cypriots to turn to the Soviets. Efforts were coordinated and Canada was instrumental in getting West Germany to block a delivery of torpedo boats to both belligerents.[110]

There was another invasion scare in June 1964. American intelligence sources provided evidence that Turkey was gearing up for invasion yet again. On 5 June, the Turkish government threatened Makarios in a public broadcast after they learned that George Grivas, the leader of the 1955-59 insurgency, had arrived back on the island. The invasion was to start at 1700 hours on 6 June (the anniversary of the Normandy landings in 1944). The situation was serious enough for NATO SACEUR to fly to Turkey and consult with Turkish military authorities and for President Johnson to sent a strongly worded letter to President Inonu. Brigadier General Tedlie was informed through Arthur Andrew that something was up and the Canadian contingent was alerted for possible action. The Turks were playing a dangerous game. The Turkish Cypriots "are said to be in high spirits and think the invasion is coming. Another letdown would increase their desperation and combined with Greek cockiness and certainty that Turkey will never invade can lead to a resumption of violence." Makarios told Tedlie that the UN forces had better get out of the way in the event of an invasion or they would be crushed.[111]

This latest Turkish move generated serious concern in Canadian quarters. Tedlie and Arthur made plans for the Canadian brigade headquarters to take command of the Dragoons recce squadron, the support elements, and the R22eR battalion and fight their way down to the SBAs if necessary where Canadian aircraft would evacuate them. Both men were concerned that in the event of an invasion "UNFICYP command might give instructions which could lead to involvement of Canadian troops with a NATO ally" or might fail to give instructions "which would enable Canadian troops to disengage from present tasks and so become exposed." No one else, with the exception of the British, had given any thought to this.[112]

Johnson, Rusk, and Ball were "deeply shaken by the Turkish invasion threat" but felt they had been used to garner more international attention to the Turkish cause. The no-notice full scale diplomatic effort, the second of that year, was something they "did not wish to repeat." There was now more than ever a search for a long term solution. Unfortunately, the Americans were concerned that U Thant and his people might come up with a series of theoretical solutions that, when leaked, might include various forms of self-determination exercises that "would be unacceptable from the Turkish point of view." The British were even thinking about reducing their participation in UNFICYP, perhaps to force the issue.[113]

The problem was now the British, who introduced a rather radical plan. In one variant of this plan, the Turkish Cypriots would be evacuated to Turkey, the Greek minority in western Turkey would be resettled in Greece, Cyprus would achieve *enosis* and the bases turned over to Greece which would maintain them for NATO purposes. This would all be done under the guise of a supposedly UN conducted plebiscite. British representatives continually used the word "Cuba" in their communications: Canadian analysts thought that "the emphasis in likening Cyprus to Cuba is clearly designed to engage USA support for a radical solution." There was also some hint that the British envisioned covertly supporting a Grivas-backed coup against Makarios to make all this happen. [114]

Paul Martin opposed this solution. He believed that Makarios "having tasted the heady wine of independence" would not want to join another country, especially since he was now non-aligned with similar backing in the UN, and a NATO country. Canada's interests in the matter were based on strict impartiality and Canada "intended to maintain this approach." It would, therefore not "be appropriate for [Canada] to become involved in the question of a search for a long term solution." This was slightly disingenuous of Martin, but his staff recommended that he avoid getting involved in solutions which might be unscrupulous.[115]

What of the Soviets? By the end of June 1964 Pravda and the Mongolian UN delegation were making virulent statements "holding NATO responsible for strife in Cyprus" and "inciting civil disturbances." Johnson, NATO, Stikker and Turkey were to blame, apparently and Makarios was a great non-aligned anti-colonial visionary. There were numerous positive remarks about Greece designed to "help consolidate the Soviet position in case Grivas makes trouble for the Cypriot Communists." More explicit threats were made by Khrushchev in which he reiterated that the Soviet Union would use force against Turkey if she intervened in Cyprus. More and more heavy weapons started to arrive by ship in the port of Limassol: anti-tank and anti-aircraft artillery, mobile radar and twenty-two trucks full of aircraft parts were seen by Canadian observers.[116]

The West's response to continued Soviet interference was to step up diplomatic efforts throughout July. Canada played a key role in this coordinated effort, particularly in NATO circles which appeared to be the best means of preventing war assuming UNFICYP was able to quell the belligerents on the island.

Paul Martin met with Inonu in New York and Papandreou in Washington on 24 and 25 June. Martin explained that Canada was impartial and had no direct interests with either side. Inonu blasted the UNFICYP forces as "unwitting tools of Makarios" and Martin was unable to make serious headway. He proposed the vague outlines of a disarmament plan, but Inonu did not think it was feasible since there was no guarantee that the sides would or could be disarmed.[117]

Papandreou was also given Canada's position but was told that if no movement could be made and if the belligerents kept trying to undermine the force, Canada would pull out of UNFICYP. The Greeks told Martin that if Turkey removed the threat of invasion, then arms smuggling and requests for Soviet aid would cease, "and the crisis would just disappear." Martin did not believe them. What about the activities of George Grivas? Papandreou gave "a slightly evasive reply...Greece was aware of Grivas' activities even though they might be unable to condone them publicly." Papandreou also implied that this was acceptable to the British as well. Martin was only able to appeal for NATO solidarity. Little was achieved, although it was adequate preparation for the planned talks sponsored by Johnson in Washington in July.

The Johnson administration established several objectives which were conveyed to Greece and Turkey in the North Atlantic Council: there had to be a permanent solution, it had to contribute to maintaining stability in the region, it could not humiliate either party and had to be acceptable to the population on the island. The Americans were clear that there could be a settlement that was not acceptable to all parties. The British and Canadians backed such conditions, but the Greek and Turkish representatives appeared not to hear the message.[118]

In the aftermath of the NAC meeting held in Ottawa, Stikker and Paul Hellyer conferred. It was now 3 July. Stikker told Hellyer that Johnson and Rusk were now pre-occupied with a little far eastern country called Vietnam and that apart from George Ball, "nobody appeared interested in Cyprus." Ball, unfortunately, accepted the British position as outlined by Noel-Baker, which was unacceptable. American intelligence sources warned Stikker that "a Turkish invasion of Cyprus was imminent." The last time this happened, Stikker sent NATO SACEUR General Lemnitzer, who believed that "we have never been so close to World War III as on the day Turkey was on the point of invasion." Stikker did not want this to happen again.[119]

Hellyer was primarily concerned with "the clandestine infiltration into Cyprus of elements of the regular Greek Army" which could trigger precipitous action if they were used against the Turkish Cypriots. In communications with Pearson, the two men agreed that a meeting of NATO foreign ministers should be called to place pressure on Greece and Turkey. This might not be enough, Stikker mused, since NATO analysis was that "the operations would not remain confined to the island but there would be fighting in Thrace as well." Hellyer's view was that peace on the island was a long term project and could only occur if two conditions were in place: "strong international guarantees against outside intervention by Greece and Turkey and an imposed internal solution by a third party." During such a process the UN contingent would have to hold the ring. Word came through that the Americans were sending Dean Acheson to Geneva to confer with Greece and Turkish representatives: both men agreed that they would await the outcome of this move.[120]

Martin coordinated his efforts in NATO with George Ball through Charles Ritchie and Senator Fulbright. The Canadian contribution to the collective pressure effort was to have George Ignatieff at NATO push for the suspension of all mutual defence aid to both Greece and Turkey. The argument was "we have been told many times of the economic and defence needs of the southeastern flank of the Alliance yet how can we take these needs seriously if the equipment provided under mutual aid and possibly NATO-assigned forces are being used contrary to the resolutions of the UN?"[121] The role of Dean Acheson as mediator was confirmed to Martin, but not all members of the American team agreed with this appointment. In Senator Fulbright's view, Acheson was "arrogant and opinionated and quite unfit to be a mediator of anything." Martin thought that Lyndon Johnson himself should be the mediator.[122]

The first Acheson mission failed: the Greeks did not appear.

Paul Martin voiced his displeasure to the Greek Ambassador, Mr. Kalegris. When Kalegris accused Martin of partiality at the start of the meeting, Martin snapped that he was tired of Greek anti-Canadian propaganda. Canada's position was twofold: the crisis "threatened the viability of [NATO] which means so much to Canada...it is obvious that Russia is enjoying the embarrassment of the West over Cyprus and is prepared to exploit any opening." Second, "if the UN is not permitted to keep the peace in Cyprus, then we must admit a tragic failure for the organization; nevertheless, this would be better than a massacre which UN troops as peacemakers must avoid even at the price of humiliation despite their recognized ability as fighters, especially the Canadians."[123]

Martin stormed at Kalegris. He had now developed "a strong interest in Cyprus and admitted deep personal involvement" but unless the "present trend was reversed [Canada] could not continue to contribute [her] resources in a hopeless cause." The Canadian media was questioning the UN effort calling it "idealism gone wild." Canadians "would get tired of devotion to UN ideals if efforts proved fruitless." Kalegris remained "stubborn" and offered no comment of substance.[124]

There could have been no better depiction of Canadian interests in the matter. Martin's exasperation, however, reflected the West's frustration with Cyprus. This led to a highly secret American-Canadian-British discussion in Washington camouflaged as two separate bi-lateral discussions: Canada-US and United Kingdom-US. The full range of American intelligence analysis was provided to all participants including confirmation that the Turks would conduct an amphibious landing at the port of Kyrenia and use it as a negotiating card.[125]

The problem was summed up thus: the Greeks were in a strong position since efforts to stop the infiltration of support to the Greek Cypriots were futile, the UNFICYP commander was unwilling to use the UN force aggressively to prevent infiltration since its mandate was fuzzy, and the United States was pressuring Turkey not to invade because of its larger interests related to the Soviet threat. Some means had to be found to curb Greece: Canada's move within NATO to stop mutual aid was favoured, as was a British proposal to confront Greece in the North Atlantic Council with intelligence demonstrating their intentions. The Americans wanted to use SACEUR to maintain pressure on the Greek and Turkish military commanders. The British agreed and committed to pressuring Greece over the presence of

George Grivas on the island. All three parties favoured exploring economic sanctions against Greece and Turkey.[126]

What about the role of UNFICYP? General Gyani was considered to be ineffective and both the British and Canadian force commanders were holding their own discussions on protective measures without consulting him. In effect UNFICYP was prepared not to oppose a Turkish invasion, ride out the predicted four to five-day period of chaos which would ensue during the fighting, emerge once a temporary settlement was found and then conduct humanitarian relief work pending a clarification of its role in the aftermath.[127]

It took several days to build a consensus in the NAC, and the pressure the three nations counted on never materialized, in part due to French intransigence and Italian cravenness. The proposal to have SACEUR attend the NAC meetings was nearly blocked by these two powers, even though all other NATO members approved.[128] SACEUR was then authorized to write the Greek and Turkish chiefs of staffs. He bluntly told them that "under the terms of MC 57/1 and related NATO documents, forces assigned to my command shall not be redeployed or used operationally within Allied Command Europe without consent of SACEUR, subject to political guidance furnished by the NAC." Using intelligence data, Lemnitzer informed them he knew there were 7400 Greek troops on the island, far in excess of the 950 authorized by the London and Zurich agreements: there were only 1000 more Turkish troops in addition to the 650 allowed. UNFICYP, particularly the Canadian contingent, verified these numbers and the Canadians were impartial assessors. All of this, SACEUR stated, degraded his capability to defend the NATO area on the southeastern flank.[129]

Lemnitzer told George Ignatieff that he was not sure it would accomplish anything, and it did not. Greece removed its forces from NATO command. Throughout the sweltering remnants of July 1964, the NAC deliberated back and forth, but no amount of cajoling could persuade the Greeks. As of 18 July, Arthur Andrew reported that "the internal situation in Cyprus has remained unchanged in its essentials" and that "UNFICYP has played a credible role in muting the outward manifestations but the essential ingredients have remained constant." For the Canadian High Commissioner, "the question the UN and the contributors must face is whether they could simply leave the Turkish minority to the mercies of their Greek compatriots. The moral and humane objections to such a course need not be stated." U Thant had to alter UNFICYP's mandate to disarm Greek Cypriot irregulars in conjunction with some form of monitoring the Greek Army withdrawal but the Soviets would oppose it. The alternative was "unpleasant" since the UN's credibility would be damaged and there would be a "violent reaction by Turkey against metropolitan Greece with all that would entail."[130]

Andrew was hinting that UNFICYP's role could be redefined to protect Turkish Cypriot enclaves within a Greek Cypriot-controlled island. This concept anticipated the safe-haven plan implemented in Bosnia in the 1990s by UNPROFOR. Like the situation encountered in the 1990s, it would mean a loss of impartiality for the UN forces since they would be seen by the Greeks as protecting Turkish interests. Canadian policymakers, Martin in particular, was adamant that Canada's impartiality be maintained.

George Ball and the Americans convened an unofficial meeting of UNFICYP troop contributors on 21 July. He used Canada's participation in the force as a lever to prevent some wavering members from withdrawing from Cyprus.[131]

Lieutenant General Walsh, the Chief of the General Staff, was seriously concerned about the status and organization of the Canadian UNFICYP contingent. In their haste to deploy the force in March, the infantry battalion had been instructed to leave behind certain heavy weapons which were not deemed necessary given the perceived nature of the mission. This included 4.2-inch heavy mortars and 106mm recoilless rifle anti-tank weapons. The battalion commander and Brigadier Tedlie noted with concern that both sides were deploying tanks to the island. Without an anti-tank capability, the lightly-armed Canadian contingent would not stand a chance. The Force Commander, General Gyani, had no serious objection.[132] This matter (essentially the deployment of four 106mm recoilless rifles and 25 men) went to Cabinet for debate, which gave assent after Paul Hellyer explained that they were necessary to deter belligerent action against Canadian forces. (This is in contrast with the UNPROFOR experience in which the Canadian contingent brought its anti-tank weapons for force protection despite UN New York's protestations and much hand-wringing in National Defence Headquarters' policy world about "provocation" and "escalation.")[133]

There was good reason to be concerned. From 7 to 9 August, the Turkish Air Force flew several retaliatory strike missions after Greek forces attacked several Turkish Cypriot villages. Sixty-four aircraft were involved, some of them dropping napalm.[134] Lieutenant General E.L.M. Burns, now serving with Canada's disarmament delegation, was queried by External Affairs on the situation. Burns was in contact with several British officials who were using him as a sounding board on Canadian opinion. Burns told them the "killing of say 20 Turkish civilians including some women and children might in the view of the Turkish community be sufficient provocation to bring about a Turkish intervention." It was possible that some Turkish extremist group might kill twenty of their own to bring about intervention. It was unlikely these invasion scares were just threats—they were serious messages. As for the Greek side, Burns thought that "Makarios had a Byzantine mentality, and liked to play many cards at once: it was always possible he might get his cards mixed."[135]

The situation was serious enough for Pearson and Martin to talk with Johnson and Rusk on 8 July. The Prime Minister told the President that the only way to avoid a war over Cyprus was to expand and "strengthen the UN force for more effective peace-keeping" but that was not enough since "it would require more drastic action by the Security Council and more dynamic leadership by the Secretary-General than had yet been shown." U Thant "had many fine qualities but perhaps he was not being positive and aggressive enough in this situation." Johnson agreed emphatically and asked if Canada was willing to remain involved. Pearson replied that Canada would do so if UNFICYP were strengthened and "adequate power and authority conferred on it by a UN Security Council Resolution." The men discussed the obstacles— Makarios and the Soviets. They were under no illusions that using the Security Council might not work. Pearson even told Rusk that he "was personally available to do anything if asked to" something Rusk "expressed great appreciation over."[136]

Martin and Paul Trembley at the UN confronted Ralph Bunche but were unable to make any headway as he was "rather hesitant and negative" since Makarios would be able to veto any increase or alteration of UNFICYP's configuration. This the Archbishop had already done when the Netherlands and Norway were considered for UNFICYP duty. Rusk then called Pearson back and requested that the Canadian Prime Minister fly down to New York and "stiffen up" U Thant: the Security Council had agreed to a ceasefire resolution, but this was just temporary. The problem, Rusk told him, was that Makarios was initiating a process to introduce Soviet intervention forces. The Soviets were leery and noncommittal, but this situation could change.[137]

Pearson composed some private notes to organize his thoughts on Cyprus and the role of the UN there. He stated that "we know that a small conventional war in any place—Cyprus or Vietnam—can lead to nuclear global war. We have a duty to do what we can as human beings to prevent this." In his view, "it is absolutely intolerable that the United Nations or NATO or the Commonwealth should not be able to prevent a war breaking out between two civilized, friendly states, actually in alliance, because of the treatment of a minority in the third state of the same race." What concerned Pearson greatly was that "it is also intolerable, and not to be admitted, that the policies of a government in a small country should be such, by omission or commission, as to provoke or give reason for the intervention of a neighbouring state; either to protect a minority or to strengthen the military strength of a majority."[138]

If the United Nations did not alter UNFICYP's terms of reference and strengthen its forces, then "failure of the United Nations and the international community in this crisis will be far more than the failure of peace-keeping in Cyprus. It will put in jeopardy the whole peace-keeping function of the United Nations, the function on which the whole concept and organization of the United Nations is based." Drawing on his experiences in the 1930s, Pearson concluded that "The League of Nations received its death blow in Ethiopia. We must prevent the United Nations from suffering the same fate through failure in Cyprus. Furthermore, armed conflict between two NATO members will end NATO in its present form."[139]

The ideas and concerns expressed in Pearson's document were the basis of a new Canadian policy. Paul Trembley would tell the UN authorities that "there is no question of UNFICYP shooting its way in Cyprus, but in [Canada's] opinion, there are at least two main areas where the UN should undertake an intensive and dynamic pacifying role in northwest Cyprus."[140] These moves indicate that Canada was contemplating a type of peacekeeping quite different from that used in the Sinai with UNEF. In effect, UNFICYP's "new look" would be more like the Congo operation.

Yet such an alteration was not implemented. The Soviets were becoming more and more vocal about Cyprus and eventually at a NATO meeting in September, the new NATO Secretary General, Manlio Brosio, privately told the Greek and Turkish representatives that if the Soviets attacked either nation in any context, NATO would not invoke Article 5 and come to their defence. Although some of the more timid Canadian analysts did not respond favourably to this approach, it appears to have been a major factor in easing tensions that fall.[141]

That lull led to a further UN Security Council resolution which reiterated the ceasefire agreement: it did not provide an adequate response to the conditions set by Canada. Nevertheless, Cabinet met and concluded that

The Canadian contingent was the largest and only really professional one in the Force and its withdrawal in present circumstances would almost certainly make the United Nations peacekeeping force in Cyprus impossible.[142]

The stakes were simply too high, so Canada accepted a partial solution. This compromise laid the groundwork for the thirty-year Canadian Army commitment to Cyprus and for the eventual Turkish intervention in 1974 which would find soldiers from the Canadian Airborne Regiment fighting Turkish paratroopers attempting to seize Nicosia airport as part of a massive invasion which would partition the island and further polarize the situation into the 21st Century.

Notes to Chapter 10

1. Lord Kinross, *The Ottoman Centuries: The Rise and Fall of the Turkish Empire* (New York: Norrow Quill, 1977), 264-266.

2. Robert Stephens, *Cyprus: A Place of Arms* (London: Pall Mall Press, 1966), introduction; Tom Pocock, *East and West of Suez: The Retreat From Empire* (London: The Bodley Head, 1986), 36; Frank Kitson, *Bunch of Five* (London: Faber and Faber, 1975), 205.

3. Kitson, *Bunch of Five*, 209-210; Jane Perry Clark Carey and Andrew Galbraith Carey, *The Web of Modern Greek Politics* (New York: Columbia University Press, 1968), 145-147.

4. Michael Carver, *War Since 1945* (New York: Putnam's 1981), 45-47; Kitson, *Bunch of Five*, 211-212; Pocock, *East and West of Suez*, 37-41; Thomas W. Adams and Alvin J. Cottrell, *Cyprus Between East and West* (Washington: Johns Hopkins, 1968), 14-17.

5. Monteagle Stearns, *Entangled Allies: US Policy Toward Greece, Turkey, and Cyprus* (New York: Council for Foreign Relations, 1992), 29-30.

6. Ibid.

7. Pocock, *East and West of Suez*, 47.

8. Kitson, *Bunch of Five*, 212

9. Ibid.; Pocock, *East and West of Suez*, 54, 59;

10. Adams and Cottrell, *Cyprus Between East and West*, 6.

11. Stavros Panteli, *The Making of Modern Cyprus: From Obscurity to Statehood* (Herts: Interworld Publications, 1990), 182-183.

12. N.M. Ertekun, *The Cyprus Dispute and the Birth of the Turkish Republic of Northern Cyprus* (Nicosia: K. Rustem and Brother, 1981), 7-8; Polyvios G. Polyviou, *Cyrpus: Conflict and Negotiation 1960-1980* (London: Duckworth, 1980), 13-14.

13. NAC RG 25, vol. 7846 file 12833-40 pt. 1, (29 Sep 59) memo DL(1) to Commonwealth Division, "Cyprus and The Commonwealth."

14. NAC RG 25, vol. 7846 file 12833-40 pt. 1, (20 Nov 59) message Athens to SSEA, "Cyprus-Relationship with the Commonwealth and NATO."

15. NAC RG 25, vol. 7846 file 12833-40 pt. 1, (4 Dec 59) message Ankara to SSEA, "Cyprus-Turkish views on membership in the Commonwealth and NATO."

16. NAC RG 25, vol. 7846 file 12833-40 pt. 1, (3 Dec 59) message Ankara to External Affairs Ottawa, "Cyprus."

17. Chris Ashworth, *RAF Bomber Command 1936-1968* (Wellingborough: Patrick Stephens Ltd., 1995), 162-166; Robert Jackson, *AVRO Vulcan* (Wellingborough: Patrick Stephens Ltd., 1987), 61; Humphrey Wynn, *RAF Nuclear Deterrent Forces* (London: HMSO, 1994), 546-549.

18. These missiles were never put into production or deployed, although an arrangement was made with the United States to supply Thor IRBMs to RAF Bomber Command to work in conjunction with V-Force and SAC. NAC RG 25 vol. 5571 file 12833-40 pt. 2 (12 Feb 60) message Ankara to SSEA, "United Kingdom Military Bases in Cyprus." See Wynn, op. cit., for information relating to Thor deployments in the UK.

19. Robert Jackson, *Canberra: The Operational Record* (Washington D.C.: Smithsonian Institution Press, 1989), 54-55; Michael Armitage, *The Royal Air Force: An Illustrated History* (London: Brockhampton Press, 1996), 232.

20. Paul Jackson, "Bin the Bomb," *The Royal Air Force Yearbook 1999*, 21-26. Note that United Arab Republic propaganda leapt on the "atomic base" aspect of Cyprus in July 1960 during the constitutional talks and tried to generate anti-British feeling by asserting that the bases were for nuclear weapons use against the UAR. NAC RG 25 vol. 6145 file 50405-E-40 pt. 1, (11 Jul 60) Summary of World Broadcasts: Cairo Home Service, "Britain's Atomic Bases Policy in Cyprus and Africa."

21. Armitage, *The Royal Air Force*, 233; Ashworth, *RAF Bomber Command 1936-1968*, 164.

22. Paul Lashmar, *Spy Flights of the Cold War* (Annapolis: Naval Institute Press, 1996), 65, 148-149, 157; Jay Miller, *Lockheed U-2* (Austin: Aerofax Inc., 1983), 29; NAC RG 25 vol. 5571 file 12833-40 pt. 3 FP, see map, "United Kingdom Sites and Installations in Cyprus."

23. James Bamford, *The Puzzle Palace: Inside the National Security Agency* (Harmondsworth: Penguin Books, 1983), 208-210, 232-239; William A. Arkin and Richard W. Fieldhouse, Nuclear Battlefields: Global Links to the Arms Race (Cambridge: Ballinger Publishing Co., 1985), 220, 233.

24. NAC RG 25 vol. 5571 file 12833-40 pt. 2, (19 Jan 60) message HiCom London to SSEA, "Cyprus"; (28 Jan 60) message Athens to SSEA, "Greek views on Recent Cyprus Conference in London."

25. NAC RG 25 vol. 5571 file 12833-40 pt. 2, (22 Feb 60) letter Rogers to Scott.

26. NAC RG 25 vol. 5571 file 12833-40 pt. 2, (25 Feb 60) message Ankara to SSEA, "Turkish Stand on Cyprus Base Question."

27. Adams and Cottrell, *Cyprus Between East and West*, 56, 59.

28. NAC RG 25 vol. 5571 file 12833-40 pt. 2, (25 Feb 60) "Interdivisional Meeting on Cyprus"; NAC RG 25 vol. 6145 file 50405-E-40 pt. 1, (17 Feb 60) letter USSEA to CCOSC, "Cyprus and NATO."

29. NAC RG 25 vol. 5571 file 12833-40 pt. 3, (29 Jun 60) letter Robertson to Miller, "British Bases in Cyprus."

30. NAC RG 25 vol. 5571 file 12833-40 pt. 3, (10 Jun 60) memo Middle Eastern Division to European Division, "Value of UK bases in Cyprus."

31. NAC RG 25 vol. 5571 file 12833-40 pt. 3, (13 Jul 60) memo for SSEA, "Decisions Regarding Cyprus."

32. Carey and Carey, *The Web of Modern Greek Politics*, 166; Stephens, *Cyprus: A Place of Arms*, 168.

33. NAC RG 25 vol. 5571 file 12833-40 pt. 3, (5 Aug 60) message Ankara to SSEA, "Cyprus."

34. NAC RG 25 vol. 5571 file 12833-40 pt. 4, (8 Feb 61) "Background Information on Cyprus"; (10 Feb 61) message Ankara to SSEA, "Cyprus and the Commonwealth."

35. NAC RG 25 vol. 5571 file 12833-40 pt. 4, (16 Jun 61) memo DL(2) Division to African and European Division, "Accreditation of a Service Advisor to Cyprus." This accreditation was later changed in 1962 because of "the extreme sensitivity of either side to outside intelligence activities and Canada's role in the UNEF" and the service advisor at the Tel Aviv embassy fulfilled these functions but in a less visible and informal capacity. See NAC RG 25 vol. 5571 file 12833-40 pt. 4, (5 Jul 62) letter Green to Andrew.

36. NAC RG 25 vol. 5578 file 12845-A-40 pt. 1, (5 Apr 61) Draft letter of Appointment for the Canadian High Commissioner to Cyprus."

37. Ibid.

38. NAC RG 25 vol. 5571 file 12833-40 pt. 4, (25 Aug 61) message HiCom Cyprus to USSEA, "United Kingdom Sovereign Base in Cyprus"; NAC RG 25 vol. 5853 file 50141-B-40 vol. 1, (24 Aug 61) message HiCom Cyprus to SSEA, "Communism in Cyprus."

39. NAC RG 25 vol. 5608 file 12946-40 pt. 1, (21 Aug 61) message HiCom Cyprus to USSEA, "Relations with Soviet and Satellite Diplomats."

40. NAC RG 25 vol. 5608 file 12946-A-40 pt 1, (22 Aug 61) message Ankara to USSEA, "Cyprus and Turkey."

41. NAC RG 25 vol. 5853 file 50141-B-40 vol. 1, (5 Sep 61) message Ankara to USSEA, "Cyprus and Turkey."

42. NAC RG 25 vol. 5571 file 12833-40 pt. 4, (12 Oct 61) memo European Division to DL(1), "RCN Visits in 1962"; (21 Nov 61) message HiCom Cyprus to USSEA, "Technical Assistance for Cyprus."

43. NAC RG 25 vol. 5571 file 12833-40 pt. 4, (10 Jan 62) message London to External Affairs Ottawa, "Cyprus."

44. NAC RG 25 vol. 5571 file 12833-40 pt. 4, (5 Jul 62) letter Green to Andrew.

45. NAC RG 25 vol. 5571 file 12833-40 pt. 4, (6 Sep 62) message Tel Aviv to External Affairs Ottawa, "External Policies: Cyprus."

46. NAC RG 25 vol. 5608 file 12946-A-40 pt. 1, (10 Apr 62) message Ankara to USSEA, "Cyprus"; (23 May 62) message Ankara to USSEA, "Cyprus."

47. NAC RG 25 vol. 5608 file 12946-B-40 pt. 1, (29 Nov 62) message Ankara to External Affairs Ottawa, "Makarios Visit to Turkey."

48. NAC RG 25 vol. 5608 file 12946-A-40 pt. 1, (14 Dec 62) message HiCom Cyprus to SSEA, "Cyprus."

49. NAC RG 25 vol. 5608 file 12946-A-40 pt. 1, (18 Apr 63) message Ankara to External, "Cyprus."

50. NAC RG 25 vol. 5608 file 12946-A-40 pt. 1, (1 Jul 63) message Ankara to USSEA, "Turkish-Greek relations"; (22 Aug 63) message Tel Aviv to External Affairs Ottawa, "Interview with Makarios: Comments on Foreign Relations."

51. Parker T. Hart, *Two NATO Allies at the Threshold of War: Cyprus, a Firsthand Account of Crisis Management, 1965-1968* (Durham: Duke University Press, 1990), 3-10; See also Kitson, *Bunch of Five*, 213-215.

52. Stephens, *Cyprus: A Place of Arms*, 174-176.

53. Hart, *Two Allies*, 10.

54. Ertekun, *The Cyprus Dispute*, 10-15.

55. Stephens, *Cyprus: A Place of Arms*, 181-182.

56. Kitson, *Bunch of Five*, 231; (30 Sep 66) US Navy Office of Naval Research, "The Navy and Sub-Limited Conflicts: Final Report", A-25-A-26; Stearns, *Entangled Allies*, 34-35.

57. Adams and Cottrell, *Cyprus Between East and West*, 66; (July 1977) Center for Naval Analysis, "US Navy Responses to International Incidents and Crisis, 1955-1975 Vol. II: Summaries of Incidents and Responses", C-47.

58. Stephens, *Cyprus: A Place of Arms*, 187-189, Adams and Cottrell, *Cyprus Between East and West*, 61.

59. Stephens, *Cyprus: A Place of Arms*, 187-189, (July 1977) Center for Naval Analysis, "US Navy Responses to International Incidents and Crisis, 1955-1975 Vol. II: Summaries of Incidents and Responses", C-48, Adams and Cottrell, *Cyprus Between East and West*, 61.

60. Paul Martin, *A Very Public Life Vol. 2*, 540-541.

61. Ibid.

62. NAC RG 2, (4 Feb 64) Cabinet Conclusions.

63. Ibid.; Martin, *A Very Public Life Vol. 2*, 542.

64. NAC RG 24 vol. 21498 file 2146.1 v.3, (10 Feb 64) message Ankara to USSEA, "Turkey and the Cyprus Problem-End of the First Phase."

65. NAC RG 24 vol. 21498 file 2146.1 v.3, (11 Feb 64) memo to USSEA from DL(1) Division, "Cyprus-Planning for Possible Canadian Participation."

66. NAC RG 24 vol. 21501 file 2146.1.1v.1 (13 Mar 64) "Intelligence Annex: Cyprus."

67. NAC RG 24 vol. 21498 file 2146.1 v.3, (13 Feb 64) message Ankara to External Affairs Ottawa, "Cyprus."

68. NAC RG 24 vol. 21498 file 2146.1 v.3, (14 Feb 63) message London to External Affairs Ottawa, "Cyprus"; (14 Feb 64) message London to External, "Cyprus" (Canadian Eyes Only). Note that the first message date time group is a typographical error.

69. NAC RG 24 vol. 21498 file 2146.1 v.3, (14 Feb 64) message HiCom Cyprus to External Affairs Ottawa, "Cyprus-Present Situation."

70. Ibid.

71. Martin, *A Very Public Life Vol. 2*, 543-545.

72. NAC RG 24 vol. 21498 file 2146.1 v.3, (15 Feb 64) message London to External Affairs Ottawa, "Cyprus"; NAC RG 24 vol 21501 file 2146.1.1 vol. 1 (13 Mar 64) "Intelligence Annex: Cyprus." See also (23 Feb 64) message Ankara to External Affairs Ottawa, "Cyprus: Turkish Military Preparations."

73. NAC RG 24 vol 21501 file 2146.1.1 vol. 1 (13 Mar 64) "Intelligence Annex: Cyprus"; NAC RG 24 vol. 21498 file 2146.1 v.4, (25 Feb 64) message Athens to External Affairs Ottawa, "Situation: Military Forces of Greece over Cyprus Crisis Relatively Calm."

74. NAC RG 24 vol. 21498 file 2146.1 v.3 (19 Feb 64) message PERMISNY to External Affairs Ottawa, "Cyprus"; NAC RG 24 vol. 21501 file 2146.1.1 v.2, (10 Aug 64) mem to MND, "Chronological List of Events Leading to Canadian Participation in Cyprus."

75. NAC RG 24 vol. 21498 file 2146.1 v.3 (19 Feb 64) message WashDC to External Affairs Ottawa, "Cyprus."

76. NAC RG 24 vol. 21498 file 2146.1 v.3 (20 Feb 64) message External Affairs Ottawa to PERMISNY, "Ref: Telecon Barton-Smith Today."

77. NAC RG 24 vol. 21498 file 2146.1 V. 4, (2 Mar 64) message NATO Paris to External Affairs Ottawa, "NAC Consultations: Cyprus."

78. NAC RG 2 (5 Mar 64) Cabinet Conclusions.

79. Ibid.

80. NAC RG 24 vol. 21498 file 2146.1 v.4, (6 Mar 64) message Tel Aviv to External Affairs Ottawa, "Cyprus-Peacekeeping Force"; (6 Mar 64) PERMISNY to External Affairs Ottawa, "Cyprus: Peacekeeping Force Request for Canadian Contingent."

81. NAC RG 24 vol. 21498 file 2146.1 v.4,(6 Mar 64) message External Affairs to PERMISNY, "Cyprus: Peacekeeping Force Request for Canadian Contingent."

82. NAC RG 24 vol. 21458 file 2146.1 v. 5, (13 Mar 64) message PERMISNY to External Affairs Ottawa, "Cyprus: UN Involvement."

83. NAC RG 24 vol. 21458 file 2146.1 v. 5, (11 Mar 64) NATO message from Standing Group Representative to Standing Group Principals, "Situation: Cyprus."

84. NAC RG 24 vol. 21498 file 2146.1 v.5, (14 Mar 64) message NATO Paris to External Affairs Ottawa, "Special NAC Meeting."

85. (July 1977) Center for Naval Analysis, "US Navy Responses to International Incidents and Crisis, 1955-1975 Vol. II: Summaries of Incidents and Responses", C-48; (30 Sep 66) US Navy Office of Naval Research, "The Navy and Sub-Limited Conflicts: Final Report," A-54; NAC RG 24 vol. 21498 file 2146.1 v.4, (11 Mar 64) message NATO Paris to External Affairs

Ottawa, "Cyprus: Deteriorating Situation"; NAC RG 24 vol. 21498 file 2146.1 v.4, (10 Mar 64) message MA Athens to External Affairs Ottawa, "Cyprus."

86. Pearson, Memoirs Vol. 3, 135.

87. NAC RG 24 vol. 21501 file 2146.1.1v.1, (13 Mar 64) "Operations Order 64/1: Op SNOW GOOSE."

88. NAC RG 24 vol. 21501 file 2146.1.1v.1, (13 Mar 64) record of Cabinet Decision.

89. Pearson, *Memoirs Vol. 3*, 135.

90. NAC RG 24 vol. 21458 file 2146.1 v. 5, (14 Mar 64) message Tel Aviv to External Affairs Ottawa, "Cyprus: Turkish Threat."

91. See Maloney, "Learning to Love The Bomb: Canada's Cold War Strategy and Nuclear Weapons, 1951-1968" (forthcoming).

92. NAC RG 24 vol. 21498 file 2146.1 v.6, (23 Mar 64) message Washington DC to External, "F-104s for Greece and Turkey"; NAC RG 24 vol. 21498 file 2146.1 v.5,(12 Mar 64) message Washington DC to External, "Joint CDA-UAS F-104 G Programme."

93. NAC RG 25 acc 80-81/22 vol. 64 file 21-14-4 CYPR-1 Pt. 1, (19 Mar 64) Statements and Speeches, "UN Peacekeeping Operations in Cyprus."

94. NAC RG 25 acc 80-81/22 vol. 64 file 21-14-4 CYPR-1 Pt. 1, (23 Mar 64) message Geneva to External Affairs Ottawa, "Cyprus—My Conversation with U Thant."

95. NAC RG 24 vol. 21498 file 2146.1 V.6, (26 mar 64) message Cairo to External Affairs Ottawa, "Cyprus"; (25 Mar 64) message Geneva to External Affairs Ottawa, "Cyprus—My Conversation with the Foreign Minister of Turkey."

96. NAC RG 24 vol. 21498 file 2146.1 V.6, (26 Mar 64) message CANDEL Geneva to External Affairs Ottawa, "Cyprus—My Conversation with Spinelli."

97. NAC RG 24 vol. 21498 file 2146.1 V.6, (25 Mar 64) memo to the chiefs from CCOSC, "UN Forces in Cyprus"; NAC RG 24 vol. 21501 file 2146.1 V.2, (1 Mar 64) memo MND to CCOS, "Canadian Forces in Cyprus."

98. UN Archive, DAG 1/2.5.5.1.1 #4 file: Cyprus-Rikhye Memos, "Appraisal of the Situation in Cyprus 27 March-16 April 1964"; DHH, file 82/139, (2 Nov 64) "Talk Given by Brigadier General A.J. Tedlie on Command and Control in UNFICYP."

99. NAC RG 25 acc 80-81/22 vol. 64 file 21-14-4 CYPR-1 Pt. 1, (7 Apr 64) message Nicosia to External Affairs Ottawa, "SITREP"; NAC RG 24 vol. 21501 file 2146.1.1 v.2, (27 Apr 64) AHQ SITREP No. 16, "Information Summary"; W. Granger Blair, "UN Force has Little to Show for Month's Effort on Cyprus," *Montreal Daily Star*, 29 April 1964; Robert Miller, "Van Doos Confront Cyprus Greeks from New Positions in Mountains," *Globe and Mail* 1 May 1964; "Cypriots Shoot at Canadian Troops," *London Telegram*, 27 May 1964.

100. NAC RG 25 acc 80-81/22 vol. 64 file 21-14-4 CYPR-1 Pt. 1, (23 Apr 64) memo to the Minister, "Cyprus: Notes for Talk with U Thant."

101. Ibid.

102. NAC RG 24 vol. 21499 file 2146.1.1 v. 8 (27 Apr 64) message HiCom Cyprus to SSEA, "Cyprus-UNFICYP-An Interim Assessment"; NAC RG 25 acc 80-81/22 vol. 64 file 21-14-4 CYPR-1 Pt. 1, (24 Apr 64) message PERMISNY to External Affairs Ottawa, "Cyprus."

103. NAC RG 25 acc 80-81/22 vol. 64 file 21-14-4 CYPR-1 Pt. 1 (28 Apr 64) message PERMISNY to External Affairs Ottawa, "Cyprus."

104. NAC RG 25 acc 80-81/22 vol. 64 file 21-14-4 CYPR-1 Pt. 2, (5 May 64) memo to DL(1) Division, "Excerpt from the Minutes of the Meeting held on April 30 with Mr. Dean Rusk."

105. NAC RG 24 vol. 21499 file 2146.1.1 v. 7, (1 May 64) message NATO Paris to External Affairs Ottawa, "Cyprus-Stikker Mission and Special NAC Meeting."

106. NAC RG 24 vol. 21499 file 2146.1.1 v. 7 (2 May 64) message NATO Paris to External Affairs Ottawa, "Cyprus-Special NAC Meeting."

107. NAC RG 24 vol. 21499 file 2146.1.1 v. 8 (14 May 64) message NATO Paris to External Affairs Ottawa, "NATO Ministerial Meeting Cyprus."

108. NAC RG 24 vol. 21499 file 2146.1.1 v. 8, (5 May 64) message Nicosia to External, "UNFICYP-Peacekeeping and Normalization."

109. Ibid.

110. NAC RG 24 vol. 21499 file 2146.1.1 v. 8, (27 May 64) message External Affairs Ottawa to NATO Paris, "Cyprus-Acquisition of Arms"; (28 May 64) message Washington DC to External Affairs Ottawa, "Cyprus-Acquisition of Arms."

111. (July 1977) Center for Naval Analysis, "US Navy Responses to International Incidents and Crisis, 1955-1975 Vol. II: Summaries of Incidents and Responses", C-48; NAC RG 24 vol. 21499 file 2146.1.1 v. 9, (6 Jun 64) message Washington DC to External Affairs Ottawa, "Cyprus-Concern over Turkish Intention"; (6 Jun 64) message Nicosia to External Affairs Ottawa, "Cyprus-Turkish Invasion Contingency."

112. NAC RG 24 vol. 21499 file 2146.1.1 v. 9, (9 Jun 64) message Nicosia to External Affaris, "Cyprus-Consultations-Invasion Contingencies."

113. NAC RG 24 vol. 21499 file 2146.1.1 v. 9, (10 Jun 64) message London to External Affairs Ottawa, "Cyprus: Ball Visit to London."

114. NAC RG 25 acc 80-81/22 vol. 64 file 21-14-4 CYPR-1 Pt. 2, (10 Jun 64) letter Noel- Baker to Martin; (10 Jun 64) "Notes on Noel-Baker Letter of 10 June 1964."

115. NAC RG 25 acc 80-81/22 vol. 64 file 21-14-4 CYPR-1 Pt. 2, (22 Jun 64) letter Martin to Noel-Baker.

116. NAC RG 24 vol. 21499 file 2146.1.1v.9 (29 Jun 64) message Moscow to External Affairs Ottawa, "Cyprus: Soviet Attitude"; (8 Jul 64) message PERMISNY to External Affairs Ottawa, "UNFICYP: Military Developments"; Adams and Cottrell, *Cyprus Between East and West*, 37.

117. NAC RG 25 acc 80-81/22 vol. 64 file 21-14-4 CYPR-1 Pt. 2, (1 Jul 64) memo for USSEA, "Minister Meeting with Prime Minister Inonu of Turkey in New York, June 24, and Prime Minister Papandreou of Greece in Washington, June 25, 1964."

118. NAC RG 24 vol. 21499 file 2146.1.1 v. 9, (1 Jul 64) message NATO Paris to External Affairs Ottawa, "Cyprus."

119. NAC RG 25 acc 80-81/22 vol. 64 file 21-14-4 CYPR-1 Pt. 2,(3 Jul 64) memo for MND.

120. Ibid.

121. NAC RG 24 vol. 21499 file 2146.1.1 v. 9, (3 Jul 64) message External Affairs Ottawa to PERMISNY, "Cyprus."

122. NAC RG 24 vol. 21499 file 2146.1.1 v. 9, (3 Jul 64) message External Affairs Ottawa to PERMISNY, "Cyprus."

123. NAC RG 25 acc 80-81/22 vol. 64 file 21-14-4 CYPR-1 Pt. 2, (7 Jul 64) message External Affairs Ottawa to PERMISNY, "Minister's Discussion with Greek Ambassador."

124. Ibid.

125. NAC RG 24 vol. 21499 file 2146.1.1 v. 9, (9 Jul 64) message WashDC to External Affairs Ottawa, "Cyprus."

126. Ibid.

127. Ibid.

128. NAC RG 24 vol. 21499 file 2146.1.1 v. 9, (14 Jul 64) message NATO Paris to External Affairs Ottawa, "Cyprus-NAC Mtg Jul 14."

129. NAC RG 24 vol. 21500 file 2146.1 v.10, (20 Jul 64) message NATO Paris to External Affairs Ottawa, "Cyprus: SACEUR's Let."

130. NAC RG 24 vol. 21500 file 2146.1 v.10, (19 Jul 64) message Nicosia to External Affairs Ottawa, "Contingency-Future of UNFICYP."

131. NAC RG 25 acc 80-81/22 vol. 64 file 21-14-4 CYPR-1 Pt. 2, (21 Jul 64) message External Affairs Ottawa to WashDC, "Cyprus: Possible Interim Report by the Mediator."

132. NAC RG 24 vol. 21501 file 2146.1.1 v.2, (4 Aug 64) memo CGS to CDS, "CCUNCYP-Organization of Infantry Battalion."

133. NAC RG 2 (6 Aug 64) Cabinet Conclusions; Maloney, *War Without Battles*, 468.

134. NAC RG 24 vol. 21500 file: 2146.1 v.11, (10 Aug 64) message Ankara to External Affairs.

135. NAC RG 25 acc 80-81/22 vol. 64 file 21-14-4 CYPR-1 Pt. 2, (7 Aug 64) message Geneva to External Affairs Ottawa, "Cyprus."

136. NAC MG 26 N6 file: Cyprus Crisis August 1964, (9 Aug 64) "Cyprus."

137. Ibid.

138. NAC MG 26 N6 file: Cyprus Crisis August 1964, (9 Aug 64) "Canada's Interest in the Cyprus Tragedy."

139. Ibid.

140. NAC RG 24 vol. 21500 file: 2146.1 v.11, (13 Aug 64) message PERMISNY to External Affairs Ottawa, "Cyprus SECGHENs mtg."

141. NAC RG 24 vol. 21501 file 2146.1.1 v. 13, (14 Sep 64) message NATO Paris to External Affairs Ottawa, "Cyprus Consideration in NATO"; (3 Sep 64) message External Affairs Ottawa to NATO Paris, "Cyprus: Watching Brief."

142. NAC RG 2 (25 Sep 64) Cabinet Conclusions.

CHAPTER 11

RECALLING THE BLUE LEGIONS: THE DECLINE OF CANADIAN UN PEACE OPERATIONS, 1964-1970

For heathen hearts that puts her trust
In reeking tube and iron shard
All valiant dust that builds on dust
And guarding, calls not thee to guard
For frantic boast and foolish word-
Thy mercy on Thy people Lord!

—Rudyard Kipling, *Recessional*

The situation in Cyprus deteriorated considerably in 1967, which brought into question UNFICYP's ability to prevent what was euphemistically called intercommunal violence. Turkey lost patience, invaded and partitioned the island in 1974.

(CF Photo)

As an important means of Canadian Cold War crisis management and intervention, UN peacekeeping entered a serious decline after 1964. This decline was manifest in two areas. First, UN peacekeeping was itself in disrepute both within UN circles and on the world stage. Financial and procedural questions continued to plague those who championed impartial UN intervention as the Blue Helmets withdrew from the Congo and The Yemen. UNMOGIP in the Kashmir only served to freeze tensions in that area and another mission, UNIPOM, had to be formed when serious fighting broke out elsewhere on the Indian subcontinent. That mission was withdrawn in less than a year. It was clear by 1967 that UNFICYP was trapped in a quagmire on the island of love. The UN was also unable to make any headway in mitigating the effects of the war in Southeast Asia. Then the crown jewel of UN peacekeeping, the United Nations Emergency Force, was forced out of the Sinai in a humiliating fashion and another desperate battle in the Middle East ensued, a battle with nuclear implications. Canada even had to plan an armed rescue of the UNEF contingent with NATO forces, much as it would four decades later with the UNPROFOR contingent in the former Yugoslavia.

The Canadian political scene was also changing. Lester Pearson was unable to match his previous international diplomatic successes with domestic ones. A troubled economy and a Marxist-oriented separatist movement in Quebec initiated a terrorist campaign against the establishment. Once Pierre Elliot Trudeau assumed control in 1968, even the utility and function of NATO as the central pillar of Canadian national security policy was questioned, while the UN was considered to be a dangerous joke. An isolationist wind was blowing as the Canadian legions withdrew from their thin blue lines abroad. The Trudeau government was not interested in intervening to mitigate the effects of the Biafran War, which in some ways was the 1960s equivalent of Rwanda in the 1990s. The period from 1964 to 1970 clearly marked the end of an era in Canadian national security policy.

DRAW DOWN, 1964

The first UN mission involving Canadian forces to draw down was ONUC in the Congo throughout 1964. It was evident to educated observers of the Congo situation that the 20 000-man UN presence in that country could not be maintained indefinitely. ONUC had served its original purpose which was to stabilize the situation and forestall or prevent Soviet interference. By late 1962, the United States and the United Nations agreed that the best means to keep the Congo stable was to build a professional Congolese army. An American team developed a plan to do so in conjunction with UN representatives in the Congo. The main problem from UN New York's perspective was that the so-called "Green Plan" had too many NATO nations participating. New York understood that "the only countries which can make a significant contribution to the training plan are NATO countries" but was sensitive to Cold War propaganda attacks from the Soviets and their allies. The Americans were asked to lower their profile, which they promptly did.[1]

Military aid flowed to the Congolese forces throughout 1963, particularly from Italy, Belgium, Norway, and even Israel, although such a project could not be completed overnight.

The Green Plan should be considered a prototype of the process in Vietnam, which the Americans would undertake later in the 1960s. The future role of the UN force in the Congo was now in doubt. By October 1963, ONUC downsized to 5200 men, a fraction of its size in 1961. ONUC's mission, which the Congolese government acceded to, was to "be used only when law and order has broken down to the extent ANC cannot exercise control."[2]

Canada continued to provide 250 signals personnel and the Chief of Staff position, now filled by Brigadier J.A. Dextraze. Dextraze's heroic adventures in the Congo are discussed elsewhere:[3] The Nigerian General commanding ONUC was portrayed by Canadian diplomatic personnel as "a playboy [who] did not know his job as a staff officer, and still less, as a force commander." A.J. Hicks, the Canadian diplomatic representative on the ground, compared Ironsi to his Indian predecessor: "The difference between the previous Force Commander and the present one is that the former, who was well trained, had every intention of doing nothing, and the latter, who has little military ability, insists on doing something....Dextraze and Green between them are patching up the holes and keeping ruffled tempers from exploding, but it is a wearying and soul-destroying task."[4]

As an example of the state to which ONUC had been reduced, Hicks reported to Ottawa that "the Brigadier often has to kick out the drunks from the Commander's house at 2, 3 or 4 o'clock in the morning, stick the Commander in bed, and make sure he is dragged out and at his desk the next morning. That next morning starts with abuses, and abuse, often of an arrogantly personal nature, often continues all day. These are trials which Dextraze is accepting (1) because he is a good professional soldier (2) because he is a Canadian and, I suppose, there are other reasons, but God knows what they are."[5]

New Soviet and Chinese-supported menaces threatened the Congo in a number of areas. Dextraze orchestrated the ONUC withdrawal with Green, while the latter coordinated the Belgian, Italian, and American military assistance groups. French, Belgian, Rhodesian, South African mercenaries who had fought for the Katangese against the central government and the UN were later hired by the Congolese government, as were Cuban exile pilots who had worked for the CIA. The Congo continued as a Cold War proxy fight well into the late 1960s, but the UN was not involved. The Canadian contingent had departed by August 1964.[6]

The situation with UNYOM in The Yemen was no better. The UNYOM Force Commander's recommendations on equipment, leave policy, lack of medical support, and mandate had been disregarded by the UN leadership in New York, in part because there was little money available and in part because of the friction between von Horn and senior UN personalities. The dispute became public and Von Horn was fired. U Thant conducted an assessment and reported to the Security Council at the end of October 1963 that if Saudi Arabia was not forthcoming with more funds, UNYOM would be terminated. Saudi Arabia relented under US pressure and the mission was extended. This financial roller coaster continued throughout 1964. UNYOM never had enough personnel or logistic support to carry out what was an increasingly irrelevent mandate: the Royalists, who had not been part of the larger peace scheme, continued their fight against the UAR far away from the UNYOM operating areas while UAR-supported terrorists infiltrated Aden and clashed with British forces.[7]

There was little discussion of UNYOM in Canadian circles. Cabinet met periodically to approve extending the Canadian contingent's stay commensurate with the mandate. By this time the Pearson Government was deeply involved in Cyprus. It is clear that UN credibility had to be maintained during that time and so the RCAF unit stayed in place, despite UNYOM's irrelevance.[8] In time, the Saudi Arabians and the UAR tired of the game. A 1964 External Affairs report merely noted, almost in passing, that "the termination was due to the decision of Saudi Arabia and the UAR, which had borne the costs of UNYOM, to withdraw their financial support."[9] The Canadian contingent rejoined its compatriots in UNEF in the fall of 1964, while some forty thousand Egyptian troops were redeployed from Yemen to Egypt over the course of the next year, just in time for the 1967 Six Day War with Israel.

UNIPOM: INDIA AND PAKISTAN, 1965-66

A small number of Canadian UN Military Observers continued the long, cold watch in the mountains of the Kashmir. In his biography of Ralph Bunche, Sir Brian Urquart noted that by 1965

> UNMOGIP suffered from a syndrome which was to afflict other successful peacekeeping operations. Because its presence reduced the number of border incidents and prevented them from escalating, its activities received very little attention, either from the Security Council or in the press, and the pressures which were building up on both sides were ignored.[10]

India had other problems, such as dealing with Chinese incursions and invading the Portuguese colony of Goa in 1961. By October 1962 at the height of the Cuban Missile Crisis, India lost a major battle with China which threw the Indian government into turmoil. American and British military support flowed into India to compensate. This was by no means a risk-free gamble for the West: Pakistan hosted a U-2 base for the CIA (Francis Gary Powers departed from Peshawar in May 1960 on his rendezvous with destiny and a Soviet SAM-2 Guideline missile) and signals intelligence gathering sites for the National Security Agency. From 1962 to 1963, the British focussed on India while the Americans wooed Pakistan.[11]

Late in 1963, however, the Muslim population in the Kashmir had had enough and agitated for Pakistani assistance. This situation was further complicated when a sacred relic (a clip of Mohammed's hair) was stolen from the Hazratbal mosque in Sringar. The Pakistani government declared that "Kashmir is to Pakistan what Berlin is to the West" and set about reinforcing underground extremist groups in the region.[12]

Ayub Khan was under increasing domestic political pressure to do something in Kashmir. He needed freedom of action, however. To gain maneouvering room Khan traveled to Moscow to try and patch up relations with the Soviets. While he was away in the spring of 1965, Indian troops escalated a border clash in the extremely remote and desolate region of the Rann of Kutch. Indian forces were defeated and withdrew. This emboldened Khan, who increased infiltration into the Kashmir and developed plans to seize the region with armoured and airborne forces. The early stages of this plan were implemented, but the Indians launched a massive armoured attack in the Lahore region.[13]

Fearing that China might get involved and the situation devolve into a major regional war, U Thant considered sending Ralph Bunche to mediate. This plan was rejected by both belligerents, each accusing UNMOGIP of being a tool of the other. American Ambassador Arthur Goldberg at the UN was, however, instrumental in getting unanimous support in the Security Council for a peace initiative. U Thant then embarked on shuttle diplomacy in the region.[14]

A combination of superpower arms embargoes and serious Soviet initiatives succeeded where U Thant failed. As the Indian and Pakistani armies ran out of spare parts, Soviet Premier Alexi Kosygin achieved a massive Soviet propaganda victory by formulating the Tashkent Declaration in January-February 1966. The UN, meanwhile, increased UNMOGIP to 102 observers and created an "administrative adjunct" to the existing force called UNIPOM: United Nations India Pakistan Observer Mission. UNIPOM was a "temporary measure" to supervise the September 1965 ceasefire in the region outside of UNMOGIP's jurisdiction.[15]

Canadian involvement with the peace process started in September 1965 when Lester Pearson offered his services to U Thant as mediator in the crisis. His offer, however, was rejected by the Secretary General.[16] Canadian interest in the continuing conflict between India and Pakistan had not dramatically changed since the 1950s. Both belligerents were members of the Commonwealth, India and Canada were still working together on the ICSC missions in southeast Asia, and the United States still maintained intelligence facilities in Pakistan which related to the larger aspects of the Cold War with the Soviet Union and China (China's nuclear test site, Lop Nor, for example, is located in western China).

Despite U Thant's rejection of Pearson's offer, Paul Martin flew to New York for discussions with the Secretary General. Martin was able to cajole U Thant to accept a Canadian force commander for UNIPOM and to have a Canadian air unit join the force.[17]

UNIPOM was a small force of around 150 observers drawn from ten nations. Twelve of the observers were Canadian as was the force commander, Brigadier General B.F. Macdonald. The Canadian UNMOGIP contingent was also expanded so that 117 Air Transport Unit could increase its observation capability to monitor both Kashmir and the Rann of Kutch. UNIPOM had ended by February 1966 and the Canadian contingent returned home.[18] Attempts to solve the Kashmir problem ground to a halt.

CRISIS YEAR IN CYPRUS: 1967

The shaky peace brokered by UNFICYP in Cyprus almost collapsed in 1967. The first inkling of change came in April 1967 when a junta consisting of extremely patriotic Greek colonels staged a revolution in Athens, overthrowing the George Papandreou government. The exact reasons for the coup did not relate to Cyprus per se: rather, the conspiratorial nature of Greek politics of the day, coupled with the rise of secret political organizations (left as well as right) within the armed forces, and the inflammatory anti-monarchist and anti-military remarks of Papandreous' son Andreas were contributing factors. The fact that George Grivas was anti-Papandreou was incidental.[19] The situation was exacerbated when an American aircraft carrier task group and a Marine Corps amphibious force arrived on the scene to prepare for the evacuation of allied diplomats and American nuclear weapons stored in Greece, if the situation deteriorated further.[20]

Events had stabilized by the end of May. The junta's policy towards Cyprus was, surprisingly, to continue negotiations through the UN. Their position was that enosis should be the ultimate objective. The Turkish Cypriots should be fairly compensated, not exterminated, however. This policy was not accepted by George Grivas, although Archbishop Makarios paid lip service to it.[21]

It is clear that Grivas embarked upon a campaign of provocation after the junta was established. Grivas then exploited ongoing tensions encompassing two small villages in south-eastern Cyprus: Kophinu and Ayios Theodhoros. The tensions here initially revolved around the use of Turkish or Greek lettering on the sides of municipal buses but escalated to the point where Greek Cypriot police patrol demanded unfettered entry. The Turkish defence organization TMT moved in as a precautionary measure but in time the local TMT leader was taking initiatives beyond his authority. Between July and October, the area was visited and re-visited by UNFICYP forces which interposed themselves between the belligerents on numerous occasions.[22]

In November 1967, a nasty incident in the Kophinou area threatened to get out of control when a Greek patrol removed a Turk roadblock, prompting a gunfight. The situation escalated when Greek armoured cars and infantry overran Ayios Theodhoros. Three UN observation positions were shelled and their blue helmeted British occupants seized by Greek forces. Nine Turkish Cypriots were killed and another nine wounded. Rifles were no match for heavy machineguns, mortars, and the 2 pounder guns on the Greek armoured cars. The Greek forces then turned 25 pounder artillery fire onto the village of Kophinou. Thirty-two Turkish Cypriots were killed.[23]

The bulk of the Fort Garry Horse Recce Squadron, part of Canada's UNFICYP contingent Quick Reaction Force, forced their way through several belligerent roadblocks with the intent of intervening in the flare-up. The local British UN commanders, who had taken fire from the Turkish Cypriots in the village, would not permit the Canadian Ferrets to move in order to allow the Greek Cypriots to continue with their assault and thereby exacting a sort of proxy revenge. The Fort Garrys were forced to sit and watch the ritual humiliation of non-combatants, shades of events in Bosnia in the 1990s.[24]

Incidents of Turkish sniping at Greek and UN forces erupted all over the island. Turkish Air Force overflights started immediately, and the Turkish Navy once again sailed for Cyprus with its Eskendrun-based amphibious forces. The Turkish First Army picked up its bridging equipment and moved to the Greek frontier opposite the Bosphorus.[25]

Tripartite diplomacy was put into action again, as it had been in 1964. The Americans worked on the Turks, the British parlayed with the Greeks, and the Canadians went to

Makarios. Paul Martin and Leo Cadieux, the Associate Minister of National Defence, told Makarios that if no movement were made in resolving the situation, Canada would withdraw from UNFICYP. They also presented the Archbishop with a joint statement of demands, the most prominent being the withdrawal of Greek mainland forces from Cyprus and a cessation of Makarios' attempts to restrict UNFICYP's mandate.[26]

Martin and Cadieux also tried to implement a Declaration of Reconciliation, but the Americans shied away from it, considering it premature. The Americans believed that Pearson and Martin were under a certain amount of domestic political pressure to bring the Canadian contingent home and this forced Martin's hand. Paul Martin, meanwhile, had a high-volume telephone conversation with U Thant in which he accused the Secretary General of criminal inaction.[27] The Canadian position remained, as it had in 1964, that UNFICYP had to be strengthened or withdrawn. Martin noted that "Although the peace had been kept in Cyprus for three and a half years, we were no closer to a settlement than in March 1964."[28]

Despite Martin's frustrations, enough NATO, American, British and Canadian and UN pressure was brought to bear. NATO Secretary General Manilio Brosio and American Secretary of the Army Cyrus Vance were key players in convincing the Greek Colonels that Grivas' actions in Cyprus were not acceptable. Eventually, "war was averted only because the Colonels finally recognized that they faced inevitable defeat in Cyprus" due to Turkish proximity to the island and the massed Turkish forces on the border of a country which had just undergone a revolution. Greek forces in Cyprus were withdrawn down to treaty-established levels.[29]

As for Canadian policy, the Pearson government was unhappy with the events of 1967 and displayed this by dramatically cutting the number of Canadian troops serving with UNFICYP—nearly in half during the early months of 1968.[30]

OPERATION LEAVEN AND THE UNEF: THE IGNOMINY OF RETREAT, 1967

The heaviest blow to fall on Canadian UN peacekeeping was the humiliating withdrawal of the United Nations Emergency Force from the Middle East in May 1967. When added to the 1964 draw down of UNYOM and ONUC, the failure of UNMOGIP to stave off war between India and Pakistan, coupled with the inability of UNFICYP to keep the peace on Cyprus, UNEF's removal generated intense questioning over the continuing value of peacekeeping in the 1960s.

As early as the spring of 1966, Canada's ambassador in Cairo, John Starnes, warned Ottawa that Nasser was shifting his position on allowing UNEF to operate on UAR territory. Under UNEF's original terms of reference, the Israelis forbade UNEF to operate on both sides of the International Frontier (IF) and Armistice Demarcation Line (ADL). Nasser's shift was directly related to Operation STEP, a substantial Israeli military operation conducted against Jordanian and al-Fatah installations near Samu village in November 1966. The Jordanian Army was defeated by the Israeli Defence Forces in a day-long raid.[31] King Hussein castigated Nasser for hiding behind UNEF and not taking his share of Israeli retaliation for al-Fatah's activities. The suggestion that Nasser remove UNEF was even raised at a meeting of the Arab

League in the fall of 1966. An April 1967 air battle between the Israeli Air Force and the Syrian Air Force (in which six Syrian MiGs were downed with no Israeli losses) prompted more inter-Arab discussion on the matter. Five days after the April air battle, the Israeli government warned that they would retaliate against Syria if al-Fatah raids from the Golan Heights against Galilee were not stopped.[32]

Superimposed on all of this activity was the problem of Israel's acquisition of a nuclear weapons capability. Canadian DND analysts predicted in 1963 that "Israel will be the first minor nation to engage in the manufacture of nuclear weapons and the probability is increased by her high state of technological competence."[33] Nasser was pre-occupied with this problem throughout 1966 and went so far as to enter into talks with the Soviets to extend their nuclear umbrella over the UAR. Publicly, Nasser told his people that the UAR would conduct a preventive war if Israel developed nuclear weapons first.[34]

On 13 May 1967, representatives of the Soviet Union in Moscow and Cairo provided Egyptian intelligence and military officials with information that Israel had mobilized ten brigades and was moving to attack the Golan Heights. Nasser then mobilized the Egyptian Army and prepared to move four armoured divisions into the Sinai. The information provided by the Soviets was, in fact, false: there was no Israeli mobilization against Syria.[35] Three days later, the Egyptian Chief of Staff General Fawzi informed General Rikhye, the UNEF commander, that UNEF was to redeploy from its forward positions back to its base areas. Paul Martin noted in his memoirs that "Nasser, with Moscow's support, had begun to beat the war drums."[36]

The debate over culpability for the Six Day War of 1967 continues today. It is clear that the Soviet inputs were critical to Nasser's decisionmaking process. Some portray the Soviet intelligence matter as an accident or mistake.[37] This is, however, unlikely given the nature of the Cold War in such a vital region. What motives could the Soviet Union have for contributing to the destabilization of the Middle East at this juncture?

Short-term Soviet objectives in the Middle East in 1967 included the containment of Israel, whose existence was believed to threaten the "progressive" (pro-Soviet) Arab regimes of Egypt, Syria, and Iraq. The Soviet leadership needed to be seen on the world stage as "a highly visible supporter and protector of Arab national security,"[38] invaluable in Cold War propaganda terms, particularly in the Third World. It also allowed the Soviet fleet access to bases in the Eastern Mediterranean from which NATO interests on the southern flank could be threatened.

The medium-term Soviet objective was the isolation of Turkey and her withdrawal from NATO. This would allow the Soviet Union control over the Bosporus Straits. It would also force NATO-committed nuclear forces out of Turkey and limit NATO's ability to strike at Soviet nuclear forces in the Soviet Union proper, thus decreasing the nuclear deterrence balance and increasing the possibility that the Soviets could fight and win a conventional war in Western Europe. The Soviets had been conducing a careful and quiet diplomatic game with Turkey after the 1964 tensions strained her relationship with NATO.[39]

Turkish tensions with Syria and Iraq had been high since 1958 and 1961. NATO members were seriously concerned about the border areas, so much so that SACEUR established several deployment areas for NATO's ACE Mobile Force along those borders to counteract any moves in the region.[40] Syria had to keep forces deployed on the Turkish border, forces which were needed to counter the Israelis. Turkey's neutralization would accomplish much for the Soviet Union and the isolation or reduction of Israel and its nuclear capability would be a significant step in that direction.

The Canadian UNEF contingent was targeted by Nasser, as part of the larger game being played out in May 1967. On 17 May, one day after Fawzi told Rikhye to pull out of the forward positions, U Thant summoned Canada's UN representative, George Ignatieff for an informal meeting. The UN, U Thant told Ignatieff, was legally obliged to withdraw since the legal basis for the force's existence was part of the agreement between Nasser and Dag Hammarskjöld. Ignatieff was "totally taken by surprise" and cautioned U Thant not to act precipitously since this was not a formal request. Ignatieff argued that the Hammarskjöld-Pearson-Nasser arrangements in 1956 specifically included consultation and discussion. Others, including Bunche, argued that this was not the case.[41]

The next day, Egyptian Army forces initiated a harassment campaign against UNEF which included artillery fire directed near UN positions. Canadian troops on the ground, "believed that it would all blow over and we continued with normal routine."[42] On 18 May, U Thant informed Ignatieff that a formal request was received from Nasser demanding the complete withdrawal of UNEF from the Sinai. Ignatieff was concerned that the UNEF would have to abandon Sharm el Sheik, the vital position at the tip of the Sinai peninsula which commanded access to the Gulf of Aqaba and thus the Israeli port of Eilat. The UN had bargained with Israel in 1956 when UNEF first deployed to get Israeli troops out of the Sinai. The UN guaranteed the security of the sea lines of communications which now posed problems for the UN's credibility with Israel. Israel would have a completely legitimate *causus belli* if the Straits of Tiran were interdicted by the UAR.[43]

The UNEF troop contributors' committee met and Brazil, Norway, and Denmark supported Canada in requesting delay tactics so that the matter could be resolved diplomatically. India and Yugoslavia, supported by Ralph Bunche, said no. U Thant backed this group. Rikhye, however, wanted to keep some part of the force on ground to facilitate negotiations.[44]

Pearson privately examined the situation in preparation for a Cabinet meeting. It was clear that Paul Martin should not handle this situation on his own: UNEF was Pearson's

The loss of UN credibility was highlighted in 1967 when President Nasser demanded the withdrawal of UNEF from the Sinai. Initially denied landing rights by Egypt, Air Transport Command and 115 ATU were permitted to evacuate UN troops after a Canadian naval task force drawn from NATO commitments entered the Mediterranean.

(CF Photo)

concern. In the Prime Minister's view, the language of the original agreement between the UN and Egypt was vague: the Egyptian Government "declared" in 1956 that it had the right to order the UNEF to leave, but the UN only "took note" of the declaration and would use the principles of "good faith" in handling how UNEF would operate. Pearson and Cabinet agreed that the matter should be dealt with in the UN General Assembly and not by the Secretary General. Pearson had in fact identified the sovereignty aspects of UNEF's existence as an Achille's heel back in 1956 when the force was established.[45]

What Pearson and his advisors could not know was that the Egyptian Air Force had conducted an unopposed overflight of the Dimona nuclear weapons facility with two MiG-21 fighter-bombers on 18 May: the aircraft proceeded to Jordan without incident. The Israeli Government had, in previous years, established a list of events which would trigger Israeli mobilization and war. An aerial attack against Dimona was one of the events on that list.[46]

UNEF's position became even more precarious on 19 May. Ralph Bunche was informed by Egyptian representatives that UN aircraft would not be allowed to land at Egyptian air bases to evacuate UNEF. When word of this reached Canada, the Chief of the Defence Staff, General Jean V. Allard, ordered his staff to develop a series of contingency plans to unilaterally evacuate the Canadian contingent under a variety of non-permissive conditions.[47]

From its earliest days, UNEF contingency planning for a withdrawal had been discouraged by UN HQ in New York. This was based on the erroneous belief that even the mention of withdrawal would undermine the mission. Consequently, there was no serious plan at the UNEF HQ level when the Egyptian demands were made. Fortunately for the Canadian contingent, such planning had been conducted by Canadian Base Units Middle East-UNEF (CBU).[48]

The Directorate of Operations (DOps) was dubbed the coordinator and personnel from DOps and Directorate of Movements (DMove) were grouped into an ad hoc planning staff in Canadian Forces HQ. This staff, when it could, communicated directly with CBU. The plan was pushed down to the Air Transport Command level which produced an airlift plan to remove the entire UNEF, not just the Canadian contingent. Other problems intervened: the Egyptians denied landing clearances for RCAF aircraft since they believed the Canadians would gather intelligence on their troop movements in the Sinai.[49]

This forced CFHQ to reassess the situation and examine a naval option. The expertise did not exist in the special planning staff (there were no naval officers tasked to it) which resulted in a request to Maritime Command to develop a sealift plan. This was readily done and MARCOM sent the supply ship HMCS *Provider*, and destroyers *Kootenay* and *Saguenay*. Mobile Command wanted to embark CH-113 Voyageur medium lift helicopters on *Provider* but were told this was not feasible. Sea King helicopters were instead substituted. The idea was to use *Saguenay's* and *Provider's* four Sea Kings and small landing craft to lift the personnel off the beach if necessary and abandon the heavy equipment.[50]

The naval task force, called Operation LEAVEN, was to proceed to the Azores and then Malta. Heavy seas damaged *Saguenay* and MARCOM tried to replace her with the destroyer *Chaudière*, which was on a training cruise and not prepared for full operations. Allard then instructed MARCOM to send the destroyer *Annapolis*. Faulty message handling and procedures, coupled with high-level commanders reaching down too far into the operational forces, produced some confusion. Similarly, MARCOM could not talk to the CBU commander and find out how much equipment would be embarked. The naval task force was held at Gibraltar pending clarification.[51]

Two events of consequence occurred on 21 May. Egyptian airborne forces occupied Sharm el Shiek on the Straits of Tiran and Prime Minister Pearson welcomed Israeli diplomatic representatives to Expo '67. Nasser immediately announced a blockade on the Straits and then proceeded to attack Canada as American-British-Israeli "stooges" in the cause of "neo-imperialism."[52] There was more to this outburst than the Expo '67 meeting. One theory suggests that the Soviets were feeding Nasser doctored signals intelligence intercepts relating to the movement of the Canadian naval task force to Gibraltar and its relationship to the situation with UNEF. Nasser probably could not distinguish between an evacuation force and an intervention force. The RCAF's 115 Air Transport Unit with its Caribous and Otters was ordered out of the Sinai by the Egyptian Government by 3 June.[53]

Cabinet met once again to consider the situation. Paul Martin explained that it was his belief that the purpose of the whole exercise was in part "directed towards strengthening his [Nasser's] leadership in the Middle East" (although other motives have been redacted by PCO censors in the released Cabinet documents). Martin noted that "for all practical purposes the effectiveness of the UNEF had been eliminated." The crisis, however, could become explosive over the Straits of Tiran/Gulf of Aqaba issue and he was consulting with the British and Americans. Pearson was apparently more concerned about "the effect of U Thant's decision on peacekeeping generally," particularly in Cyprus.[54]

The Pearson government's stance had suddenly changed to accepting the legitimacy of the UAR action. Starnes, meanwhile, had been summoned to the UAR foreign ministry and told bluntly that "any efforts by UNGA or the Security Council would be considered as an attempt to aid Israel and as an unfriendly act" and "any attempt to delay the UNEF withdrawal would not be tolerated." In a situation that UNPROFOR would be confronted with twenty-five years later, the Canadian UNEF contingent was being held hostage to the UN's good behaviour; that is, behaviour acceptable to one of the belligerents with a significant military advantage over the UN force. Paul Martin was dispatched to New York to represent Canadian interests in the UN. He was told that "We believe it would be unwise not to take these UAR views seriously, particularly in the present inflamed state of feelings in the Middle East."[55]

The Americans and British were working on a solution to the closure of the Straits of Tiran matter. Generally, the plan was to form an international naval force to escort ships past UAR naval forces, something similar to an American plan in the 1980s to escort Kuwaiti tankers in the Iran-Iraq conflict. Martin was instructed, however, that Canada should not give the appearance of being involved in such planning since it might compromise Canada's ability to be part of a post-UNEF peacekeeping or peace observation solution in the region.[56]

None of this in any way ameliorated the anxiety felt within the ranks of UNEF. The Canadian guard company shot and killed an intruder and an RCAF Caribou was harassed by Israeli Air Force fighters. The Canadian contingent finally was ensconced in Rafah Camp in Gaza and El Arish air base, but UN New York would not permit RCAF transports to pull out the force. As an internal analysis put it, "There was now a possibility that an almost totally defenceless Canadian force would be stranded in an area liable to erupt into hostilities."[57]

Pearson then talked to the American President about the naval force in the Straits of Tiran. Word of the discussion leaked and Nasser once again launched a tirade of anti-Canadian rhetoric accusing Canada of colluding with the British and Americans. Canadian attempts to use UN forums to resolve the problems were "proved useless owing to the tactics of the USSR and the Arabs" a situation that was exacerbated by "the aggressive attitude of senior Israeli officers and their confidence of ready victory over the Arabs was a source of concern." The Director General of Intelligence informed Paul Hellyer that war was inevitable.[58]

Cabinet was split, with Hellyer operating in a worst case scenario mode according to Martin, who was not convinced war would occur.[59] George Ignatieff was instructed to go directly to the UN Secretariat and tell them that Canada was not going to stand idly by and allow her forces to be caught up in hostilities because the UN would not permit Canadian aircraft to evacuate the contingent.[60] If there was no movement on UN New York's part, Canada would do the job herself since she had pre-positioned Yukon and Hercules transport aircraft to forward bases in West Germany. Bunche and the UN Secretariat were upset and "argued against a precipitate withdrawal," almost opposite to the stance taken earlier. Bunche did not believe Ignatieff when the latter explained that Canadian assessments of the situation were dire: Bunche was in communication with General Rikhye "and there was no need to accelerate the UN withdrawal plan."[61]

The next day, 27 May, Nasser sent a diplomatic note to Canada. Canada was exhibiting an intolerable "pro-Israeli attitude" and the dispatch of Canadian naval forces had inflamed public opinion to a degree that the Canadian UNEF contingent was no longer welcome in Egypt. El Arish was now opened to RCAF aircraft so that the Canadian contingent could be withdrawn. Canada had 48 hours to get out.[62] Bunche reconsidered and U Thant ordered Rikhye to "permit" the Canadian withdrawal. The withdrawal was conducted under a great deal of sanctioned Egyptian military interference and harassment by local forces: three Canadian soldiers were shot and wounded by Egyptian Army personnel.[63] To add insult to injury, Canadian media outlets noted that "Egyptian newspapers have cast Canada in recent days with the Imperialist powers and have referred to Prime Minister Lester Pearson as 'stupid,'" and: "Nasser Boots Out Our Troops: A Loss of Face for Canada, says Dief."[64]

Cabinet considered more active measures on 29 May. If the planned international naval force secured passage in the Straits of Tiran, Israel might not initiate hostilities. The legal basis was examined and the Gulf of Aqaba was considered to be international waters by some, but not by others. Although the records have been censored by the PCO, it appears as though Canada was contemplating pursuing this option and even taking the lead with the American and British naval forces in the Mediterranean. Most ministers supported some Canadian military action since "there appears to be little point in stating what the law was if one was not prepared to actively support it." Others believed that "Canadian intervention would not make much of a difference" and that "it would be a mistake to get involved in a ground war."[65]

As to the larger Cold War aspects of the crisis Pearson believed:

> The crisis could readily be resolved if the United States and the USSR were interested in getting together. The USSR in particular apparently was not, but preferred to encourage the alienation of the Arab world from the UN and the West. The deepening of the Middle Eastern crisis also served Soviet purposes by increasing US difficulties in Vietnam. Undoubtedly the Soviet Government did not intend to let the crisis deepen into disaster but the danger was that it might slide beyond the control of any powers.[66]

Four days later on 5 June, the first Israeli air strikes completely destroyed the UAR air forces on the ground. The Six Day War had begun. Fourteen Indian UNEF members were killed in the crossfire because New York was adhering to its prolonged withdrawal timetable.

Pearson pessimistically assumed that the belligerents would not want another UN peacekeeping mission in place once hostilities ended since "the Israelis have never been great admirers of United Nations operations in the Mideast and the circumstances of withdrawal of UNEF will have reinforced this view." Moreover,"the USSR position on peacekeeping has been enhanced by the way in which UNEF was dissolved since it now appears that peacekeeping arrangements made outside the Security Council depend nevertheless on great power unanimity if they are to be effective when they are really needed."[67]

The Prime Minister told Cabinet in the wake of the ceasefire that "it seemed obvious that the Russians wanted to prevent a peaceful settlement in the Middle East. They seemed to look forward to building their won position, possibly even through support to future 'liberation movements.'....it might be best [for Canada] to avoid undue diplomatic activity."[68]

In the aftermath of the 1967 affair, George Ignatieff reported to External Affairs:

> I have reluctantly come to the conclusion that, so long as the present management is in charge on the 38th floor, we may have eloquent expressions of philosophy and an admirable tone of high aspiration, but I would have hesitations about entrusting to them any substantial operational responsibility involving Canadian personnel....there is an unfortunate attitude of oriental passivity on the part of the Secretary General himself which limits any likelihood of initiative, except on matters of direct concern to him in Asia such as Vietnam and China.[69]

Paul Martin believed that "the whole affair made the UN look irrelevant."[70] At National Defence, Colonel R.L. Raymont told General Allard that "it would seem that in the ultimate result all our presence did for ten years was to give both the Israelis and the Arabs time to build up sufficient strength to have another go at each other."[71] General E.L.M. Burns noted that after the withdrawal of UNEF, "Peacekeeping seemed to be discredited, and there were many voices in Canada calling for abandonment of our efforts in this field."[72] Some of these voices included the new Prime Minister, Pierre Elliott Trudeau, and his advisors.

THE TRUDEAU GOVERNMENT AND UN PEACEKEEPING

Pierre Elliott Trudeau has best been described by journalist Richard Gwyn as:

distant, pagan, ageless, like the photographs of Nijinsky: the aquiline nose and high Slavic cheekbones, the taut, sculptured face, the ambiguous grace. His countenance, chilly and cerebral, flared nostrils hinting at a sneer, gives him a natural aristocratic quality of dominion over others. Above all, there are the pale and predatory eyes that tell one of skepticism, inquiry, ferocity.[73]

Jesuit-trained in Montreal and Harvard-educated in Boston, Trudeau was a well-traveled upper-class Quebecois (he had been behind the Iron Curtain, in the middle of the first Arab-Israeli troubles and had even been to China).[74] In 1949, a young Trudeau worked within Louis St. Laurent's Privy Council Office. He went on to establish Cite Libre magazine along with his friends Gerard Pelletier and Jean Marchand, both of whom would become Cabinet ministers under Pearson, and Trudeau would follow as Justice Minister in 1967.[75]

Lester Pearson set his retirement date for April 1968. Two members of the PCO who were close friends of Trudeau, Marc Lalonde and Michael Pitfield, convinced him to run. In a stunning election campaign, Trudeaumania swept the land and the Liberal Party was returned to power in June 1968.[76]

One former External Affairs analyst noted that Trudeau's outlook was not formed by the Second World War. He was from a new generation, skeptical about military solutions to political problems. He even questioned Canada's role in the United Nations:

As a delegate to the UN General Assembly in 1966, Trudeau appears to have been impressed principally by the inefficacy of the organization and shocked by the contrast between the reality he observed and the image then current in Canada of the country's exaggerated influence within the UN.[77]

Another foreign policy analyst maintains that Trudeau was motivated by the pursuit of individual freedom and a belief that the government's purpose was to improve the quality of life and thus encourage self improvement. He abhorred ethnic nationalism, which he took to be the primary threat to peace and stability. If ethnic nationalism could be eliminated in addition to over-robust claims of sovereignty, war could be eliminated too. Above all, Trudeau was an anti-separatist. The largest threat to Canada was clamor for independence in Quebec, and the main objective was national unity. The best means to achieve this was economic growth through an aggressive search for new markets and exports.[78] Thomas Axworthy, Principal Secretary to the Prime Minister, notes that Trudeau's pre-1968 writings revealed a deep skepticism of the "simplistic" Cold War "system," that Canada had her "eyes closed" to the possibilities inherent in the emerging Third World. In some of his election campaign speeches, Trudeau asserted that there was too much foreign policy emphasis on NATO.[79]

As Mitchell Sharp once put it, "Pearson was merely one of us, whereas Trudeau was not— he was someone extraordinary."[80] This extraordinary man was about to turn Pearson's world upside down. Trudeau did not like Parliament: it was in his mind a bunch of posturing "old boys" behaving childishly. He held even more contempt for the bureaucracy, which he considered ossified and also an old boys' club.[81]

Trudeau's solution was "counter bureaucracy," better known at the time by journalists and professional civil servants as the "Supergroup." One journalist recounted a story by an anonymous senior civil servant who complained that "I was heard, but not listened to. Supergroup had been there before me."[82] The Supergroup was best described by Richard Gwyn:

> Supergroup, of course, was and is a myth, in the same way that the Establishment is a myth. Just as no businessman or society matron dares ignore the standards of behaviour laid down by the mythical Establishment, no Liberal politician or upwardly mobile civil servant dared to ignore the political codes laid down by the non-existent Supergroup.[83]

In effect, Trudeau established "a parallel power to the bureaucracy."[84] Although Trudeau participated in these changes, he was influenced by Marc Lalonde, Gordon Robertson (who had been Clerk of the PCO under Pearson) and Michael Pitfield.[85]

Philosopher John Ralston Saul observed:

> [Pitfield] experimented so well that the individual ministers were gradually drained of power and kept off balance by the young bureaucrats in his central Privy Council Office. They maintained an atmosphere in which the ministers were constantly afraid of losing their jobs and increasingly in the dark as to what was really going on in the Prime Minister's mind....Pitfield was certainly the finest practitioner yet seen of that bizarre management method which consists of using massive quantities of information to create confusion which in turn creates ignorance and thus removes power from those who receive the information....Pitfield's organization was the final nail in the coffin of Canadian foreign policy.[86]

The other group was a somewhat ill defined "informal, loosely organized ring of advisors, some of them on Trudeau's staff, some of them public servants, some elected, some appointed."[87] The key personalities included Pitfield, Gordon Robertson, Marc Lalonde, and Ivan Head. Essentially, these men constituted Trudeau's informal, unelected Cabinet.

Of the men in the inner circle, Ivan Head had the most influence on foreign policy. Journalist Peter Newman once described Head as "a sub-Arctic Henry Kissinger, flying about the world on the Prime Minister's behalf by-passing apoplectic officials."[88] Head was an Albertan who, like Trudeau, had studied at Harvard. He was a law professor at the University of Alberta and had worked for External Affairs. As Trudeau notes in his memoirs, "Ivan Head, who had been an officer in the Department of External Affairs, became my most important personal foreign policy adviser throughout the 1970s."[89]

The more traditional Cabinet strategic policy team under Trudeau consisted of Mitchell Sharp and Leo Cadieux. Cadieux, the first French Canadian Minister of National Defence, had served under Hellyer as the Associate Minister since 1965 and had borne the brunt of the unification debate. The fact that he was both French Canadian and in charge of the military was probably a deliberate message to Quebec separatists. Sharp assumed power from Paul Martin, who was eased out by Trudeau due to increasing philosophical differences. Paul Hellyer had been shifted to Housing and sidelined there. He would eventually resign from Cabinet, "convinced that the country was being run by closet fellow-travelers at best."[90]

From 1968 to 1970, the Trudeau government was at war with itself over Canadian national security policy, a story too complex to be told in detail here.[91] In essence, General Allard and Leo Cadieux were asked to put together a presentation for Cabinet in 1968. Allard's staff had already prepared a document the previous year, the *Rationale for Canadian Defence Forces*, that was used within CFHQ as a touchstone for military personnel operating in the political environment. *Rationale* was based on St Laurent's original foreign policy points as established in 1947: national unity, political liberty, the international rule of law, and acceptance of international responsibility. The primary means by which Canada exerted influence was based on her participation in NATO and in bi-lateral Canada-US defence projects like NORAD. As before, the main theatres of operations in the Cold War were Europe and North America.[92]

Rationale did not ignore the peripheries, however. There was an entire section on "The Promotion of International Stability in Other Areas." The UN was grouped in this section with other methods such as the provision of Military Assistance to the Third World and Canadian participation in other regional groupings like the OAS or SEATO. *Rationale* noted that "the principle functions of the UN's military activities have been to place a check on tensions [and] to keep conflicts from spreading."[93] Consequently, "it is unlikely that the scope for United Nations military operations will be significantly enlarged in the foreseeable future." Superpower games would interfere with the ability of the UN to fulfill its original purpose, and would continue to do so. Other regional powers were less and less interested in UN operations since "their own interests might some day be adversely affected if the UN were able to develop an ability to carry out military operations without necessarily obtaining the consent of all concerned."[94]

The study noted that:

> The possibility of being drawn into a conflict of unforeseen dimensions, the risk of causing a confrontation with the USSR or China, and perhaps above all the problem of governments of explaining to their own populations the reason for being involved in a conflict "in a faraway land between people of whom we know nothing" could all be expected to serve as decisive influences against such operations.[95]

Trudeau rejected the Allard/Cadieux paper as a basis for Canadian national security policy, despite its pessimistic view of UN operations. A number of Cabinet members were upset that a neutral option had not been considered and that the proposed paper was too pro-NATO. Allard and Cadieux then generated a study which gave Cabinet a vision of Canada's world if it was "non-aligned." This document was Defence Policy Review 1969 (DPR 69).

DPR 69 essentially demonstrated that Canada would need its own nuclear weapons program and quadruple the size of the armed forces in order to guarantee sovereignty, let alone project power.[96] DPR 69 noted that "a non-aligned Canada...might also be hopeful of increased opportunities to play a conciliatory role between the blocs at the UN or elsewhere." However, as Canada would lose influence with the United States and the NATO allies, the gains were not worth the price. As for UN peacekeeping, Canada would be a less valuable player, since "Canadian participation was desired precisely because Canada enjoyed the confidence of the USA and other major Western countries." DPR 69 was pessimistic about the future of UN peacekeeping for the usual reasons: the ongoing financial crisis, East-West deadlock and the fact that there was a "lack of sustained support from the Afro-Asians for the concept."[97]

Finally, DPR 69 noted:

> The uncertain future of international peacekeeping missions, when considered with Canada's experience of the forces required, suggests that Canada, during the next few years, should not maintain armed forces trained and equipped solely to meet the possibility of international peacekeeping operations throughout the world....efforts to keep the peace must for the time being take the form of support for NATO's policy of maintaining a stable military balance.[98]

DPR 69 was rejected by members of Cabinet who did not support "the detested status quo."[99] A joint External Affairs-National Defence body was then formed to report to Cabinet once again, since the anti-military proponents were not hearing what they wanted to hear from the professionals in those agencies charged with the defence of Canadian interests. This group was called the Special Task Force on Europe or STAFFEUR. STAFFEUR's composition was notable: it included External Affairs' greatest realist Ambassador Robert Ford, Ambassador Paul Trembley, General W.A.B. Anderson, and General Henri Tellier, men who had considerable experience in NATO circles.

The STAFFEUR report was tabled in 1969. STAFFEUR defined several principles which formed the basis of Canadian national security: Security, National Unity, National Identity, and Economic Interests. UN peacekeeping fell under the Security principle were its role was the containment of conflicts which could lead to nuclear war. STAFFEUR did note that peacekeeping was important in developing the Canadian identity elsewhere because it could serve a role in "diversifying and balancing our relations with the United States," but the point of main effort for Canada was still Europe and NATO.[100]

STAFFEUR did, however, explore alternatives to a European focus:

> One reason [for doing so] is simply the widespread and often unarticulated desire for a "new look," a new role for Canada. Another is that there is a feeling abroad that Europe does not offer as much opportunity as do other regions of the world for Canada to play a distinctive and satisfying role. Partly this seems to be because Europe is associated in people's minds with power politics, military alliances and other "immoral" aspects of international affairs....another reason is that Canadians are more aware of and interested in other parts of the world than they used to be and are often attracted by the possibilities of doing good there.[101]

STAFFEUR examined the "Third World Option" wherein Canada changed focus away from Europe. The members concluded that "It would enable Canada to make a significant contribution to alleviate the world's poverty....in the process it would bring opportunities for influence and prestige that would be flattering to the Canadian psyche." On the other hand,

> The prestige and influence that might accrue to Canada would have very strict limits and in many areas would be more illusory than real. The Latin Americans and Afro-Asians are no more likely than any other to allow outsiders to intervene in quarrels of vital interest to them (eg: Nigeria-Biafra) and we, for our part, would have no direct interest in doing so. If we were involved in such quarrels, our energies would be spent on problems that would have no real bearing on Canada's own development....
> The truth is, that although Canada can make a contribution to the Third World, the Third World has very little to contribute to or to do with the fabric of Canadian life or, indeed, in terms of our security.[102]

STAFFEUR, DPR 69, and the Defence Rationale paper all were grist for the mill when the Trudeau government formulated its 1970s policy documents. *Foreign Policy for Canadians and Defence in the 70s* did not heed the professional advice on not getting too involved in the Third World and remaining players in Europe: the documents compromised in those areas. Canada's NATO commitment was halved, while the Third Option became an economic strategy with little or no security focus. Neither document gave credence to the UN as a significant factor in Canadian national security policy.[103]

These beliefs were confirmed by the Trudeau government's handling of the Biafra crisis. When queried about the possibility of sending a battalion group to Nigeria-Biafra in 1968, Cabinet noted:

> The civil war has been fought in a primitive and brutal fashion, in jungle terrain with which Canadian troops are not familiar. It might be disastrous to commit Canadians to an unfamiliar environment where the political situation is tense and the necessary guarantee that they will not have to defend themselves against unruly tribesmen is, at best, uncertain.

> Canada should not take a decision about the proposed peacekeeping or observer force at this time but care should be taken that the impression is not conveyed that Canada is not interested in Nigeria....[104]

Trudeau's reluctance to get involved in UN peacekeeping would not last throughout his tenure as Prime Minister. By 1973 Trudeau and his advisors had developed a more mature outlook on the place of Canada in the world.[105] Canada would join another United Nations Emergency Force (UNEF II) in the Sinai and the United Nations Disengagement Force (UNDOF) on the Golan Heights after the October War of 1973. The next year, Turkey would invade Cyprus and Canada was forced to decide whether fighting for peace was worthwhile: the Trudeau government did and sent in the Canadian Airborne Regiment to assist the UN in stabilizing the de facto partition of the island. Trudeau also re-engaged with the ICCS peace observation mission in Vietnam, although this was not a UN mission but essentially an extension of the ICSC. By 1978, Lebanon had exploded into a tragic and needless civil war. This time, Trudeau was more circumspect and sent a limited liability contingent for a year to serve with the increasingly ineffectual United Nations Interim Force Lebanon.[106]

All four of these commitments—UNDOF, UNEF II, UNFICYP and UNIFL—should be considered extensions of the UN Middle East missions generated over the previous two decades. When the Camp David Accords abandoned UNEF II in favour of the non-UN Multinational Force Organization (MFO), Canadian UN peacekeeping entered yet another decline until the late 1980s when some limited observer missions were conducted in Central America and a signals unit deployed to assist in the aftermath of the Iran-Iraq war. It was only in the first post-Cold War decade that Canadian UN peacekeeping exploded into a vast proliferation of missions, although this time the term "peacekeeping" was almost obsolete and "peacemaking" was the new fad.

The direction of Canadian UN peacekeeping was unclear once Pierre Trudeau took over in 1968: unimpressed with the pedantic nature of the UN, Trudeau's government nevertheless was drawn into four major peacekeeping operations in the 1970s.

(CF Photo)

Notes to Chapter 11

1. NAC RG 24 vol. 21487 file 2137.3 v.9, (23 Jan 63) message PERMISNY to USSEA, "ANC-Green Plan."

2. NAC RG 24 vol. 21487 file 2137.3 v. 11 (21 Oct 63) message PERMISNY to External Affairs Ottawa, "Congo: ANC-ONUC."

3. See Sean M. Maloney, "Mad Jimmy Dextraze: The Tightrope of UN Command," in Bernd Horn (ed) *Warrior Chiefs: Perspectives on Senior Canadian Military Leaders* (Toronto: Dundurn Press, 2001) Ch. 14.

4. NAC RG 24 vol. 21487 file 2137.3 v. 12 (21 Feb 64) message Leopoldville to External Affairs Ottawa, "Staff Relations: ONUC."

5. NAC RG 24 vol. 21487 file 2137.3 v. 12 (21 Feb 64) message Leopoldville to External Affairs Ottawa, "Staff Relations: ONUC."

6. NAC RG 24 vol. 21487 file 2137.3 v.12 (28 Aug 64) message Leopoldville to USSEA, "Military Assistance to the Congo."

7. See von Horn, *Soldiering for Peace* and O'Ballance, *The War in Yemen* Chapter 5.

8. NAC, RG 2, Cabinet Conclusions, 23 June 1964.

9. *Report of the Department of External Affairs 1964*, 6

10. Urquart, *Ralph Bunche*, 376.

11. Victoria Schofield, *Kashmir in Conflict: India, Pakistan, and the Unfinished War* (New York: I.B. Taurus, 2000), 99-100.

12. Ibid., 102; Eric S. Margolis, *War at the Top of the World: The Clash for Mastery of Asia* (Toronto: Key Porter Books, 1999), 71.

13. Schofield, *Kashmir in Conflict*, 106-110; U Thant, *View from the UN*, 400-402.

14. U Thant, *View from the UN*, 402-410; Alastair Lamb, *Crisis in Kashmir 1947 to 1966* (London: Routledge and Kegan Paul, 1966), 122-123.

15. Ibid.; *Blue Helmets* (1996 ed.), 137-139.

16. *Report of the Department of External Affairs 1965*, 16.

17. Martin, *A Very Public Life Volume 2*, 492.

18. "Mission Accomplished," Sentinel, April 1966, 33.

19. See C.M. Woodhouse, *The Rise and Fall of the Greek Colonels* (New York: Franklin Watts, 1985), 3-7.

20. CNA, "US Navy Responses to International Incidents and Crises, 1955-1975", C-58.

21. Ibid., 41.

22. Parker T. Hart, *Two NATO Allies at the Threshold of War: A Firsthand Account of Crisis Management, 1965-1968* (Durham, NC: Duke University Press, 1990), 38-40.

23. Ibid., 44-48.

24. Interview with the Canadian on-site commander.

25. Hart, *Two NATO Allies at the Threshold of War*, 52-55.

26. UN Archive, DAG 1/5.2.2.5.1, file: "Cyprus: Correspondence with Canada"; (23 Nov 67) "Paper Given to Archbishop Makarios by the Ambassadors of Canada, the United Kingdom, and the USA on 22 November 1967."

27. Martin, *A Very Public Life Volume 2*, 559; Hart, *Two NATO Allies at the Threshold of War*, 62.

28. Martin, *A Very Public Life Volume 2*, 558.

29. Woodhouse, *The Rise and Fall of the Greek Colonels*, 42.

30. Sean M. Maloney, "Directorate of Peacekeeping Policy Study 00/01: Canada and UN Commanded Operations, 1948-2000."

31. Samuel Ktaz, *Soldier Spies: Israeli Military Intelligence* (Novato: Praesidio Press, 1992), 178.

32. Richard B. Parker (ed) *The Six Day War: A Retrospective* (Gainesville: University Press of Florida, 1996), 6; DHH, file 78/70, Syd Wise, "Directorate of History Report No. 16: The Withdrawal of UNEF from Egypt May June 1967 (Canadian Aspects)", 6.

33. DHH (30 Sep 63) "Report of the Ad Hoc Committee on Defence Policy," 54.

34. Avner Cohen, *Israel and the Bomb* (New York: Columbia University Press, 1998), 257-261.

35. See extensive discussion of this throughout Richard B. Parker (ed) *The Six Day War: A Retrospective*.

36. Martin, *A Very Public Life Volume 2*, 562.

37. See Parker (ed) *The Six Day War: A Retrospective*.

38. Stephen S. Kaplan, *Diplomacy of Power: Soviet Armed Forces as a Political Instrument* (Washington: The Brookings Institute, 1981), 416.

39. Walter Laqueur, *The Struggle for the Middle East: The Soviet Union in the Mediterranean 1958-1968* (London: Macmillan and Co., 1969), 15-25; see also *Red Star on the Nile: The Soviet-Egyptian Influence Relationship Since the June War* (Princeton: Princeton University Press, 1977).

40. Sean M. Maloney, "Fire Brigade or Tocsin? NATO's ACE Mobile Force." (unpublished paper).

41. Ignatieff, *The Making of a Peacemonger*, 219-220. see also Ignatieff Papers, file 985.0039/005(21) (17 May 67) Verbatim Record of Information Meeting of Representatives of Governments Providing Contingents for UNEF."

42. Howie Langan, "The Operational Withdrawal of the Canadian Contingent from the UNEF," *The Springbok* Volume 4, 49-52.

43. Ibid., 221. See also Ignatieff Papers, file 985.0039/005(21) (17 May 67) Verbatim Record of Information Meeting of Representatives of Governments Providing Contingents for UNEF."

44. Ibid., 221-222.

45. NAC MG 26 N6 Middle East UNEF file, (18 May 67) "UNEF-Problem of Consent of Host Country"; NAC RG 2 Cabinet Conclusions, 18 May 1967. The Canadian position was not considered legitimate according to Sir Brian Urquart in a 1992 conference on the Six Day War. See Parker (ed) *The Six Day War: A Retrospective.*

46. Cohen, *Israel and the Bomb*, 269-270.

47. DHH, file 78/70, Syd Wise, "Directorate of History Report No. 16: The Withdrawal of UNEF from Egypt May June 1967 (Canadian Aspects)", 34; John Starnes notes that the Mobile Command planning exercise may have been called Exercise LAZARUS or PHOENIX, but that documentation has not yet been found to explain what all the options were. See John Starnes, *Closely Guarded: A Life in Canadian Security and Intelligence* (Toronto: University of Toronto Press, 1998), 122-124.

48. DHH, file 78/70, Syd Wise, "Directorate of History Report No. 16: The Withdrawal of UNEF from Egypt May June 1967 (Canadian Aspects)," 28-33.

49. Ibid., 35-38.

50. Ibid., 38-47.

51. Ibid., 52-53.

52. Martin, *A Very Public Life Vol. 2*, 565; Ignatieff, *The Making of a Peacemonger*, 222.

53. Starnes, *Closely Guarded*, 123-124; DHH, file 78/70, Syd Wise, "Directorate of History Report No. 16: The Withdrawal of UNEF from Egypt May June 1967 (Canadian Aspects)", 34.

54. NAC RG 2 Cabinet Conclusions, 23 May 1967.

55. NAC MG 26 N6 file: Middle East UNEF, "(22 May 67) memo for the Minister, "Status of UNEF and Timing of its Withdrawal."

56. Ibid.

57. DHH, file 78/70, Syd Wise, "Directorate of History Report No. 16: The Withdrawal of UNEF from Egypt May June 1967 (Canadian Aspects)", 42.

58. NAC RG 2 Cabinet Conclusions, 25 May 1967; DHH, file 78/70, Syd Wise, "Directorate of History Report No. 16: The Withdrawal of UNEF from Egypt May June 1967 (Canadian Aspects)", 51; Hellyer, *Damn the Torpedoes*, 235.

59. NAC RG 2 Cabinet Conclusions, 26 May 1967.

60. Ignatieff, *Making of a Peacemonger*, 35.

61. NAC MG 26 N6 file: Middle East UNEF, (28 Apr 67) "48 Hours Evacuation."

62. DHH, file 78/70, Syd Wise, "Directorate of History Report No. 16: The Withdrawal of UNEF from Egypt May June 1967 (Canadian Aspects)", 59.

63. Ibid., 75.

64. Anthoney Westall, "Canadians Pull out after Cairo Demand," *Globe and Mail* 29 May 1967; ; Nasser Boots Out Our Troops," *Toronto Telegram* 29 May 1967.

65. NAC RG 2 Cabinet Conclusions, 29 May 1967.

66. NAC RG 2 Cabinet Conclusions, 1 June 1967.

67. NAC MG 26 N6 file: Middle East UNEF, (Jun 67) notes on situation as of June 1967.

68. NAC RG 2 Cabinet Conclusions, 15 June 1967.

69. Trinity College Archives, Ignatieff Papers, 985-0039/002(03) (20 May 68) message PERMISNY to USSEA, "Review of Canadian Foreign Policy."

70. Martin, *A Very Public Life Vol. 2*, 565.

71. DHH, Raymont Collection, file 1082 (24 Aug 67) memo to CDS from ESO.

72. ELM Burns, "Canada's Peacekeeping Role in the Middle East," in Tareq Y. Ismael (ed) *Canada and the Arab World* (Edmonton: University of Alberta Press, 1985), 42.

73. Richard Gwyn, *The Northern Magus* (Toronto: McClelland and Stewart, 1980), 13.

74. Pierre Elliot Trudeau, *Memoirs* (Toronto: McClelland and Stewart, 1993) Ch. 1.

75. Gwyn, *The Northern Magus*, 17, 29, 41-44.

76. Ibid., 64.

77. Peter C. Dobell, *Canada's Search for New Roles: Foreign Policy in the Trudeau Era* (Toronto: Oxford University Press, 1972), 10.

78. Bruce Thordarson, *Trudeau and Foreign Policy: A Study in Decisionmaking* (Toronto: Oxford University Press, 1972), 55-63, 81-83.

79. Thomas S. Axworthy, "To Stand Not So High Perhaps but Always Alone: The Foreign Policy of Pierre Elliott Trudeau," *Towards a Just Society: The Trudeau Years* (Markham, Ontario: Viking Books Ltd., 1990), 17-18.

80. Gwyn, *The Northern Magus*, 50.

81. Ibid., 58.

82. Walter Stewart, *Shrug: Trudeau in Power* (Toronto: New Press, 1971), 173.

83. Ibid., 73.

84. Gwyn, *The Northern Magus*, 72.

85. Ibid.; *Radwinski, Trudeau*, 147-148.

86. John Ralston Saul, *Voltaire's Bastards: The Dictatorship of Reason in the West* (New York: Vintage Books, 1992), 91-92.

87. Stewart, *Shrug*, 174.

88. Ibid., 83.

89. Trudeau, *Memoirs*, 202.

90. Gwyn, *The Northern Magus*, 297.

91. See Sean M. Maloney, "To the Left, March: The Trudeau Government, De- NATOization and Denuclearization, 1967-1971," (forthcoming).

92. DHH, Raymont Collection, CFP 243 *Rationale for Canadian Defence Forces.*

93. Ibid.

94. Ibid.

95. Ibid.

96. ATI, PCO, "The Defence Policy Review, February 1969."

97. Ibid.

98. Ibid.

99. See Sean M. Maloney, "To the Left, March: The Trudeau Government, De- NATOization and Denuclearization, 1967-1971," (forthcoming).

100. ATI PCO, "Canada and Europe: Report of the Special Task Force on Europe, February 1969."

101. Ibid.

102. Ibid.

103. Bothwell and Granatstein, *Pirouette.*

104. ATI PCO, Cabinet Conclusions, 19 July 1968.

105. See Bothwell and Granatstein, *Pirouette.*

106. The information necessary to examine peacekeeping operations in the 1970s to the same levels as those operations conducted from 1948 to 1970 is not yet in the public domain and will be the subject of a sequel to this work.

CONCLUSION

*Peacekeeping is the ultimate Canadian endeavour.
Not just because it is noble and selfless and nice, but because it is such
a nonsolution. Rather than confront a problem head on, you diffuse it by
creating separate solitudes, by living parallel lives, by maintaining duality and
by limiting contact. Sound familiar? It should. It is the very blueprint
of our nation. Peacekeeping is simply Canada projected outwards onto the world.*

—Will Ferguson, *Why I Hate Canadians*

*The lessons of the Canadian peacekeeping experience were lost over time. By 1995 the UN's credibility
was so badly damaged that NATO had to step into the breech. It took the rest of the 1990s to relearn the relationship
between strong general-purpose combat capable forces and Canadian national interests.*

(Author's Collection)

The twenty-five-year peacekeeping journey from 1945 to 1970 was indeed Canada projected onto the world, but in ways different from Will Ferguson's interpretation. Though some of the situations in the early Cold War resembled the 1990s, Canada of the early Cold War was not the nation of the 1990s. Canada was a tougher, more realistic country with clearly articulated national interests and the means to protect them. UN peacekeeping was but one of those means. The reputation that Canadians built in subsequent years as "peacekeepers" was related more to participation in NATO than to announcing "ready aye ready" every time UN New York called for more Blue Berets. Several new aspects of Canadian UN peacekeeping emerge from this study.

First, Canada became involved in UN peacekeeping for reasons that are unrelated to the existing "noble, selfless, and nice" mythology. In most of the operations discussed in this book, UN peacekeeping was used by Canada as part of a Western effort to deny the Soviet Union influence and control over potential base areas they might use to degrade NATO's ability to deter and/or fight a third world war.

Initially, the Mackenzie King government endorsed isolationism but this was superseded by the St Laurent government's new internationalism. The UN was a failure as a collective security arrangement, which led to the creation of NATO and the ABC relationship in the West. The first peace observation missions, UNMOGIP and UNTSO, were part of ABC-related pre-NATO stability with the dual purpose of staving off Soviet interference in Commonwealth countries and protecting potential wartime nuclear base areas. In the case of United Nations Emergency Force in 1956, there was a clear immediate nuclear threat to NATO from a Middle East crisis that must be controlled.

In Asia, the stalemate in the Korean war and the loss of French control over Indochina undermined the West's ability to continue fighting Communism in the region. Outright withdrawal was not an option since Asian interests were vital for the economic survival of many NATO nations. Thus, "economy of effort" peacekeeping operations like the ICSC were implemented: UNMOGIP efforts had similar objectives. Canadian UN peacekeeping operations under St Laurent were directly related to global Western interests in containing Communism. No unique Canadian force structure was necessary: peacekeeping support and observation forces were drawn from existing Cold War forces.

Under the Diefenbaker government, Canadian UN peacekeeping was for the most part directly related to NATO interests in peripheral areas, but the Diefenbaker government veered off into areas where UN peacekeeping could not succeed. UNOGIL was similar to UNEF in the threat of nuclear weapons use, the assistance to be provided to allies, and the issue of Middle East stabilization. ONUC in the Congo was an intervention to stamp out a brushfire war before it became a proxy fight. In that operation Canada assisted NATO allies in denying the enemy wartime base areas in a peripheral but vital area.

Laos was an extension of the ICSC problem: it was another "economy of effort" mission, but was badly fumbled by the Diefenbaker government. UNTEA was NATO-related in terms of Dutch-American relations, but was also mishandled by the participants. The crises in Berlin and Cuba demonstrated the limits of a UN solution in direct superpower confrontation. With the exception of ONUC in the Congo, the Diefenbaker government was practicing "flash minimalism;" that is, the appearance of Canadian involvement without the deployment of significant resources. Even then the deployment of Canadians to the Congo was a limited liability deployment. The only actual peacekeeping force deployed during this time by Canada was a recce squadron, the rest were support or observation personnel. There were, however, initial attempts at creating a specialized peacekeeping force structure in the period from 1957 to 1963.

Under the Pearson government, Canadian peacekeeping missions were even more directly related to NATO concerns. UNFICYP and UNYOM dealt with Cold War basing issues, while UNFICYP was geared to maintaining NATO proper as the primary bulwark against Communism. UNIPOM was basically an extension of UNMOGIP. The Pearson government created and sanctioned a multi-purpose military force structure but only partially implemented it. Unlike the Diefenbaker government, the Pearson government committed Canadian combat troops to keep the peace as opposed to deploying troops for peacekeeping support.

Peacekeeping as a Cold War tool, however, declined in the 1960s. Long term problems unrelated to the Cold War, such as ethnic nationalism, could not be solved by UN peace-keeping. Peacekeeping could only hold the line for so long before the legal contradictions and institutional stresses showed. There was also the loss of will on the part of the Pearson government to remain deeply involved in UN peacekeeping after UNEF was withdrawn in 1967.

Second, Canadian peacekeeping efforts would have been impossible or disregarded by other powers if Canada had not been a member of NATO, had not possessed strong and effective military forces and leaders, or had conformed to the peacekeeping mythology. Participation in NATO, the ABC relationship, and the Commonwealth generated many positive outcomes for Canada. They helped improve Canada's place in the world by seasoning Canadian diplomatic and military personnel in co-equal alliance politics.

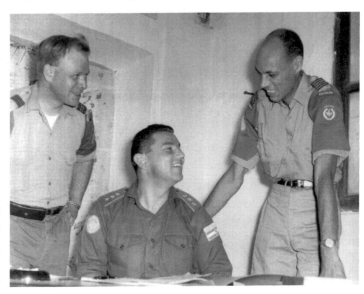

Who would have guessed that the descendants of these Canadian and Yugoslav UN peacekeeping troops would face off in fractured Croatia, Bosnia, and Kosovo in the 1990s?

(CF Photo)

Effective participation in NATO provided Canada with strong general purpose military forces. These forces were capable of fighting across the spectrum of conflict. Canada had strategic airlift and globally deployable naval forces. Canadian military forces were demonstrably competent through annual participation in NATO and bi-lateral exercises and would not have existed without the 1951 NATO commitments and the subsequent expansion of the armed forces for the Cold War. Similarly, the effective conduct of peacekeeping operations would have been impossible without good military leadership at all levels. Again, this would not have existed without the NATO-committed force structure. Canada's massive and significant participation in NATO's nuclear umbrella also provided a subtle backdrop to UN diplomatic negotiations involving Canada. Canadian governments of the day generally recognized there as a relationship between Canadian involvement in UN peacekeeping and the potential use of Canadian force in a non-UN context.

The Canadian national character also played a positive role in attaining objectives. Despite the myths that have developed since the 1970s, the Canadian image of the 1950s was that of a young, tough, and resourceful nation. In essence, Canada could afford to cultivate impartiality since its people could not be bullied.

Third, United Nations peacekeeping operations during the 1950s and 1960s are closer to 1990s concepts of UN peacekeeping than is commonly believed. A number of theorists have attempted to differentiate between so-called "first" and "second" generation peacekeeping and have adopted convoluted means to reconcile the events of the 1990s with the more traditional visions of peacekeeping.[1] Similarly, in the Canadian public domain, peacekeeping was considered to be "thin blue line" interpositionary operations like UNEF: impartial and inoffensive, with the use of minimal force.

Throughout the Cold War Canada's diplomats and soldiers were dealing with ethnic cleansing, heavily armed, uncontrolled and violent stateless actors, tribal bloodbaths, Machiavellian politics at all levels, and complex emergencies. The decolonization period during the Cold War was similar to the post-Cold War disengagement period of "empires" breaking down, with similar results requiring settlements brokered through the UN. The primary difference was that the stakes were higher during the Cold War due to the overarching possibility of a nuclear exchange between the Soviets and the West.

Fourth, the role of personalities is the paramount factor in the success of peacekeeping operations. At the diplomatic-strategic level, the personality of the UN Secretary General and his relationship with Canadian leaders was critical to achieving Canadian objectives. The fact that Dag Hammarskjöld was sympathetic to preventing the surge of Communism was crucial in stabilizing Central Africa and the Middle East. The ability of Canadian diplomatic and military personnel to adapt to rapidly changing situations on the ground and communicate effectively so that Ottawa could make timely decisions served Canadian interests time and time again. Personal vanity and ambition also made appearances however, mostly during the Diefenbaker years. U Thant's indecisiveness perhaps placed obstacles in Canada's way during the course of the 1960s.

Finally, we must seriously re-assess the relative importance of Lester B. Pearson in the development of Canadian UN peacekeeping. It is clear that Canada acted as part of a team with her allies in many of the crises handled by the United Nations during the subsequent diplomatic maneouverings. It is equally clear that Paul Martin played as positive a role in averting war over Cyprus as Pearson had in the Suez Crisis of 1956. It is absolutely critical that senior Canadian military personnel receive equal recognition, particularly Generals E.L.M. Burns and Charles Foulkes, as well as many staff officers who assisted them in conceptualizing and implementing Canadian peacekeeping operations.

In the end, Canadians should view their involvement in UN peacekeeping as an honourable and generally successful means of preventing nuclear war, and not surrendering vital positions to the scourge of totalitarianism as the West had in the 1930s. Canada used the UN actively to further her interests: the forward security of Canadians and their economic prosperity. UN peacekeeping was but one blue-feathered arrow in Canada's Cold War quiver: the others had nuclear and conventional heads.

1. See John Hillen, *Blue Helmets: The Strategy of Military Operations* (London: Brassey's, 1998); Christopher Bellamy, *Knights in White Armor: the New Art of War and Peace* (London: Hutchison, 1996); Steven R. Ratner, *The New UN Peacekeeping: Building Peace in Lands of Conflict after the Cold War* (New York: St Martin's 1995). The exception is Anthony Parsons, *From Cold War to Hot Peace: UN Interventions 1947-1994* (London: Michael Joseph, 1995).

PRIMARY SOURCES

John G. Diefenbaker Centre, Saskatoon:
John G. Diefenbaker Papers

Declassified Documents Record System:
Annual releases

Dwight D. Eisenhower Library, Abilene:
Christian Herter Papers; Ann Whitman Collection;
National Security Collection

National Archives of Canada, Ottawa: RG 2 Cabinet
Conclusions; RG 24 Department of National
Defence; RG 25 Department of External Affairs;
E.L.M. Burns Papers; Brooke Claxton Papers;
Howard Green Papers; Douglas Harkness Papers;
George Pearkes Papers; Lester B. Pearson Papers

National Defence Directorate of History and
Heritage, Ottawa: Jean V. Allard Papers; Chiefs of
Staff Committee Records; the Raymont Collection

Public Record Office, Kew: DEFE 6 Joint
Planning Staff

United Nations Archives, New York: Organization
Nations Unies au Congo records; United Nations
Emergency Force records; United Nations Forces in
Cyprus records

U.S. National Archives and Records Administration,
Washington: RG 59 State Department

DOCUMENT COLLECTIONS AND
OFFICIAL DOCUMENTS

Department of External Affairs. *Report of the
Department of External Affairs 1959*,
Ottawa: Queen's Printer, 1960.

Department of Foreign Affairs and International
Trade. *Documents on Canadian External Relations
Vol. 15 1949*, Ottawa: Supply and Services, 1995.

Department of National Defence. *White Paper on
Defence: March 1964*, Ottawa: Queen's Printer and
Controller of Stationery, 1964.

House of Commons. 1963 Special Committee on
Defence. *Minutes of Proceedings and Evidence*, Ottawa:
Queen's Printer and Controller of Stationery, 1963.

Foreign Relations of the United States series:

U.S. State Department. *FRUS 1948 Vol. V:
The Near East South Asia, and Africa Part 1.*
Washington: US GPO, 1975.

U.S. State Department. *FRUS 1956 Vol. XVI:
The Suez Crisis: July 26-31 December 1956.*
Washington: US GPO, 1990.

U.S. State Department. *FRUS 1958-1960 Vol. VIII:
Berlin Crisis 1958-1959.* Washington: US GPO, 1993.

U.S. State Department. *FRUS 1958-1960 Vol. XI:
Lebanon and Jordan.* Washington: US GPO, 1992.

U.S. State Department. *FRUS 1958-1960 Vol. XIV:
Africa.* Washington: US GPO, 1993.

U.S. State Department. *FRUS 1958-1960 Vol. XVI:
Asia.* Washington: US GPO, 1992.

U.S. State Department. FRUS 1961-1963 Vol. XXIV
Laos Crisis. Washington: US GPO, 1994.

U.S. State Department. FRUS 1961-1963 Vol XIII:
West Europe and Canada. Washington: US GPO,
1994.

U.S. State Department. FRUS 1961-1963: Cuban
Missile Crisis and Aftermath. Washington: US GPO,
1997.

U.S. State Department. FRUS 1961-63 Vol. XXIII
Southeast Asia. Washington: US GPO, 1995.

OFFICIAL HISTORIES

Hilliker, John, and Donald Barry. *Canada's
Department of External Affairs Volume II: Coming
of Age, 1946-1968.* Kingston: McGill-Queens
University Press, 1995.

U.S. JCS. *The History of the Unified Command Plan
1946-1993.* Washington: Joint History Office, Office
of the Chairman of the Joint Chiefs of Staff, 1995.

Wynn, Humphrey. *RAF Nuclear Deterrent Forces.*
London: HMSO, 1994.

MEMOIRS AND BIOGRAPHIES

Bingham, June. *U Thant: The Search for Peace.* New
York: Alfred Knopf, 1966.

Burns, E.L.M. *Between Arab and Israeli*. Toronto: Clark Irwin and Co., 1962.

Dayal. *Mission for Hammarskjöld: The Congo Crisis*. (Princeton: Princeton University Press, 1976).

English, John. *The Shadow of Heaven: The Life of Lester Pearson Volume 1 1897-1948*. Montreal: Vintage UK, 1989.

_____. *The Worldly Years: The Life of Lester B. Pearson 1949-1972*. Toronto: Vintage Books, 1992.

Fleming, Donald M. *So Very Near: The Political Memoirs of the Honourable Donald M. Fleming Vol. Two: The Summit Years*. Toronto: McClelland & Stewart, 1985.

Gordon, Walter. *A Political Memoir*. Toronto: McClelland & Stewart, 1977.

Granatstein, J.L. *A Man of Influence: Norman A. Robertson and Canadian Statecraft 1929-68*. Ottawa: Deneau Publishers, 1981.

Gwyn, Richard. *The Northern Magus*. Toronto: McClelland & Stewart Inc, 1980.

Hellyer, Paul. *Damn the Torpedoes: My Fight to Unify Canada's Armed Forces*. Toronto: McClelland & Stewart, 1990.

Ignatieff, George. *The Making of a Peacemonger: The Memoirs of George Ignatieff*. Toronto: University of Toronto Press, 1985.

Ilan, Amitzur. *Bernadotte in Palestine, 1948: A Study in Contemporary Knight-Errantry*. New York: St. Martin's 1989.

Lie, Trygve. *In the Cause of Peace: Seven Years with the United Nations*. Toronto: Macmillan Co., 1954.

Martin, Paul. *A Very Public Life Volume 2*. Toronto: Deneau Publishers, 1985.

_____. *Paul Martin Speaks for Canada: A Selection of Speeches on Foreign Policy, 1964-67*. Toronto: McClelland & Stewart, 1967.

O'Brien, Conor Cruise. *To Katanga and Back: A UN Case History*. New York: Simon and Schuster 1962.

Pearson, Lester B. *Mike: The Memoirs of the Rt. Hon. Lester B. Pearson, Volume Two 1948- 1957*. Toronto: University of Toronto Press, 1973.

_____. *Mike: The Memoirs of the Rt. Hon. Lester B. Pearson, Volume Three 1957-1968*. Toronto: University of Toronto Press, 1975.

Pocock, Tom. *East and West of Suez: the Retreat from Empire*. London: The Bodley Head, 1986.

Reid, Escott. *Time of Fear and Hope: The Making of the North Atlantic Treaty 1947-1949*. Toronto: McClelland & Stewart, 1977.

Rikhye, Indar Jit. *Military Adviser to the Secretary General*. New York: St Martins Press, 1993.

Robinson, H. Basil. *Diefenbaker's World: A Populist in World Affairs*. Toronto: University of Toronto Press, 1989.

Spaak, Paul-Henri. *The Continuing Battle: Memoirs of a European*. Toronto: Little, Brown and Company, 1971.

Starnes, John. *Closely Guarded: A Life in Canadian Security and Intelligence*. Toronto: University of Toronto Press, 1998.

Swettenham, John *McNaughton: Volume 3 1944-1966*. Toronto: Ryerson Press, 1969.

Thant, U. *View from the UN*. New York: Doubleday, 1978.

Thompson, Dale C. *Louis St Laurent: Canadian*. Toronto: Macmillan of Canada, 1967.

Trudeau, Pierre Elliot. *Memoirs*. Toronto: McClelland & Stewart, 1993.

Urquart, Brian. *Ralph Bunche: An American Life*. New York: W.W. Norton, 1993.

_____. *A Life in Peace and War*. New York: W.W. Norton, 1987.

_____. *Hammarskjöld*. New York: W.W. Norton, 1994.

von Horn, Carl. *Soldiering for Peace*, New York: David McKay, 1966.

Ziegler, Philip. *Mountbatten*. London: Harper and Row, 1985.

BOOKS

Adams, Thomas W. and Alvin J. Cottrell, *Cyprus Between East and West*. Washington: Johns Hopkins, 1968.

Adamson, David. *The Last Empire: Britain and the Commonwealth*. London: I.B. Taurus and Co. Ltd., 1989.

Ambrosius, Lloyd. *Wilsonian Statecraft: Theory and Practice of Liberal Internationalism during World War I*. Wilmington: Scholarly Resources Inc, 1991.

Anrys, Henri, et al. *La Force Naval: De l'amiraute de Flandre a la Force Naval Belge*. Tielt: Iannoo, 1992.

Arkin, William A. and Richard W. Fieldhouse, *Nuclear Battlefields: Global Links to the Arms Race*. Cambridge: Ballinger Publishing Co., 1985.

Armitage, Michael. *The Royal Air Force: An Illustrated History*. London: Brockhampton Press, 1996.

Ashworth, Chris. *RAF Bomber Command 1936-1968*. Wellingborough: Patrick Stephens Ltd., 1995.

Bamford, James. *The Puzzle Palace: Inside the National Security Agency*. Harmondsworth: Penguin Books, 1983.

Beahen, William. and Stan Horrall, *Red Coats on the Prairies: The North-West Mounted Police 1886-1900*. Regina: Centex Books, 1998.

Beker, Avi. *The United States and Israel: From Recognition to Reprehension*. Toronto: Lexington Books, 1988.

Berton, Pierre. *Why We Act Like Canadians: A Personal Exploration of Our National Character*. Toronto: Penguin Books, 1982.

Bickerton, Ian J. and Carla L. Klausner, *A Concise History of the Arab-Israeli Conflict (2nd ed.)*. New York: Prentice Hall, 1995.

Bland, Douglas L. *Chiefs of Defence*. Toronto: Canadian Institute for Strategic Studies, 1995.

Blaufarb, Douglas S. *The Counter-Insurgency Era: U.S. Doctrine 1950 to Present*. New York: The Free Press, 1977.

Blechman, Barry and Stephen S. Kaplan, *Force Without War: U.S. Armed Forces as a Political Instrument*. Washington D.C.: The Brookings Institution, 1978.

Bloomfield, Lincoln P., ed. *International Military Forces: The Question of Peacekeeping in an Armed and Disarming World*. New York: Little, Brown and Co., 1964.

Brackman, Arnold C. *Southeast Asia's Second Front: The Power Struggle in the Malay Archipelago*. London: Frederick A. Praeger, 1966.

Bradsher, Henry S. *Afghanistan and the Soviet Union*. Durham: Duke University Policy Studies, 1983.

Brown, Neville. *Strategic Mobility*. London: Chatto & Windus, 1963.

Brugioni, Dino. *Eyeball to Eyeball: The Inside Story of the Cuban Missile Crisis*. New York: Random House, 1991.

Buchan, Alastair. "Commonwealth Military Relations,"in W.B. Hamilton et al. *A Decade of the Commonwealth 1955-1964*. Durham: Duke University Press, 1966.

Bumstead, J.M. *The Red River Rebellion*. Winnipeg: Watson and Dwyer, 1996.

Bunge, Frederica M., ed. *Indonesia: A Country Study*. Washington: Department of the Army, 1983.

Caplan, Gerald L. and James Laxer. "Perspectives on un-American Traditions in Canada," in *Close the 49th Parallel etc: The Americanization of Canada*. Toronto: University of Toronto Press, 1970.

Carey, Jane Perry Clark and Andrew Galbraith Carey. *The Web of Modern Greek Politics*. New York: Columbia University Press, 1968.

Carver, Michael. *War Since 1945*. New York: Putnam and Sons, 1981.

Castle, Timothy N. *At War in the Shadow of Vietnam: U.S. Military Aid to the Royal Lao Government 1955-1975*. New York: Columbia University Press, 1997.

Charters, David. and James LeBlanc. "Peace-keeping and Internal Security: the Canadian Army in Low Intensity Operations," *Armies in Low Intensity Conflict: A Comparative Analysis*. Toronto: Brassey, 1989.

Charters, David. "From October to Oka: Peacekeeping in Canada, 1970-1990," *Canadian Military History: Selected Readings*. Toronto: Copp Clark Pittman, 1993.

Clayton, Anthony. *The Wars of French Decolonization*. New York: Longman, 1994.

Cohen, Avner. *Israel and the Bomb*. New York: Columbia University Press, 1998.

Conrad, Joseph. *Heart of Darkness.* New York: W.W. Norton and Co, 1988.

Crouch, Harold. *The Army and Politics in Indonesia.* Ithaca: Cornell University Press, 1978.

Cruise, David and Alison Griffiths. *The Great Adventure: How the Mounties Conquered the West.* Toronto: Penguin Books, 1998.

de Domenico, John E.G. *Land of a Million Elephants: Memoirs of a Canadian Peacekeeper.* Burnstown: General Store Publishing house, n/d.

Dean, Arthur H. *Test Ban and Disarmament: The Path of Negotiation.* New York: Harper and Row, 1966.

Dobell, Peter C. *Canada's Search for New Roles: Foreign Policy in the Trudeau Era.* Toronto: Oxford University Press, 1972.

Durch, William, ed. *The Evolution of UN Peacekeeping: Case Studies and Comparative Analysis.* New York: St Martin's Press, 1993.

Dyer, Gwynne and Tina Viljoen. *The Defence of Canada: In the Arms of the Empire 1790-1939.* Toronto: Macmillan of Canada, 1990.

_____. *War.* Toronto: Stoddart Publishing, 1985.

Eayrs, James *In Defence of Canada: Peacemaking and Deterrence.* Toronto: University of Toronto Press, 1972.

Ertekun, N.M. *The Cyprus Dispute and the Birth of the Turkish Republic of Northern Cyprus.* Nicosia: K. Rustem and Brother, 1981.

Fall, Bernard B. *Anatomy of a Crisis: The Story of the Laotian Crisis of 1960-61.* New York: Doubleday, 1969.

Fraser, Blair. *The Search for Identity: Canada Postwar to Present 1945-1967.* Toronto: Doubleday Books, 1967.

Foot, Rosemary. *The Wrong War: American Policy and the Dimensions of the Korean Conflict, 1950-1953.* Ithaca: Cornell University Press, 1985.

Fullick, Roy and Geoffrey Powell, *Suez: The Double War.* London: Leo Cooper, 1990.

Gaddis, John Lewis. *The United States and the Origins of the Cold War 1941-1947.* New York: Columbia, University Press, 1972.

Gaffen, Fred. *In the Eye of the Storm: A History of Canadian Peacekeeping.* Ottawa: Deneau and Wayne, 1989.

Geraghty, Tony. *Who Dares Wins: The Special Air Service 1950 to the Gulf War* (rev ed). New York: Warner Books, 1997.

Gavshon, Arthur L. *The Mysterious Death of Dag Hammarskjöld.* New York: Walker and Co., 1962.

George, Alexander and Richard Smoke. *Deterrence in American Foreign Policy: Theory and Practice.* New York: Columbia University Press, 1974.

Goodrich, Leland M. *The United Nations.* New York: Thomas Y. Crowell, 1959.

Granatstein, J.L. and David Bercuson. *War and Peacekeeping: From South Africa to the Gulf- Canada's Limited Wars.* Toronto: Key Porter Books, 1991.

_____. *The Ottawa Men.* Toronto: University of Toronto Press, 1982.

Greenhous, Brereton, ed. *Guarding the Goldfields: The Story of the Yukon Field Force.* Toronto: Dundurn Press, 1987.

Griffiths, Ieuan L. *The Atlas of African Affairs* (2nd ed). London: Routledge, 1993.

Grove, Eric J. *Vanguard to Trident: British Naval Policy Since World War Two.* Annapolis: Naval Institute Press, 1987.

Hanks, Robert J. *The Cape Route: Imperiled Western Lifeline.* Washington: Institute for Foreign Policy Analysis, 1981.

Halle, Louis J. *The Cold War as History.* New York: Harper Collins, 1991.

Hanly, Charles. "The Ethics of Independence," Stephen Clarkson, ed. *An Independent Foreign Policy for Canada?* Toronto: McClelland & Stewart, 1968.

Hannah, Norman B. *The Key to Failure: Laos and the Vietnam War.* London: Madison Books, 1987.

Harbottle, Michael. *The Blue Berets: The Story of The United Nations Peacekeeping Forces.* Harrisburg: Stackpole Books, 1972.

Hargreaves, J.D. *Decolonization in Africa.* New York: Longman, 1988.

Hart, Parker T. *Two NATO Allies at the Threshold of War: Cyprus, a Firsthand Account of Crisis Management, 1965-1968.* Durham: Duke University Press, 1990.

Haydon, Peter. *When Military Plans and Policies Collide: The Case of Canada's General Purpose Frigate Problems.* Toronto: Canadian Institute for Strategic Studies, 1991.

Heinemann, Winfried *Vom Zusammenwaschen des Bundnisses: Die Funktionsweise der NATO in ausgewahlten Krisenfallen 1951-1956.* Munchen: Oldenbourg, 1998.

Hiscocks, Richard. *The Security Council: A Study in Adolescence.* New York: The Free Press, 1973.

Hochschild, Adam. *King Leopold's Ghost: A Story of Greed, Terror, and Heroism in Colonial Africa.* New York: Mariner Books, 1999.

Holmes, John. *The Shaping of Peace: Canada and the Search for World Order Volume I 1943- 1957.* Toronto: University of Toronto Press, 1979.

Hood, Hugh. "Moral Imagination: Canadian Thing," William Kilbourn, ed. *Canada: A Guide to the Peaceable Kingdom.* Toronto: Macmillan, 1970.

Hutchison, E.H. *Violent Truce: A Military Observer Looks at the Middle East Conflict, 1951- 1955.* New York: Devin Adair Co., 1956.

Immerman, Richard. "Between the Unattainable and the Unacceptable: Eisenhower and Dienbienphu," in Melanson and Mayers, eds. *Re-evaluating Eisenhower: American Foreign Policy in the Fifties.* Chicago: University of Illinois Press, 1989.

Ismael, Tareq Y., ed. *Canada and the Arab World.* Edmonton: University of Alberta Press, 1985.

Jackson, William. *Britain's Defence Dilemma: An Inside View.* London: B.T. Batsford, 1990.

Jackson, Robert. *AVRO Vulcan.* Wellingborough: Patrick Stephens Ltd., 1987.

Jackson, Robert. *Canberra: The Operational Record.* Washington: Smithsonian Institution Press, 1989.

James, Lawrence. *Raj: The Making and the Unmaking of British India.* London: Little, Brown and Co., 1997.

Kahin, George McT. *Intervention: How America Became Involved in Vietnam.* Garden City: Anchor Books, 1987.

Kaplan, Stephen S. *Diplomacy of Power: Soviet Armed Forces as a Political Instrument.* Washington: The Brookings Institution, 1981.

Katz, Samuel. *Soldier Spies: Israeli Military Intelligence.* Novato: Presidio Press, 1992.

Kinross, Lord. *The Ottoman Centuries: The Rise and Fall of the Turkish Empire.* New York: Norrow Quill, 1977.

Kitson, Frank. *Bunch of Five.* London: Faber and Faber, 1977.

_____. *Low Intensity Operations: Subversion, Insurgency, Peace-Keeping.* Harrisburg: Stackpole Books, 1971.

Kosut, Hal, ed. *Indonesia: The Sukarno Years.* New York: Facts on File Interim History, 1967.

Kuniholm, Bruce R. *The Origins of the Cold War in the Near East: Great Power Conflict and Diplomacy in Iran, Turkey, and Greece.* Princeton: Princeton University Press, 1980.

Kyle, Keith. *Suez.* New York: St. Martin's Press, 1991.

Laqueur, Walter. *The Struggle for the Middle East: The Soviet Union in the Mediterranean 1958-1968.* London: Macmillan and Co., 1969.

Lamb, Alastair. *Crisis in Kashmir 1947 to 1966.* London: Routledge and Kegan Paul, 1966.

Langille, Howard Peter. *Changing the Guard: Canada's Defence in a World of Transition.* Toronto: University of Toronto Press, 1990.

Lashmar, Paul. *Spy Flights of the Cold War.* Annapolis: Naval Institute Press, 1996.

Lefever, Ernest W. *Crisis in the Congo: A UN Force in Action.* Washington: The Brookings Institution, 1965.

LePan, Douglas. "In Frock Coat and Moccasins," William Kilbourn, ed. *Canada: A Guide to the Peaceable Kingdom.* Toronto: Macmillan, 1970.

Levant, Victor. *Quiet Complicity: Canadian Involvement in the Vietnam War.* Toronto: Between the Lines Press, 1986.

Levin Jr., N. Gordon. *Woodrow Wilson and World Politics: America's Response to War and Revolution.* New York: Oxford University Press, 1968.

Levitt, Joseph. *Pearson and Canada's Role in Nuclear Disarmament and Arms Control Negotiations 1945-1957.* Kingston: McGill-Queen's University Press, 1993.

Low, D.A. *Eclipse of Empire.* Cambridge: Cambridge University Press, 1993.

Lyon, Peyton. *Canada in World Affairs 1961-1963.* Toronto: Oxford University Press, 1968.

McGhee, George. *The US-Turkish-NATO Middle East Connection: How the Truman Doctrine and Turkey's NATO Entry Contained the Soviets.* London: Macmillan, 1990.

McMahon, Robert J. *The Cold War on the Periphery: The United States, India, and Pakistan.* New York: Columbia University Press, 1994.

Mackenzie, Lewis. *Peacekeeper: The Road to Sarajevo.* Toronto: Douglas and MacIntyre, 1993.

Macmillan, Alan and John Baylis. *A Reassessment of the British Global Strategy Paper of 1952.* Nuclear History Program Occasional Paper 8, Center for International and Security Studies at Maryland School of Public Affairs, University of Maryland, 1994.

Maloney, Sean M. *Securing Command of the Sea: NATO Naval Planning 1948-1954.* Annapolis: Naval Institute Press, 1995.

_____. *War Without Battles: Canada's NATO Brigade in Germany, 1951-1993.* Toronto: McGraw-Hill Ryerson, 1997.

_____. "Learning to Love The Bomb: Canada's Cold War Strategy and Nuclear Weapons, 1951-1968" (forthcoming).

Manning, Patrick. *Francophone Sub-Saharan Africa 1880-1995.* Cambridge: Cambridge University Press, 1998.

Margolis, Eric S. *War at the Top of the World: The Clash for Mastery of Asia.* Toronto: Key Porter Books, 1999.

Meisner, Stanley. *United Nations: The First Fifty Years.* New York: Atlantic Monthly Press, 1995.

Milberry, Larry. *The AVRO CF-100.* Toronto: CANAV Books, 1981.

Miller, Carmen. *Painting the Map Red: Canada and the South Africa War, 1899-1902.* Kingston: McGill-Queen's University Press, 1993.

Miller, Jay. *Lockheed U-2.* Austin: Aerofax Inc., 1983.

Nicholas, H.G. *The United Nations as a Political Institution.* London: Oxford University Press, 1967.

Noer, Thomas J. "Africa," Thomas G. Paterson ed. *Kennedy's Quest for Victory: American Foreign Policy 1961-1963.* New York: Oxford University Press, 1989.

Novick, Peter. *That Noble Dream: The Objectivity Question and the American Historical Profession.* Cambridge: Cambridge University Press, 1988.

O'Ballance, Edgar. *The War in Yemen.* London: Faber and Faber, 1971.

Padelford Norman J. and Leland M. Goodrich. *The United Nations in the Balance: Accomplishments and Prospects.* New York: Praeger Books, 1965.

Paget, Julian. *Last Post: Aden 1964-1967.* London: Faber and Faber, 1969.

Palmer, Michael A. *Guardians of the Gulf: A History of America's Expanding Role in the Persian Gulf, 1833-1992.* New York: The Free Press, 1992.

Panteli, Stavros. *The Making of Modern Cyprus: From Obscurity to Statehood.* Herts: Interworld Publications, 1990.

Parker, Richard B., ed. *The Six Day War: A Retrospective.* Gainesville: University Press of Florida, 1996.

Polyviou, Polyvios G. *Cyprus: Conflict and Negotiation 1960-1980.* London: Duckworth, 1980.

Qubain, Fahim I. *Crisis in Lebanon.* Washington: The Middle East Institute, 1961.

Resnick, Phillip. "Canadian Defence Policy and the American Empire," *Close the 49th Parallel etc: The Americanization of Canada.* Toronto: University of Toronto Press, 1970.

Rikhye, Indar Jit. *Military Adviser to the Secretary General: UN Peacekeeping and the Congo Crisis.* New York: St. Martin's Press, 1993.

Ross, Douglas. *In the Interests of Peace: Canada and Vietnam 1954-73.* Toronto: University of Toronto Press, 1984.

Rotter, Andrew. *The Path to Vietnam: Origins of the American Commitment to Southeast Asia.* Ithaca: Cornell University Press, 1987.

Saul, John Ralston. *Voltaire's Bastards: The Dictatorship of Reason in the West.* New York: Vintage Books, 1992.

Schoenbaum, David. *The United States and Israel.* New York: Oxford University Press, 1993.

Schultz Jr., Richard H. *The Secret War Against Hanoi: Kennedy's and Johnson's Use of Spies, Saboteurs, and Covert Warriors in North Vietnam.* New York: Harper Collins, 1999.

Schick, Jack. *The Berlin Crisis 1958-1962.* Philadelphia: University of Pennsylvania Press, 1971.

Schofield, Victoria. *Kashmir in Conflict: India, Pakistan, and the Unfinished War.* New York: I.B. Taurus, 2000.

Schwartz, David N. *NATO's Nuclear Dilemmas.* Washington: The Brookings Institution, 1983.

Smith, Charles D. *Palestine and the Arab-Israeli Conflict,* (3rd ed.) New York: St. Martin's Press, 1996.

Smith, Dan. *Pressure: How The US Runs NATO.* London: Bloomsbury, 1989.

Smith, Denis. *Diplomacy of Fear: Canada and the Cold War 1941-1948.* Toronto: University of Toronto Press, 1988.

Spaak, Paul-Henri. *The Continuing Battle: Memoirs of a European 1936-1966.* Toronto: Little, Brown and Co., 1971.

Stacey, C.P. *Canada and the Age of Conflict Vol. 1: 1867-1921.* Toronto: University of Toronto, 1984.

_____. *Canada and the Age of Conflict Vol. 2 1921-1948.* Toronto: University of Toronto Press, 1981.

Stanley, George. *Canada's Soldiers: The Military History of an Unmilitary People* (rev ed). Toronto: Macmillan and Co., 1960.

Stearns, Monteagle. *Entangled Allies: U.S. Policy Toward Greece, Turkey, and Cyprus.* New York: Council for Foreign Relations, 1992.

Stephens, Robert. *Cyprus: A Place of Arms.* London: Pall Mall Press, 1966.

Stewart, Walter. *Shrug: Trudeau in Power.* Toronto: New Press, 1971.

Stromseth, Jane E. *The Origins of Flexible Response: NATO's Debate over Strategy in the 1960s.* Oxford: Macmillan Press, 1988.

Stuart-Fox, Martin. *A History of Laos.* Cambridge: Cambridge University Press, 1997.

Taylor, Alastair, ed. *Peacekeeping: International Challenge and Canadian Response.* Toronto: University of Toronto Press, 1968.

Thompson, Robert. *Defeating Communist Insurgency.* London: Chatto and Windus, 1966.

Thordarson, Bruce. *Trudeau and Foreign Policy: A Study in Decisionmaking.* Toronto: Oxford University Press, 1972.

Trinquier, Roger. *Modern Warfare: The French View of Counterinsurgency.* New York: Praeger, 1964.

Tusa, Ann. *The Last Division: A History of Berlin 1945-1989.* London: Hodder and Stoughton, 1997.

United Nations Department of Public Information, *The Blue Helmets: A Review of United Nations Peace-keeping,* (3rd ed.). New York: UNDPI, 1996.

Verrier, Anthony. *International Peacekeeping: UN Forces in a Troubled World.* London: Penguin Books, 1981.

Wainhouse, David. *International Peace Observation.* Baltimore: John Hopkins University Press, 1966.

Walker, Andrew. *The Commonwealth: A New Look.* Toronto: Pergamon Press, 1978.

Weigley, Russell F. *The American Way of War: A History of United States Military Strategy and Policy.* Bloomington: Indiana University Press, 1973.

Wood, Herbert Fairlie. *Strange Battleground: The Official History of the Canadian Army in Korea.* Ottawa: Queen's Printer, 1966.

Woodhouse, C.M. *The Rise and Fall of the Greek Colonels.* New York: Franklin Watts, 1985.

ARTICLES AND CONFERENCE PRESENTATIONS

Ben, Philippe. "The Limits of the UN ." *Survival* Vol. 8 No. 4 (1966): 130-133.

Claude Jr, Inis L. "United Nations Use of Military Force." *Conflict Resolution* Vol.7 No. 2: 117-129.

de Lee, Nigel. "More Like Korea than Suez: British and American Intervention in the Levant in 1958." *Small Wars and Insurgencies* Vol. 8 No.2 (Autumn 1997): 1-24.

Gordon, D.J. "Guarding the Right Flank." *The Royal Air Forces Quarterly* Vol. 1 No. 1 (Feb 1961) 19-23.

Greenhous, Brereton and Bill McAndrew. "The Canadian Military Marches North: The Yukon Field Force 1998-1900." *Canadian Defence Quarterly* Vol. 10 No. 4 (Spring 1981): 30-41.

Hero Jr., Alfred O. "The American Public and the UN 1954-1966." *Conflict Resolution* Vol. 10 No. 4: 436-475.

Hessler, William H. "Norway's Role in U.S. Defence." *U.S. Naval Institute Proceedings* (July 1960): 31-37.

Hoffmann, Stanley. "Erewhon or Lilliput? A Critical View of the Problem." *International Organization* Vol. 17 (1963): 404-424.

Jackson, Paul. "Bin the Bomb." *The Royal Air Force Yearbook 1999*: 21-26.

Korbel, Josef. "The Kashmir Dispute and the United Nations." *International Organization* Vol. 2 (1949): 278-287.

Lauria, Joe. "Ouellet proposes 5 000-strong UN force." *Edmonton Sun* (27 September 1995).

Lourie, Sylvain. "The United Nations Military Observer Group in India and Pakistan." *International Organization* Vol. 9 (1955): 19-31.

Love, Kenneth. "Burns: the Man in the Middle." *Globe and Mail* (18 November 1955).

Maloney, Sean M. "Domestic Operations: The Canadian Approach." Parameters (Autumn 1997): 135-152.

Maloney, Sean M. "Maple Leaf Over the Caribbean: Gunboat Diplomacy Canadian-Style?" Conference paper presented at the Halifax Naval Conference on the Diplomatic uses of Canadian Naval Forces (June 1998).

Maloney, Sean M. "Insights into Canadian Peacekeeping Doctrine." *Military Review* (March- April 1996): 12-23.

Maloney, Sean M. "Notfallplanung fur Berlin: Vorlaufer der Flexible response 1958-1963." *Militargeschichte* 7 Jahrgang Heft 1.1 Quartal (1997).

Maloney, Sean M. "Fire Brigade or Tocsin? ACE Mobile Force and Flexible Response, 1958-1993" unpublished paper.

Maloney, Sean M. "To the Left, March: The Trudeau Government, De-NATOization and Denuclearization 1967-1971 " (forthcoming).

Morris, Chris. "Canada's plan outlined for new UN force." *The Edmonton Journal* (26 September 1995).

Nicholas, H.G. "The United Nations in Crisis." *Survival* vol. 7 (1965): 257-262.

Pedlow, Gregory W. "Multinational Contingency Planning During the Second Berlin Crisis: The LIVE OAK Organization, 1959-1963 " Nuclear History Program Third Study and Review Conference (Ebenhause) (26-29 June 1991).

Preston, Richard A. "The RCN and Gun-Boat Diplomacy in the Caribbean." *Military Affairs* Vol. 36 No. 2 (April 1972): 41-44.

Schelling, Thomas. "Strategic Problems of an International Armed Force." *International Organization* Vol. 17 (1963): 465-485.

Stursberg, Peter. "Project to Form U.N. Army Means Red Troops or Veto." *The Toronto Star* (16 February 1956).

Watkins, Tarleton H. "Operation NEW TAPE: The Congo Airlift." *Air University Quarterly Review* Vol. 13 No. 1 (Summer 1961): 18-35.

Wyndham, E.H. "NATO: The Flanks." *Brassey's Annual* 1960: 149-162.

ABOUT THE AUTHOR

Dr. Sean M. Maloney served in Germany as the historian for 4 Canadian Mechanized Brigade, the Canadian Army's contribution to NATO during the Cold War. He is the author of several works dealing with the modern Canadian Army and peacekeeping history including *Chances for Peace: The Canadians and UNPROFOR 1992-1995* and the forthcoming Operation KINETIC: The Canadians in Kosovo 1999-2000. Dr. Maloney has gained extensive field research experience throughout the Balkans, the Middle East, and Central Asia. He currently teaches in the War Studies Program at the Royal Military College, Kingston, and is a research fellow at the Queen's University School for Policy Studies. Dr. Maloney is also the academic advisor to the Land Force Doctrine and Training System's Army Doctrine and Training Bulletin. His graduate work at the PhD level dealt with Canadian Cold War strategy and will soon be published as Learning to Love the Bomb: Canada's Cold War Strategy and Nuclear Weapons, 1951-1968, a study which complements *Canada and UN Peacekeeping: Cold War by Other Means, 1945-1970*. In his spare time, he undertakes cross-continental journeys on his VT 750 Shadow ACE and instructs in the martial arts. He is from Kingston, Ontario.